Web Data Management Practices:
Practices:
Emerging Techniques and Technologies

Athena Vakali
Aristotle University of Thessaloniki, Greece

George Pallis
Aristotle University of Thessaloniki, Greece

IDEA GROUP PUBLISHING
Hershey • London • Melbourne • Singapore

Acquisition Editor:	Michelle Potter
Senior Managing Editor:	Jennifer Neidig
Managing Editor:	Sara Reed
Development Editor:	Kristin Roth
Copy Editor:	Shanelle Ramelb
Typesetter:	Marko Primorac
Cover Design:	Lisa Tosheff
Printed at:	Integrated Book Technology

Published in the United States of America by
   Idea Group Publishing (an imprint of Idea Group Inc.)
   701 E. Chocolate Avenue
   Hershey PA 17033
   Tel: 717-533-8845
   Fax: 717-533-8661
   E-mail: cust@idea-group.com
   Web site: http://www.idea-group.com

and in the United Kingdom by
   Idea Group Publishing (an imprint of Idea Group Inc.)
   3 Henrietta Street
   Covent Garden
   London WC2E 8LU
   Tel: 44 20 7240 0856
   Fax: 44 20 7379 3313
   Web site: http://www.eurospan.co.uk

Library of Congress Cataloging-in-Publication Data

Web data management practices : emerging techniques and technologies / Athena Vakali and George Pallis, editors.
   p. cm.
   Summary: "This book provides an understanding of major issues, current practices and the main ideas in the field of Web data management, helping readers to identify current and emerging issues, as well as future trends. The most important aspects are discussed: Web data mining, content management on the Web, Web applications and Web services"--Provided by publisher.
   ISBN 1-59904-228-2 (hardcover) -- ISBN 1-59904-229-0 (softcover) -- ISBN 1-59904-230-4 (ebook)
   1. Web databases. 2. Database management. 3. Data warehousing. 4. Web services. I. Vakali, Athena, 1963- II. Pallis, George, 1978-
   QA76.9.W43W4155 2006
   005.74--dc22
                                        2006019124

British Cataloguing in Publication Data
A Cataloguing in Publication record for this book is available from the British Library.

Web Data Management Practices: Emerging Techniques and Technologies

Table of Contents

Section I: Web Data Mining

Chapter I
    Dušan Húsek, Academy of the Sciences of the Czech Republic,
      Czech Republic
    Jaroslav Pokorný, Charles University, Czech Republic
    Hana Řezanková, University of Economics, Prague, Czech Republic
    Václav Snášel, Technical University of Ostrava, Czech Republic

Chapter II
    Athena Vakali, Aristotle University of Thessaloniki, Greece
    George Pallis, Aristotle University of Thessaloniki, Greece
    Lefteris Angelis, Aristotle University of Thessaloniki, Greece

Foreword

The Web revolution currently under way is making the Internet more and more central to our everyday lives. The amount of information available on the Web is increasing at an enormous rate, and almost everyday new services become available. The Internet is now widely used not only for B2B (business-to-business) and B2C (business-to-consumer) communications, but also to carry on our everyday activities, such as making a phone call, booking seats at a theatre, searching for information, and so on.

The richness of the Web is fascinating: It is an infinite repository of up-to-date information and services able to fulfill everybody's needs. However, all of us have experienced that accessing Web information and services can be very frustrating as it is very easy to get lost in an apparently chaotic environment. Additionally, interacting with the Web is very often a time-consuming activity resulting in an increasingly frustrating user experience. So, how can access to such a heterogeneous and highly dynamic environment be managed best? The explosive growth of the Web calls for new models, techniques, and technologies for Web data management upon which efficient and effective services can be built.

The current volume is a major contribution in the field of Web data management. It presents many of the most relevant current developments and research results in a coherent and self-contained manner. What I really like about this book is its ability to balance theoretical and practical aspects. Each chapter contains case studies or real-world examples that enable the reader to understand and evaluate the illustrated techniques immediately. The book provides exhaustive coverage of the most important fundamental issues related to Web data management, such as Web data models and integration techniques, and Web data clustering.

It also provides interesting insights on the most relevant applications, such as Web services and e-mail systems. Finally, the most crucial issues related to efficiency are covered, too, such as caching and prefetching. The variety of topics found in this book makes it a valuable reference for all professionals, researchers, and students that are interested in Web data-management issues.

Elena Ferrari
University of Insubria at Como, Italy

Preface

The explosive growth of the Web has dramatically changed the way in which information is managed and accessed. In particular, nowadays, the Web has evolved rapidly from a simple information-sharing environment (offering only static text and images) to a rich framework of dynamic and interactive services (such as video and audio conferencing, e-commerce, and distance learning). This enormous growth and diversity in terms of access devices, bandwidth, information sources, and content has complicated Web data-management frameworks and practices.

The Web is actually a distributed global information resource containing a large spectrum of applications in which users interact with (or within) companies, organizations, governmental agencies, and educational or collaborative environments. The popularity of the Web originates from its potential to deliver readily dynamic, distributed, heterogeneous, and unstructured data all over the world. In this context, the Web is evolving at an alarming rate and is becoming increasingly chaotic without any specific, consistent organization. Therefore, the need of various Web data-management techniques and mechanisms has become obligatory toward providing information (that is actually useful to users) and improving information circulation and dissemination over the Web. Furthermore, new tools and techniques are needed to effectively manage these data since managing Web data with conventional tools is becoming almost impossible.

Efficient and effective Web data-management practices may form the basis for developing intelligent, personalized, and business-optimal Web services. Such enabling practices include Web data mining, scalable data warehousing, and preprocessing, sequence discovery, real-time processing, users and documents clustering and classification, user modeling, and evaluation models. These issues may provide valuable information about user preferences and expectations, together with usage, content, and structural patterns as practiced over the Web.

As the demand for data and information management increases, there is also a critical need for effectively managing Web content. Specifically, Web data mining has a major effect on the performance of Web data accessing and querying. Therefore, new implementations (such as Web data clustering, Web data caching, and Web services) have emerged to manage the (continuously growing) number of documents, their dynamic content, and services under quality-of-service (QoS) guarantees. The term QoS refers to certain technical characteristics, such as performance, scalability, reliability, and speed. So, current Web data-management issues are enforced with specific capabilities to design new Web applications and improve Web data searching and workload balancing.

In this framework, the chapters of this book provide an overview of current research and development activities in the area of Web data management. Following our call for chapters in 2005, we received 25 chapter proposals. All chapters underwent a rigorous, double-blind refereeing process before final acceptance. Eventually, 12 chapters were accepted for inclusion in this book. This book brought together academic and industrial researchers and practitioners from many different countries, including Australia, Brazil, Canada, Cyprus, Czech Republic, France, Greece, Italy, Spain, and the USA. Authors' research and industrial experience are reflected in their work and will certainly offer to readers in-depth knowledge of their areas of expertise.

Organization of This Book

The broad range of topics of the present book makes it an excellent reference on Web data management. The book is organized so that it could cover a wide range of audiences including undergraduate university students, postgraduate students, research engineers, and system developers. Because each chapter is self-contained, readers can focus on the topics that most interest them. Most of the chapters (if not all) in this book have great practical utility. Each chapter is accompanied by examples or case studies to show the applicability of the described techniques or methodologies. Each chapter opens with an abstract, which is the summary of the chapter, and an introduction, and then closes with a conclusion in order to give readers adequate background and knowledge for understanding the subject. All chapters also include an extensive list of references to allow readers to understand the subject thoroughly by not only studying the topic in depth, but also by referring to other works related to their topic of interest.

Overall, this book includes work in some of the most breaking topics, such as Web modeling, clustering over Web data, XML (extensible markup language) data management, Web services, and Web data prefetching and caching. A short outline of the material presented in each of the chapters of this book follows to help readers understand the chapter within their interests.

The book is divided into four major sections:

I.   Web Data Mining
II.   Content Management on the Web
III.   Web Information Integration and Applications
IV.   Web Services for Data Accessing

Section I deals with the issues concerned with Web data clustering and association rules, providing a pathway for current research and development activities in this area. This section is further divided into four chapters:

Chapter I, entitled "Data Clustering: From Documents to the Web" by Dušan Húsek, Jaroslav Pokorný, Hana Řezanková, and Václav Snášel, presents an overview of approaches to clustering in the Web environment. Particularly, this chapter deals with clustering Web search results, in which clustering search engines arrange the search results into groups around a common theme. Furthermore, some considerations are given concerning the justification of so many clustering algorithms and their application in the Web environment.

Chapter II, entitled "Clustering Web Information Sources" by Athena Vakali, George Pallis, and Lefteris Angelis, focuses on the topic of clustering information over the Web in an effort to provide an overview and survey on the theoretical background and the adopted practices of the most popular emerging and challenging clustering research efforts. An up-to-date survey of the existing clustering schemes is given to be of use for both researchers and practitioners interested in the area of Web data mining.

Chapter III, entitled "An Overview of Similarity Measures for Clustering XML Documents" by Giovanna Guerrini, Marco Mesiti, and Ismael Sanz, presents the most indicative research efforts for clustering XML documents relying on contents, structures, and link-related properties of XML documents. Specifically, the most relevant similarity measures are evaluated, providing a systematic comparison of all the presented measures that allows one to determine which measure applies in a particular context.

Chapter IV, entitled "Mining Association Rules from XML Documents" by Laura Irina Rusu, Wenny Rahayu, and David Taniar, presents some of the existing mining techniques for extracting association rules out of XML documents in the context of rapid changes in the Web knowledge-discovery area. Specifically, it presents the latest discoveries in the area of mining association rules from XML documents, both static and dynamic, in a well-structured manner, with examples and explanations so the reader will be able to easily identify the appropriate technique for his or her needs and replicate the algorithm in a development environment. At the same time, this chapter includes research work with a high level of usability, in which concepts and models are easy to be applied in real situations without imposing knowledge of any high-level mathematics concepts.

Section II presents interesting techniques for effectively managing the Web content. There are three chapters in this section:

Chapter V, entitled "Dynamically Generated Web Content: Research and Technology Practices" by Stavros Papastavrou, George Samaras, Paraskevas Evripidou, and Panos Chrysanthis, deals with the dynamic Web content technology, which is definitely one of the most emerging research areas due to the exponential increase in the information circulation and dissemination over the Web. This chapter covers past and present research approaches, practices, and available technologies that facilitate the extraction of information from Web databases and its dissemination to Web users.

Chapter VI, entitled "Caching on the Web" by Mehregan Mahdavi and Boualem Benatallah, studies Web caching techniques with focus on dynamic content. Caching is a key technique that addresses some of the performance issues in today's Web-enabled applications. Deploying dynamic data, especially in an emerging class of Web applications, called Web portals, makes caching even more interesting. This chapter discusses the limitations of caching in Web portals and studies a solution that addresses these limitations. The solution is based on the collaboration between the portal and its providers.

Chapter VII, entitled "Information-Theoretic Methods for Prediction in the Wireless and Wired Web" by Dimitrios Katsaros, presents information-theoretic techniques for discrete sequence prediction. It surveys, classifies, and compares the state-of-the-art solutions, suggesting routes for further research by discussing the critical issues and challenges of prediction in wired and wireless networks.

Section III is about information integration and Web-based applications and includes three chapters:

Chapter VIII, entitled "Designing and Mining Web Applications: A Conceptual Modeling Approach" by Rosa Meo and Maristella Matera, presents the usage of a modeling language, WebML, for the design of Web applications. It discusses the advantages of adopting conceptual modeling for the design and maintenance of a Web data-intensive application. Furthermore, it presents a case study about the analysis of the conceptual logs for testifying to the effectiveness of WebML and its conceptual modeling methods. The methodology of the analysis of Web logs is based on the data-mining paradigm of item sets and frequent patterns and makes full use of constraints on the conceptual logs' content. Many interesting patterns are obtained, such as recurrent navigation paths, the most frequently visited page's contents, and anomalies.

Chapter IX, entitled "Integrating Heterogeneous Data Sources in the Web" by Angelo Brayner, Marcelo Meirelles, and José de Aguiar Moraes Filho, describes an extension to the XQuery language, called MXQuery, which supports queries over several data sources and solves integration problems as semantic heterogeneity and incomplete information. The proposed language provides the necessary support for integrating a variable number of data sources with different degrees of autonomy. MXQuery solves problems of data integration, such as semantics heterogeneity, and copes with incomplete information. Furthermore, this chapter presents an architecture to process MXQuery queries over multiple heterogeneous databases available on the Web.

Chapter X, entitled "E-Mail Mining: Emerging Techniques for E-Mail Management" by Ioannis Katakis, Grigorios Tsoumakas, and Ioannis Vlahavas, deals with e-mail mining. In particular, this chapter discusses how disciplines like machine learning and data mining can contribute to the solution of the problem by constructing intelligent techniques that automate e-mail managing tasks, and what advantages they hold over other conventional solutions. It also discusses the particularity of e-mail data and what special treatment e-mail requires. Some interesting e-mail mining applications like mail categorization, summarization, automatic answering, and spam filtering are also presented.

Section IV presents insights and perspectives for Web services and contains two chapters:

Chapter XI, entitled "Web Services: Technology Issues and Foundations" by Bernd Amann, Salima Benbernou, and Benjamin Nguyen, introduces the concept of service-oriented computing (SOC) on the Web and the current standards enabling the definition and publication of Web services. Moreover, this chapter illustrates the complexity of the Web-service composition problem and provides a representative overview of the existing approaches.

The chapter concludes with a short presentation of two research projects exploiting and extending the Web-service paradigm.

Chapter XII, "Web-Services Management: Toward Efficient Web Data Access" by Farhana Zulkernine and Pat Martin, presents an overview and the state-of-the-art of various management approaches, models, and architectures for Web-services systems toward achieving QoS in Web data access. Moreover, it discusses the importance of autonomic or self-managing systems and provides an outline of the current research on autonomic Web services.

What Makes This Book Different

Several research efforts have already appeared in the area of Web data management, and this field seems to be of high importance for a wide academic and technical group due to the difficulties raised by the diversity of Web data structure and representation, information distribution, and communication and accessing costs. However, a dedicated book on important issues in Web data-management systems is still difficult to find. Most books are about either Web technology focusing on developing Web warehouses, or very specific areas such as Web modeling, Web mining, and Web replication.

This book provides a complete overview on important aspects in the Web data-management practice in order to be used either as a class textbook or as a complementary course text in a Web data-management course; in that case, its level is suitable for undergraduate- or graduate-level courses.

This book is, therefore, different in that it covers an extensive range of topics, including related issues about Web modeling, Web mining, Web caching and replication, Web semantics, and the XML standard. Furthermore, the main advantage of this book is the integration of both theoretical and practical aspects in the Web data-management research area.

Intended Audience

Web Data Management Practices: Emerging Techniques and Technologies is intended for academic institutions and for working professionals, and for technical and non-technical readers. The broad range of topics in this book makes it a pathway for current research and development activities in the area of Web data management. The book is organized so that it could cover a wide range of audiences including undergraduate university students, postgraduate students, research engineers, and system developers.

Computer science instructors could use this book to teach Web data-management issues to senior undergraduate or postgraduate students. The chapters are organized such that they provide a great deal of flexibility; emphasis can be given to different chapters depending on the scope of the course and the instructor's interests. Equivalently, computer-science students could use it in the context of a course or as a supplementary book for their independent study.

Computer-science researchers could also benefit from this book because it surveys a vast content of recent research in the area of Web data management. The research coverage is likely to benefit researchers and students from academia as well as industry. Moreover, this book is also ideal for researchers from other computer-science disciplines who wish to get acquainted with this area and integrate it with their own fields. The general computer community will benefit from this book through its technical as well as practical overview of the area.

Finally, the chapters in this book can be used by Web application developers as a reference to use the correct techniques for modeling and designing Web services, as well as efficiently handling a huge amount of Web information.

How to Read This Book

The book as a whole is meant for anyone professionally interested in Web data-management techniques and who in some way wants to gain an understanding of how data-mining applications are implemented on the Web. The organization of the book has been carefully selected to help the reader. Each chapter may be studied separately or in conjunction with other chapters. Thus, it is not mandatory to study the topics in their order of appearance. If the reader wishes to perform an in-depth study of a particular subject, then he or she could focus on the corresponding section.

Although how the book is read largely depends on the personal interests of the reader, two possible paths are recommended. For readers who are interested in the Web applications and implementations, it is recommended to read Sections II, III, and IV. For the reader who wants to acquire a theoretical knowledge about Web data management issues, it is recommended to read Sections I and II, and at least "scan" Section IV.

A Closing Remark

The authors have made significant efforts to provide high-quality chapters despite space restrictions. The authors are well-known researchers in the area of Web data management, and they have already offered significant contributions to the literature. We hope that the reader will benefit from the works presented in this book.

Acknowledgments

The editors would like to acknowledge the help of all people involved in the collation and review process of the book, without whose support this project could not have been completed.

We thank all the chapter reviewers for their dedicated effort to review chapters in their areas of expertise in a timely manner. Special thanks go to all the staff at Idea Group Inc., whose contributions throughout the whole process from inception of the initial idea to final publication have been invaluable. In particular, the editors are thankful to Mehdi Khosrow-Pour, senior academic editor of Idea Group Inc., for his support and encouragement in publishing this book. The authors are grateful to Kristin Roth, development editor, for her timely and professional cooperation, and for her decisive and kind support of this project.

In closing, we wish to thank all of the authors for their insights and excellent contributions to this book. We also want to thank Professor Elena Ferrari for kindly accepting to write a foreword for this book. Finally, we thank our families for their support and understanding throughout this project.

We hope that the readers will find these chapters informative and enlightening. Comments from readers will be greatly appreciated. Please contact us at avakali@csd.auth.gr and gpallis@ccf.auth.gr.

Athena Vakali and George Pallis
Thessaloniki, Greece
June 2006

Special Thanks to Reviewers

This project depends on the efforts of our volunteers to help us deliver high-quality peer-reviewed chapters. We thank the following reviewers for their gracious efforts.

- Lefteris Angelis, Aristotle University, Greece
- Nikos Bassiliades, Aristotle University, Greece
- Salima Benbernou, University of Lyon 1, France
- Barbara Catania, University of Genova, Italy
- Elena Ferrari, University of Insubria, Italy
- Fang Li, Shanghai Jiao Tong University, China
- Rosa Meo, University of Torino, Italy
- Marco Mesiti, University of Milano, Italy
- Giovanna Guerrini, University of Pisa, Italy
- Carlos Hurtado, University of Chile, Chile
- Dimitrios Katsaros, Aristotle University, Greece
- Vassiliki Koutsonikola, Aristotle University, Greece
- Jaroslav Pokorny, Charles University, Czech Republic
- Yucel Saygin, Sabanci University, Turkey

Section I

Web Data Mining

Chapter I

Data Clustering:
From Documents to the Web

Dušan Húsek, Academy of the Sciences of the Czech Republic, Czech Republic

Jaroslav Pokorný, Charles University, Czech Republic

Hana Řezanková, University of Economics, Prague, Czech Republic

Václav Snášel, Technical University of Ostrava, Czech Republic

Abstract

*This chapter provides a survey of some clustering methods relevant to clustering docu-
ment collections and, in consequence, Web data. We start with classical methods of cluster
analysis that seem to be relevant in approaching the clustering Web data. Graph clustering
is also described since its methods contribute significantly to clustering Web data. The use
of artificial neural networks for clustering has the same motivation. Based on previously
presented material, the core of the chapter provides an overview of approaches to clustering
in the Web environment. Particularly, we focus on clustering Web search results, in which
clustering search engines arrange the search results into groups around a common theme.*

We conclude with some general considerations concerning the justification of so many clustering algorithms and their application in the Web environment.

Introduction

Document and information retrieval (IR) is an important task for Web communities. In this chapter, we introduce some clustering methods and focus on their use for the clustering, classification, and retrieval of Web documents.

The aim of clustering is either to create groups of similar objects or to create a hierarchy of such groups (Jain & Dubes, 1988). Clustering is often confused with classification, but there is some difference between the two techniques. In classification, the objects are assigned to predefined classes, whereas in clustering, the classes are also to be defined. We focus here mainly on document clustering, for example, in which objects are texts, Web pages, phrases, and so forth. Any clustering technique relies on four concepts:

1.   the model of the data to be clustered,
2.   the similarity measure,
3.   the cluster model, and
4.   the clustering algorithm that builds the clusters using the data model and the similarity measure.

By a data model, we mean the common notion used in IR. For example, in the Boolean model, text is represented by a set of significant terms; in the vector space model, documents are modeled by vectors of term weights. The way objects are clustered is called the cluster model. This approach is in accordance with Jain and Dubes (1988), in which objects are called patterns and the following steps are considered:

•   pattern representation (optionally including feature extraction and/or selection),
•   the definition of a pattern proximity measure appropriate to the data domain,
•   clustering or grouping,
•   data abstraction (if needed), and
•   the assessment of output (if needed).

The last two steps concern the application of clustering. Data abstraction influences the description of clusters, for example, labels of folders when clustering with snippets in the Web environment. A difficult task is the assessment of output, that is, evaluating the quality of the clustering. Various statistical approaches are used in this context, while in IR we make this evaluation using the usual measures such as precision and recall. In the past, clustering was mainly addressed in exploratory data analysis. In consequence, most data clustering methods come from statistics. The other application area is the fast retrieval of relevant information from databases, particularly from huge text collections. In this chapter, we will present clustering from this perspective. As texts become more and more multimedia oriented, a lot of special clustering techniques can be applied in this context (e.g., image clustering). Consider the Web or a set of Web search results as a text collection. Web pages are modeled from various points of view. In a Web model, we can combine:

- textual information,
- the hyperlink structure,
- co-citation,
- metadata,
- pictures, and
- the HTML (HyperText Markup Language) or XML (eXtensible Markup Language) structure of Web pages.

We can observe that the hyperlink structure or combining data and metadata in XML documents, for example, extend usual assumptions about texts to be clustered. Consequently, new issues appear.

As different communities use clustering, the associated terminology varies widely. We will freely take up the taxonomy presented in Jain, Murty, and Flynn (1999).

- **Hierarchical vs. Flat:** In the former case, a hierarchy of clusters is found and objects can be assigned to a different number of clusters. The result of flat clustering is an assignment of objects to certain numbers of clusters determined before analysis. These methods are sometimes divided into partitioning methods if classes are mutually exclusive and use clumping methods, in which an overlap is allowed.

- **Agglomerative vs. Divisive (Hierarchical Clustering):** Agglomerative methods start with each object in a separation group, and then proceed until all objects are in a single group. Divisive methods start with all objects in a single group and proceed until each object is in a separate group.

- **Monothetic vs. Polythetic (Hierarchical Clustering):** Monothetic methods use single-feature-based assignment to divide objects into clusters. Polythetic algorithms consider multiple-feature-based assignment.

- **Hard vs. Fuzzy:** In nonfuzzy or hard clustering, objects are divided into crisp clusters, where each object belongs to exactly one cluster. In fuzzy clustering, the object can belong to more than one cluster, and associated with each of the objects are membership grades that indicate the degree to which the objects belong to the different clusters.

- **Deterministic vs. Stochastic:** Deterministic clustering methods, given a data set, always arrive at the same clustering. Stochastic clustering methods employ stochastic elements (e.g., random numbers) to find a good clustering.

- **Incremental vs. Nonincremental:** Non-incremental clustering methods mainly rely on having the whole data set ready before applying the algorithm. For example, a hierarchical agglomerative clustering belongs to this class. Incremental clustering algorithms work by assigning objects to their respective clusters as they arrive.

Besides flat and hierarchical methods, some authors (e.g., Han & Kamber, 2001; Mercer, 2003) distinguish three to four further categories. These are density-based approaches, grid-based approaches, model-based approaches, and also hybrid approaches, which are based on all mentioned approaches.

This chapter provides a survey of some clustering methods relevant to clustering document collections. We start with classical methods of cluster analysis. In general, the choice of methods has been influenced by progress appearing recently in approaching the clustering Web data. Graph clustering contributes to this issue. The section about artificial neural networks (ANNs) is built with the same motivation. Based on previously presented material, the chapter then tries to provide an overview of approaches to clustering in the Web environment. Particularly, we focus on clustering Web search results, in which clustering search engines arrange the search results into groups around a common theme. Finally, the chapter concludes with some considerations about clustering in Web environment.

Methods of Cluster Analysis

The following terms and notation will be used throughout this chapter.

- An *object* (or pattern, feature vector, or Web page) $\mathbf{x}$ is a single data item used by the clustering algorithm. It typically consists of a vector of p components $\mathbf{x} = (x_1,..., x_p)$.
- The individual scalar components x_i of an object $\mathbf{x}$ are called *features* (or attributes or values of variables).
- p is the dimensionality of the objects or of the feature space.
- An object set will be denoted by $X = \{\mathbf{x}_1,...,\mathbf{x}_n\}$ The ith object in X will be denoted by $\mathbf{x}_i = (x_{i1},..., x_{ip})$ In many cases, an object set to be clustered is viewed as an $n \times p$ object matrix.

Clustering is a division of the object set into subsets (groups) of similar objects. Each group, called a *cluster*, consists of objects that are similar between themselves and dissimilar to objects of other groups.

Clustering can be realized by means of such techniques as multivariate statistical methods, neural networks, genetic algorithms, and formal concept analysis. In the terminology of machine learning, we can talk about *unsupervised learning*. Statistical methods for clustering can be classified into groups like cluster analysis, multidimensional scaling (Gordon, 1999; Jain & Dubes, 1988), factor analysis, and correspondence analysis.

The following tasks should be solved in connection with the clustering of documents: the clustering of large data sets, clustering in high-dimensional spaces, a sparse matrix approach, and outlier detection and handling.

We can start with methods for the *vector space model* (VSM; Salton & Buckley, 1988), which represents a document as a vector of the terms that appear in the document set. Each feature vector contains term weights of the terms appearing in that document. The term weighting scheme is usually based on the *tf×idf* method in IR.

A collection of documents can be represented by a term-document matrix. *Similarity* between documents is measured using one of several similarity measures that are based on the relations of feature vectors, for example, by the cosine of feature vectors or, equivalently, by a distance measure (generally, we will use the term *proximity measure*). We can consider both documents (Web pages) and terms (topics) as objects of clustering. In the latter case, the searching of clusters is very close to the reduction of dimensionality. For example, factor analysis can be used both for the reduction of dimensionality and for clustering (Hartigan, 1975).

We can mention the following basic requirements for clustering techniques for large data sets (Han & Kamber, 2001): scalability (clustering techniques must be scalable, both in terms of computing time and memory requirements), the independence of the order of input (i.e., the order of objects that enter into analysis), and the ability to evaluate the validity of the produced clusters. The user usually wants to have a robust clustering technique that is strong in the following areas: dimensionality (the distance between two objects must be distinguishable in a high-dimensional space), noise and outliers (an algorithm must be able to detect noise and outliers and eliminate their negative effects), statistical distribution, cluster shape, cluster size, cluster density, and cluster separation (an algorithm must be able to detect overlapping clusters).

Particular attention is paid to the problem of high-dimensional data. Clustering algorithms based on proximity measures work effectively for dimensions below 16. Therefore, Berkhin (2002) claims that data with more than 16 attributes are high-dimensional. Two general techniques are used in the case of high dimensionality: *attributes transformation and domain decomposition*.

In the former case, for certain types of data, aggregated attributes can be used. If it is impossible, *principal component analysis* (PCA) can be applied. However, this approach is problematic since it leads to a cluster with poor interpretability. In the area of IR, the *singular value decomposition* (SVD) technique is used to reduce dimensionality. As concerns domain decomposition, it divides the data into subsets (canopies) using some inexpensive similarity measure. The dimension stays the same, but the costs are reduced. Some algorithms were designed for *subspace clustering*, for example, CLIQUE (CLustering In QUEst) and MAFIA (Merging of Adaptive Finite Intervals, And more than a CLIQUE).

For large data sets, hybrid methods, which combine different techniques, are often suggested. In the past 10 years, new approaches to clustering large data sets were suggested and some surveys of clustering methods were prepared, for example, in Berkhin (2002), Jain et al. (1999), Mercer (2003), and Řezanková, Húsek, and Snášel (2004).

Several approaches are used for clustering large data sets by means of traditional methods of cluster analysis. One of them can be characterized in the following way. Only objects of the sample (either random or representative) are clustered to the desired number of clusters. Other objects are assigned to these created clusters. In the second approach, the data set is divided into blocks (their size is determined by the capability of used software product), and in each block, objects are clustered. As results we obtain *centroids*, which characterize created clusters (a centroid is a vector of average values of object features computed on the base of objects assigned to the cluster). At the final stage, the centroids are clustered for obtaining the desired number of clusters. The centroids can be obtained also by other ways, for example, by incremental clustering.

For easier searching of document clusters, we can find groups of similar terms (topics). We can repeat the clustering of terms and documents for the achievement of interesting co-occurrences. We can find second-order co-occurrences of documents.

In the following text, we will focus only on the clustering of documents (Web pages) and subspace clustering. When clusters of documents (Web pages) are found, each cluster can be characterized in a certain way, for example, by a centroid or *medoid* (an object of the cluster that was chosen as a representative). In the process of IR, we can calculate similarity coefficients between the query and the centroid or medoid, and search for clusters of documents that best correspond to the query. This way of calculation is less time consuming for searching documents with high similarity than the calculation of similarity coefficients between the query and individual documents.

Dissimilarity and Similarity Measures

A *dissimilarity* (or *distance*) between object x and y (or distance measure) is represented by the function $d(x, y) : X \times X \rightarrow R$, which satisfies the following conditions:

$d(x, x) = 0$

$d(x, y) \geq 0$

$d(x, y) = d(y, x)$

For distance, we require triangle inequality to be satisfied; that is, for any objects x, y, and z:

$d(x, z) = d(x, y) + d(y, z)$

A *similarity* $s(x, y)$ between object x and y is the function $s(x, y) : X \times X \rightarrow R$, which satisfies the following conditions:

$s(x, x) = 1$

$s(x, y) \geq 0$

$s(x, y) = s(y, x)$

Both dissimilarity and similarity functions are often defined by a matrix.

Some clustering algorithms operate on a dissimilarity matrix (they are called distance-space methods in Mercer, 2003). How the dissimilarity between two objects is computed depends on the type of the original objects.

Here are some of the most frequently used dissimilarity measures for continuous data:

- *Minkowski L_q distance (for $1 \geq q$)*

$$d(\mathbf{x}_i, \mathbf{x}_j) = \sqrt[q]{\sum_{l=1}^{P} |x_{il} - x_{jl}|^q}$$

- *City*-block (or Manhattan distance or L_1)

$$d(\mathbf{x}_i, \mathbf{x}_j) = \sum_{l=1}^{P} |x_{il} - x_{jl}|$$

- *Euclidean distance (L_2)*

$$d(\mathbf{x}_i, \mathbf{x}_j) = \sqrt{\sum_{l=1}^{P} (x_{il} - x_{jl})^2}$$

- *Chebychev distance metric* (or maximum or L_∞)

$$d(\mathbf{x}_i, \mathbf{x}_j) = \max_{l=1,\dots,P} (|x_{il} - x_{jl}|)$$

In the case of Chebychev distance, the objects with the largest dispersion will have the largest impact on the clustering. If all objects are considered equally important, the data need to be standardized first. If continuous measurements are on an unknown scale (*continuous ordinal variables*), each value x_{ip} must be replaced by its rank, and the rank scale must be transformed to <0,1> Then dissimilarities, as for interval-scaled variables, can be used.

A relation between two objects can be expressed also as a similarity (Berry & Browne, 1999). It can be measured as a correlation between feature vectors. For interval-scaled data, the Pearson correlation coefficient is used, but values are from the interval $< -1,1 >$. A further possibility is a *cosine measure*. The cosine of feature vectors is calculated according to the following formula:

$$s(\mathbf{x}_i, \mathbf{x}_j) = \frac{\sum_{l=1}^{P} x_{il} x_{jl}}{\sqrt{\sum_{l=1}^{P} x_{il}^2} \sqrt{\sum_{l=1}^{P} x_{jl}^2}} \; .$$

Furthermore, we can use the *Jaccard coefficient* or *Dice coefficient*. The former can be expressed as:

$$s(\mathbf{x}_i, \mathbf{x}_j) = \frac{\sum_{l=1}^{P} x_{il} x_{jl}}{\sum_{l=1}^{P} x_{il}^2 + \sum_{l=1}^{P} x_{jl}^2 - \sum_{l=1}^{P} x_{il} x_{jl}}$$

and the latter as:

$$s(\mathbf{x}_i,\mathbf{x}_j) = \frac{2 \times \sum_{l=1}^{p} x_{il} x_{jl}}{\sum_{l=1}^{p} x_{il}^2 + \sum_{l=1}^{p} x_{jl}^2}.$$

Concerning *binary* variables, we distinguish symmetric ones (both categories are equally important, e.g., male and female) and asymmetric ones (one category carries more importance than the other). For document clustering, the latter has to be considered. Let us consider the following contingency table:

$\mathbf{x}_i / \mathbf{x}_j$	1	0
1	a	b
0	c	d

with frequencies a, b, c, and d. For asymmetric variables, we can use, for example, the Jaccard coefficient or Dice coefficient. The former can be expressed as:

$$s(\mathbf{x}_i,\mathbf{x}_j) = \frac{a}{a+b+c}$$

and the latter as:

$$s(\mathbf{x}_i,\mathbf{x}_j) = \frac{2a}{2a+b+c}.$$

We can also use the cosine of feature vectors, that is, the Ochiai coefficient:

$$s(\mathbf{x}_i,\mathbf{x}_j) = \sqrt{\frac{a}{a+b} \times \frac{a}{a+c}}.$$

If the data set is a contingency table with frequencies of categories, we can use dissimilarity measures based on the *chi*-square test of equality for two sets of frequencies:

$$d(\mathbf{x}_i,\mathbf{x}_j) = \sqrt{\sum_{l=1}^{p} \frac{(x_{il} - E(x_{il}))^2}{E(x_{il})} + \sum_{l=1}^{p} \frac{(x_{jl} - E(x_{jl}))^2}{E(x_{jl})}},$$

where $E(x_{il})$ and $E(x_{jl})$ are expected values on the assumption of independency in the contingency table:

$$E(x_{il}) = \frac{\sum_{m=1}^{p}(x_{im}) \times (x_{il} + x_{jl})}{\sum_{m=1}^{p}x_{im} + \sum_{m=1}^{p}x_{jm}}.$$

We can also use *phi*-square between sets of frequencies: The *chi*-square statistic is divided by the total number of cases, and the square root of this value is computed.

There are a lot of measures for clustering. We will mention how the distance between clusters can be measured. The log-likelihood distance between clusters a and b is:

$$d(a,b) = z_a + z_b - z_{<a,b>},$$

where $<a,b>$ denotes a cluster created by joining objects from clusters a and b, and:

$$z_v = -n_v \sum_{l=1}^{p} \frac{1}{2}\log(s_l^2 + s_{vl}^2),$$

where n_v is the number of objects in the vth cluster, p is the number of variables, s_l^2 is a sample variance of the lth continuous variable, and s_{vl}^2 is a sample variance of the lth continuous variable in the vth cluster. This measure can also be used for investigating the distance between objects.

Partitioning Algorithms

These methods divide the data set into k clusters, where the integer k needs to be specified by the user. An initial classification is modified by moving objects from one group to another if this will reduce the sum of the squares. The algorithm of k-means is very often described in the literature. For large data sets, some algorithms are based on the PAM (partitioning around medoids) algorithm. The algorithms k-means and k-medoids belong to methods of hard clustering. However, we have to consider also the possibility of overlapping clusters. One approach to solve this task is fuzzy clustering.

Partitioning around Medoids. The algorithm proceeds in two steps. First, for a given cluster assignment, centrally located objects (medoids) are selected by minimizing the total distance to other objects in the cluster. At the second step, each object is assigned to the closest medoid. Object $\mathbf{x}_i$ is put into cluster v when medoid m_v is nearer than any other medoid m_w; that is:

$$d(\mathbf{x}_i, m_v) \leq d(\mathbf{x}_i, m_w) \text{ for all } w = 1, 2, ..., k.$$

These two steps are repeated until assignments do not change.

The PAM algorithm was extended to the CLARA (Clustering LARge Applications) method (Kaufman & Rousseeuw, 1990). CLARA clusters a sample from the data set and then assigns all objects in the data set to these clusters. The process is repeated several times, and then the clustering with the smallest average distance is selected.

The improvement of the CLARA algorithm is CLARANS (Clustering Large Applications based on a RANdomized Search; Ng & Han, 1994). It proceeds by searching a random subset of the neighbours of a particular solution. Thus, the search for the best representation is not confined to a local area of the data.

Fuzzy Cluster Analysis. The aim of these methods is to compute memberships u_{iv} for each object $\mathbf{x}_i$ and each cluster v. Memberships have to satisfy the following conditions (Gordon, 1999; Höppner, Klawon, Kruse, & Runkler, 2000):

$$u_{iv} \geq 0 \text{ for all } i = 1,...,n \text{ and all } v = 1,...,k,$$

$$\sum_{v=1}^{k} u_{iv} = 1 \text{ for all } i = 1,...,n$$

The memberships are defined through the minimization of function f:

$$f = \sum_{v=1}^{k} \frac{\sum_{i,j=1}^{n} u_{iv}^2 u_{jv}^2 d(\mathbf{x}_i, \mathbf{x}_j)}{2 \times \sum_{j=1}^{n} u_{jv}^2},$$

where dissimilarities $d(\mathbf{x}_i,\mathbf{x}_j)$ are known and memberships u_{iv} and u_{jv} are unknown.

Hierarchical Algorithms

A hierarchical agglomerative algorithm starts with each object in a group of its own. Then the algorithm merges clusters until only one large cluster remains, which is the whole data set. The user must select variables, and choose dissimilarity or similarity measures and the agglomerative procedure. At the first step, when each object represents its own cluster, the dissimilarity $d(\mathbf{x}_i,\mathbf{x}_j)$ between objects $\mathbf{x}_i$ and $\mathbf{x}_j$ is defined by the chosen dissimilarity measure. However, once several objects have been linked together, we need a linkage or amalgamation rule to determine when two clusters are sufficiently similar to be linked together. Numerous linkage rules have been proposed.

The distance between two different clusters can be determined by the distance of the two closest objects in the clusters (single-linkage method), the greatest distance between two objects in the clusters (complete-linkage method), or the average distance between all pairs of objects in the two clusters (unweighted pair-group average method). Furthermore, this distance can be determined by the weighted average distance between all pairs of objects in the two clusters (the number of objects in a cluster is used as a weight), or the distance between centroids (unweighted or weighted). Moreover, we can use the method that attempts to minimize the sum of squares of differences of individual values from their average in the cluster (Ward's method).

The hierarchical approach is used in some algorithms proposed for clustering large data sets. We can mention the BIRCH (balanced iterative reducing and clustering using hierarchies;

Zhang, Ramakrishnan, & Livny, 1996) method as an example. Objects in the data set are arranged into subclusters, known as cluster features (CFs). These cluster features are then clustered into *k* groups using a traditional hierarchical clustering procedure. A CF represents a set of summary statistics on a subset of the data. The algorithm consists of two phases. In the first one, an initial CF tree is built (a multilevel compression of the data that tries to preserve the inherent clustering structure of the data). In the second one, an arbitrary clustering algorithm is used to cluster the leaf nodes of the CF tree. The disadvantage of this method is its sensitivity to the order of the objects.

Two-Way Joining Algorithm

Two-way joining is useful in (the relatively rare) circumstances when one expects that both objects and variables (documents and features) will simultaneously contribute to the uncovering of meaningful patterns of clusters. The difficulty with interpreting these results may arise from the fact that the similarities between different clusters may pertain to (or be caused by) somewhat different subsets of variables. Thus, the resulting structure (clusters) is by nature not homogeneous. However, this method offers a powerful exploratory data analysis tool (the detailed description of this method is in Hartigan, 1975).

We can explain the use of this method by a simple example. Let us suppose that we have three variables. Two of them are categorical. We know only one value of the third variable corresponding to the certain combination of categories of categorical variables. This value is 0 or 1. We investigate the similarity of categories for each categorical variable on the basis of values of the third variable. If values of the third variable are written into a cross-table, where categories of one variable are situated in rows and categories of the second one in columns, both row clusters and column clusters can be distinguished.

At each step of the algorithm, such pairs of rows or columns that are closest in a certain distance measure are joined. The closest pair of rows (columns) makes a new row (column) by using a certain linkage rule. This algorithm can be generalized to many-way tables.

Subspace Clustering

In high-dimensional spaces, clusters often lie in a *subspace*. To handle this situation, some algorithms are suggested. Instead of the creation of reduced matrices based on new features (obtained, for example, by linear combinations of original features), subspaces of the original data space are investigated. The task is based on the original features, which have real meaning while linear combinations of many dimensions may be sometimes hard to interpret. Subspace clustering is based on a density-based approach. The aim is to find subsets of features for which projections of the input data include high-density regions. The principle is the partitioning of each dimension into the same number of equal-length intervals. The clusters are unions of connected high-density units within a subspace.

CLIQUE, suggested for numerical variables by Agrawal, Gehrke, Gunopulos, and Raghavan (1998), is a clustering algorithm that finds high-density regions by partitioning the data space into cells (hyperrectangles) and finding the dense cells. Clusters are found by taking the union of all high-density cells. For simplicity, clusters are described by expressing a cluster as a DNF (disjunctive normal form) expression and then simplifying the expression.

MAFIA is a modification of CLIQUE that runs faster and finds better quality clusters. pMAFIA is the parallel version. MAFIA was presented by Goil, Nagesh, and Choudhary (1999), and Nagesh, Goil, and Choudhary (2001). The main modification is the use of an adaptive grid. Initially, each dimension is partitioned into a fixed number of cells.

Moreover, we can mention the algorithm ENCLUS (entropy-based clustering) suggested by Cheng, Fu, and Zhang (1999). In comparison with CLIQUE, it uses a different criterion for subspace selection.

Graph Clustering

Networks arising from real life are concerned with relations between real objects and are an important part of modern life. Important examples include links between Web pages, citations of references in scientific papers, social networks of acquaintance, or other connections between individuals, such as those for electric power grids and so forth. A word network is usually used for what mathematicians and a few computer scientists calls graphs (Newman, 2003). A *graph* (*network*) is a set of items called *nodes* (*vertices*) with connections between them called *edges* (*links*). The study of graph theory is one of the fundamental pillars of discrete mathematics.

A *social network* is a set of people or groups of people with some pattern of contacts or interactions between them. Social networks have been studied extensively since the beginning of the 20th century, when sociologists realized the importance of understanding how human society functions. The traditional way to analyze a graph is to look at its picture, but for large networks, this is not useful. A new approach to examine properties of graphs has been driven largely by the availability of computers and communication networks that allow us to analyze data on a scale far larger than before (Guimerà, Danon, Díaz-Guilera, Giralt, & Arenas, 2003; Newman, Balthrop, Forrest, & Williamson, 2004).

An interesting source of reliable data about personal connections between people is communication records of certain kinds. For example, one could construct a network in which each node represents an e-mail address and directed edges represent messages passing from one address to another.

Complex networks such as the Web, social networks, or e-mail often do not have an engineered architecture, but instead are self-organized by the actions of a large number of individuals. From these local interactions, nontrivial global phenomena can emerge as, for example, small-world properties or a scale-free distribution of the degree (Newman et al., 2003). In *small-world networks*, short paths between almost any two sites exist even though nodes are highly clustered. *Scale-free networks* are characterized by a power-law distribution of a node's degree, defined as the number of its next neighbours, meaning that the structure and dynamics of the network are strongly affected by nodes with a great number of connections. It is reported in Ebel, Mielsch, and Bornholdt (2002) that networks composed of persons connected by exchanged e-mails show both the characteristics of small-world networks and scale-free networks.

The Web can be considered a graph where nodes are HTML pages and edges are hyperlinks between these pages. This graph is called the *Web graph*. It has been the subject of a variety of recent works aimed at understanding the structure of the Web (Huang & Lai, 2003).

A *directed graph* $G = (V, E)$ consists of a set of nodes, denoted as V, and a set of edges, denoted as E. Each edge is an ordered pair of nodes (u, v) representing a directed connection from u to v. The graph $G = (V, E)$ is often represented by the *adjacency matrix* W by $|V| \times |V|$, where $w_{ij} = 1$ if $(v_i, v_j) \in E$ and $w_{ij} = 0$ in other cases. The *out-degree* of a node u is the number of distinct edges $(u, v_1) \ldots (u, v_k)$ (i.e., the number of links from u), and the *in-degree* is the number of distinct edges $(v_1, u) \ldots (v_k, u)$ (i.e., the number of links to u). A *path* from node u to node v is a sequence of edges $(u, u_1), (u_1, u_2), \ldots (u_k, v)$. One can follow such a sequence of edges to walk through the graph from u to v. Note that a path from u to v does not imply a path from v to u. The *distance* from u to v is one more than the smallest k for which such a path exists. If no path exists, the distance from u to v is defined to be infinity. If (u, v) is an edge, then the distance from u to v is 1.

Given a directed graph, a *strongly connected* component (*strong component* for brevity) of this graph is a set of nodes such that for any pair of nodes u and v in the set, there is a path from u to v. In general, a directed graph may have one or many strong components. The strong components of a graph consist of disjoint sets of nodes. One focus of our studies will be in understanding the distribution of the sizes of strong components on the Web graph.

An *undirected graph* consists of a set of nodes and a set of edges, each of which is an unordered pair {u,v} of nodes. In our context, we say there is an edge between u and v if there is a link between u and v, without regard to whether the link points from u to v or the other way around. The *degree deg(u)* of a node u is the number of edges incident to u. A path is defined as in directed graphs, except that now the existence of a path from u to v implies a path from v to u. A *component* of an undirected graph is a set of nodes such that for any pair of nodes u and v in the set, there is a path from u to v. We refer to the components of the undirected graph obtained from a directed graph by ignoring the directions of its edges as the weak components of the directed graph. Thus, two nodes on the Web may be in the same weak component even though there is no directed path between them (consider, for instance, a node u that points to two other nodes v and w; then v and w are in the same weak component even though there may be no sequence of links leading from v to w or vice versa). The interplay of strong and weak components on the (directed) Web graph turns out to reveal some unexpected properties of the Web's connectivity.

Informally, we can say that two nodes are considered *similar* if there are many short paths connecting them. On the contrary, the shortest path distance does not necessarily decrease when connections between nodes are added, and thus it does not capture the fact that strongly connected nodes are at a smaller distance away from each other than weakly connected nodes.

The main findings about the Web structure are as follows.

- A power-law distribution of degrees (Kumar, Raghavan, Rajagopalan, & Tomkins, 1999): The in-degree and out-degree distribution of the nodes of the Web graph follows the power law.

- A bow-tie shape (Broder et al., 2000): the Web's macroscopic structure.

- The average path length between two Web pages: 16 (Broder et al., 2000) and 19 (Barabasi & Albert, 1999).

- Small-world phenomenon (Adamic, 1999): Six degrees of separation between any two Web pages.

- Cybercommunities (Kumar et al., 1999): groups of individuals who share a common interest, together with the most popular Web pages among them.

- Self-similarity structure (Dill, Kumar, McCurley, Rajagopalan, Sivakumar, & Tomkins, 2002): The Web shows a fractal structure in many different ways.

Link analysis plays an import role in understanding the Web's structure. There are three well-known algorithms for ranking pages: HITS (hypertext induced topic selection), PageRank, and SALSA (stochastic approach for link-structure analysis; Schenker, Kande, Bunke, & Last, 2005).

Schenker et al. (2005) describe exciting new opportunities for utilizing robust graph representations of data with common machine-learning algorithms. Graphs can model additional information that is often not present in commonly used data representations, such as vectors. Through the use of graph distance, a relatively new approach for determining graph similarity, the authors show how well-known algorithms, such as k-means clustering and k-nearest-neighbours classification, can be easily extended to work with graphs instead of vectors. This allows for the utilization of additional information found in graph representations, while at the same time employing well-known, proven algorithms.

Linear Algebra Background

Any $m \times n$ matrix A can be expressed as:

$$A = \sum_{t=1}^{r} s_t(A)u(t)v(t)^T,$$

where r is the rank of A, $\sigma_1(A) \geq \sigma_2(A) \geq ... \geq \sigma_r(A) > 0$ are its singular values, and $u(t) \in R^m$, $v(t) \in R^n$, $t = 1,...,r$ are its left and right singular vectors, respectively. The $u(t)$ and the $v(t)$ are orthonormal sets of vectors; namely, $u(i)^T u(j)$ is 1 if $i = j$, and 0 otherwise. We also remind the reader that:

- Frobenius norm

$$\|A\|_F^2 = \sum_{i,j} A_{i,j}^2 = \sum_{i=1}^{r} \sigma_i^2(A)$$

- 2-norm

$$\|A\|_2 = \max_{x \in R^n, \|x\|=1} \|Ax\| = \max_{x \in R^m, \|x\|=1} \|x^T A\| = \sigma_1(A)$$

In matrix notation, SVD is defined as $A = U \Sigma V^T$, where U and V are orthogonal matrices (thus, $U^T U = I$ and $V^T V = I$, and an I matrix is the identity matrix $I = \{d_{ij}\}$, where d_{ij} is the Kronecker symbol) of dimensions $m \times r$ and $n \times r$ respectively, containing the left and right singular vectors of A $\Sigma = diag(\sigma_1(A),..., \sigma_r(A))$ is an $r \times r$ diagonal matrix containing the singular values of A. If we define $A_l = \sum_{t=1}^{l} \sigma_t(A) u(t) v(t)^T$, then A_l is the best rank l approximation to A with respect to the 2-norm and the Frobenius norm. Thus, for any matrix D of rank at most l $\|A - A_k\|_2 \leq \|A - D\|_2$ and $\|A - A_k\|_F \leq \|A - D\|_F$. A matrix A has a good rank l approximation if $A - A_l$ is small with respect to the 2-norm and the Frobenius norm. It is well known that $\|A - A_k\|_F^2 = \sum_{t=l+1}^{r} \sigma_t^2(A)$ and $\|A - A_k\|_2 = \sigma_{l+1}(A)$. From basic linear algebra, $A_l = U_l \Sigma_l V_l^T = A V_l V_l^T = U_l U_l^T A$, where U_l and V_l are submatrices of U and V containing only the top k left and right singular vectors of A respectively; for a detailed treatment of SVD, see Golub and Van Loan (1989).

Eigenvector Clustering of Graphs

Donath and Hoffman (1973) introduced the use of eigenvectors for the purpose of partitioning an undirected graph in a balanced way. Since then, there has been a lot of work on spectral approaches for graph partitioning. See Chung (1997) for an excellent overview of the field. Shi and Malik (2000) showed that the eigenvectors of different matrices based on the adjacency matrix of a graph are related to different kinds of balanced cuts in a graph. Let W be the adjacency matrix of an undirected graph $G = (V,E)$ with nodes $1,2,...,n$, and let D be a diagonal matrix with $d_i = deg(i)$. Let A and B be sets of nodes and let $E(A,B)$ be the set of edges (u,v) with $u \in A$ and $v \in B$. Two subsets A and B of V, such that $A \cup B = V$ and $A \cap B = \varnothing$, define a *cut* in G, which we denote as (A, B).

The average association of a set A is:

$|E(A,A)| / |A|$.

The average cut of a set A is:

$|E(A,V-A)| / |A| + |E(A,V-A)| / |V-A|$.

The normalized cut of a set A is:

$|E(A,V-A)| / |E(A,V)| + |E(A,V-A)| / |E(V-A,V)|$.

Then Shi and Malik (2000) show that:

- the second largest eigenvector of W is related to a set that maximizes the average association,

- the second smallest eigenvector of $D - W$ (also known as the algebraic connectivity or Fiedler value; Fiedler, 1975) is related to a set that minimizes the average cut, and

- the second smallest eigenvector of the generalized eigenvector problem $(D - W)x = \lambda Dx$ gives an approximation of the smallest normalized cut.

These results hold for undirected graphs, but the Web graph is a directed graph. Thus, it would be interesting to understand what the above relationships are for directed graphs, that is, whether the eigenvectors of the corresponding matrices of a directed graph are also related to balanced decompositions of the directed graph. It is possible that this would lead to an interesting clustering of the Web graph or to a topic-specific subgraph. The first step in this direction was taken by Gibson, Kleinberg, and Raghavan (1998). They used the eigenvectors of the matrix AA^T and the matrix A^TA, where A is the adjacency matrix of a topic-specific subgraph, to decompose topic-specific subgraphs. They show that the principal eigenvector and the top few nonprincipal eigenvectors decompose the topic graphs into multiple hyperlinked communities, that is, clusters of pages on the same subtopic (Henzinger, 2003). Lots of examples of eigenvector computations can be found in the survey paper of Langville and Meyer (2005).

Roughly speaking, from spectral analysis, we obtain the decomposition of a graph to a high-order connected component (Fiedler, 1973, 1975). The work by He, Ding, Zha, and Simon (2001) compares clustering based on the Fiedler vector with the k-means clustering method and found that the results of spectral partitioning are usually much better.

Connectivity Clustering of Graphs

Although there are numerous algorithms for cluster analysis in the literature, we briefly review the approaches that are closely related to the structure of a graph.

Matula (1970, 1972, 1977) uses high connectivity in similarity graphs for cluster analysis, which is based on the cohesiveness function. The function defines every node and edge of a graph to be the maximum edge connectivity of any subgraph containing that element. The *k-connected subgraphs* of the graph are obtained by deleting all elements with cohesiveness less than k in the graph, where k is a constant value. It is hard to determine the connectivity values in real clustering applications with this approach.

There are approaches using biconnected components (two connected subgraphs). The work of Canutescu, Shelenkob, and Dunbrack (2003) introduces a new algorithm for protein structure prediction based on biconnected components. In Henzinger (1997), the author presents fully dynamic algorithms for maintaining the biconnected components.

There is a recent work related to the clustering of a graph. The HCS (highly connected subgraphs) algorithm (Hartuv & Shamir, 2000) use a similarity graph as the input data. The algorithm recursively partitions a current set of elements into two subsets. It then identifies highly connected subgraphs in which the number of edges exceeds half the number of their corresponding nodes as kernels among them. A kernel is considered a cluster. Unfortunately, the result of the clustering is not uniquely determined.

The CLICK (CLuster Identification via Connectivity Kernal) algorithm (Sharan & Shamir, 2000) builds on a statistical model. It uses the same basic scheme as HCS to form kernels, and includes the following processing: singleton adoption, a recursive clustering process on the set of remaining singletons, and an iterative merging step.

CAST (cluster affinity search technique; Ben-Dor, Shamir, & Yakhini, 1999) uses a single parameter t and starts with a single object. Objects are added or removed from the cluster if their affinities are larger or lower than t, respectively, until the process stabilizes.

In Huang and Lai (2003), definitions of homogeneity and separation to measure the quality of a graph clustering are introduced.

In Newman (2006), Newman's Q function is used for graph embedding into Euclidean space. This representation is used for fast geometric clustering.

Combined Methods

Cai, He, Li, Ma, and Wen (2004) described a method to organize Web image search results. Based on the Web context, they proposed three representations for Web images, that is, representation based on a visual feature, representation based on a textual feature, and representation induced from the image link graph. Spectral techniques were applied to cluster the search results into different semantic categories. They show that the combination of textual-feature-based representation and graph-based representation actually reflects the semantic relationships between Web images.

In Lian, Cheung, Mamoulis, and Yiu (2004), the algorithm S-GRACE (s-graph-based clustering algorithm for query performance enhancement) is presented. S-GRACE is a hierarchical clustering algorithm on XML documents that applies a categorical clustering algorithm ROCK (RObust Clustering using linKs; Guha, Rastogi, & Shim, 1999) on the s-graphs (structure graphs) extracted from the XML documents.

For two XML documents $\mathbf{x}_i$ and $\mathbf{x}_j$, the distance between them is defined by:

$$d(\mathbf{x}_i, \mathbf{x}_j) = 1 - \frac{|sg(\mathbf{x}_i) \cap sg(\mathbf{x}_j)|}{\max(|sg(\mathbf{x}_i)|, |sg(\mathbf{x}_j)|)},$$

where $sg(\mathbf{x}_i)$ is a structure graph ($i = 1, 2$), $|sg(\mathbf{x}_i)|$ is the number of edges in $sg(\mathbf{x}_i)$, and $sg(\mathbf{x}_i) \cap sg(\mathbf{x}_j)$ is the set of common edges of $sg(\mathbf{x}_i)$ and $sg(\mathbf{x}_j)$.

Artificial Neural Networks

Artificial neural networks (ANNS) belong to the adaptive class of techniques in the machine-learning area. ANNs try to mimic the biological neural network — the brain — to solve basic, computationally hard problems of AI (artificial intelligence).

There are three important and attractive features of ANNs:

1.   their capability of learning from example (extracting knowledge from data),

2.   they are naturally parallel and thus should be computationally effective, and

3.   they work incrementally — the whole data set is not necessary at once.

These features make ANNs a very interesting and promising clustering choice for large data sets including multimedia and text files.

Most models of ANNs are organized in the form of a number of processing units (also called artificial neurons or simply neurons; McCulloch, 1943) and a number of weighted connections (artificial synapses) between the neurons. The process of building an ANN, similar to its biological inspiration, involves a learning episode (also called training). During the learning episode, the network observes a sequence of recorded data and adjusts the strength of its synapses according to a learning algorithm and the observed data. The process of adjusting the synaptic strengths in order to be able to accomplish a certain task, much like the brain, is called learning. Learning algorithms are generally divided into two types: supervised and unsupervised. The supervised algorithms require labeled training data. In other words, they require more a priori knowledge about the training set.

There is a very large body of research that has resulted in a large number of ANN designs. For a more complete review of the various ANN types, see Hassoun (1995) and Rumelhart and McClelland (1988). In this chapter, we discuss only some of the types that have been used in the data mining area.

Layered, Feed-Forward, and Back-Propagation Neural Networks

These are a class of ANNs whose neurons are organized in layers. The layers are normally fully connected, meaning that each element (neuron) of a layer is connected to each element of the next layer. However, self-organizing varieties also exist in which a network either starts with a minimal number of synaptic connections between the layers and adds new ones as training progresses (*constructive*), or starts as a fully connected network and prunes connections based on the data observed in training (*destructive*; Hassoun, 1995; Rumelhart & McClelland, 1988).

Back propagation (Rumelhart & McClelland, 1988) is a learning algorithm that, in its original version, belongs to the gradient-descent optimization methods (Wu, 1996b). The combination of the back-propagation learning algorithm and the feed-forward, layered networks provides the most popular type of ANNs. These ANNs have been applied to virtually all pattern-recognition problems and are typically the first networks tried on a new problem. The reason for this is the simplicity of the algorithm and the vast body of research that has studied these networks. As such, in sequencing, many researchers have also used this type of network as a first line of attack. Examples can be found in Wu, Zhao, Chen, Lo, and McLarty (1996) and Wu (1995). In Wu (1995), the author has developed a system called the gene-classification artificial neural system (GenCANS), which is based on a three-layered, feed-forward, back-propagation network.

Self-Organizing Neural Networks

These networks are a very large class of neural networks whose structure (number of neurons, number of synaptic connections, number of modules, or number of layers) changes during learning based on the observed data. There are two classes of this type of networks: destructive and constructive. Destructive networks are initially a fully connected topology, and the learning algorithm prunes synapses (sometimes entire neurons, modules, or layers) based on the observed data. The final remaining network after learning is complete usually is a sparsely connected network. Constructive algorithms start with a minimally connected network and gradually add synapses (neurons, modules, or layers) as training progresses in order to accommodate for the complexity of the task at hand.

Self-Organizing Map. A self-organizing map (SOM; Kohonen, 2001) is a neural-network paradigm first proposed by Kohonen (1991). SOMs have been used as a divisive clustering approach in many areas. Several groups have used SOMs to discover pattern clusters in Web pages or in textual documents (Anonymous, 2005a, b). A special version of this paradigm, WEBSOM, was developed for Web-page clustering (Kaski, Honkela, Lagus, & Kohonen, 1998; Kohonen et al., 2000). With the WEBSOM method, a textual document collection is organized onto a graphical map display that provides an overview of the collection and facilitates interactive browsing. Interesting documents can be located on the map using a content-directed search. Each document is encoded as a histogram of term categories that are formed by the SOM algorithm based on the similarities in the contexts of the terms. The encoded documents are organized on another self-organizing map — a document map — on which nearby locations contain similar documents. Special consideration is given to the computation of very large document maps, which is possible with general-purpose computers if the dimensionality of the term-category histograms is first reduced with a random mapping method and if computationally efficient algorithms are used in computing the SOMs.

SOM as a clustering method has some disadvantages. One of them is the necessity for the introduction of a decay coefficient that stops the learning (clustering) phase. If the map is allowed to grow indefinitely, the size of the SOM is gradually increased to a point at which clearly different sets of expression patterns are identified. Therefore, as with k-means clustering, the user has to rely on some other source of information, such as PCA, to determine the number of clusters that best represents the available data. For this reason, Sásik, Hwa, Iranfar, and Loomis (2001) believe that SOM, as implemented by Tamayo et al. (1999), is essentially a restricted version of k-means: Here, the k clusters are linked by some arbitrary user-imposed topological constraints (e.g., a 3×2 grid), and as such, the SOM suffers from all of the problems mentioned above for k-means (and more), except that the constraints expedite the optimization process. There are many varieties of SOM, among which the self-organizing feature maps (SOFM) should be mentioned (Kohonen, 1991, 2001). The growing cell structure (GCS; Fritzke, 1974) is a derivative of SOFM. It is a self-organizing and incremental (constructive) neural learning approach.

Self-Organizing Trees. Self-organizing trees are normally constructive neural network methods that develop into a tree (usually a binary tree) topology during learning. Among examples of these networks, the work of Dopazo and Carazo (1997), Wang, Dopazo, and Carazo (1998), and Herrero, Valencia, and Dopazo (2001) can be mentioned. Dopazo and Carazo introduce the self-organizing tree algorithm (SOTA). SOTA is a hierarchical neural network that grows into a binary tree topology. For this reason, SOTA can be considered a hierarchical clustering algorithm. SOTA is based on Kohonen's SOM discussed above and Fritzke's growing cell (Fritzke, 1974). SOTA's performance is superior to that of classical hierarchical clustering techniques. Among the advantages of SOTA as compared to hierarchical cluster algorithms are its lower time complexity and its top-to-bottom hierarchical approach. SOTA's runtimes are approximately linear with the number of items to be classified, making it suitable for large data sets. Also, because SOTA forms higher clusters in the hierarchy before forming the lower clusters, it can be stopped at any level of the hierarchy and still produces meaningful intermediate results. There are many other types of self-organizing trees.

Recurrent ANNs

ART and its Derivatives. Adaptive resonance theory (ART) was introduced by Stephen Grossberg (1976a, b). Networks based on ART are unsupervised and self-organizing, and they only learn in the so-called resonant state. ART can form (stable) clusters of arbitrary sequences of input patterns by learning (entering resonant states) and self-organizing. Since its inception, many derivatives of ART have emerged. Among these, ART-1 (the binary version of ART that forms clusters of binary input data; Carpenter & Grossberg, 1987b), ART-2 (analog version of ART; Carpenter & Grossberg, 1987a), ART-2A (fast version of ART-2; Carpenter, Grossberg, & Rosen, 1991a), ART-3 (includes chemical transmitters to control the search process in a hierarchical ART structure; Carpenter & Grossberg, 1990), and ARTMAP (supervised version of ART; Carpenter, Grossberg, & Reynolds, 1991) can be mentioned. Many hybrid varieties such as fuzzy ART (Carpenter, Grossberg, & Rosen, 1991b), fuzzy ARTMAP (supervised Fuzzy-ART; Carpenter, Grossberg, Markuzon, Reynolds, & Rosen, 1992; Carpenter, Grossberg, & Reynolds, 1995), and simplified fuzzy ARTMAP (SFAM; Kasuba, 1993) have also been developed.

These networks have a broad application in virtually all areas of clustering. In general, in problem settings when the number of clusters is not previously known a priori, researchers tend to use unsupervised ART; when the number of clusters is known a priori, usually the supervised version, ARTMAP, is used. Among the unsupervised implementations, the work of Tomida, Hanai, Honda, and Kobayashi (2001) should be mentioned. Here the authors used fuzzy ART for expression-level data analysis. Fuzzy ART incorporates the basic features of all ART systems, notably, pattern matching between bottom-up input and top-down learned prototype vectors. This matching process leads either to a resonant state that focuses attention and triggers stable prototype learning or to a self-regulating parallel memory search. If the search ends by selecting an established category, then the category's prototype may be refined to incorporate new information in the input pattern. If the search ends by selecting a previously untrained node, then learning of a new category takes place. Fuzzy ART performs best in noisy data. Although ART has been used in several research works as a text clustering tool, the level of the quality of the resulting document clusters has not been clearly established. In Massey (2003), the author presents experimental results with binary ART that address this issue by determining how close the clustering quality is to an upper bound on the quality.

Associative clustering neural networks. Since the introduction of the concept of auto-associative memory by Hopfield (1982), there have been many associative-memory models built with neural networks (Kawamura, Okada, & Hirai, 1999; Kosko, 1987). Most of them can be considered store-recall models, and the correlation between any two D-bit bipolar patterns $s(\mathbf{x}_i,\mathbf{x}_j)$, $x_{id} \in \{-1,1\}$ for all $l = 1,...,p$ is often determined by a static measurement such as:

$$s(\mathbf{x}_i,\mathbf{x}_j) = \frac{1}{p}\sum_{l=1}^{p} x_{il}x_{jl}.$$

The human mind, however, associates one pattern in memory to others in a much more sophisticated way than merely attempting to homogeneously link vectors. Such associations would interfere with each other (Hinton & Anderson, 1989). To mimic the formation of such associations in cybernetics, Yao, Chen, and Chen (2001) built a recurrent neural network to dynamically evaluate the association of any pairwise patterns through the interaction among a group of patterns, and incorporate the results of interaction into data clustering. The novel rule based on the characteristics of clusters has been proposed to determine the number of clusters with a reject option. The hybrid model was named associative clustering neural network (ACNN). The performance of ACNN has been studied by authors on simulated data only, but the results have demonstrated that ACNN has the feasibility to cluster data with a reject option and label the data robustly.

Bayesian neural networks. There are a number of recent networks that have been suggested as solutions to clustering. For instance, Bayesian neural networks (BNNs) are another technique that has been recently used for Web clustering. Her, Jun, Choi, and Lee (1999) have used BNNs for clustering Web query results. Their BNN is based on SOM and differs in the last step when n documents are assigned under each cluster by the Bayesian rule. The BNNs are an important addition to the host of ANN solutions that have been offered to the problem at hand as they represent a large group of hybrid ANNs that combine classical ANNs with statistical classification and prediction theories.

Web Clustering

The Web has undergone exponential growth since its birth, which is the cause of a number of problems with its usage. Particularly, the quality of Web search and the corresponding interpretation of search results are often far from satisfying due to various reasons like the huge volume of information and diverse requirements for search results.

The lack of a central structure and freedom from a strict syntax allow the availability of a vast amount of information on the Web, but they often cause the difficult retrieval of data that is not meaningful. Although ranked lists of search results returned by a search engine are still popular, this method is highly inefficient since the number of retrieved search results can be high for a typical query. Most users just view the top 10 results and therefore might miss relevant information. Moreover, the criteria used for ranking may not reflect the needs of the user. A majority of the queries tend to be short and, consequently, nonspecific or imprecise. Moreover, as terms or phrases are ambiguous in the absence of their contexts, a large amount of search results is irrelevant to the user.

In an effort to keep up with the tremendous growth of the Web, many research projects were targeted on how to deal with its content and structure to make it easier for the users to find the information they want more efficiently and accurately. In the last years, mainly data-mining methods applied in the Web environment created new possibilities and challenges.

Methods of Web data mining can be divided into a number of categories according to the kind of mined information and the goals that particular categories set. In Pal, Talwar, and Mitra (2002), three categories are distinguished: *Web structure mining* (WSM), *Web usage mining* (WUM), and *Web content mining* (WCM). Particularly, WCM refers broadly to the process of uncovering interesting and potentially useful knowledge from Web documents.

WCM shares many concepts with traditional text-mining techniques. One of these, *clustering*, groups similar documents together to make information retrieval more effective. When applied to Web pages, clustering methods try to identify inherent groupings of pages so that a set of clusters is produced in which clusters contain relevant pages (to a specific topic); irrelevant pages are separated. Generally, text-document clustering methods attempt to collect the documents into groups, where each group represents some topic that is different than those topics represented by the other groups. Such clustering is expected to be helpful for discrimination, summarization, organization, and navigation for unstructured Web pages.

In a more general approach, we can consider Web documents as collections of Web pages including not only HTML files, but also XML files, images, and so forth. An important research direction in Web clustering is Web XML data clustering, stating the clustering problem with two dimensions: content and structure (Vakali, Pokorný, & Dalamagas, 2004).

WUM techniques use the Web log data coming from users' sessions. In this framework, Web log data provide information about activities performed by a user from the moment the user enters a Web site to the moment the same user leaves it. In WUM, the clustering tries to group together users' navigation sessions having similar characteristics (Vakali et al., 2004). Concerning WSM techniques, graph-oriented methods can be used.

Considering Web clustering techniques, it is important to be aware of two main categories of approaches:

1.   clustering Web pages in a space of resources to facilitate some search services and

2.   clustering Web search results.

In Boley et al. (1999), these categories are called *off-line clustering* and *online clustering*, respectively. We mention approaches of both categories, although the main accent is put on the latter.

Application of Web Clustering

Web clustering is currently one of the crucial IR problems related to the Web. It is used by many intelligent software agents in order to retrieve, filter, and categorize Web documents. Various forms of clustering are required in a wide range of applications: efficient information retrieval by focusing on relevant subsets (clusters) rather than whole collections, clustering documents in collections of digital libraries, clustering search results to present them in an organized and understandable form, finding mirrored Web pages, and detecting copyright violations, among others.

Clustering techniques are immensely important for Web applications to assist the automated (or semiautomated) generation of proper categories of documents and organize repositories of search engines. The hierarchical categorization of documents is often used (see Google, Yahoo, Open Directory, and LookSmart as examples). The reason for this is that the search results are not summarized in terms of topics; they are not well suited for browsing tasks. One possible solution is to create manually a static hierarchical categorization of a reasonable part of the Web and use these categories to organize the search results of a particular query. However, this solution is feasible only for small collections. To categorize the entire Web either manually or automatically is, unfortunately, not realistic.

In Pierrakos, Paliouras, Papatheodorou, Karkaletsis, and Dikaiakos (2003), document clustering and a WUM technique are used for the construction of Web community directories as a means of personalizing Web services. Also, the effective summarization of Web page collections becomes more and more critical as the amount of information continues to grow on the Web. The significance of Web collection clustering for automatic Web collection summarization is investigated in Zamir and Etzioni (1999).

Clustering is also useful in extracting salient features of related Web documents to automatically formulate queries and search for other similar documents on the Web.

Principles of Web Clustering Methods

Most of the document-clustering methods that are in use today are based on the VSM. The similarity between documents is measured using one of several similarity measures that are based on relations of feature vectors, for example, the cosine of feature vectors. Many of the traditional algorithms based on VSM, however, falter when the dimensionality of the feature space becomes high relative to the size of the document space. In a high-dimensional space, the distance between any two documents tends to be constant, making clustering on the basis of distance ill defined. This phenomenon is called the *curse of dimensionality*. Therefore, the issue of reducing the dimensionality of the space is critical. The methods presented earlier are often used.

Traditional clustering algorithms either use a priori knowledge of document structures to define a distance or similarity among these documents, or use probabilistic techniques such as Bayesian classification.

Taxonomies are generated using document clustering algorithms that typically result in topic or concept hierarchies. These classification and clustering techniques are combined.

Concept hierarchies expose the different concepts presented in the Web page (or search-result) collection. The user can choose the concept he or she is interested in and can browse it in detail.

Classification of Web Clustering Methods

Generally, clustering approaches could be classified in two broad categories (Y. Wang & Kitsuregawa, 2002): *term-based clustering* and *link-based clustering*. Recent work in online clustering has included both link-based and term-based methods.

Term-based clustering. We start with methods in which each term is a single word. Zamir, Etzioni, Madanim, and Karp (1997) mention a very simple *word-intersection clustering* method in which words that are shared by documents are used to produce clusters. Let n denote the number of documents to be clustered. The method runs in $O(n^2)$ and produces good results for Web documents originating rather from a corpus of texts. We point out that standard methods such as k-means are also in this category since they usually exploit single words as features. Most of the methods based on VSM belong to this category. They do not make use of any word proximity or phrase-based approach.

Word-based clustering that is used on common words shared among documents does not adapt well to the Web environment since it ignores the availability of hyperlinks between Web pages and is susceptible to spam. Also, the curse of dimensionality restricts the usability of these methods. A more successful clustering in this case (also ignoring links among documents) is based on multiword terms (phrases or sentences). Here we speak about *term-based clustering* (Zamir & Etzioni, 1999). Extracting terms significantly reduces the high dimensionality. Zamir and Etzioni show that this reduction is almost on an order of magnitude while maintaining comparable performance with the word-based model.

Among the first works using phrases in clustering, we find the approach based on *suffix-tree clustering* (STC; Zamir & Etzioni, 1998). STC first transforms the string of text representing each document into a sequence of stems. Second, it identifies the sets of documents that share a common phrase as base clusters by a suffix tree. Finally, these base clusters are combined into clusters. Tree building often requires $O(n \log n)$ time and produces high-quality clusters. On the other hand, the suffix-tree model can have a high number of redundancies in terms of the suffixes stored in the tree. However, STC based on phrases shared between documents generates inferior results to those based on the full text of the document.

In Hammouda and Kamel (2004), a system for Web clustering is based on two key concepts. The first is the use of weighted phrases as an essential constituent of documents. Similarity between documents will be based on matching phrases and their weights. The similarity calculation between documents combines single-word similarity and phrase-based similarity. The latter is proven to have a more significant effect on the clustering quality due to its insensitivity to noisy terms that could lead to incorrect similarity measures. The second concept is the incremental clustering of documents using a histogram-based method to maximize the tightness of clusters by carefully watching the similarity distribution inside each cluster. In the system, a novel phrase-based document-index model is used — the document index graph (DIG) — that captures the structure of sentences in the document set rather than single words only. The DIG model is based on graph theory and utilizes graph properties to match any-length phrases from a document to any number of previously seen documents in a time nearly proportional to the number of words of the document. Improvement over traditional clustering methods was 10 to 29%.

- **Link-based clustering:** Links among Web pages could provide valuable information to determine the related pages since they give objective opinions for the topics of the pages they point to. Many works tried to explore link analysis to improve the term-based methods. In general, these methods belong to the category of graph clustering. Kleinberg (1999) suggested that there are two kinds of pages on the Web for a specific query topic — hub and authority — and they reinforce each other. The HITS algorithm, which was used to locate hubs and authorities from the search results given a query topic, provided a possible way to alleviate the problems. However, sometimes one's most authoritative pages are not useful for others. It is also observable that many authority pages contain very little text. The work of Y. Wang and Kitsuregawa (2002) successfully combines link-based features (co-citations and bibliographic coupling) and content information in clustering. Co-citation measures the number of citations (out-links) in common between two documents, and coupling measures the number of documents (in-links) that cites both of the two documents under consideration.

- **Structure of clusters:** Two clustering algorithms that can effectively cluster documents, even in the presence of a very high-dimensional feature space, are described in Haveliwala, Gionis, and Indyk (2000). These clustering techniques, which are based on generalizations of graph partitioning, do not require prespecified ad hoc distance functions and are capable of automatically discovering document similarities or associations.

As we mentioned in the introduction, most clustering methods can be divided into two categories: hierarchical clusters and flat clusters. Hierarchical clustering is exceedingly slow when it is used online for very high n Its implementing time can be from $O(n^2)$ up to $O(n^3)$.

The flat clustering algorithms are model-based algorithms that search for the model parameters given the data and prior expectation. For example, k-means is an $O(nkT)$ algorithm, where T is the number of iterations, but the task to determine a model describing the data complicates its use for large collections, particularly in a Web environment.

Clustering with Snippets

Today, search engines return with a ranked list of search results some contextual information in the form of a Web-page excerpt, the so-called *snippet*. *Web snippet clustering* is an innovative approach to help users in searching the Web. It consists of clustering the snippets returned by a (meta-) search engine into a hierarchy of folders each labeled with a term. The term expresses latent semantics of the folder and of the corresponding Web pages contained in the folder. The folder labels vary from a bag of words to variable-length sentences.

Web snippet clustering methods are classified in Ferragin and Gulli (2005) according to two dimensions: words vs. terms, and flat vs. hierarchical. Four categories of approaches are distinguished.

1. **Word-based and flat clustering:** This category includes systems like SCATTER-GATHER and WEBCAT. Other systems use, for example, fuzzy relations (Joshi & Jiang, 2002) or take into account in-linking and out-linking pages to improve precision.

2. **Term-based and flat clustering:** Zamir and Etzioni (1999) used sentences of variable length to label the folders, but these sentences were drawn as contiguous portions of the snippets by means of a suffix-tree data structure. Other systems use SVD on a term-document matrix to find meaningful long labels. This approach is restricted by the time complexity of SVD applied to a large number of snippets. In addition, the similar snippets can lead to very high overlap.

3. **Word-based and hierarchical clustering:** These are approaches based on the frequent item-sets problem and a concept lattice on single words (Rice & Siff, 2001) in order to construct the folder hierarchy.

4. **Term-based and hierarchical clustering:** This class includes the best metasearch engines of the years 2000 to 2003: Vivisimo and Dogpile. These tools add to the flat list of search results a hierarchy of clusters built on the fly over snippets. They improve precision over recall by using a snippet representation made of pairs of words (not necessarily contiguous) linked by a lexical affinity, that is, a correlation of their common appearance. Among older approaches, there is a simple extension of Grouper (Zamir & Etzioni, 1998) to hierarchical clustering based on the size of folder overlaps. A hierarchical engine SNAKET introduced in Ferragin and Gulli (2005) organizes on the fly the search results from 16 commodity search engines and offers folder labeling with variable-length sentences. Hierarchies are overlapping because snippets might cover multiple themes.

Conclusion

Clustering is currently one of the most crucial techniques for:

*   dealing with a massive amount of heterogeneous information on the Web, and
*   organizing Web search results.

Unlike clustering in other fields, Web clustering separates unrelated pages and clusters related pages (to a specific topic) into semantically meaningful groups, which is useful for the discrimination, summarization, organization, and navigation of unstructured Web pages. In this chapter, we have presented a lot of general approaches to clustering as well as a lot of various classifications of clustering algorithms. Consequently, two important questions arise:

1. Why are there so many clustering algorithms and
2. Which of them are usable for Web clustering?,

In his paper, Estivill-Castro (2002) tries to answer the first question in terms of the model of the data to be clustered and the cluster model (inductive principle, in his terminology). For a single model of data and a cluster model, there are many clustering algorithms. Why are there so many clustering models? There are so many because clustering is in part beholder dependent. Cluster models are just formal models of what researchers believe is the definition of a cluster. Thus, it is very hard to compare particular approaches.

To answer the second question, we can first consider the techniques that are not usable for Web clustering. Observe that clustering in a Web environment eliminates naturally the use of some general clustering techniques. The reason is easy to see. Since clustering translates into an optimization problem, its computational complexity is typically intractable in the case of huge Web data collections.

Another reason for the inapplicability of some classical techniques is associated with the usability of the clustering achieved. Given a large document collection, it is difficult to provide the number of real categories for users when they attempt to categorize the documents. Organizing Web search results into a hierarchy of topics and subtopics facilitates browsing the collection and locating results of interest. Traditional clustering techniques are inadequate for the Web since they do not generate clusters with highly readable names. It seems that Web snippet clustering methods deal successfully with this issue. We have also mentioned how link information can be used to improve classification results for Web collections. In practice, it is desirable to combine term-based clustering and link-based clustering.

This survey represents only a small part of the research being conducted in the area. Furthermore, as new techniques and algorithms are being proposed for Web data sets, it makes a survey such as this highly time dependent.

Acknowledgements

This work was partly supported by the project 1ET100300419 of the Program Information Society of the Thematic Program II of the National Research Program of the Czech Republic, and the project 201/05/0079 of the Grant Agency of the Czech Republic.

References

Adamic, L. A. (1999). The small world Web. In S. Abiteboul & A. M. Vercoustre (Eds.), *Lecture notes in computer science: Vol. 1696. ECDL'99* (pp. 443-452). Springer.

Agrawal, R., Gehrke, J., Gunopulos, D., & Raghavan, P. (1998). Automatic subspace clustering of high dimensional data for data mining applications. *ACM SIGMOD Record, 27*(2), 94-105.

Anonymous. (2005a). *5384 works that have been based on the self-organizing map (SOM) method developed by Kohonen: Part I.* Retrieved from http://www.cis.hut.fi/research/som-bibl/references_a-k.ps

Anonymous. (2005b). *5384 works that have been based on the self-organizing map (SOM) method developed by Kohonen: Part II.* Retrieved from http://www.cis.hut.fi/research/som-bibl/references_l-z.ps

Barabasi, A. L., & Albert, R. (1999). Emergence of scaling in random networks. *Science, 286*(5439), 509-512.

Ben-Dor, A., Shamir, R., & Yakhini, Z. (1999). Clustering gene expression patterns. *Journal of Computational Biology, 6*(3/4), 281-297.

Berkhin, P. (2002). *Survey of clustering data mining techniques.* Accrue Software, Inc. Retrieved from http://www.ee.ucr.edu/barth/EE242/clustering_survey.pdf

Berry, M. W., & Browne, M. (1999). *Understanding search engines: Mathematical modeling and text retrieval: Software, environments, tools.* Society for Industrial & Applied Mathematics.

Boley, D., Gini, M., Gross, R., Han, E.-H., Hastings, K., Karypis, G., et al. (1999). Partitioning-based clustering for Web document categorization. *Journal of Decision Support Systems, 27*(3), 329-341.

Broder, A., Kumar, R., Maghoul, R., Raghavan, P., Rajagopalan, P., Stata, R., et al. (2000). Graph structure in the Web. *The 9th International WWW Conference (2000).* Retrieved from http://www9.org/w9cdrom/160/160.html

Cai, D., He, X., Li, Z., Ma, W., & Wen, J. (2004). *Hierarchical clustering of WWW image search results using visual, textual and link information.* Proceedings of ACM MM'04, New York.

Canutescu, A. A., Shelenkov, A. A., & Dunbrack, R. L. (2003). A graph-theory algorithm for rapid protein side-chain prediction. *Protein Science, 12*, 2001-2014.

Carpenter, G. A., & Grossberg, S. (1987a). Art 2: Self organisation of stable category recognition codes for analog input patterns. *Applied Optics, 26*, 4919-4930.

Carpenter, G. A., & Grossberg, S. (1987b). Invariant pattern recognition and recall by an attentive self-organizing art architecture in a nonstationary world. *Proceedings of the IEEE 1st International Conference on Neural Networks* (737-745).

Carpenter, G. A., & Grossberg, S. (1990). Art3: Hierarchical search using chemical transmitters in self-organizing pattern recognition architectures. *Neural Networks, 3*, 129-152.

Carpenter, G. A., Grossberg, S., Markuzon, N., Reynolds, J. H., & Rosen, D. B. (1992). Fuzzy artmap: A neural network architecture for incremental supervised learning of analog multidimensional maps. *IEEE Transactions on Neural Networks, 3*(5), 698-713.

Carpenter, G. A., Grossberg, S., & Reynolds, J. H. (1991). Artmap: Supervised real-time learning and classification of nonstationary data by a self-organizing neural network. *Neural Networks, 4*, 565-588.

Carpenter, G. A., Grossberg, S., & Reynolds, J. H. (1995). A fuzzy artmap nonparametric probability estimator for nonstationary pattern recognition problems. *IEEE Transactions on Neural Networks, 6*(6), 1330-1336.

Carpenter, G. A., Grossberg, S., & Rosen, D. B. (1991a). Art2-a: An adaptive resonance algorithm for rapid category learning and recognition. *Neural Networks, 4*, 493-504.

Carpenter, G. A., Grossberg, S., & Rosen, D. B. (1991b). Fuzzy art: Fast stable learning and categorization of analog patterns by an adaptive resonance system. *Neural Networks, 4*, 759-771.

Cheng, C., Fu, A. W., & Zhang, Y. (1999). Entropy-based subspace clustering for mining numerical data. *Proceedings of 5th ACM SIGKDD International Conference on Knowledge Discovery and Data Mining* (84-93).

Chung, F. R. K. (1997). Spectral graph theory. *CBMS Regional Conference Series in Mathematics, 92.*

Dill, S., Kumar, R., McCurley, K., Rajagopalan, S., Sivakumar, D., & Tomkins, A. (2002). Self-similarity in the Web. *ACM Transactions on Internet Technology, 2*(3), 205-223.

Donath, W. E., & Hoffman, A. J. (1973). Lower bounds for the partitioning of graphs. *IBM Journal of Research and Development, 17*, 420-425.

Dopazo, J., & Carazo, J. M. (1997). Phylogenetic reconstruction using an unsupervised growing neural network that adopts the topology of a phylogenetic tree. *Journal of Molecular Evolution, 44*, 226-233.

Ebel, H., Mielsch, L. I., & Bornholdt, S. (2002). Scale-free topology of e-mail networks. *Phys. Rev. E, 66.*

Estivill-Castro, V. (2002). Why so many clustering algorithms: A position paper. *ACM SIGKDD Explorations Newsletter, 4*(1), 65-75.

Ferragin, P., & Gulli, A. (2005). A personalized search engine based on Web-snippet hierarchical clustering. *Proceedings of 14th International Conference on World Wide Web 2005* (801-810).

Fiedler, M. (1973). Algebraic connectivity of graphs. *Czech. Math. J., 23*, 298-305.

Fiedler, M. (1975). A property of eigenvectors of non-negative symmetric matrices and its applications to graph theory. *Czech. Math. J., 25*(100), 619-633.

Fritzke, B. (1974). Growing cell structures: A self-organizing network for unsupervised and supervised learning. *Neural Network, 7*, 1141-1160.

Gibson, D., Kleinberg, J., & Raghavan, P. (1998). Inferring Web communities from link topology. *Proceedings of the 9th ACM Conference on Hypertext and Hypermedia* (225-234).

Goil, S., Nagesh, H., & Choudhary, A. (1999). *MAFIA: Efficient and scalable subspace clustering for very large data sets* (Tech. Rep. No. CPDC-TR-9906-010). Northwestern University.

Golub, G., & Van Loan, C. (1989). *Matrix computations.* Johns Hopkins University Press.

Gordon, A. D. (1999). *Classification* (2nd ed.). Boca Raton, FL: Chapman & Hall/CRC.

Grossberg, S. (1976). Adaptive pattern recognition and universal recoding: II. Feedback, expectation, olfaction, and illusions. *Biological Cybernetics, 23*, 187-202.

Grossberg, S. (1988). Adaptive pattern classification and universal recoding: I. Parallel development and coding of neural feature detectors. In Anderson & Rosenfeld (Eds.), (pp. 121-134). (Reprinted from *Biological Cybernetics, 23*)

Guha, S., Rastogi, R., & Shim, K. (1999). ROCK: A robust clustering algorithm for categorical attributes. *Proceedings of 15th International Conference on Data Engineering* (512-521).

Guimerà, R., Danon, L., Díaz-Guilera, A., Giralt, F., & Arenas, A. (2003). Self-similar community structure in a network of human interactions. *Physical Review, 68.*

Hammouda, K. M., & Kamel, M. S. (2004). Efficient phrase-based document indexing for Web document clustering. *IEEE Transactions on Knowledge and Data Engineering, 18*(10), 1279-1296.

Han, J., & Kamber, M. (2001). *Data mining: Concepts and techniques.* San Francisco: Morgan Kaufmann Publishers.

Hartigan, J. A. (1975). *Clustering algorithms.* New York: John Wiley & Sons.

Hartuv, E., & Shamir, R. (2000). A clustering algorithm based on graph connectivity. *Information Processing Letters, 76*(4-6), 175-181.

Hassoun, M. H. (1995). *Fundamentals of artificial neural networks.* MIT Press.

Haveliwala, T., Gionis, A., & Indyk, P. (2000). Scalable techniques for clustering the Web. *Proceedings of WebDB.*

He, X., Ding, C. H. Q., Zha, H., & Simon, H. D. (2001). Automatic topic identification using Webpage clustering. *Proceedings of the 2001 IEEE International Conference on Data Mining (ICDM 01)* (195-203).

Henzinger, M. R. (1997). *Improved data structures for fully dynamic biconnectivity.* Digital Equipment Corporation.

Henzinger, M. R. (2003). Algorithmic challenges in Web search engines. *Internet Mathematics, 1*(1), 115-126.

Her, J. H., Jun, S. H., Choi, J. H., & Lee, J. H. (1999). A Bayesian neural network model for dynamic Web document clustering. *Proceedings of the IEEE Region 10 Conference (TENCON 99)* (vol. 2, 1415-1418).

Herrero, J., Valencia, A., & Dopazo, J. (2001). A hierarchical unsupervised growing neural network for clustering gene expression patterns. *Bioinformatics, 17,* 126-136.

Hinton, G. E., & Anderson, J. A. (1989). *Parallel models of associative memory.* Hillsdale, NJ.

Hopfield, J. J. (1982). Neural network and physical systems with emergent collective computational abilities. *Proceedings of Acad. Sci. USA,* (vol. 79, 2554-2558).

Höppner, F., Klawon, F., Kruse, R., & Runkler, T. (2000). *Fuzzy cluster analysis: Methods for classification, data analysis and image recognition.* New York: Wiley.

Huang, X., & Lai, W. (2003). Identification of clusters in the Web graph based on link topology. *Proceedings of the 7th International Database Engineering and Applications Symposium (IDEAS'03)* (pp. 123-130).

Jain, A. K., & Dubes, R. C. (1988). *Algorithms for clustering data.* NJ: Prentice Hall.

Jain, A. K., Murty, M. N., & Flynn, P. J. (1999). Data clustering: A review. *ACM Computing Surveys, 31*(3), 264-323.

Joshi, A., & Jiang, Z. (2002). *Retriever: Improving Web search engine results using clustering*. Idea Group Publishing.

Kaski, S., Honkela, T., Lagus, K., & Kohonen, T. (1998). WEBSOM: Self-organizing maps of document collections. *Neurocomputing, 21*, 101-117.

Kasuba, T. (1993). Simplified fuzzy ARTMAP. *AI Expert*, 18-25.

Kaufman, L., & Rousseeuw, P. (1990). *Finding groups in data: An introduction to cluster analysis*. New York: Wiley.

Kawamura, M., Okada, M., & Hirai, Y. (1999). Dynamics of selective recall in an associative memory model with one-to-many associations. *IEEE Transactions on Neural Networks, 10*(3), 704-713.

Kleinberg, J. M. (1999). Authoritative sources in a hyperlinked environment. *JACM, 46*(5) (pp. 604-632).

Kohonen, T. (1991). Self-organizing maps. *Proceedings of IEEE 78* (pp. 1464-1480).

Kohonen, T. (2001). *Self-organizing maps* (3rd extended ed.). Berlin, Germany: Springer.

Kohonen, T., Kaski, S., Lagus, K., Salogärui, J., Honkela, J., Paatero, V., et al. (2000). Self organization of a massive document collection. *IEEE Transactions on Neural Networks, 11*, 574-585.

Kosko, B. (1987). Adaptive bidirectional associative memories. *Appl. Opt., 26*(23), 4947-4960.

Kumar, S. R., Raghavan, P., Rajagopalan, S., & Tomkins, A. (1999). Trawling the Web for emerging cyber communities. *Proceedings of the 8th WWW Conference* (pp. 403-416).

Langville, A. N., & Meyer, C. D. (2005). A survey of eigenvector methods for Web information retrieval. *SIAM Review, 47*(1), 135-161.

Lian, W., Cheung, D. W. L., Mamoulis, N., & Yiu, S. M. (2004). An efficient and scalable algorithm for clustering XML documents by structure. *IEEE Transactions on Knowledge Data Engineering, 16*(1), 82-96.

Massey, L. (2003). On the quality of ART1 text clustering. *Neural Networks, 16*(5-6), 771-778.

Matula, D. W. (1970). Cluster analysis via graph theoretic techniques. *Proceedings of the Louisiana Conference on Combinatorics: Graph Theory and Computing* (pp. 199-212).

Matula, D. W. (1972). K-components, clusters and slicings in graphs. *SIAM Journal of Applied Mathematics, 22*(3), 459-480.

Matula, D. W. (1987). Graph theoretic techniques for cluster analysis algorithms. In J. Van Ryzin (Ed.), *Classification and clustering* (pp. 95-129).

McCulloch, W. S., & Pitts, W. (1943). A logical calculus of the ideas immanent in nervous activity. *Bulletin of Mathematical Biophysics, 5*, 115-133.

Mercer, D. P. (2003). *Clustering large datasets*. Linacre College.

Nagesh, H., Goil, S., & Choudhary, A. (2001). Adaptive grids for clustering massive data sets. *Proceedings of the 1st SIAM ICDM* (p. 477).

Newman, M. E. J. (2003). The structure and function of complex networks. *SIAM Review, 45*, 167-256.

Newman, M. E. J., Balthrop, J., Forrest, S., & Williamson, M. M. (2004). Technological networks and the spread of computer viruses. *Science, 304*, 527-529.

Ng, R. T., & Han, J. (1994). Efficient and effective clustering methods for spatial data mining. *Proceedings of the 20ᵗʰ International Conference on Very Large Data Bases* (pp. 144-155).

Pal, S. K., Talwar, V., & Mitra, P. (2002). Web mining in soft computing framework: Relevance, state of the art and future directions. *IEEE Transactions on Neural Networks, 13*(5), 1163-1177.

Pierrakos, D., Paliouras, G., Papatheodorou, C., Karkaletsis, V., & Dikaiakos, M. (2003). Construction of Web community directories using document clustering and Web usage mining. *ECML/PKDD 2003: First European Web Mining Forum*.

Řezanková, H., Húsek, D., & Snášel, V. (2004). Clustering as a tool for data mining. In M. Klíma (Ed.), *Applications of mathematics and statistics in economy* (pp. 203-208). Praha: Professional Publishing.

Rice, M. D., & Siff, M. (2001). Clusters, concepts, and pseudo-metrics. *Electronic Notes in Theoretical Computer Science, 40*, 323-346.

Rumelhart, D. E., & McClelland, J. L. (1988). *Parallel distributed processing: Explorations in the microstructure of cognition* (Vols. 1 & 2). Cambridge, MA: MIT Press.

Salton, G., & Buckley, C. (1988). Term weighting approaches in automatic text retrieval. *Information Processing and Management, 24*(5), 513-523.

Sásik, R., Hwa, T., Iranfar, N., & Loomis, W. F. (2001). Percolation clustering: A novel approach to the clustering of gene expression patterns. *Dictyostelium Development PSB Proceedings* (vol. 6, pp. 335-347).

Schenker, A., Kande, A., Bunke, H., & Last, M. (2005). *Graph-theoretic techniques for Web content mining*. World Scientific Publishing.

Sharan, R., & Shamir, R. (2000). CLICK: A clustering algorithm for gene expression analysis. In S. Miyano, R. Shamir, & T. Takagi (Eds.), *Currents in computational molecular biology* (pp. 6-7). Universal Academy Press.

Shi, J., & Malik, J. (2000). Normalized cuts and image segmentation. *IEEE Transactions on Pattern Analysis and Machine Intelligence, 22*(8), 888-905.

Tamayo, P., Slonim, D., Mesirov, J., Zhu, Q., Kitareewan, S., Dmitrovsky, E., et al. (1999). Interpreting patterns of gene expression with self-organizing maps: Methods and application to hematopoietic differentiation. *Proceedings of the National Acad. Sci. USA* (vol. 96, pp. 2907-2912).

Tomida, S., Hanai, T., Honda, H., & Kobayashi, T. (2001). Gene expression analysis using fuzzy ART. *Genome Informatics, 12*, 245-246.

Vakali, A., Pokorný, J., & Dalamagas, T. (2004). An overview of Web clustering practices. In *Lecture notes in computer science: Vol. 3268. Current Trends in Database Technology: International Workshop on Database Technologies for Handling XML Information on the Web, DataX, EDBT 2004* (pp. 597-606). Springer Verlag.

Wang, H. C., Dopazo, J., & Carazo, J. M. (1998). Self-organizing tree growing network for classifying amino acids. *Bioinformatics, 14*(4), 376-377.

Wang, Y., & Kitsuregawa, M. (2002). Evaluating contents-link Web page clustering for Web search results. *CIKM'02* (pp. 499-506).

White, S., & Smyth, P. (2005). A spectral clustering approach to finding communities in graph. *SDM.*

Wu, C., Zhao, S., Chen, H. L., Lo, C. J., & McLarty, J. (1996). Motif identification neural design for rapid and sensitive protein family search. *CABIOS, 12*(2), 109-118.

Wu, C. H. (1995). Gene classification artificial neural system. In R. F. Doolittle (Ed.), *Methods in enzymology: Computer methods for macromolecular sequence analysis.* New York: Academic Press.

Yao, Y., Chen, L., & Chen, Y. Q. (2001). Associative clustering for clusters of arbitrary distribution shapes. *Neural Processing Letters, 14*, 169-177.

Zamir, O., & Etzioni, O. (1998). Web document clustering: A feasibility demonstration. *Proceedings of the 21st International ACM SIGIR Conference on Research and Development in Information Retrieval* (pp. 46-54).

Zamir, O., & Etzioni, O. (1999). Grouper: A dynamic clustering interface to Web search results. *Computer Networks: The International Journal of Computer and Telecommunications Networking Archive, 31*(11-16), 1361-1374.

Zamir, O., Etzioni, O., Madanim, O., & Karp, R. M. (1997). Fast and intuitive clustering of Web documents. *Proceedings of the 3rd International Conference on Knowledge Discovery and Data Mining* (pp. 287-290).

Zhang, T., Ramakrishnan, R., & Livny, M. (1996). BIRCH: An efficient data clustering method for very large databases. *ACM SIGMOD Record, 25*(2), 103-114.

Chapter II

Clustering Web
Information Sources

Athena Vakali, Aristotle University of Thessaloniki, Greece

George Pallis, Aristotle University of Thessaloniki, Greece

Lefteris Angelis, Aristotle University of Thessaloniki, Greece

Abstract

The explosive growth of the Web has drastically increased information circulation and dissemination rates. As the numbers of both Web users and Web sources grow significantly every day, crucial data management issues, such as clustering on the Web, should be addressed and analyzed. Clustering has been proposed toward improving both information availability and the Web users' personalization. Clusters on the Web are either users' sessions or Web information sources, which are managed in a variation of applications and implementation test beds. This chapter focuses on the topic of clustering information over the Web in an effort to provide an overview and survey on the theoretical background and the adopted practices of the most popular emerging and challenging clustering research efforts. An up-to-date survey of the existing clustering schemes is given to be of use for both researchers and practitioners interested in the area of Web data mining.

Introduction

The explosive growth of the Web has dramatically changed the way in which information is managed and accessed. Thus, several data management solutions such as clustering have been proposed. Specifically, clustering is the process of collecting Web sources into groups so that similar objects are in the same group and dissimilar objects are in different groups.

Clustering on the Web has been proposed based on the idea of identifying homogeneous groups of objects from the values of certain attributes (variables; Jain, Murty, & Flynn, 1999). In the context of the Web, many clustering approaches have been introduced for identifying Web source clusters evaluated under a wide range of parameters (such as their size, content, or complexity). A clustering scheme is considered to be efficient if it results in reliable Web data grouping within a reasonable time.

Clustering algorithms have their origins in various areas such as statistics, pattern recognition, and machine learning. An optimal clustering scheme should mainly satisfy the following criteria:

1. **Compactness:** The data within each cluster should be as close to each other as possible. A common measure of compactness is the variance, which should be minimized.

2. **Separation:** The clusters should be widely spaced. The notion of cluster distance is commonly used for indicating the measure of separation, which should be maximized.

In general, the Web consists of a variety of Web sources. In order to facilitate data availability and accessing, and to meet user preferences, the Web sources are clustered with respect to a certain parameter or characteristic such as their popularity, structure, or content. Clustering on the Web can be one of the following types:

*   **Web User Clustering:** The establishment of groups of users exhibiting similar browsing patterns. Such knowledge is especially useful for inferring user statistics in order to perform various actions such as market segmentation in e-commerce applications, personalized Web content for users, and so forth. This type of clustering helps in better understanding the users' navigation behavior and in improving Web users' request servicing (by decreasing the lengths in Web navigation pathways).

*   **Web Document Clustering:** The grouping of documents with related content. This information is useful in various applications, for example, in Web search engines toward improving the information retrieval process (i.e., clustering Web queries). In addition, the clustering of Web documents increases Web information accessibility and improves content delivery on the Web.

Figure 1 depicts the overall clustering idea as employed on users' accessing of data over the Web. Considering the complexity and the diversity of the information sources on the Web, it is important to understand the relationships between Web data sources and Web users. Due to the fact that the Web data clustering topic is quite challenging and complex, this chapter

Figure 1. Clustering information over the Web

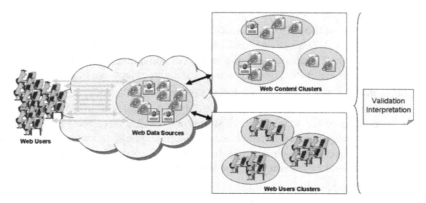

contributes to understanding the role of clustering mechanisms and methodologies in accessing Web information (such as documents, users' patterns). Thus, it provides a complete view for the existing Web data clustering practices, which is essential both for computing practitioners (e.g., Web site developers) and for researchers as well.

Considerable research efforts have focused on clustering information on the Web, and earlier studies have shown that the clustering of Web sources is beneficial toward better Web data management (Baldi, Frasconi, & Smyth, 2003; Cadez, Heckerman, Meek, Smyth, & White, 2003). Some of these benefits are listed:

- **The improvement of the Web searching process:** Clustering Web content allows efficient query processing over the large amount of documents stored on Web servers.

- **The interaction with information retrieval systems:** Query clustering helps in discovering frequently asked questions or the most popular topics on a search engine.

- **The construction and maintenance of more intelligent Web servers:** Intelligent servers that are able to dynamically adapt their designs to satisfy future user needs, providing clues about improvements in site design, might be useful.

- **The improvement of caching and prefetching schemes** This will help to deliver the appropriate content (products) to the interested users in a timely, scalable, and cost-effective manner.

- **The adaptation of e-commerce sites to customers' needs:** Understanding Web users' navigation behavior through e-commerce Web sites can provide valuable insights into customer behavior, and can help end users, for example, by recommending new products to Web site visitors based on their browsing behavior.

In order to identify the Web data clusters, a number of clustering algorithms has been proposed and is available in the literature (Baldi, Franconi, & Smyth, 2003; Jain, Murty, & Flynn,

1999). In general terms, the existing clustering approaches do not provide an indication of the quality of their outcomes. For instance, questions such as "How many clusters are there in the data set?", "Does the resulting clustering scheme fit the data set?", and "Is there a better partitioning for the data set?" show the need for clustering result validation. However, the evaluation of the quality of a clustering algorithm is not an easy task since the correct clustering is not a priori known, and it depends on the different information sources and on the nature of the underlying applications. In this context, a validation scheme is often used for evaluating whether the objects have been assigned correctly to the resulting clusters (Stein, Eissen, & Wibrock, 2003; Zaïane, Foss, Lee, & Wang, 2002). Another aspect of cluster validation is to justify the number of clusters in a clustering result. Moreover, a further analysis of the resulting clusters is also important since it helps to extract useful information that is often hidden. For example, the experts in an application area have to integrate the clustering results with other experimental evidence and analysis in order to draw the right conclusion. Data mining techniques, statistical analysis, and visualization tools are usually used in order to interpret the clusters.

The rest of the chapter is organized as follows. The types of Web sources used for clustering are described, then a presenation of how these are processed toward clustering is given. The most representative Web data clustering schemes and algorithms are presented. An overview of the most indicative validation and interpretation techniques for clustering information over the Web is given. The most popular Web applications that are favored for clustering are highlighted. Finally, conclusions are made.

Information Sources Used for Clustering

A wide range of information sources are available on the Web. These sources might lie at the server side, at the client side, or at proxy servers. Each type of Web information collection differs not only in the location of the Web data source, but also in the formats of data available. In the following paragraphs, we classify the sources that are most commonly available on the Web and describe the way they are processed in order to be used by a clustering scheme.

Web Documents

Web documents are all the objects that are stored in Web servers around the world and can be accessed via a browser. In general, each Web site is considered as a collection of Web documents (a set of related Web resources, such as HTML [HyperText Markup Language] files, XML [eXtensible Markup Language] files, images, applets, multimedia resources, etc.). Typically, documents on the Web have a very large variety of topics; they are differently structured and most of them are not well structured. Therefore, Web documents need to be represented in an effective manner in order for them to be clustered. A typical approach is to preprocess them (either by their content or by their structure) prior to clustering.

Web Server Logs

A Web user may visit a Web site from time to time and spend an arbitrary amount of time between consecutive visits. All this traffic is logged in a Web server-side log file. In particular, a common log file of any given Web server is a simple text file with one user access record per line. Each user access record consists of the following fields: the user's IP (Internet protocol) address (or host name), the access time, the request method (e.g., GET, POST, etc.), the URL (uniform resource locator) of the document accessed, the protocol, the return code, and the number of bytes transmitted. The format of a common log-file line has the following fields separated by a space:

[remotehost rfc931 authuser date request status bytes]

- **remotehost:** The remote host name (or IP address number if the DNS [domain name system] host name is not available or was not provided);

- **rfc931:** The remote log-in name of the user (if not available, a minus sign is typically placed in the field);

- **authuser:** The user name with which the user has authenticated himself or herself (if not available, a minus sign is typically placed in the field);

- **date:** Date and time of the request;

- **request:** The request line exactly as it came from the client (i.e., the file name and the method used to retrieve it, typically GET);

- **status:** The HTTP (hypertext transfer protocol) response code returned to the client. It indicates whether or not the file was successfully retrieved, and if not, what error message was returned; and

- **bytes:** The number of bytes transferred.

The access logs provide most of the data needed for Web servers' workload characterization. However, they do not provide all of the information that is of interest, such as identifying the Web users' navigation patterns, and certain processing should take place before getting valuable information from Web logs.

Web Proxy Logs

A Web proxy acts as an intermediate level of caching between client browsers and Web servers. Proxy caching can be used to reduce the loading time of a Web document experienced by users as well as the network traffic load at the server and client sides (Pallis, Vakali, Angelis, & Hacid, 2003). Proxy traces may reveal the actual HTTP requests from multiple clients to multiple Web servers. This may serve as a data source for characterizing the browsing behavior of a group of anonymous users sharing a common proxy server.

Proxy servers can be configured to record (in an access log) information about all of the requests and responses processed by the Web servers. Specifically, a proxy log file records all the requests made to Web documents by a certain population of users (e.g., the set of users of a certain Internet service provider). Each line from the access log contains information on a single request for a document. From each log entry, it is possible to determine the name of the host machine making the request, the time that the request was made, and the name of the requested document. The entry also provides information about the server's response to this request, such as if the server was able to satisfy the request (if not, a reason why the response was unsuccessful is given) and the number of bytes transmitted by the server, if any. The access logs provide most of the data needed for workload characterization studies of Web servers. The format of a proxy* log-file line consists of the following fields separated by a space:

[time duration remotehost code bytes method URL rfc931 peerstatus/peerhost type]

- **time:** The time when the client socket was closed. The format is Unix time (seconds since January 1, 1970) with millisecond resolution;

- **duration:** The elapsed time of the request, in milliseconds. This is the time between the acceptance and close of the client socket;

- **remotehost:** The client IP address;

- **code:** It encodes the transaction result. The cache result of the request contains information on the kind of request, how it was satisfied, or in what way it failed;

- **bytes:** The amount of data delivered to the client;

- **method:** The HTTP request method;

- **URL:** The requested URL;

- **rfc931:** The remote log-in name of the user (if not available, a minus sign is typically placed in the field);

- **peerstatus/peerhost:** A description of how and where the requested object was fetched; and

- **type:** The content type of the object as seen in the HTTP reply header (if not available, a minus sign is typically placed in the field).

Information Processing Toward Clustering

Document Preprocessing

The clustering of documents depends on the quality of the representation of the documents' content. This representation is characterized by the amount and type of information to be encapsulated, and, in practice, the most important features from each document should be extracted (Moore et al., 1997). However, since each Web document has a variety of content formats (such as text, graphics, scripts), feature extraction should be facilitated by evicting useless content. Thus, the so-called cleaning process is an important part of preprocessing and involves several tasks including parsing, decoding encoded characters, removing tags, and detecting word and sentence boundaries. Some learning mechanisms to recognize banner ads and redundant and irrelevant links to Web documents have already been discussed in Jushmerick (1999) and Bar-Yossef and Rajagopalan (2002), in which the preprocessing of Web documents is defined as a frequent template-detection problem (a frequency-based data mining algorithm detects templates as noise).

After cleaning, each Web document might be represented by a vector or a graph (Hammouda & Kamel, 2004; Yang & Pedersen, 1997; Zamir, Etzioni, Madanim, & Karp, 1997). The goal here is to transform each Web document (unstructured format) into a structured format using a vector of feature or attribute values (which may be binary, nominal, ordinal, interval, or ratio variables). Most document clustering methods (Baldi et al., 2003; Chakrabarti, 2003; Jain et al, 1999; Modha & Sprangler, 2003) that are in use today are based on the vector space model (VSM), which is a very widely used data model for text classification and clustering (Salton, Wong, & Yang, 1975). In particular, the VSM represents documents as feature vectors of the terms (words) that appear in all of the document sets, and each such feature vector is assigned term weights (usually term frequencies) related to the terms appearing in that document. In its simplest form, each document is represented by the (TF) vector $v_{tf} =$ $(tf_1, tf_2, ..., tf_v)$, where tf_i is the frequency of the ith term in the document. Normally, very common words are stripped out completely and different forms of a word are reduced to one canonical form. Finally, in order to account for documents of different lengths, each document vector is usually normalized so that it is of unit length. Then, the dissimilarity between two Web documents is measured by applying a metric (such as Euclidean or Manhattan distance) or a cost function to their feature vectors.

Web Server Log Preprocessing

Web server access logs undergo a certain preprocessing, such as data cleaning and session identification. Data cleaning removes the records that do not include useful information for the users' navigation behavior, such as graphics, javascripts, small pictures of buttons, advertisements, and so forth. The remaining document requests are usually categorized into different categories.

Users' Session Identification

A user session is defined as a sequence of requests made by a single user over a certain navigation period, and a user may have a single or multiple sessions during a period of time. The most popular session identification methods include the following:

- Use a time-out threshold, in which a user poses a sequence of consecutive requests that are separated by an interval less than a predefined threshold. This session identification suffers from the difficulty of setting the time threshold since different users may have different navigation behaviors, and their time intervals between sessions may significantly vary. In order to define the optimal time threshold, earlier research efforts proposed a time threshold of 25.5 minutes based on empirical data (Catledge & Pitkow, 1995), whereas Goker and He (2000) used a wide range of values and concluded that a time range of 10 to 15 minutes was an optimal session interval threshold. In general, the optimal time threshold clearly depends on the specific context and application. Up to now, the most common choice was to use 30 minutes as a default time threshold.

- Consider the reference length (Cooley, Mobasher, & Srivastava, 1999), that is, identify sessions by the amount of time a user spends on viewing that document for a specific log entry. The reference-length session identification is based on the assumption that the amount of time a user spends on a document correlates to whether the document should be classified as an auxiliary or content document for that user. In addition, in M. S. Chen, Park, and Yu (1998), the users' sessions are identified by their maximal forward reference. In this approach, each session is defined as the set of documents from the first document in a request sequence to the final document before a backward reference is made. Here, a backward reference is defined to be a document that has already occurred in the current session. One advantage of the maximal forward reference method is that it does not have any administrative parameters (e.g., time threshold). However, it has the significant drawback that backward references may not be recorded by the server if caching is enabled at the client site.

- Identify dynamically the sessions' boundaries (X. Huang, Peng, An, & Schuurmans, 2004) based on an information-theoretic approach by which session boundary detection is based on a statistical n-gram language modeling. In particular, this model predicts the probability of natural requests' sequences. According to this approach, a session boundary is identified by measuring the change of information (known as entropy) in the sequence of requests. Specifically, when a new object is observed in the sequence, an increase in the entropy of the sequence is observed. Therefore, such an entropy increase serves as a natural signal for session boundary detection, and if the change in entropy passes a specific threshold, a session boundary is placed before the new object.

Web Proxy Log Preprocessing

These data should also be preprocessed in order to extract useful conclusions for the workload and characterize the entire structure of the Web (Pallis et al., 2003). In general, the Web proxy logs are more difficult to manage than the Web server ones. Thus, a wide range of tools[1] has been implemented in order to manage the Web proxy log file in an efficient way. Furthermore, the Web proxy logs are preprocessed in order to extract users' sessions from them. A lot of approaches have been developed in order to identify users' sessions from Web access logs. However, these approaches may lead to poor performance in the context of proxy Web log mining. In Lou, Liu, Lu, and Yang (2002), an algorithm is proposed, called cut-and-pick, for identifying users' sessions from Web proxy logs. According to this algorithm, the sessions' boundaries are determined by using a Web site clustering algorithm based on site traversal graphs constructed from the proxy logs. In particular, if two consecutive document requests in a proxy log visit two Web sites that fall in two clusters, the two visits are regarded as irrelevant and are therefore classified into two user sessions.

Clustering Algorithms

Identifying Web Document Clusters

The main contribution of grouping Web documents is to improve both Web information retrieval (e.g., search engines) and content delivery. The clustering of Web documents helps to discover groups of documents having related content. In general, the process of grouping Web documents into categories is a usual practice (Cadez et al., 2003; Pallis, Angelis, Vakali, & Pokorny, 2004) since it improves data management and, in addition, eliminates the complexity of the underlying problem (since the number of document categories is smaller than the number of Web documents in a Web site). The approaches that have been proposed in order to group Web documents into categories can be summarized as follows (Baldi et al., 2003):

- **Content based:** The individual documents are grouped into semantically similar groups (as determined by the Web site administrator).
- **Functionality based:** Scanning for specific keywords that occur in the URL string of the document request makes the assignment of the document requests to a category.
- **Directory based:** The documents are categorized according to the directory of the Web server where they have been stored.

The schemes that have been developed for clustering Web documents can be categorized into the following two types.

Text-Based Clustering Approach

The text-based clustering approach uses textual document content to estimate the similarity among documents. In text-based clustering, the Web documents are usually represented by VSMs in a high-dimensional vector space where terms are associated with vector components. Once the Web documents are vectorized, clustering methods of vectors provide Web document clusters (Jain et al, 2003; Modha & Spangler, 2003; Wong & Fu, 2000). Similarity between documents is measured using one of several similarity measures that are based on such vectors. Examples include the cosine measure and the Jacard measure (Jain et al.). However, clustering methods based on this model make use of single-term analysis only. In Hammouda and Kamel (2004) and Zamir et al. (1997), the similarity between documents is based on matching phrases (sequences of words) rather than single words. A drawback of all these approaches is that they are time consuming since it is required to decompose the texts into terms.

Link-Based Clustering Approach

According to this approach, the Web is treated as a directed graph, where the nodes represent the Web documents with URL addresses and the edges among nodes represent the hyperlinks among Web documents. Link-based techniques use the Web site topology in order to cluster the Web documents. In Masada, Takasu, and Adachi (2004), the Web documents are grouped based only on hyperlink structure. Specifically, each cluster is considered to be a subset of a strongly connected component. In Zhu, Hong, and Hughes (2004), the authors presented a hierarchical clustering algorithm, called PageCluster, that clusters documents on each conceptual level of the link hierarchy based on the in-link and out-link similarities between these documents. The link hierarchy of each Web site is constructed by using the Web server log files.

In the same context, other works use link-based clustering techniques in order to identify Web communities (Flake, Tarjan, & Tsioutsiouliklis, 2004). A Web community is defined as a set of Web documents that link to more Web documents in the community than to documents outside of the community. A Web community enables Web crawlers to effectively focus on narrow but topically related subsets of the Web. In this framework, a lot of research has been devoted to efficiently identifying them. In Flake et al., communities can be efficiently computed by calculating the s-t minimum cut of the Web site graph (s and t denote the source and sink nodes, respectively). In Ino, Kudo, and Nakamura (2005), the authors propose a hierarchical partitioning through repeating partitioning and contraction. Finally, an efficient method for identifying a subclass of communities is given. A different technique for discovering communities from the graph structure of Web documents has been proposed in Reddy and Kitsuregawa (2001). The idea is that the set of documents composes a complete bipartite graph such that every hub document contains a link to all authorities. An algorithm for computing Web communities defined as complete bipartite graphs is also proposed. In Greco, Greco, and Zumpano (2004), the authors study the evolution of Web communities and find interesting properties. A new technique for identifying them is proposed on the basis of the above properties.

The notion of Web communities has also been used (implicitly or explicitly) in other contexts as well, but with different meanings and different objectives. For instance, there is a growing interest in compound documents and logical information units (Eiron & McCurley, 2003). A compound document is a logical document authored by (usually) one author presenting an extremely coherent body of material on a single topic, which is split across multiple nodes (URLs). A necessary condition for a set of Web documents to form a compound document is that their link graph should contain a vertex that has a path to every other part of the document. Similarly, a logical information unit is not a single Web document, but it is a connected subgraph corresponding to one logical document, organized into a set of documents connected via links provided by the document author as standard navigation routes.

Identifying XML Document Clusters

With the standardization of XML as an information exchange language over the Web,[2] documents formatted in XML have become quite popular. Similarly, clustering XML documents refers to the application of clustering algorithms in order to detect groups that share similar characteristics. Although there have been considerable works on clustering Web documents, new approaches are being proposed in order to exploit the advantages that offers the XML standard. The existing approaches for clustering XML documents are classified as follows:

- **Text-based approach:** The clustering of XML documents is based on the application of traditional information-retrieval techniques (Baeza-Yates & Ribiero-Neto, 1999) in order to define distance metrics that capture the content similarity for pieces of text. Text-based approaches aim at grouping the XML documents of similar topics together. The existing approaches should consider both statistical information for the various parts of the XML documents (e.g., the frequency of a term) and hierarchical indexes for calculating efficiently the distance metrics.

- **Link-based approach:** It is based on distances that estimate similarity in terms of the structural relationships of the elements in XML documents. In this approach, each document is represented by a tree model. So, the clustering problem is replaced by a tree-clustering one. Therefore, most research works focus on finding tree edit distances in order to define metrics that capture structural similarity. Recently, in Nierman and Jagadish (2002), a method was proposed to cluster XML documents according to the structural similarity between trees using the edit distance. A quite different approach is presented in Lian, Cheung, Mamoulis, and Yiu (2004), where the XML document is represented as a structured graph (s-graph), and a distance metric is used to find similarities.

Identifying Web User Clusters

In order to cluster the Web users' sessions, each one is usually represented by an n-dimensional vector, where n is the number of Web pages in the session. The values of each vector are the requested Web pages. For simplicity, it is common to group the pages into groups. In addition, a user session may be represented by a graph where the nodes are the visited pages (Baldi et al., 2003; Lou et al., 2002). Up to now, several clustering algorithms have been proposed assigning the Web users' sessions with common characteristics into the same cluster (Jain et al., 1999). These may be classified into the following approaches:

- **Similarity-Based Approach:** In order to decide whether two sessions are clustered together, a distance function (similarity measure) must be defined in advance. Distance functions (e.g., Euclidean, Manhattan, Levenshtein [Scherbina & Kuznetsov, 2004], etc.) can be determined either directly or indirectly, although the latter is more common in applications. Hierarchical and partitional approaches are the most indicative that belong to this category. Hierarchical clustering approaches proceed successfully by either merging smaller clusters into larger ones (agglomerative methods) or splitting larger clusters (divisive methods). In general, differences among the techniques that use hierarchical clustering arise mainly because of the various ways of defining distance (similarity) between two individuals (sessions) or between two groups of individuals.[3]

Since the distances have been computed, a hierarchical clustering algorithm is used either to merge or to divide the sessions. The result is represented by a tree of clusters (a two-dimensional diagram that is called a dendrogram) and illustrates the relations among them. On the other hand, the partitional algorithms determine a flat clustering into a specific number of clusters (e.g., k-means, k-mode, etc.). Specifically, a partition-based clustering scheme decomposes the data set into a predefined set of disjoint clusters such that the individuals within each cluster are as homogeneous as possible. Homogeneity is determined by an appropriate score function, such as the distance between each individual and the centroid of the cluster to which it is assigned.

- **Model-Based Approach:** Model-based clustering is a framework that combines cluster analysis with probabilistic techniques. The objects in such an approach are supposed to follow a finite mixture of probability distributions such that each component distribution expresses a cluster (each cluster has a data-generating model with different parameters for each cluster). The issue in model-based approaches is to learn the parameters for each cluster. Then, the objects are assigned to clusters using a hard assignment policy.[4] In order to learn the set of parameters for each cluster, the expectation-maximization (EM) algorithm is usually used. The EM algorithm originates from Dempster, Laird, and Rubin (1977). In Cadez et al. (2003), a method for employing EM on users' sessions is proposed. The EM algorithm is an iterative procedure that finds the maximum-likelihood estimates of the parameter vector by repeating the following steps:

  o The expectation E-step: Given a set of parameter estimates, the E-step calculates the conditional expectation of the complete data-log likelihood given the observed data and the parameter estimates.

  o The maximization M-step: Given a complete data-log likelihood, the M-step finds the parameter estimates to maximize the complete data-log likelihood from the E-step.

The two steps are iterated until convergence. The complexity of the EM algorithm depends on the complexity of the E- and M-steps at each iteration (Dempster et al., 1977). It is important to note that the number of clusters on model-based schemes is estimated by using probabilistic techniques. Specifically, the BIC (Bayesian information criterion) and AIC (Akaike information criterion) are widely used (Fraley & Raftery, 1998).

Similarity Based vs. Model Based

The benefits of similarity-based algorithms are their simplicity and their low complexity. However, a drawback of these algorithms is that they do not contain a metric about the structure of the data being clustered. For instance, in hierarchical approaches, the entire hierarchy should be explored a priori, and for partitioning approaches, it is essential to predetermine the appropriate number of clusters. On the other hand, the model-based approaches try to solve the above problems by building models that describe the browsing behavior of users on the Web. Modeling can generate insight into how the users use the Web as well as provide mechanisms for making predictions for a variety of applications (such as Web prefetching,

Table 1. Web data clustering approaches

Information Source: Web Documents		
Research Work	**Cluster Content**	**Clustering Approach**
k-means (Modha & Spangler, 2003)	*Web documents*	*Text based*
Suffix-Tree Clustering (Zamir et al, 1997)	*Web documents*	*Text based*
Hierarchical Clustering Algorithm (Wong & Fu, 2000)	*Web documents*	*Text based*
Similarity Histogram-Based Clustering (SHC; Hammouda & Kamel, 2004)	*Web documents*	*Text based*
Strongly Connected Components Clustering (Masada et al., 2004)	*Web documents*	*Link based*
The s-t Minimum Cut Algorithm (Flake et al., 2004)	*Web communities*	*Link based*
PageCluster (Zhu et al., 2004)	*Web documents*	*Link based*
Distance-Based Clustering Algorithm (Baeza-Yates & Ribiero-Neto, 1999)	*XML documents*	*Text based*
S-GRACE clustering algorithm (Lian et al., 2004)	*XML documents*	*Link based*
Information Source: Web Server Logs		
Research Work	**Cluster Content**	**Clustering Approach**
Sequence-Alignment Method (SAM; Wang & Zaïane, 2002)	*Web users' sessions*	*Similarity based*
Generalization-Based Clustering (Fu, Sandhu, & Shih, 1999)	*Web users' sessions*	*Similarity based*
Weighted Longest Common Subsequences Clustering (Banerjee & Ghosh, 2001)	*Web users' sessions*	*Similarity based*
Cube-Model Clustering (Huang, Ng, Cheung, Ng, & Ching, 2001)	*Web users' sessions*	*Similarity based*
Path-Mining Clustering (Shahabi, Zarkesh, Adibi, & Shah, 1997)	*Web users' sessions*	*Similarity based*
Hierarchical Clustering Algorithm (Scherbina & Kuznetsov, 2004)	*Web users' sessions*	*Similarity based*
EM (Cadez et al., 2003)	*Web users' sessions*	*Model based*
Self-Organizing Maps (SOMs) Clustering (Smith & Ng, 2003)	*Web users' sessions*	*Model based*

the personalization of Web content, etc.). Therefore, the model-based schemes are usually favored for clustering Web users' sessions.

In fact, there are a number of reasons why probabilistic modeling is usually selected for describing the dynamic evolution of the Web instead of the other clustering approaches (Baldi et al., 2003). First of all, model-based schemes enable the compact representation of complex data sets (such as Web log files) by being able to exploit regularities present in many real-world systems and the data associated with these systems. Second, model-based schemes can deal with uncertainty and unknown attributes, which is often the typical case in Web data applications. The Web is a high-dimensional system, where the measurement of all relevant variables becomes unrealistic, so most of the variables remain hidden and must be revealed using probabilistic methods. Furthermore, the probabilistic models are supported by a sound mathematical background. Another advantage is that model-based schemes can utilize prior knowledge about the domain of interest and combine this knowledge with observed data to build a complete model.

Table 1 presents a summary of the Web data clustering approaches.

Validation and Interpretation of Clusters

One of the main challenges with clustering algorithms is that it is difficult to assess the quality of the resulted clusters (Chen & Liu, 2003; Halkidi, Batistakis, & Vazirgiannis, 2002a, 2002b; Pallis et al., 2004). So, an important issue is the evaluation and validation of a clustering scheme.

Another major challenge with clustering algorithms is to efficiently interpret the resulting clusters. No matter how effective a clustering algorithm is, the clustering process might be proven to be inefficient if it is not accompanied by a sophisticated interpretation of the clusters. An analysis of the clusters can provide valuable insights about users' navigation behavior and about the Web site structure. In the following paragraphs, the most representative validating and interpreting approaches are presented.

Clustering Validation

In general, a validation approach is used to decide whether a clustering scheme is valid or not. A cluster validity framework provides insights into the outcomes of the clustering algorithms and assesses the quality of them. Furthermore, a validation technique may be used in order to determine the number of clusters in a clustering result (Fraley & Raftery, 1998).

Most of the existing validation approaches for Web data clustering rely on statistical hypothesis testing (Halkidi et al., 2002a, 2002b). The basic idea is to test whether the points of a data set are randomly structured or not. This analysis involves a null hypothesis (H_o) expressed as a statement of a random structure of a data set. To test this hypothesis, statistical tests are widely used, which lead to a computationally complex procedure. In the literature (Halkidi et al., 2002a, 2002b), several statistical tests have been proposed for clustering validation, such as Rand statistic (R), cophenetic correlation coefficient (CPCC), and the χ^2 test (Pallis et al., 2004). The major drawback of all these approaches is their high computational demands.

A different approach for evaluating cluster validity is to compare the underlying clustering algorithm with other clustering schemes, modifying only the parameter values. The challenge is to choose the best clustering scheme from a set of defined schemes according to a prespecified criterion, the so-called cluster validation index (a number indicating the quality of a given clustering). Several cluster validation indices have been proposed in the literature.

The most indicative are the Davies-Bouldin index (DB; Günter & Bunke, 2003), Frobenius norm (Z. Huang et al., 2001), and SD validity index (Halkidi et al., 2002a, 2002b).

Clustering Interpretation

It is quite probable that the information that is obtained by the clusters needs further analysis, such as in cases involving clusters of Web users' sessions for a commercial Web site, which without any analysis may not provide useful conclusions. An interpretation of the resulting clusters could be important for a number of tasks, such as managing the Web site, identifying malicious visitors, and targeted advertising. It also helps in understanding the Web users' navigation behavior, and therefore helps in organizing the Web site to better suit the users' needs. Furthermore, interpreting the results of Web data clusters contributes to identify and provide customized services and recommendations to Web users. However, the interpretation of clusters is a difficult and time-consuming process due to large-scale data sets and their complexity.

Several research works in various industrial and academic research communities are focusing on interpreting Web data clusters (e.g., Cadez et al., 2003; Wu, Yu, & Ballman, 1998). Statistical methods are usually used in order to interpret the resulting clusters and extract valuable information. For example, a further analysis of the Web users' session clusters may reveal interesting relations among clusters and the documents that users visit (Pallis et al., 2004).

A valuable help in cluster interpretation is visualization, which can help the Web administrators to visually perceive the clustered results and sometimes discover hidden patterns in data. In Vesanto and Alhoniemi (2000), a visualization method is used in order to interpret Web document clusters based on the self-organizing map. The SOM is an artificial neural-network model that is well suited for mapping high-dimensional data into a two-dimensional representation space where clusters can be identified. However, it requires the preprocessing and normalization of the data, and the prior specification of the number of clusters. Furthermore, in Gomory, Hoch, Lee, Podlaseck, and Schonberg (1999), a parallel coordinate system has been deployed for the interpretation and analysis of users' navigation sessions of online stores. They define microconversion rates as metrics in e-commerce analysis in order to understand the effectiveness of marketing and merchandising efforts. Moreover, a tool called INSITE has also been developed for knowledge discovery from users' Web site navigation in a real-time fashion (Shahabi, Faisal, Kashani, & Faruque, 2000). INSITE visualizes the result of clustering users' navigation paths in real time. In Cadez et al. (2003), a mixture of Markov models is used to predict the behavior of user clusters and visualize the classification of users. The authors have developed a tool, called WebCANVAS (Web Clustering ANalysis and VisuAlization Sequence), that visualizes user navigation paths in each cluster. In this system, user sessions are represented using categories of general topics for Web documents. Another graphical tool, called CLUTO[5]: A clustering toolkit (software for clustering high-dimensional datasets), has been implemented for clustering data sets and for analyzing the characteristics of the various clusters. Finally, in Pallis, Angelis, and Vakali (2005) a visualization method for interpreting the clustering results is presented, revealing interesting features for Web users' navigation behavior and their interaction with the content and structure of Web sites. This method is based on a statistical method, namely, the correspondence analysis (CO-AN), which is used for picturing both the intercluster and intracluster associations.

Integrating Clustering in Applications

A wide range of Web applications can be favored for clustering. Specifically, clustering schemes may be adopted in Web applications in order to manage effectively the large collections of data. Such applications include the following:

- **Web Personalization Systems:** In general, Web personalization is defined by Mobasher, Cooley, and Srivastava (2000) as any action that adapts the information or services provided by a Web site to the needs of a particular user or a set of users, taking advantage of the knowledge gained from the users' navigational behavior and individual interests in combination with the content and the structure of the Web site. The challenge of a Web personalization system is to provide users with the information they want without expecting them to ask for it explicitly. Personalization effectiveness heavily relies on user-profile reliability, which, in turn, depends on the accuracy with which user navigation behavior is modeled. In this context, the clustering of Web users' sessions improves significantly this process since an analysis of the resulting clusters helps in modeling and understanding better human behavior on the Web (Baldi et al., 2003; Cadez et al., 2003; Spiliopoulou & Faulstich, 1998).

- **Web Prefetching:** Web prefetching is the process of predicting future requests for Web objects and bringing those objects into the cache in the background before an explicit request is made for them (Nanopoulos, Katsaros, & Manolopoulos, 2003). Therefore, for a prefetching scheme to be effective, there should be an efficient method to predict users' requests. Sophisticated clustering schemes may be adopted in Web prefetching systems, reducing the user-perceived Web latency and improving the content-management process. The prefetching process is facilitated by determining clusters of Web documents that are probably requested together. In addition, clustering Web users' sessions helps in predicting the future requests so that objects can be prefetched before a request is made for them.

- **Web Search Engines:** Search engines are the most widely used tools for retrieving Web data. Their goal is to crawl over the Web and retrieve the requested documents with low communication costs in a reasonable interval of time. Recently, Web search engines have enhanced sophisticated clustering schemes in their infrastructures in order to improve the Web search process (Chakrabarti, 2003). The objects are clustered either by their popularity statistics or by their structure. Considerable work has also been done on clustering Web queries (Wen, Nie, & Zhang, 2001) and Web search results (Zeng, He, Chen, Ma, & Ma, 2004) toward the improvement of user satisfaction.

- **E-Mail Mining:** E-mail overload has grown significantly over the past years, becoming a personal headache for users and a financial issue for companies. In order to alleviate this problem, Web mining practices have been developed that compute the behavior profiles or models of user e-mail accounts (Vel, Anderson, Corney, & Mohay, 2001). Thus, e-mail clustering is useful for report generation and the summarization of e-mail archives, as well as for detecting spam mail.

- **Content Delivery Networks:** Content (different types of information) delivery over the Web has become a mostly crucial practice in improving Web performance. Content delivery networks (CDNs) have been proposed to maximize bandwidth, improve accessibility, and maintain correctness through content replication. Web data clustering techniques seem to offer an effective trend for CDNs since CDNs manage large collections of data over highly distributed infrastructures (Pallis & Vakali, 2006).

Table 2 highlights some indicative Web applications and systems that have been favored for clustering in an effort to understand the importance and the challenge in adopting clustering under frameworks.

Table 2. Integrating Web data clustering on Web applications

Web Applications	Systems	Improve Information Retrieval	Reduce Traffic	Improve Quality of Service	Improve Content Management	Improve Security
Web personalization	WebPersonalizer (Mobasher et al., 2000), NETMIND[6] (a commercial system from Mindlab that produces multi-user recommendations), WUM (Web usage miner; Spiliopoulou & Faulstich, 1998), SpeedTracer (Wu et al., 1998)	√		√		√
Web prefetching	CacheFlow, NetSonic, Webcelerator		√	√	√	
Search engines	Google, Niagara[7]	√		√	√	
E-mail mining	Popfile,[8] SwiftFile, eMailSift			√		√
CDNs	Akamai,[9] Limelight Network,[10] Mirror Image[11]		√	√	√	

Conclusion

The explosive growth of the Web has dramatically changed the way in which information is managed and accessed. Web data mining is an evolving field of high interest to a wide academic and technical community. In this framework, clustering data on the Web has become an emerging research area, raising new difficulties and challenges for the Web community. This chapter addresses the issues involved in the effect of Web data clustering on increasing Web information accessibility, decreasing lengths in navigation patterns, improving user servicing, integrating various data representation standards, and extending current Web information organization practices. Furthermore, the most popular methodologies and implementations in terms of Web data clustering are presented.

In summary, clustering is an interesting, useful, and challenging problem. Although, a great deal of research works exists, there is a lot of room for improvement in both theoretical and practical applications. For instance, the emergence of the XML standard has resulted in the development of new clustering schemes. Finally, the rich assortment of dynamic and interactive services on the Web, such as video and audio conferencing, e-commerce, and distance learning, has opened new research issues in terms of Web data clustering.

References

Baeza-Yates, R., & Ribiero-Neto, B. (1999). *Modern information retrieval.* Boston: Addison-Wesley.

Baldi, P., Frasconi, P., & Smyth, P. (2003). *Modeling the Internet and the Web.* New York: Wiley.

Banerjee, A., & Ghosh, J. (2001). Clickstream clustering using weighted longest common subsequences. *Proceedings of the Workshop on Web Mining, SIAM Conference on Data Mining,* 33-40.

Bar-Yossef, Z., & Rajagopalan, S. (2002). Template detection via data mining and its applications. *Proceedings of the 11th International World Wide Web Conference (WWW2002)* (pp. 580-591).

Cadez, I. V., Heckerman, D., Meek, C., Smyth, P., & White, S. (2003). Model-based clustering and visualization of navigation patterns on a Web site. *Journal of Data Mining and Knowledge Discovery, 7*(4), 399-424.

Catledge, L., & Pitkow, J. (1995). Characterizing browsing behaviors on the World Wide Web. *Computer Networks and ISDN Systems, 6*(27), 1065-1073.

Chakrabarti, S. (2003). *Mining the Web.* San Francisco: Morgan Kaufmann.

Chen, K., & Liu, L. (2003). Validating and refining clusters via visual rendering. *Proceedings of the 3rd IEEE International Conference on Data Mining (ICDM 2003)* (pp. 501-504).

Chen, M. S., Park, J. S., & Yu, P. S. (1998). Efficient data mining for path traversal patterns. *IEEE Transactions on Knowledge and Data Engineering, 10*(2), 209-221.

Cooley, R., Mobasher, B., & Srivastava, J. (1999). Data preparation for mining World Wide Web browsing patterns. *Knowledge Information Systems, 1*(1), 5-32.

Dempster, A. P., Laird, N. P., & Rubin, D. B. (1977). Maximum likelihood from incomplete data via the EM algorithm. *Journal of the Royal Statistical Society, B, 39*, 1-22.

Eiron, N., & McCurley, K. S. (2003). Untangling compound documents on the Web. *Proceedings of the 14th ACM Conference on Hypertext and Hypermedia* (pp. 85-94).

Flake, G. W., Tarjan, R. E., & Tsioutsiouliklis, K. (2004). Graph clustering and minimum cut trees. *Internet Mathematics, 1*(4), 385-408.

Fraley, C., & Raftery, A. (1998). How many clusters? Which clustering method? Answers via model-based cluster analysis. *Computer Journal, 41*, 578-588.

Fu, Y., Sandhu, K., & Shih, M. Y. (1999). A generalization-based approach to clustering of Web usage sessions. In *Proceedings of the International Workshop on Web Usage Analysis and User Profiling (WEBKDD1999)* (LNCS 1836, pp. 21-38). San Diego: Springer Verlag.

Goker, A., & He, D. (2000). Analysing Web search logs to determine session boundaries for user-oriented learning. In *Proceedings of the International Conference of Adaptive Hypermedia and Adaptive Web-Based Systems (AH2000)* (LNCS 1892, pp. 319-322). Trento, Italy: Springer Verlag.

Gomory, S., Hoch, R., Lee, J., Podlaseck, M., & Schonberg, E. (1999). Analysis and visualization of metrics for online merchandising. In *Proceedings of the International Workshop on Web Usage Analysis and User Profiling (WEBKDD1999)* (LNCS 1836, pp. 126-141). San Diego, CA: Springer Verlag.

Greco, G., Greco, S., & Zumpano, E. (2004). Web communities: Models and algorithms. *World Wide Web Journal, 7*(1), 58-82.

Günter, S., & Bunke, H. (2003). Validation indices for graph clustering. *Pattern Recognition Letters, 24*(8), 1107-1113.

Halkidi, M., Batistakis, Y., & Vazirgiannis, M. (2002a). Cluster validity methods: Part I. *SIGMOD Record, 31*(2), 40-45.

Halkidi, M., Batistakis, Y., & Vazirgiannis, M. (2002b). Cluster validity methods: Part II. *SIGMOD Record, 31*(3), 19-27.

Hammouda, K. M., & Kamel, M. S. (2004). Efficient phrase-based document indexing for Web document clustering. *IEEE Transactions on Knowledge Data Engineering, 16*(10), 1279-1296.

Huang, X., Peng, F., An, A., & Schuurmans, D. (2004). Dynamic Web log session identification with statistical language models. *Journal of the American Society for Information Science and Technology (JASIST), 55*(14), 1290-1303.

Huang, Z., Ng, J., Cheung, D. W., Ng, M. K., & Ching, W. (2001). A cube model for Web access sessions and cluster analysis. In *Proceedings of the International Workshop on Web Usage Analysis and User Profiling (WEBKDD2001)* (LNCS 2356, pp. 48-67). Hong Kong, China: Springer Verlag.

Huang, Z., Ng, M. K., & Cheung, D. (2001). An empirical study on the visual cluster validation method with fastmap. *Proceedings of the 7th International Conference on Database Systems for Advanced Applications (DASFAA 2001)* (pp. 84-91).

Ino, H., Kudo, M., & Nakamura, A. (2005). Partitioning of Web graphs by community topology. *Proceedings of the 14th International Conference on World Wide Web (WWW 2005)*, 661-669.

Jain, A. K., Murty, M. N., & Flynn, P. J. (1999). Data clustering: A review. *ACM Computing Surveys, 31*(3), 264-323.

Jushmerick, N. (1999). Learning to remove Internet advertisements. *Proceedings of the 3rd Annual Conference on Autonomous Agents* (pp. 175-181).

Lian, W., Cheung, D. W., Mamoulis, N., & Yiu, S. (2004). An efficient and scalable algorithm for clustering XML documents by structure. *IEEE Transactions on Knowledge Data Engineering, 16*(1), 82-96.

Lou, W., Liu, G., Lu, H., & Yang, Q. (2002). Cut-and-pick transactions for proxy log mining. *Proceedings of the 8th International Conference on Extending Database Technology (EDBT 2002)* (pp. 88-105).

Masada, T., Takasu, A., & Adachi, J. (2004). Web page grouping based on parameterized connectivity. *Proceedings of the 9th International Conference on Database Systems for Advanced Applications (DASFAA 2004)* (pp. 374-380).

Mobasher, B., Cooley, R., & Srivastava, J. (2000). Automatic personalization based on Web usage mining. *Communications of the ACM, 43*(8), 142-151.

Modha, D., & Spangler, W. (2003). Feature weighting in *k*-means clustering. *Machine Learning, 52*(3), 217-237.

Moore, J., Han, E., Boley, D., Gini, M., Gross, R., Hastings, K., et al. (1997). Web page categorization and feature selection using association rule and principal component clustering. Proceedings of the *7th Workshop on Information Technologies and Systems*, Atlanta, GA.

Nanopoulos, A., Katsaros, D., & Manolopoulos, Y. (2003). A data mining algorithm for generalized Web prefetching. *IEEE Transactions on Knowledge Data Engineering, 15*(5), 1155-1169.

Nierman, A., & Jagadish, H. V. (2002). Evaluating structural similarity in XML documents. *Proceedings of the 5th International Workshop on the Web and Databases (WebDB 2002)* (pp. 61-66).

Pallis, G., Angelis, L., & Vakali, A. (2005). Model-based cluster analysis for Web users sessions. In *Proceedings of the 15th International Symposium on Methodologies for Intelligent Systems (ISMIS 2005)* (LNCS 3488, pp. 219-227). Saratoga Springs, NY: Springer Verlag.

Pallis, G., Angelis, L., Vakali, A., & Pokorny, J. (2004). A probabilistic validation algorithm for Web users' clusters. *Proceedings of the IEEE International Conference on Systems, Man and Cybernetics (SMC 2004)* (pp. 4129-4134).

Pallis, G., & Vakali, A. (2006). Insight and perspectives for content delivery networks. *Communications of the ACM, 49*(1), 101-106.

Pallis, G., Vakali, A., Angelis, L., & Hacid, M. S. (2003). A study on workload characterization for a Web proxy server. *Proceedings of the 21st IASTED International Multi-Conference on Applied Informatics (AI 2003)* (pp. 779-784).

Reddy, P. K., & Kitsuregawa, M. (2001). An approach to relate the Web communities through bipartite graphs. *WISE, 1*, 301-310.

Salton, G., Wong, A., & Yang, C. (1975). A vector space model for automatic indexing. *Communications of the ACM, 18*(11), 613-620.

Scherbina, A., & Kuznetsov, S. (2004). Clustering of Web sessions using Levenshtein metric. In *Proceedings of the 4th Industrial Conference on Data Mining (ICDM 2004)* (LNCS 3275, pp. 127-133). San Jose, CA: Springer Verlag.

Shahabi, C., Faisal, A., Kashani, F. B., & Faruque, J. (2000). INSITE: A tool for interpreting users' interaction with a Web space. *Proceedings of the 26th International Conference on Very Large Data Bases (VLDB 2000)* (pp. 635-638).

Shahabi, C., Zarkesh, A. M., Adibi, J., & Shah, V. (1997). *Knowledge discovery from users Web page navigation.* Proceedings of the 7th International Workshop on Research Issues in Data Engineering (IEEE RIDE), Birmingham, United Kingdom.

Smith, K., & Ng, A. (2003). Web page clustering using a self-organizing map of user navigation patterns. *Decision Support Systems, 35*(2), 245-256.

Spiliopoulou, M., & Faulstich, L. (1998). WUM: A tool for WWW utilization analysis. In *Proceedings of the International Workshop on World Wide Web and Databases (WebDB 1998)* (LNCS 1590, pp. 184-203). Valencia, Spain: Springer Verlag.

Stein, B., Eissen, S. M., & Wibrock, F. (2003). *On cluster validity and the information need of users.* Proceedings of the 3rd IASTED International Conference on Artificial Intelligence and Applications (AIA 2003), Benalmadena, Spain.

Vel, O. D., Anderson, A., Corney, M., & Mohay, G. (2001). Mining e-mail content for author identification forensics. *Special Interest Group on Management of Data Record (SIGMOD Rec.), 30*(4), 55-64.

Vesanto, J., & Alhoniemi, E. (2000). Clustering of self-organizing map. *IEEE Transactions on Neural Networks, 11*(3), 586-600.

Wang, W., & Zaïane, O. R. (2002). Clustering Web sessions by sequence alignment. In *Proceedings of the 13th International Workshop on Database and Expert Systems Applications (DEXA 2002)* (LNCS 2453, pp. 394-398). Aix-en-Provence, France: Springer Verlag.

Wen, J. R., Nie, J. Y., & Zhang, H. (2001). Clustering user queries of a search engine. *Proceedings of the 10th International World Wide Web Conference (WWW2001)* (pp. 162-168).

Wong, W., & Fu, A. (2000). *Incremental document clustering for Web page classification.* Proceedings of the IEEE International Conference on Information Society in the 21st Century: Emerging Technologies and New Challenges (IS2000), Fukushima, Japan.

Wu, K., Yu, P. S., & Ballman, A. (1998). Speedtracer: A Web usage mining and analysis tool. *IBM Systems Journal, 37*(1), 89-105.

Yang, Y., & Pedersen, J. O. (1997). A comparative study on feature selection in text categorization. *Proceedings of the 14th International Conference on Machine Learning (ICML 1997)* (pp. 412-420).

Zaïane, O. R., Foss, A., Lee, C.-H., & Wang, W. (2002). On data clustering analysis: Scalability, constraints, and validation. In *Proceedings of the 6th Pacific-Asia Conference of Advances in Knowledge Discovery and Data Mining (PAKDD 2002)* (LNCS 2336, pp. 28-39). Taipei, Taiwan: Springer Verlag.

Zamir, O., Etzioni, O., Madanim, O., & Karp, R. M. (1997). Fast and intuitive clustering of Web documents. *Proceedings of the 3rd International Conference on Knowledge Discovery and Data Mining (KDD 1997)* (pp. 287-290).

Zeng, H. J., He, Q. C., Chen, Z., Ma, W. Y., & Ma, J. (2004). Learning to cluster Web search results. *Proceedings of the 27th Annual International ACM SIGIR Conference on Research and Development in Information Retrieval* (pp. 210-217).

Zhu, J., Hong, J., & Hughes, J. (2004). PageCluster: Mining conceptual link hierarchies from Web log files for adaptive Web site navigation. *ACM Transactions on Internet Technologies, 4*(2), 185-208.

Endnotes

[1]   http://www.squid-cache.org/Scripts

[2]   http://www.w3.org/

[3]   The term proximity is often used as a general term to denote either a measure of similarity or dissimilarity.

[4]   In a hard assignment policy, each object is assigned to only one cluster. On the other hand, a soft assignment policy allows degrees of membership in multiple clusters, which means that one object can be assigned to multiple clusters with certain membership values.

[5]   http://www-users.cs.umn.edu/~karypis/cluto/index.html

[6]   http://www.mindlab.de

[7]   http://www.cs.wisc.edu/niagara/Introduction.html

[8]   http://popfile.sourceforge.net

[9]   http://www.akamai.org

[10]   http://www.limelightnetworks.com/

[11]   http://www.mirror-image.com

Chapter III

An Overview of Similarity Measures for Clustering XML Documents

Giovanna Guerrini, Università degli Studi di Milano, Italy

Marco Mesiti, Università degli Studi di Genova, Italy

Ismael Sanz, Universitat Jaume I, Spain

Abstract

The large amount and heterogeneity of XML documents on the Web requires the development of clustering techniques to group together similar documents. Documents can be grouped together according to their content, their structure, and the links inside and among the documents. For instance, grouping together documents with similar structure has interesting applications in the context of information extraction, heterogeneous data integration, personalized content delivery, access-control definition, Web site structural analysis, and the comparison of RNA secondary structures. Many approaches have been proposed for evaluating the structural and content similarity between tree-based and vector-based rep-

resentations of XML documents. Link-based similarity approaches developed for Web data clustering have been adapted for XML documents. This chapter discusses and compares the most relevant similarity measures and their employment for XML document clustering.

Introduction

XML stands for the eXtensible Markup Language introduced by World Wide Web Consortium (W3C; 1998) that allows one to structure documents by means of nested, tagged elements. The element tag allows the annotation of the semantic description of the element content and can be exploited in order to effectively retrieve only relevant documents. Thus, the document structure can be exploited for document retrieval. Moreover, through the Xlink Language (W3C, 2001), different types of links can be specified among XML documents. In Xlink, a link is a relationship among two or more resources that can be described inside an XML document. These relationships can be exploited as well to improve document retrieval.

The exponential growing of XML-structured data available on the Web has raised the need of developing clustering techniques for XML documents. Web data clustering (Vakali, Pokorný, & Dalamagas, 2004) is the process of grouping Web data into clusters so that similar data belong to the same cluster and dissimilar data to different clusters. The goal of organizing data in such a way is to improve data availability and to make data access faster so that Web information retrieval and content delivery are improved. Moreover, clustering together similar documents allows the development of homogeneous indexing structures and schemas that are more representative of such documents.

XML documents can also be used for annotating Web resources (like articles, images, movies, and also Web services). For example, an image can be coupled with an XML document representing the image author and the date on which it has been shot as well as a textual description of its content or theme. A search engine can be coupled with an XML document containing information on the domain in which it works (e.g., document retrieval, image retrieval, Web-service retrieval) as well as information on the period of time during which the engine is available to answer queries. Web services can be coupled with a description of the services they provide as well as links to analogous providers on the Web. An important activity in this respect is to identify resources on the Web that are similar by considering the similarity of the XML documents containing the annotations in order to provide users with similar resources. Thus, developing approaches for clustering together similar documents that share similar characteristics is an important research direction.

XML document clustering is realized through algorithms that rely on the similarity between two documents computed exploiting a distance metric. The algorithms should guarantee that documents in the same cluster have a high similarity degree (low distance), whereas documents in different clusters have a low similarity degree (high distance). As far as the clustering of XML data is concerned, the document content and the document structure as well as links among documents can be exploited for identifying similarities among documents. Several measures have been proposed for computing the structural and content similarity among XML documents, but few XML-specific approaches exist for computing link similarity (even if the approaches developed for Web data can be easily applied). The purpose of the chapter is to present and compare the research efforts for developing similarity measures for clustering XML documents relying on their content, structure, and links. Approaches are presented relying on the adopted representation of the documents. Vector-based as well as tree-based representations are the most commonly adopted, though more seldom graph and alternative representations have been adopted as well.

The chapter starts by introducing the basics of XML documents and clustering approaches. Then, we present measures for evaluating the similarity among XML documents exploited for clustering, discussing first those based on tree and on vector representation of documents, and then those adopting alternative representations. We then compare the different approaches by specifying a methodology for the identification of the suitable measure for an application context. Finally, we conclude by discussing further research issues that should be addressed in the next years.

Background

In this section, we first introduce some basic notions of XML documents. Then, we introduce the different granularity levels at which similarity measures can be defined. Finally, we sketch the basics of clustering approaches the similarity measures can be employed in.

XML Documents

XML documents, as shown in Figure 1, simply consist of a sequence of nested, tagged elements. An element contains a portion of the document delimited by a start tag (e.g., <recipe>) at the beginning, and an end tag (e.g., </recipe>) at the end. Empty elements of the form <tagname/> are also possible. The outermost element containing all the elements of the document, the element recipes in Figure 1a, is referred to as the document element. Each element can be characterized by one or more attributes that are name-value pairs appear-

Figure 1. XML documents containing recipes

```
<?xml version="1.0" encoding="UTF-8"?>
<recipes>
 <summary> Some recipes of my GranMa </summary>
 <recipe num="1">
  <title>Pizza Margherita</title>
  <preparation>
   <ingredients>
    <ingredient name="Tomato" amount="1" unit="Kg"/>
    <ingredient name="Mozzarella" amount="3" unit="pieces"/>
    ...
   </ingredients>
   <step> Preheat oven to 180 degrees C</step>
   ... <step>...</step>
  </preparation>
  <cost amount="5" unit="euro"/>
  <note>Chunk Tomato in little pieces, ...</note>
 </recipe>
 ...
</recipes>                          (a)
```

```
<?xml version="1.0" encoding="UTF-8"?>
<collection>
 <description> Some recipes of Aunt Carol </description>
 <recipe>
  <name>Pizza Margherita</name>
  <ingredient name="Tomato" qty="1.5"/>
  <ingredient name="Mozzarella" qty="2"/>
   ...
  <preparation>
   <step> Preheat oven to 180 degrees C</step>
   <step> ...</step>
   ...
  </preparation>
  <comment>Chunk Tomato in little pieces, ...</comment>
  <nutrition calories="500" fat="20" protein="18"/>
 </recipe>
 ...
</collection>                          (b)
```

Figure 2. (a) DTD of document in Figure 1b, and an Xlink link declaration and use (b)

```
<!DOCTYPE collection[
<!ELEMENT collection (description,recipe*, comment?)>
<!ELEMENT recipe(name,ingredient*,preparation?,comment,nutrition)>
<!ELEMENT preparation(step|comment)*>
<!ELEMENT description (#PCDATA)>
<!ELEMENT name (#PCDATA)>
<!ELEMENT ingredient EMPTY>
<!ELEMENT comment (#PCDATA)>
<!ELEMENT nutrition EMPTY>
<!ATTLIST ingredient name CDATA qty CDATA>
<!ATTLIST nutrition calories CDATA fat CDATA protein CDATA>
]!>
```
(a)

```
<!ELEMENT aLink ANY>
<!ATTLIST aLink
        xmlns:xlink="http://www.w3.org/1999/xlink"
        xlink:type (simple|extended)
        xlink:href CDATA
        xlink:show (new|replace|embed|undefined)
        xlink:actuate (onLoad|onRequest|undefined)>

<aLink xlink:type="simple" xlink:href="www.unimi.it"
        xlink:show = "new" xlink:actuate="onLoad">
        University of Milano
</aLink>
```
(b)

ing just after the element name in the start or empty tag (e.g., amount="1"), and by textual content, which is the portion of text appearing between the start tag and the end tag (e.g., Pizza Margherita). XML documents can be coupled with schema information either in the form of a DTD (document-type definition) or an XML schema for specifying constraints on the allowed contents of the documents. Figure 2a shows an example of DTD associated with the document in Figure 1b. This schema can be easily converted into an XML schema, adding further constraints (e.g., the minimal and maximal cardinality of element occurrences, the built-in types for data content elements) whose specification the DTD does not support. Links among elements or among documents can be specified through ID/IDREF(S) attributes or Xlink specifications. In Xlink, both simple links, representing one-to-one relationships between two documents, and extended links, representing many-to-many relationships among documents, can be specified. Independently from the type, a link can be associated with an actuate attribute specifying when it should be traversed (e.g., on load, on request) and a show attribute specifying the presentation of the target resource (e.g., open in a new window, load the referenced resource in the same window, embed the pointed resource). Figure 2b shows the DTD declaration of a link following the Xlink standard and an element that points to the Web page of the University of Milano.

Composition of Similarity Measures for XML Documents

In the definition of a similarity measure, we have to point out the objects on which the measure is evaluated and the relationships existing among such objects. In the XML case, documents are hierarchical in nature and can be viewed as compositions of simpler constituents, including elements, attributes, links, and plain text. The hierarchy of composition is quite rich: Attributes and text are contained in elements, and elements themselves are organized in higher order structures such as paths and subtrees. We will refer to each level in the compositional structure of an XML document as a *granularity level*. The following levels occur in the literature:

- The whole XML document
- Subtrees (i.e., portions of documents)
- Paths

Figure 3. Structural granularities in an XML document

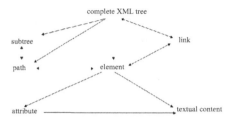

- Elements
- Links
- Attributes, and
- Textual content (of attributes and data content elements)

The relationships between the granularity levels are depicted in Figure 3 through arrows. An arrow from a granularity level A to a granularity level B means that a similarity measure at level A can be formulated in terms of objects at granularity B. Similarity measures for XML are usually defined according to these natural relations of composition. For instance, a measure for complete XML documents can be defined by evaluating the similarity of paths, which in turn requires some criterion to compare the elements contained in the path.

In addition to composition, other relationships among elements and documents that can be exploited for measuring structural similarity include the following:

- Father-children relationship, that is, the relationship between each element and its direct subelements or attributes
- Ancestor-descendant relationship, that is, the relationship between each element and its direct and indirect subelements or attributes
- Order relationship among siblings
- Link relationship among documents and elements

In measuring similarity at the textual granularity, common information retrieval (IR) approaches can be applied on text. Words that are deemed irrelevant are eliminated (e.g., stop list) as well as punctuation. Words that share a common stem are replaced by the stem word. A list of terms is then substituted to the actual text.

The approaches developed in the literature take some of these objects and relationships into account for the specification of their measures. Approaches can be classified relying on the representation of documents. Some approaches represent documents through labeled trees (eventually extended as graphs to consider links) and mainly define the similarity measure as an extension of the tree edit distance. Others represent the features of XML documents through a vector model and define the similarity measure as an extension of the distance between two vectors. The tree representation of documents allows pointing out the hierarchical relationships existing among elements and attributes.

Clustering Approaches

Different algorithms have been proposed for clustering XML documents that are extensions of the classical hierarchical and partitioning clustering approaches. We remind the reader that agglomerative algorithms find the clusters by initially assigning each document to its own cluster and then repeatedly merging pairs of clusters until a certain stopping criterion is met. The end result can be graphically represented as a tree called a dendrogram. The dendrogram shows the clusters that have been merged together and the distance between these merged clusters (the horizontal length of the branches is proportional to the distance between the merged clusters). By contrast, partitioning algorithms find clusters by partitioning the set of documents into either a predetermined or an automatically derived number of clusters. The collection is initially partitioned into clusters whose quality is repeatedly optimized until a stable solution, according to a criterion function, is found. Hierarchical clustering in general produces clusters of better quality, but its main drawback is the quadratic time complexity. For large documents, the linear time complexity of partitioning techniques has made them more popular, especially in IR systems where clustering is employed for efficiency reasons.

Cluster quality is evaluated by internal and external quality measures. The external quality measures use an (external) manual classification of the documents, whereas the internal quality measures are evaluated by calculating average inter- and intra-clustering similarity. Standard external quality measures are the entropy (which measures how the manually tagged classes are distributed within each cluster), the purity (which measures how much a cluster is specialized in a class by dividing its largest class by its size), and the F-measure (which combines the precision and recall rates as an overall performance measure). Table 1 reports the formulas of the external quality measures (Zhao & Karypis, 2004) relying on the recall and precision formulas. Specifically, we report the measure for a single cluster and for the entire set of clusters determined. A specific external quality measure specifically tailored for XML documents has been proposed by Nierman and Jagadish (2002). They

Table 1. External quality measures

Quality Measure	Formula		
Recall and precision	$R(i,j) = \dfrac{n_{ij}}{n_i}$	$P(i,j) = \dfrac{n_{ij}}{n_j}$	i – a class of the q classes j – a cluster of the k clusters n – number of items n_i – items of class i n_j – items in cluster j n_{ij} – items of class i in cluster j
Entropy	$E(j) = -\dfrac{1}{\log q}\sum_{i=1}^{q} P(i,j)\log P(i,j)$		$Entropy = \sum_{j=1}^{k}\dfrac{n_j}{n}E(j)$
Purity	$Q(j) = max_{i=1}^{q} P(i,j)$		$Purity = \sum_{j=1}^{k}\dfrac{n_j}{n}Q(j)$
F-measure	$F(i,j) = \dfrac{2R(i,j)P(i,j)}{R(i,j)+P(i,j)}$		$F = \sum_{j=1}^{k}\dfrac{n_j}{n}F(i,j)$

Figure 4. Tree representation of XML documents containing recipes

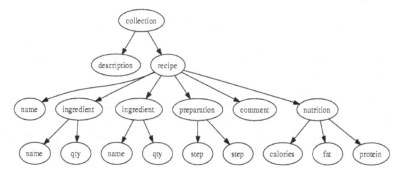

introduce the notion of "misclustering" for the evaluation of the obtained cluster of XML documents. Given a dendrogram, the misclustering degree is equal to the minimal number of documents in the dendrogram that would have to be moved so that the documents from the same schema are grouped together.

The unweighted pair-group method (UPGMA) is an example of an internal quality measure. The distance between clusters C and C', given $|C|$ is the number of objects in C, is computed as follows:

$$Sim(C,C') = \frac{\sum_{o \in C} \sum_{o' \in C'} Sim(o,o')}{|C||C'|}.$$

Tree-Based Approaches

In this section, we deal with approaches for measuring the similarity between XML documents that rely on a tree representation of the documents. We first discuss the document representation as trees, the basics of measures for evaluating tree similarity, and then approaches specifically tailored to XML.

Document Representation

XML documents can be represented as labeled trees. In trees representing documents, internal nodes are labeled by element or attribute names, and leaves are labeled by textual content. In the tree representation, attributes are not distinguished from elements: Both are mapped to the tag name set; thus, attributes are handled as elements. Attribute nodes appear as children of the element they refer to and, concerning the order, they are sorted by

Figure 5. Mapping

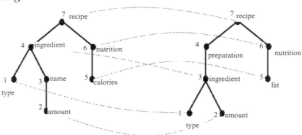

attribute name and appear before all subelement siblings. XML document elements may actually refer to, that is, contain links to, other elements. Including these links in the model gives rise to a graph rather than a tree. Even if such links can contain important semantic information that can be exploited in evaluating similarity, most approaches disregard them and simply model documents as trees. The tree representation of the document in Figure 1b is reported in Figure 4.

Tree Similarity Measures

The problem of computing the distance between two trees, also known as the tree editing problem, is the generalization of the problem of computing the distance between two strings (Wagner & Fischer, 1974) to labeled trees. The editing operations available in the tree edit-ing problem are changing (i.e., relabeling), deleting, and inserting a node. To each of these operations a cost is assigned that can depend on the labels of the involved nodes. The problem is to find a sequence of such operations transforming a tree T_1 into a tree T_2 with minimum cost. The distance between T_1 and T_2 is then defined to be the cost of such a sequence.

The best known and referenced approach to compute edit distance for ordered trees is given in Zhang and Shasha (1989). The authors consider three kinds of operations for ordered labeled trees. Relabeling a node n means changing the label on n. Deleting a node n means making the children of n become the children of the parent of n and then removing n. Insert-ing n as the child of m will make n the parent of a consecutive subsequence of the current children of m. Let Σ be the node label set and let λ be a unique symbol not in Σ denoting the null symbol. An edit operation is represented as $a \rightarrow b$, where a is either λ or the label of a node in T_1, and b is either λ or the label of a node in T_2. An operation of the form $\lambda \rightarrow b$ is an insertion, and an operation of the form $a \rightarrow \lambda$ is a deletion. Finally, an operation of the form $a \rightarrow b$, with $a, b \neq \lambda$, is a relabeling. Each edit operation $a \rightarrow b$ is assigned a cost, that is, a nonnegative real number $\gamma(a \rightarrow b)$, by a cost function γ. Function γ is a distance metric, that is,

$$\gamma(a \rightarrow b) \geq 0, \ \gamma(a \rightarrow a) = 0; \ \gamma(a \rightarrow b) = \gamma(b \rightarrow a); \ \gamma(a \rightarrow c) \leq \gamma(a \rightarrow b) + \gamma(b \rightarrow c).$$

Table 2. Tree edit-distance algorithms (* operations are restricted to leaves)

	Edit Operations	Complexity
Selkow (1977)	insert node,* delete node,* relabel node	$4^{\min(N \times M)}$ M, N numbers of nodes of the trees
Zhang & Shasha (1989)	insert node, delete node, relabel node	$O(M \times N \times b \times d)$ M, N numbers of nodes of the trees; b, d depths of the trees
Chawathe, Rajaraman, Garcia-Molina, & Widom (1996)	insert node,* delete node,* relabel node, move subtree	$O(N \times D)$ N numbers of nodes of both trees; D number of misaligned nodes
Chawathe (1999)	insert node,* delete node,* relabel node	$O(M \times N)$ M, N dimension of the matrix that represents the edit graph

Function γ is extended to a sequence of edit operation $S = s_1, \ldots, s_k$ s. t. $\gamma(S) = \sum_{i=1}^{k} \gamma(s_i)$.

The edit distance between two trees T_1 and T_2 is defined as the minimum-cost edit-operation sequence that transforms T_1 to T_2, that is, $D(T_1, T_2) = \min_S \{\gamma(S) \mid S$ is an edit-operation sequence taking T_1 to $T_2\}$.

The edit operations give rise to a mapping, which is a graphical specification of which edit operations apply to each node in the two trees. Figure 5 is an example of a mapping showing a way to transform T_1 to T_2. It corresponds to the edit sequence *name* $\rightarrow \lambda$; *calories* $\rightarrow$ *fat*; $\lambda \rightarrow$ *preparation*. The figure also shows a left-to-right postorder of nodes, which is commonly used to identify nodes in a tree.

For a tree T, let $t[i]$ represent the ith node of T. A mapping (or matching) from T_1 to T_2 is a triple (M, T_1, T_2) where M is a set of pairs of integers (i,j) such that:

- $1 \leq i \leq |T_1|$, $1 \leq j \leq |T_2|$, and
- for any pair (i_1, j_1) and (i_2, j_2) in M,
  - $i_1 = i_2$ iff $j_1 = j_2$ (one-to-one),
  - $t_1[i_1]$ is to the left of $t_1[i_2]$ iff $t_2[j_1]$, which is to the left of $t_2[j_2]$ (sibling order preserved), and
  - $t_1[i_1]$ is an ancestor of $t_1[i_2]$ iff $t_2[j_1]$, which is an ancestor of $t_2[j_2]$ (ancestor order preserved).

The mapping graphically depicted in Figure 5 consists of the pairs $\{(7,7), (4,3), (1,1), (2,2), (6,6), (5,5)\}$. Let M be a mapping from T_1 to T_2; the cost of M is defined as:

$$\gamma(M) = \sum_{(i,j)\in M}\gamma\ (t_1[i] \to t_2[j]) + \sum_{\{i|\neg\exists js.t.(i,j)\in M\}}\gamma\ (t_1[i] \to \lambda) + \sum_{\{j|\neg\exists is.t.(i,j)\in M\}}\gamma\ (\lambda \to t_2[j])$$

There is a straightforward relationship between a mapping and a sequence of edit operations. Specifically, nodes in T_1 not appearing in M correspond to deletions, nodes in T_2 not appearing in M correspond to insertions, and nodes that participate in M correspond to relabelings if the two labels are different or to null edits otherwise.

Different approaches (Chawathe, 1999; Chawathe et al., 1996; Selkow, 1977) to determine tree edit distance have been proposed as well. They rely on similar tree edit operations with minor variations. Table 2 (Dalamagas, Cheng, Winkel, & Sellis, 2006) summarizes the main differences among the approaches. The corresponding algorithms are all based on similar dynamic programming techniques. The Chawathe (1999) algorithm is based on the same edit operations (i.e., insertion and deletion at leaf nodes and relabeling at any nodes) considered by Selkow, but it significantly improves the complexity by reducing the number of recurrences needed through the use of edit graphs.

XML-Specific Approaches

The basic ideas discussed above for measuring the distance among two trees have been specialized to XML context through the following approaches.

Nierman & Jagadish (2002). They introduce an approach to measure the structural similarity specifically tailored for XML documents with the aim of clustering together documents presumably generated from the same DTD. Since the focus is strictly on structural similarity, the actual values of document elements and attributes are not represented in their tree representations (i.e., leaf nodes of the general representation are omitted from the tree). They suggest to measure the distance between two ordered labeled trees relying on a notion of tree edit distance. However, two XML documents produced from the same DTD may have very different sizes due to optional and repeatable elements. Any edit distance that permits changes to only one node at a time will necessarily find a large distance between such a pair of documents, and consequently will not recognize that these documents should be clustered together, being derived by the same DTD.

Thus, they develop an edit-distance metric that is more indicative of this notion of structural similarity. Specifically, in addition to the insert, delete, and relabel operations of Zhang and Shasha (1989), they also introduce the insert subtree and delete subtree editing operations, allowing the cutting and pasting of whole sections of a document. Specifically, the operation *insertTree*$_T$(A,i) adds A as a child of T at position i+1, and operation *deleteTree*$_T$(T_i) deletes

Figure 6. Contained-in relationship

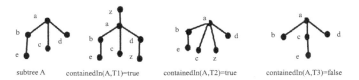

subtree A   containedIn(A,T1)=true   containedIn(A,T2)=true   containedIn(A,T3)=false

Figure 7. (a) The structure of a document, (b) its s-graph, (c) its structural summary

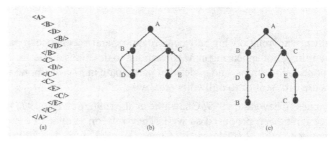

T_i as the ith child of T. They impose, however, the restriction that the use of the *insertTree* and *deleteTree* operations is limited to when the subtree that is being inserted (or deleted) is shared between the source and the destination tree. Without this restriction, one could delete the entire source tree in one step and insert the entire destination tree in a second step, thus making completely useless the insert and delete operations. The subtree A being inserted or deleted is thus required to be contained in the source or destination tree *T*: That is, all its nodes must occur in *T* with the same parent-child relationships and the same sibling order; additional siblings may occur in *T* (to handle the presence of optional elements) as graphically shown in Figure 6. A second restriction imposes that a tree that has been inserted via the *insertTree* operation cannot subsequently have additional nodes inserted, and, analogously, a tree that has been deleted via the *deleteTree* operation cannot previously have had nodes deleted. This restriction provides an efficient means for computing the costs of inserting and deleting the subtrees found in the destination and source trees, respectively. The resulting algorithm is a simple bottom-up algorithm obtained as an extension of the Zhang and Shasha basic algorithm, with the difference that any subtree T_i has a graft cost, which is the minimum among the cost of a single *insertTree* (if allowable) and any sequence of insert and (allowable) *insertTree* operations; similarly, any subtree has a prune cost.

Lian, Cheung, Mamoulis, & Yiu (2004). They propose a similarity measure for XML documents that, though based on a tree representation of documents, is not based on the tree edit distance. Given a document *D*, they introduce the concept of the structure graph (s-graph) of *D*; $sg(D)=(N,E)$ is a direct graph such that *N* is the set of all elements and attributes in document *D* and $(a,b) \in E$ if $a \nu \delta$ only if *a* is in the parent-child relationship with *b*. The notion of a structure graph is very similar to that of a data guide introduced by Goldman and Widom (1997) for semistructured data. Figure 7b shows the s-graph of the document in Figure 7a. The similarity between two documents D_1 and D_2 is then defined as:

$$Sim(D_1, D_2) = \frac{|sg(D_1) \cap sg(D_2)|}{max\{|sg(D_1)|, |sg(D_2)|\}},$$

where $|sg(Di)|$ is the cardinality of edges in $sg(Di)$, $i=1,2$ and $sg(D_1), \cap sg(D_2)$ is the set of common edges between $sg(D_1)$ and $sg(D_2)$. Relying on this metric, if the number of common parent-child relationships between D_1 and D_2 is large, the similarity between the s-graphs will be high, and vice versa. Since the definition of an s-graph can be easily applied to sets of documents, the comparison of a document with respect to a cluster can be easily

Figure 8. Two simple s-graphs

accomplished by means of their corresponding s-graphs. However, as outlined by Costa, Manco, Ortale, and Tagarelli (2004), a main problem with this approach relies on the loose-grained similarity that occurs. Indeed, two documents can share the same s-graph and still have significant structural differences. Thus, the approach fails in dealing with application domains, such as wrapper generation, requiring finer structural dissimilarities. Moreover, the similarity between the two s-graphs in Figure 8 is 0 according to their definition. Thus, the measure fails to consider similar documents that do not share common edges even if they have many elements with the same labels.

Dalamagas et al. (2006). They present an approach for measuring the similarity between XML documents modeled as rooted, ordered labeled trees. The motivating idea is the same of Nierman and Jagadish (2002), that is, that XML documents tend to have many repeated elements; thus, they can be large and deeply nested, and, even if generated from the same DTD, can have quite different size and structure. Starting from this idea, the approach of Dalamagas et al. is based on extracting structural summaries from documents by nesting and repetition reductions. Nesting reduction consists of eliminating nonleaf nodes whose labels are the same as the ones of their ancestors. In contrast, repetition reduction consists of eliminating, in a preorder tree traversal, nodes whose paths (starting from the root down to the node itself) have already been traversed. Figure 7c shows the structural summary of the document structure in Figure 7a. The similarity between two XML documents is then the tree edit distance computed through an extension of the basic Chawathe (1999) algorithm. Dalamagas et al. claim, indeed, that restricting insertions and deletions only on leaves fits better in the XML context.

Vector-Based Approaches

In this section, we deal with approaches for measuring the similarity that rely on a vector representation of documents. We first discuss the possible document representations as vectors and the different measures that can be exploited for evaluating vector similarity, and then present some approaches specifically tailored to XML.

Document Representation

Vector-based techniques represent objects as vectors in an abstract n-dimensional feature space. Let $O = (o_1, \ldots, o_m)$ be a collection of m objects; in our context, these can be whole XML documents, but also paths, individual elements, text, or any other component of a document as reported in Figure 3. Each object is described in terms of a set of features $F = (F_1, ..., F_n)$, where each feature F_i, $i \in [1,n]$, has an associated domain D_i that defines its allowed values. For instance, the level of an element is a feature whose domain is the positive integers (0 for the root, 1 for first-level elements, and so on). Feature domains can be either quantitative (continuous or discrete) or qualitative (nominal or ordinal). An object $o \in O$ is described as a tuple $(F_1(o), ..., F_n(o))$, where each $F_i(o) \in D_i$.

Consider, for instance, the two documents in Figure 1; we can represent them taking the elements as the objects to be compared. The simplest possible feature is the label of the document element, whose domain is a string according to the standard XML rules; in this case, the roots of both documents are described as the tuples recipes and collections, respectively. Of course, other features are usually considered, possibly of different structural granularities. A typical example is the path to the root; for example, consider the left-most ingredient element in each document. Both can be represented using the label and the path as features:

$F_{ingredient1}$ = ('ingredient', '/recipes/recipe/preparation/ingredients')

$F_{ingredient2}$ = ('ingredient', '/collection/recipe').

Some authors suggest restricting the length of the paths to avoid a combinatorial explosion. For example, Theobald, Schenkel, and Weikum (2003) use paths of length 2.

Another important feature of elements is the k-neighbourhood, that is, the set of elements within distance k of the element. For example, consider the 1-neighbourhood (that is, parent and children) of the ingredient elements:

$F_{ingredient1}$ = ('ingredient', {'ingredients', 'name', 'amount', 'unit'})

$F_{ingredient2}$ = ('ingredient', {'recipe', 'name', 'qty'}).

Many variations are possible; for example, one of the components of the Cupid system by Madhavan, Bernstein, and Rahm (2001) uses as features the label, the vicinity (parent and immediate siblings), and the textual contents of leaf elements.

Vector-Based Similarity Measures

Once the features have been selected, the next step is to define functions to compare them. Given a domain D_i, a comparison criterion for values in D_i is defined as a function $C_i : D_i \times D_i \rightarrow G_i$, where G_i is a totally ordered set, typically the real numbers. The following property must hold: $C_i(f_i, f_i) = max_{y \in G_i}\{y\}$; that is, when comparing a value with itself, the comparison function yields the maximum possible result. The simplest example of a comparison criterion is strict equality:

$$C_i(f_i, f_j) = \begin{cases} 1 & \text{if } f_i = f_j \\ 0 & \text{otherwise} \end{cases}$$

A similarity function $S: (D_1, \dots, D_n) \times (D_1, \dots, D_n) \to L$, where L is a totally ordered set, can now be defined that compares two objects represented as feature vectors and returns a value that corresponds to their similarity. An example of a similarity function is the weighted sum, which associates a weight w_i ($w_i \in [0,1], \sum_{i=1}^{n} w_i = 1$) with each feature:

$$S(o, o') = \frac{1}{n} \sum_{i=1}^{n} w_i C_i(F_i(o), F_i(o')).$$

If feature vectors are real vectors, metric distances induced by norms are typically used. The best known examples are the L_1 (Manhattan) and L_2 (Euclidean) distances. Other measures have been proposed based on the geometric and probabilistic models.

The most popular geometric approach to distance is the vector-space model used in information retrieval (Salton & McGill, 1983). Originally it was intended to be used to compare the similarity among the textual content of two documents, but for the XML case, it has been adapted for structural features as well.

The similarity in vector-space models is determined by using associative coefficients based on the inner product of the document vectors, where feature overlap indicates similarity. The inner product is usually normalized since, in practice, not all features are equally relevant when assessing similarity. Intuitively, a feature is more relevant to a document if it appears more frequently in it than in the rest of the documents. This is captured by *tfidf* weighting. Let $tf_{i,j}$ be the number of occurrences of feature i in document j, df_i the number of documents containing i, and N the total number of documents. The *tfidf* weight of feature i in document j is:

$$w_{i,j} = tf_{i,j} \log \frac{N}{df_i}.$$

The most popular similarity measure is the cosine coefficient, which corresponds to the angle between the vectors. Other measures are the Dice and Jaccard coefficients:

$$\cos(u, v) = \frac{uv}{|u| \, |v|} \qquad \text{Dice}(u, v) = \frac{2uv}{|u|^2 |u|^2} \qquad \text{Jac}(u,v) = \frac{uv}{|u|^2 |v|^2 - uv}.$$

Another vector-based approach considers the objects as probability mass distributions. This requires some appropriate restrictions on the values of the feature vectors $(f_1, \dots, f_n)$; namely, all values must be nonnegative real number, and $\sum_{i=1}^{n} f_i = 1$. Intuitively, the value of f_i is the probability that the feature F_i is assigned to the object. In principle, correlation statistics can be used to measure the similarity between distributions. The most popular are Pearson's and Spearman's correlation coefficients and Kendall's τ (Sheskin, 2003). In addition, some information-theoretic distances have been widely applied in the probabilistic framework, especially the relative entropy, also called the Kullback-Leibler divergence.

$$KL(p_k \| q_k) = \sum_k p_k log_2 \frac{p_k}{q_k},$$

where p_k and q_k are the probability functions of two discrete distributions. Another measure of similarity is the mutual information.

$$I(X;Y) = \sum_{x \in X} \sum_{y \in Y} P(x,y) log_2 \frac{P(x,y)}{P(x)P(y)},$$

where $P(x, y)$ is the joint probability density function of x and y (i.e., $P(x, y) = Pr[X = x, Y = y]$), and $P(x)$ and $P(y)$ are the probability density functions of x and y alone.

An important use of information-theoretical measures is to restrict the features and objects to be included in similarity computations by considering only the most informative. For example, Theobald et al. (2003) use the Kullback-Leibler divergence to cut down the number of elements to be compared in an XML classification system.

XML-Specific Approaches

Standard vector-based approaches previously presented can easily be applied to XML documents whenever clustering is performed on a single granularity (e.g., clustering based on contents, on elements, or on paths). Specifically tailored approaches have been developed for XML documents that take more than one granularity along with their relationships into account. In these cases, given C as the number of granularities, documents are represented through a C-dimensional matrix M in a Euclidean space based on one of two models: Boolean and weighted. With the Boolean model, $M(g_1,...,g_C)=1$ if the feature corresponding to the matrix intersection among granularities $g_1,...,g_C$ exists; $M(g_1,...,g_C)=0$ otherwise. With the weighted model, $M(g_1,...,g_C)$ is the frequency of the feature corresponding to the matrix intersection among granularities. Figure 9 reports a three-D dimensional Boolean matrix on granularities (document, path, term) stating the presence (or absence) of a term w_j in the element reached by a path P_j in a document D_m. As suggested by Liu and Yu (2005), once the documents are represented in the Euclidean space, standard approaches can be applied for measuring their similarity and creating clusters. The big issue that should be faced is that

Figure 9. Three-dimensional Boolean matrix

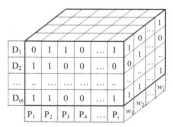

the matrix can be sparse. Therefore, approaches for reducing the matrix dimension should be investigated along with the possibility to obtain approximate results.

Yoon, Raghavan, Chakilam, & Kerschberg (2001). According to our classification, they propose a Boolean model with granularities (document, path, term) in which the path is a root-to-leaf path (ePath). A document is defined as a set of (p,v) pairs, where p denotes an ePath and v denotes a word or a content for an ePath. A collection of XML documents is represented through a three-dimensional matrix, named *BitCube*, $BC(d, p, v)$, where D denotes a document, p denotes an ePath, v denotes a word or content for p, and $BC(d, p, v)=1$ or 0 depending on the presence or absence of v in the ePath p in D. The distance between two documents is defined through the Hamming distance as:

$$Sim(D_1,D_2) = |\, xOR(BC(D_1), BC(D_2))\,|,$$

where *xOR* is a bit-wise exclusive OR operator applied on the representations of the two documents in the BitCube.

J. Yang, Cheung, & Chen (2005). According to our classification, they exploit a weighted model with granularities (document, element, term). They employ the structured link vector model (SLVM) to represent XML documents. In the model of SLVM, each document D_x in a document collection C is represented as a matrix $d_x \in R^{n\times m}$, such that $d_x = <d_{x(1)},\ldots, d_{x(n)}>^T$ and $d_{x(i)} = <d_{x(i,1)},\ldots, d_{x(i,m)}>$, where m is the number of elements; $d_{x(i,1)} \in R^m$ is a feature vector related to the term w_i for all subelements; $d_{x(i,j)}$ is a feature related to the term w_i and specific to the element e_j, given as $d_{x(i,j)}=TF(w_i,D_x.e_j)\times IDF(w_i)$; $TF(w_i,D_x.e_j)$ is the frequency of the term w_i in the element e_j of the document D_x; and $IDF(w_i)$ is the inverse document frequency of w_i based on C (each $d_{x(i,j)}$ is then normalized by $\sum_i d_{x(i,j)}$). The similarity measure between two documents D_x and D_y is then simply defined as:

$$Sim(D_x,D_y) = cos(d_x,d_y) = d_x \bullet d_y = \sum_{i=1}^{n} d_{x(i)} \cdot d_{y(i)},$$

where $\bullet$ denotes the vector dot product, and d_x, d_y are the normalized document feature vectors of D_x and D_y. A more sophisticated similarity measure is also presented by introducing a kernel matrix:

$$Sim(D_x,D_y) = \sum_{i=1}^{n} d_{x(i)}^{T} \bullet M_e \bullet d_{y(i)},$$

where M_e is an $m\times m$ kernel matrix that captures the similarity between pairs of elements as well as the contribution of a pair to the overall similarity. An entry in M_e being small means that the two elements should be semantically unrelated, and some words appearing in the two elements should not contribute to the overall similarity and vice versa. An interactive estimation procedure has been proposed for learning a kernel matrix that captures both the element similarity and the element relative importance.

Figure 10. (a) A tree document, (b) its full binary tree, and (c) the binary branch vector

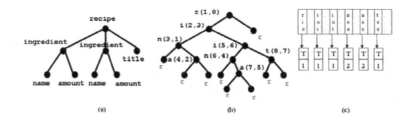

R. Yang, Kalnis, & Tung (2005). They propose an approach for determining a degree of similarity between a pair of documents that is easier to compute with respect to tree edit distance and forms a lower bound for the tree edit distance. Their approach thus allows filtering out very dissimilar documents and computes the tree edit distance only with a restricted number of documents. Starting from a tree representation of XML documents (as the one in Figure 10a), they represent them as standard full binary trees (Figure 10b). A full binary tree is a binary tree in which each node has exactly zero or two children (the first child represents the parent-child relationship, whereas the second child represents the sibling relationship). Whenever one of the children is missing, it is substituted with ε.

The binary branch of the full binary tree (i.e., all nodes with their direct children) are then represented in a binary branch vector $BRV(D)=(b_1,...,b_G)$, in which b_i represents the number of occurrences of the ith binary branch in the tree, and G is the size of the binary-branch space of the data set. The binary-branch vector for the document in Figure 10a is shown in Figure 10c. The binary-branch distance between XML documents D_1 and D_2, such that $BRV(D_1)=$ $(b_1,...,b_G)$ and $BRV(D_2)=(b_1',...,b_G')$, is computed though the Manhattan distance:

$$BDist(D_1,D_2) = |\ BRV(D_1) - BRV(D_2)|_1 = \sum_{i=1}^{\Gamma} |b_i - b_i'|.$$

In this approach, the authors consider three granularities (element, element, element) that are bound by the parent-child and the sibling relationships. Then, thanks to the transformation of the document tree structure into a full binary tree structure, they are able to use a one-dimensional vector for the representation of a document.

Other Approaches

We now present some approaches for evaluating similarity that exploit neither the vector-based nor the tree-based representation of documents.

Time-Series-Based Approach. Flesca, Manco, Masciari, Pontieri, and Pugliese (2002) represent the structure of an XML document as a time series in which each occurrence of a tag corresponds to a given impulse. Thus, they take into account the order in which tags appear in the documents. They interpret an XML document as a discrete-time signal in which numeric values summarize some relevant features of the elements enclosed within the document. If, for instance, one simply indents all tags in a given document according to their nesting level, the sequence of indentation marks, as they appear within the document rotated by 90 degrees, can be looked at as a time series whose shape roughly describes the document structure. These time-series data are then analysed through their discrete Fourier transform (*DFT*), leading to abstract or structural details that should not affect the similarity estimation (such as the different number of occurrences of an element or a small shift in its position). More precisely, during a preorder visit of the XML document tree, as soon as a node is visited, an impulse is emitted containing the information relevant to the tag. Thus, (a) each element is encoded as a real value, (b) the substructures in the documents are encoded using different signal shapes, and (c) context information can be used to encode both basic elements and substructures so that the analysis can be tuned to handle in a different way mismatches occurring at different hierarchical levels.

Once having represented each document as a signal, document shapes are analysed through *DFT*. Some useful properties of this transform, namely, the concentration of the energy into few frequency coefficients and its invariance of the amplitude under shifts, allow one to reveal much about the distribution and relevance of signal frequencies more efficiently without the need of resorting to edit-distance-based algorithms. As the encoding guarantees that each relevant subsequence is associated with a group of frequency components, the comparison of their magnitudes allows the detection of similarities and differences between documents. With variable-length sequences, however, the computation of the *DFT* should be forced on *M* fixed frequencies, where *M* is at least as large as the document sizes; otherwise, the frequency coefficients may not correspond. To avoid increasing the complexity of the overall approach, the missing coefficients are interpolated starting from the available ones. The distance between documents D_1 and D_2 is then defined as:

$$\text{Dist}(D_1, D_2) = \left(\sum_{k=1}^{M/2} (|[\widetilde{DFT}(enc(D_1))](k)| - |[\widetilde{DFT}(enc(D_2))](k)|)^2 \right)^{1/2},$$

where *enc* is the document encoding function, $\widetilde{DFT}$ denotes the interpolation of *DFT* to the frequencies appearing in both D_1 and D_2, and *M* is the total number of points appearing in the interpolation. Comparing two documents using this technique costs $O(n \log n)$, where $n = max(|D_1|, |D_2|)$ is the maximum number of tags in the documents. The authors claim their approach is practically effective as those based on tree edit distance.

Link-Based Similarity. Similarity among documents can be measured relying on links. Links can be specified at element granularity through ID/IDREF(S) attributes, or at document granularity through Xlink specifications. To the best of our knowledge, no link-based similarity measures have been specified tailored for XML documents at element granularity. At this granularity, a measure should consider the structure and content of the linked elements in order to be effective.

The problem of computing link-based similarity at document granularity has been investigated both for clustering together similar XML documents (Catania & Maddalena, 2002) and for XML document visualization as a graph partitioning problem (Guillaume & Murtagh, 2000). An XML document can be connected to other documents by means of both internal and external Xlink link specifications. A weight can be associated with the link depending on a variety of factors (e.g., the type of link, the frequency it is used, its semantics). The similarity between two documents can be expressed in terms of the weight of the minimum path between two nodes. Given a connection graph $G=(V,E)$ where each v_i in V represents an XML document D_i, and each (v_i, v_j, w) is a direct w-weighted edge in E, Catania and Maddalena specify the similarity between documents D_i and D_j as:

$$Sim(D_1, D_2) = \begin{cases} 1 - \dfrac{1}{2^{\cos t(\min Path(v_1,v_2)) + \cos t(\min Path(v_2,v_1))}} & \text{if existPath}(v_i, v_j) = \text{true, i,j} \in \{1,2\} \\ 0 & \text{otherwise} \end{cases},$$

where $minPath(v_1,v_2)$ is the minimal path from v_1 to v_2, $cost(minPath(v_1,v_2))$ is the sum of the weights on the edge in the minimal path, and $existPath(v_1,v_2)=true$ if a path exists from v_1 to v_2. A key feature of their approach is assigning a different weight to edges depending on the possible type (and, therefore, semantics) an Xlink link can have (simple or extended, on load or on demand).

A Methodology for the Choice of a Similarity Measure

The presented approaches represent the current efforts of the research community in the evaluation of similarity between XML documents for clustering together similar documents. Most of the measures have been developed either as an extension of vector-based measures employed in the information-retrieval field for content-based unstructured document clustering, or as an adaptation of tree-based measures developed for evaluating the similarity among trees in the combinatorial pattern matching field, with well-known applications in natural language processing, biology (ribonucleic acid [RNA] secondary-structure comparisons), neuroanatomy, and genealogy. Advanced applications of similarity measures are the following.

- Web search engines that exploit similarity measures for clustering together documents dealing with the same kind of information, and thus improve the precision of the returned answers and associate them with scores that evaluate the goodness of the obtained results

- Data-integration systems that can identify similarities and dissimilarities among different sources dealing with the same kind of data and thus specify data translation rules that allow one to convert a query expressed on a source in a meaningful query to another source

- Access-control modules that, by clustering together similar documents, can specify in a single shot access-control policies for documents with similar content

- Schema generators that, by clustering together structurally similar documents, can produce DTDs that strictly represent the structure and content of the documents; such schemas can then be exploited for the generation of suitable indexing structures or for the definition of eXtensible Stylesheet Language (XSL) documents that allow one to translate an XML document into another format (like HTML [HyperText Markup Language], PDF [Portable Document Format], or Word documents)

Table 3 summarizes the presented measures and the clustering approach adopted (when reported). As Table 3 shows, these basic measures are applied in a wide variety of contexts, which makes it difficult to state general rules for deciding which measure is best suited for a particular application context. An experimental analysis is required to compare the different measures on the same set of documents in order to establish the one that works better depending on the document characteristics. However, such a kind of analysis has not been performed yet.

Though we are not able to present an analytical comparison of the different similarity measures, we can provide a qualitative methodology based on our experience in the choice of the similarity measure depending on the application context.

First, the characteristics of the XML collection in which the system is intended to work should be pointed out. The product of this task should be a set of relevant granularity levels occurring in the collection, that is, the features encoded in the documents that are relevant for the application context and on which the similarity measure should be employed. For instance, one should take into account whether textual content is important or not for the

Table 3. Summary of XML-tailored approaches

	Similarity Measures and Features	Clustering Approach
Dalamagas et al. (2006)	Chawathe's (1999) tree edit distance using structural summaries	Hierarchical, single link
Nierman & Jagadish (2002)	Tree edit distance with subtree operations	Hierarchical agglomerative
Lian et al. (2004)	Structural graph similarity using elements and attributes	-
Yoon et al. (2001)	Manhattan metric between paths	Top down, bottom up
J. Yang et al. (2005)	Cosine distance between elements, weighted using *tfidf* and a learned kernel matrix	-
R. Yang et al. (2005)	Manhattan between binary branches, using parent-child and sibling relationships between elements	-
Flesca et al. (2002)	Fast Fourier transform	-
Catania & Maddalena (2002)	XLink based	-

documents, or whether the organization of elements into paths is significant or not. Liu and Yu (2005) survey techniques for feature selection applied to classification and clustering problems.

Moreover, this task should also emphasize interesting relationships that occur among the granularity levels and should be considered in the evaluation of similarity. The resulting feature set and the relationships should drive the choice of a particular set of similarity measures. Nevertheless, some general guidelines can be given based on practical experience.

- If the structure is comparatively simple (a flat structure), simple IR-like measures such as *tfidf* cosine similarity usually suffice.

- Vector-based approaches are a good choice for structured collections when the structure is not particularly relevant and only the occurrence of paths in the documents is relevant.

- Variants of tree edit distance are a good choice for structured XML collections when the structure is particularly relevant.

- If the structures of documents seem too complex, some kind of structural simplification can improve the results. These include the following.

- The application of information-theoretical measures for identifying which elements actually carry the most information and which can be ignored

- Structural summarization techniques, such as those used by Lian et al. (2004) and Dalamagas et al. (2006)

There are some attempts to automate the process of evaluating suitable similarity measures for specific domains. Bernstein, Kaufmann, and Bürki (2005) apply a machine-learning algorithm to several ontology-oriented measures in order to obtain a combined measure that adapts to human judgements obtained experimentally. In the biological domain, Müller, Selinski, and Ickstadt (2005) use statistical clustering-of-clustering methods to compare a number of matching coefficients for a genetic data-clustering problem.

Conclusion and Future Trends

In this chapter, we have provided an overview of different measures developed for XML document clustering. Though most of the discussed approaches have been experimentally validated either on synthetic or on real document sets, a systematic comparison of all the presented measures is missing that allows one to determine which measure applies in a particular context. This is also due to the lack of reference-document collections for evaluating different approaches as those being used in the INEX evaluation initiative (Kazai, Gövert, Lalmas, & Fuhr, 2003), which, however, are mainly focused on content and still exhibit little structural heterogeneity.

An interesting future research direction would be mining from document collections the structural, content, and link characteristics, particularly interesting for performing clustering following the approaches proposed by Bernstein et al. (2005) and Müller et al. (2005) in other contexts. This would lead one to identify the relevant granularity levels occurring in the documents and thus to choose the best suited measure for clustering such kinds of documents. For instance, this can lead to a better understanding of for which kinds of document collections a vector-based approach is preferable to a tree-based one, or a Boolean approach to a weighted one, and an understanding of the most adequate granularity and relationship for a document collection. Another interesting direction would be that of investigating and validating those granularities and relationships that have not been explored in the space of possible vector-based approaches.

Finally, most approaches are based on equality comparisons concerning the evaluation of the similarity at single elements or nodes. A more semantic approach, relying on ontologies and thesauri for allowing multilingual document handling and concept-based clustering, would certainly be useful.

References

Bernstein, A., Kaufmann, E., & Bürki, C. (2005). How similar is it? Towards personalized similarity measures in ontologies. In O. K. Ferstl, E. J. Sinz, S. Eckert, & T. Isselhorst (Eds.), *Wirstchaftinformatik 2005: eEconomy, eGovernment, eSociety* (Vol. 7, pp. 1347-1366). International Tagung Wirstchaftinformatik 2005, Bamberg. Physica-Verlag.

Catania, B., & Maddalena, A. (2002). A clustering approach for XML linked documents. *Proceedings of International Workshop on Database and Expert Systems Applications* (pp. 121-128).

Chawathe, S. S. (1999). Comparing hierarchical data in external memory. *Proceedings of International Conference on Very Large Databases* (pp. 90-101).

Chawathe, S. S., Rajaraman, A., Garcia-Molina, H., & Widom, J. (1996). Change detection in hierarchically structured information. *Proceedings of the ACM International Conference on Management of Data* (pp. 493-504).

Costa, G., Manco, G., Ortale, R., & Tagarelli, A. (2004). A tree-based approach for clustering XML documents by structure. *Proceedings of European Conference on Principles and Practice of Knowledge Discovery in Databases* (pp. 137-148).

Dalamagas, T., Cheng, T., Winkel, K.-J., & Sellis, T. (2006). A methodology for clustering XML documents by structure. *Information Systems, 31*(3), 187-228.

Flesca, S., Manco, G., Masciari, E., Pontieri, L., & Pugliese, A. (2002). Detecting structural similarities between XML documents. *Proceedings of the 5th International Workshop on the Web and Databases* (pp. 55-60).

Goldman, R., & Widom, J. (1997). DataGuides: Enabling query formulation and optimization in semistructured databases. *Proceedings of International Conference on Very Large Databases* (pp. 436-445).

Guillaume, D., & Murtagh, F. (2000). Clustering of XML documents. *Computer Physics Communication, 127*, 215-227.

Kazai, G., Gövert, N., Lalmas, M., & Fuhr, N. (2003). The INEX evaluation initiative. In *Intelligent search on XML data, applications, languages, models, implementations, and benchmarks* (LNCS 2818, pp. 279-293). Berlin: Springer-Verlag.

Lian, W., Cheung, D., Mamoulis, N., & Yiu, S.-M. (2004). An efficient and scalable algorithm for clustering XML documents by structure. *IEEE Transactions on Knowledge and Data Engineering, 16*(1), 82-96.

Liu, H., & Yu, L. (2005, April). Toward integrating feature selection algorithms for classification and clustering. *IEEE Transactions on Knowledge and Data Engineering, 17*(4), 491-502.

Madhavan, J., Bernstein, P. A., & Rahm, E. (2001). Generic schema matching with Cupid. *Proceedings International Conference on Very Large Databases* (pp. 49-58).

Müller, T., Selinski, S., & Ickstadt, K. (2005). Cluster analysis: A comparison of different similarity measures for SNP data. *Second IMS-ISBA Joint Meeting.*

Nierman, A., & Jagadish, H. V. (2002). Evaluating structural similarity in XML documents. *Proceedings of International Workshop on the Web and Databases* (pp. 61-66).

Salton, G., & McGill, M. J. (1983). *Introduction to modern information retrieval.* New York: McGraw-Hill.

Selkow, S. M. (1977). The tree-to-tree editing problem. *Information Processing Letters, 6*, 184-186.

Sheskin, D. (2003). *Handbook of parametric and nonparametric statistical procedures* (3rd ed.) (p. 719). Boca Raton, FL: CRC Press.

Theobald, M., Schenkel, R., & Weikum, G. (2003). Exploiting structure, annotation, and ontological knowledge for automatic classification of XML data. *Proceedings of the 6th International Workshop on the Web and Databases* (pp. 1-6).

Vakali, A., Pokorný, J., & Dalamagas, T. (2004). An overview of Web data clustering practices. In *Current Trends in Database Technology: EDBT 2004 Workshops* (LNCS 3268, pp. 597-606). Berlin: Springer-Verlag.

World Wide Web Consortium (W3C). (1998). *Extensible Markup Language (XML).*

World Wide Web Consortium (W3C). (2001). *XML Linking Language (Xlink).*

Wagner, R., & Fischer, M. (1974). The string-to-string correction problem. *Journal of the ACM, 21*(1), 168-173.

Yang, J., Cheung, W. K., & Chen, X. (2005). Learning the kernel matrix for XML document clustering. *IEEE International Conference on e-Technology, e-Commerce and e-Service* (pp. 353-358).

Yang, R., Kalnis, P., & Tung, A. (2005). Similarity evaluation on tree-structured data. *Proceedings of the ACM International Conference on Management of Data* (pp. 754-765).

Yoon, J., Raghavan, V., Chakilam, V., & Kerschberg, V. (2001). BitCube: A three-dimensional bitmap indexing for XML documents. *Journal of Intelligent Information Systems, 17*, 241-254.

Zhang, K., & Shasha, D. (1989). Simple fast algorithms for the editing distance between trees and related problems. *SIAM Journal of Computing, 18*(6), 1245-1262.

Zhao, Y., & Karypis, G. (2004). Empirical and theoretical comparisons of selected criterion functions for document clustering. *Machine Learning, 55*(3), 311-331.

Chapter IV

Mining Association Rules from XML Documents

Laura Irina Rusu, La Trobe University, Australia

Wenny Rahayu, La Trobe University, Australia

David Taniar, Monash University, Australia

Abstract

This chapter presents some of the existing mining techniques for extracting association rules out of XML documents in the context of rapid changes in the Web knowledge discovery area. The initiative of this study was driven by the fast emergence of XML (eXtensible Markup Language) as a standard language for representing semistructured data and as a new standard of exchanging information between different applications. The data exchanged as XML documents become richer and richer every day, so the necessity to not only store these large volumes of XML data for later use, but to mine them as well to discover interesting information has became obvious. The hidden knowledge can be used in various ways, for example, to decide on a business issue or to make predictions about future e-customer behaviour in a Web application. One type of knowledge that can be discovered in a collection of XML documents relates to association rules between parts of the document, and this chapter presents some of the top techniques for extracting them.

Introduction

The amount of data stored in XML (eXtensible Markup Language) format or changed between fferent types of applications has been growing during the last few years, and more companies are considering XML now as a possible solution for their data-storage and data-exchange needs (Laurent, Denilson, & Pierangelo, 2003). The first immediate problem for the researchers was how to represent the data contained in the old relational databases using this new format, so various techniques and methodologies have been developed to solve this problem. Next, the users realised that they not only required storing the data in a different way, which made it much easier to exchange data between various applications, but they required getting interesting knowledge out of the entire volume of XML data stored as well. The acquired knowledge might be successfully used in the decisional process to improve business outcomes. As a result, the need for developing new languages, tools, and algorithms to effectively manage and mine collections of XML documents became imperative.

A large volume of work has been developed, and research is still pursued to get solutions that are as effective as possible. The general idea and goal for researchers is to discover more powerful XML mining algorithms that are able to find representative patterns in the data, achieve higher accuracy, and be more scalable on large sets of documents. The privacy issue in knowledge discovery is also a subject of great interest (Ashrafi, Taniar, & Smith, 2004a).

XML mining includes both the mining of structures as well as the mining of content from XML documents (Nayak, 2005; Nayak, Witt, & Tonev, 2002). The mining of structure is seen as essentially mining the XML schema, and it includes intrastructure mining (concerned with mining the structure inside an XML document, where tasks of classification, clustering, or association rule discovering could be applied) and interstructure mining (concerned with mining the structures between XML documents, where the applicable tasks could be clustering schemas and defining hierarchies of schemas on the Web, and classification is applied with name spaces and URIs [uniform resource identifiers]). The mining of content consists of content analysis and structure clarification. While content analysis is concerned with analysing texts within the XML document, structural clarification is concerned with determining similar documents based on their content (Nayak, 2005; Nayak et al., 2002).

Discovering association rules is looking for those interesting relationships between elements appearing together in the XML document, which can be used to predict future behaviour of the document. To our knowledge, this chapter is the first work that aims to put together and study the existing techniques to perform the mining of association rules out from XML documents.

Background

The starting point in developing algorithms and methodologies for mining XML documents was, naturally, the existing work done in the relational database mining area (Agrawal, Imielinski, & Swami, 1993; Agrawal & Srikant, 1998; Ashrafi, Taniar, & Smith, 2005; Ashrafi,

2004; Daly & Taniar, 2004; Tjioe & Taniar, 2005). In their attempt to apply various relational mining algorithms to the XML documents, researchers discovered that the approach could be a useful solution for mining small and not very complex XML documents, but not an efficient approach for mining large and complex documents with many levels of nesting.

The XML format comes with the acclaimed extensibility that allows the change of structure, that is, adding, removing, and renaming nodes in the document according to the information necessary to be encoded in. Furthermore, using the XML representation, there are a lot of possibilities to express the same information (see Figure 1 for an example) not only between different XML documents, but inside the same document as well (Rusu, Rahayu, & Taniar, 2005a).

In a relational database, it is not efficient to have multiple tables to represent the same data with different field names, types, and relationships as the constraints and table structures are defined at the design time. In an opposite manner, a new XML document can be added to a collection of existing XML documents even though it represents the same type of data using a totally different structure and element names, that is, a different XML schema. As a result, researchers concluded that the logic of the relational mining techniques could be maintained, but they needed to assure that the steps of the existing algorithms were looking to the specific characteristics of the XML documents.

Among other XML mining methods, association rule discovery, and the classification and clustering of XML documents have been the most studied as they have a high degree of usability in common user tasks or in Web applications. In this chapter, we present a number of techniques for mining association rules out of XML documents. We chose to analyse this particular type of mining because (a) it is, in our opinion, the most useful for general types of applications in which the user just wants to find interesting relationships in his or her data and wants help to make better business decisions, and (b) the techniques used are easy to understand, replicate, and apply for the common user who does not have a high degree of knowledge of mathematics or statistics, often required by some techniques for performing classification or clustering.

Figure 1. Different formats to express the same information using the XML structure

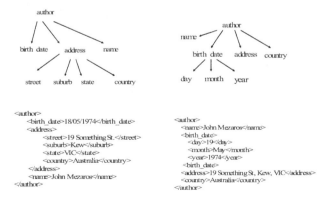

Overview of the Generic Association Rule Concepts

The concept of association rules was first introduced by Agrawal (1993) for relational-database data to determine interesting rules that could be extracted from some data in a market basket analysis. The algorithm is known as the Apriori algorithm, and an example of an association rule extracted could be "If the user buys the product A, he or she will buy the product B as well, and this happens in more than 80% of transactions." The generic terms and concepts related to the Apriori algorithm are as follows. If I represents the set of distinct items that need to be mined, let D be the set of transactions, where each transaction T from D is a set of distinct items $T \subseteq I$. An association rule R is an implication $X \rightarrow Y$, where $X, Y \subset I$ and $X \cap Y = \varnothing$. The rule R has the support s in D if $s\%$ of transactions in D contain both X and Y, and the confidence c if $c\%$ of transactions in D that contain X also contain Y. If we use a freq(X,D) function to calculate the percentage of transactions in D that contain X, the support and confidence for the association rule R could be written as the following formulas:

$$\text{Support } (X \rightarrow Y) = \text{freq } (XUY, D) \text{ and Confidence } (X \rightarrow Y) = \text{freq } (XUY, D) / \text{freq } (X, D).$$

The minimum support and minimum confidence are set at the beginning of the mining process, and it is compulsory that they are observed by the determined rules. In the Apriori algorithm, all the large k-itemsets are determined, starting from $k=1$ (itemsets with only one item) and looping through D (the set of all transactions) to calculate its support and the confidence. If they are not validated against the minimum required, the k-itemset is considered to be not large and is pruned. The algorithm assumes that any subset of items that is not large determines its parent (i.e., the itemset that contains it) to not be large, and this improves the speed of the process a lot. At the end, when all the large itemsets are found, association rules are determined from the set of large itemsets.

Overview of XML Association Rules

For the XML documents, finding association rules means finding relationships between simple or complex elements in the document: in other words, finding relationships between substructures of the XML document. For example, in an XML document containing details of the staff members and students in a computer-science university department, including details of their research publications, an association rule could be "Those staff members who publish their papers with X publisher received an award, and this happens in 75% of cases." Later in the chapter (see the section on Apriori-based approaches), we give some examples of how the generic concepts of *transaction* and *item* are perceived by the XML association rules. We will also show how the concepts of *support* and *confidence* are used by the presented approaches as they need to be correct with regard to the total number of XML transactions that need to be mined.

Our analysis is split in two subsections based on the type of XML documents mined, that is, (a) static XML documents and (b) dynamic XML documents. Static XML documents contain data gathered for a specific period of time that do not change their content (for example, details about purchases in a store for March 2005 and June 2005 might come as two separate static XML documents if the business process stores the data at the end of each month). Dynamic XML documents contain data that are continuously changing in time (an online bookstore, for example, will change its content, represented as an XML document, from one day to another, or even multiple times during the same day depending on the e-customers' behaviour).

Most of the work done in the area of mining association rules from static XML documents use classical algorithms based on the Apriori algorithm, described before in the overview section, while a number of non-Apriori-based approaches have been developed as well. In this chapter we will analyse at least one of each type of algorithms.

In case of dynamic XML documents, the focus is on mining association rules out of historic versions of the documents or out of the effective set of changes extracted between two successive versions. The difference between two versions of the same XML document is named delta, and it can be (a) structural delta, when the difference between versions is done at the schema level, or (b) content delta, when the difference is calculated at the content level (Chen, Browmick, & Chia, 2004).

Discovering Association Rules from Static XML Documents

As specified in the background section, some of the XML association rule mining techniques use the Apriori general algorithm (Agrawal et al., 1993; Agrawal & Srikant, 1998) as a starting point for developing new methodologies specific to the XML document format and extensibility, while completely different techniques have been developed as well. The following analysis is split in two subsections depending on the type of mining algorithm used, that is, (a) Apriori-based approaches and (b) non-Apriori-based approaches.

Apriori-Based Approaches

A first thing to do is to see how the generic concepts related to the association rules (mentioned in the previous section), that is, transactions and items, are mapped to the particular XML format. Even though most of the papers detailed further in the chapter (Braga, Campi, & Ceri, 2003; Braga, Campi, Klemettinen, & Lanzi, 2002; Braga, Campi, Ceri et al., 2002; Wan & Dobbie, 2003, 2004) do not give certain definitions for these concepts, we can determine their view on the matter by analysing the algorithms. If an XML document is seen as a tree (see the example in Figure 3), the set of transactions D will be a list of complex nodes formed by querying the XML document for a specific path, a single complex node will form a transaction, and the children of the transaction node will be the items. The main difference from the generic concepts is that, while a generic transaction contains only a limited number of items and is easier to quantify, one XML tree transaction can have a different number of items depending on the level of nesting of the document. A similar definition is given in Ding, Ricords, and Lumpkin (2003), but at a more general level; that is, all the nesting depths (paths) in an XML document are considered to be records starting with the root, so for any node in the document, each child is viewed as a record relative to the other records at the same depth or with similar tags.

A simple and direct method to mine association rules from an XML document by using XQuery (*XQuery*, 2005) was proposed by Wan and Dobbie (2003, 2004). Based on the fact that XQuery was introduced by W3C (World Wide Web Consortium) to enable XML data extraction and manipulation, the algorithm is actually an implementation of the Apriori algorithm's phases using the XQuery Language. In Figure 2, we exemplify the algorithm on an XML document containing information about items purchased in a number of transactions in a store (Figure 2a). The algorithm loops through the XML document, generates the large itemsets in the "large.xml" document (Figure 2b), and then builds the association rule document (Figure 2c). For details on the XQuery code implementation of the *apriori* function and the other functions involved, we refer the reader to the original papers (Wan & Dobbie, 2003, 2004).

The significance of this approach is that the authors demonstrated for the first time that XML data can be mined directly without the necessity of preprocessing the document (for example, mapping it to another format, such as a relational table, which would be easier to mine). The algorithm could work very well in case of XML documents with a very simple structure (as in our example in Figure 2), but it is not very efficient for complex documents. Also, a major drawback, assumed by the authors, is that in the XQuery implementation, the first part of the algorithm, that is, discovering large itemsets (Figure 2b), is more expensive regarding time and processor performance than in other language implementations (e.g., in C++). This drawback is explained by the lack of update operations in XQuery: a large number of loops through the document is required in order to calculate the large itemsets. However, the algorithms promise a high speed when the update operations are finally implemented in XQuery.

Other methodologies for discovering association rules from XML documents are proposed by Braga et al. (2003) and Braga, Campi, Ceri et al. (2002); they are also based on the Apriori algorithm as a starting point and mine the association rules in three major steps, that is,

Figure 2. Example of a direct association-rule mining algorithm using XQuery (Wan & Dobbie, 2003, 2004)

```
<transactions>
  <transaction id='1'>
    <items>
      <item>a</item>
      <item>d</item>
      <item>e></item>
    </items>
  </transaction>
  <transaction id='2'>
    <items>
      <item>b</item>
      <item>c</item>
      <item>d</item>
    </items>
  </transaction>
    ..........
</transactions>
```

(a)

```
let $src:=document("transactions.xml")//items
let $minsup:=0.4
let $total:=count($src)*1.00
let $C:=distinct-values($src/*)
let $l:=(for $itemset in $C
        let $items:=(for $item in $src/*
                where $itemset=$item
                return $item)
        let $sup:=(count($items)*1.00) div $total
          where $sup>=$minsup
          return <largeItemset>
            <items>{$itemset}</items>
            <support>{$sup}</support>
          </largeItemset>)
let $L:=$l
return <largeItemsets> {apriori($l, $L, $minsup, $
$src)}
        </largeItemsets>
```

(b)

```
let $minconf:=1.00
let $src:=document("large.xml")//largeItemset
for $itemset1 in $src
let $items1:=$itemset1/items/*
  for $itemset2 in $src
  let $items2:=$itemset2/items/*
  where count(items1)>count(items2) and
          count(commonIts($items1,$items2))=
          count($items2) and $itemset1/support div
            $itemset2/support>=$minconf
  return <rule support="{$itemset1/support}"
            confidence="{(itemset1/support *1.0) div
                        ($itemset2/support *1.0)}">
              <antecedent>{$items2}</antecedent>

<consequent>{removeItms($items1,$items2)}
              </consequent>
          </rule>
```

(c)

(a) preprocessing data, (b) extracting association rules, and (c) postprocessing association rules. In our opinion, due to the specific XML format, when many levels of nesting could appear inside of a document, simple loops and counts (as in Figure 2) are no longer possible, so the three-step approach seems to be more appropriate for mining various types of XML documents.

Preprocessing Phase

At this stage, a lot of operations are done to prepare the XML document for extracting association rules. In the following, we discuss some important terms and concepts appearing during this step, noting that this phase is the most extended one because a proper identification of all the aspects involved in mining preparation will significantly reduce the amount of work during the other two phases (extracting and postprocessing rules).

The concept of the *context* of the association rules refers to the part(s) of the XML documents that will be mined (similar to the generic concept of a set of transactions). Sometimes, we do not want to mine all of the information contained in an XML document, but only a part of it. For example, in an XML document containing university staff and student information (see Figure 3), we may want to find association rules among people appearing as coauthors. In this case, the *identified context* includes the multitude of nodes relating to publications, no matter if they belong to PhD students or professors. This means the algorithm will not consider the <PhD_courses> nodes or <Personal_info> nodes as they are not relevant to the proposed rules to discover.

Context selection refers to the user's opportunity to define constraints on the set of transactions D relevant to the mining problem (Braga, Campi, Ceri et al., 2002). Referring again to our example (Figure 3), we may want to look for association rules considering all the authors in the document, but only for publications after the year 2000, so a constraint needs to be defined on the "year" attribute of each publication element (not visible in the graph, but existing in the original XML document).

If we talk about an association rule as an implication $X \rightarrow Y$, X is the *body* of the rule and Y is the *head* of the association rule. The body and head are always defined with respect to the context of the rule as the support and the confidence will be calculated and relevant only with respect to the established context. In the XML association rule case, the body and the head will be, in fact, two different lists of nodes, that is, substructures of the context list of nodes; only nodes from these two lists will be considered to compose valid XML association rules.

We exemplify the above described concepts, that is, context identification, context selection, and the head and body of the rules, by using the XMINE RULE operator (Braga et al., 2003) on the working example in Figure 3, that is, the "research.xml" document.

We visually identify the mentioned concepts in Figure 4, which details the algorithm proposed by Braga et al. (2003) and Braga, Campi, Ceri, et al. (2002).

The working document is defined in the first line, then the *context*, *body*, and *head* areas are defined together with the *minimum support* and *minimum confidence* required for the rules. The WHERE clause allows constraint specification; in this example, only publications after 2000 will be included in the context of the operator.

Figure 3. Example of an XML document presented as a tree (research.xml) with the identified context, body, and head

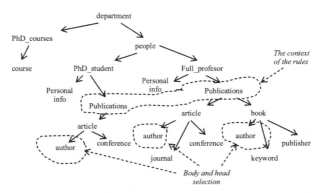

Figure 4. Mining association rules from an XML document using the XMINE RULE syntax

```
XMINE RULE
IN document ("research.xml")
FOR ROOT IN //People/*/Publications/*                    Context identification
LET BODY:=ROOT/author,
    HEAD:=ROOT/author              Body & Head
WHERE ROOT//@year>2000                                   Context selection
EXTRACTING RULES WITH
    SUPPORT = 0.1 AND CONFIDENCE =0.2
RETURN
    <Rule support={SUPPORT}
        confidence={CONFIDENCE}>
        <BODY>{ FOR $item IN BODY
                RETURN <Item>{$item}</Item>}
        </BODY>
        <HEAD>{ FOR $item IN HEAD
                RETURN <Item>{$item} </Item>}
        </HEAD>
```

The XMINE RULE operator brings some improvements, which could not be solved by the direct association rule mining algorithm in one step which uses XQuery, described at the beginning of the section, as follows:

- The context, body, and head of the operator can be as wide as necessary by specifying multiple areas of interest for them as parts of the XML document or even from different XML documents.

- When specifying the context, body, and head segments, a variable can be added to take some specific values that enhance the context selection facility.

- A GROUP clause can be added to allow the restructuring of the source data.

We exemplify how the first feature can be implemented using the same working example, that is, the "research.xml" document. Suppose we now want to determine rules between publishers and keywords, that is, to find which publishing companies are focusing on specific areas of research. See Figure 5 for a visual representation of the new body and head selections.

The main difference from the one-step mining approach (Wan & Dobbie, 2003, 2004) is that the three-step algorithm (Braga et al., 2003; Braga, Campi, Ceri et al., 2002; Braga, Campi, Klemettinen et al., Klemettinen, 2002) does not work directly on the XML document all the way down to the phase of extracting the association rules; instead, the first phase, that is, preprocessing, has as a final output a relational binary table (R). The table is built as follows (the authors suggest the use of the Xalan, 2005, as an XPath interpreter in the actual implementation): (a) The fragments of the XML document specified in the context, body, and head are extracted and filtered by applying the constraints in the WHERE clause (in case one exists), (b) the XML fragments obtained by filtering the body and head will become columns in the relational table R, (c) the XML fragments obtained by filtering the context will become rows in the table R, and (d) by applying a *contains* function (which, for a given XML fragment x and an XML fragment y, returns 1 if x contains y, and 0 otherwise), the binary relational table R is obtained, which will be used during the rule-extraction step to determine binary association rules applicable to the XML document.

The selection done during the preprocessing phase, by specifying the context, the body, and the head of the association rules, is considered by some researchers not generic enough (Ding et al., 2003) because it limits from the beginning the possibility to find and extract other rules (involving other parts of the documents).

Extracting Association Rules

For the one-step mining approach, Figure 2 exemplifies the XQuery implementation of the generic Apriori algorithm. It mainly performs the following steps. Starting from the 1-itemsets (i.e., itemsets with one single item), a k-itemset ($k>1$) is built by extending the $(k-1)$-itemset with a new item. For each itemset, the support is calculated as a percentage of the total number of transactions that contain all the items of the itemset. If the itemset is not frequent (large) enough (i.e., its support is less than the minimum support required), it will be removed (pruned), and the algorithm continues with the next itemset until all the large

Figure 5. The syntax of the XMINE RULE operator introduced by Braga et al. (2003)

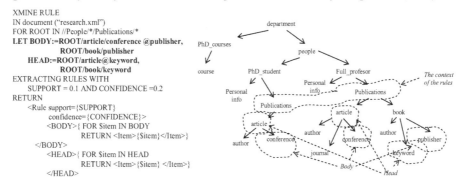

itemsets are determined. Before the calculation of an itemset's support to decide on pruning or keeping it, the itemset is considered to be a candidate itemset (i.e., possibly large) if all its sub sets are large (i.e., observe the minimum support required). The association rules are determined from the largest itemsets extracted, and for each of them a confidence is calculated as follows: For a rule X→Y, its confidence is equal to the percentage of transactions containing X that also contain Y.

In the three-step approaches presented in the previous subsection, after obtaining the binary table R in the preprocessing phase, any relational association rule algorithm can be applied (e.g., generic a priori) to get the relationship between the binary values in the table, which represent the existence of an XML fragment inside another XML fragment. The steps of the generic Apriori algorithm have been detailed in the previous paragraph. In the particular case of the binary matrix R, the rows of the matrix will be transactions to be mined by the algorithm. The binary knowledge extracted at this step will signify the simultaneous presence of fragments from the body or head in the selected context.

Postprocessing Phase

After the extraction of the binary association rules from the relational table during the second step, they will be transformed back into XML-specific representations of the discovered rules. We remember from the preprocessing step that the filtered XML fragments obtained by applying the body and head path queries on the XML document became columns in the table, while filtered XML fragments obtained by applying the context path queries became rows. Reversing the process, together with the new knowledge determined, that is, the association rules between the binary values, we get an XML structure in which each <rule> element has two attributes, support and confidence, and two child elements, <body> and <head>, where the fragments of the body and head participating in the rule are listed. An example of the result of applying the XMINE algorithm is presented in Figure 6, in which the following rules are given: "Author A → Author H has 85% support and 20% confidence" and "Author H and Author B → Author A has 70% support and 22% confidence."

Figure 6. Example of XML association rules obtained by applying the XMINE RULE algorithm

```
<RULE support='0.85' confidence='0.20'?
  <BODY>
    <Item><Author>Author A</Author></Item>
  </BODY>
  <HEAD>
    <Item><Author>Author H</Author></Item>
  </HEAD>
</RULE>
<RULE support='0.70' confidence='0.22'?
  <BODY>
    <Item><Author>Author H</Author></Item>
    <Item><Author>Author B</Author></Item>
  </BODY>
  <HEAD>
    <Item><Author>Author A</Author></Item>
  </HEAD>
</RULE>
```

Non-Apriori-Based Approach

In this section, we present one framework for discovering association rules that is different from the earlier described approaches, which were based on the Apriori algorithm sequence. The main feature is that this framework (Feng, Dillon, Wiegand, & Chang, 2003) considers in more detail the specific format of the XML documents, that is, their possible representation as trees. We recall that at the beginning of the section on Apriori-based approaches, we proposed a translation of the terms *transaction* and *item* into some concepts more specific to XML association rule mining. The non-Apriori-based framework discussed in the current section proposes a different mapping of the above terms to tree-like structured XML documents.

The work of Feng et al. (2003) aims to discover association rules from a collection of XML documents rather than from a single document, hence each XML document or tree corresponds to a database record (transaction), where each XML fragment (subtree) corresponds to an item in the transaction. In this context, the framework proposed intends to discover association rules among trees in XML documents rather than among simple-structured items. Each tree is named a *tree-structured item* and is a rooted, ordered tree having its nodes classified into (a) basic nodes with no edges emanating from them and (b) complex nodes, which are internal nodes with one or more edges emanating from them. In Figure 7 we present some of the concepts introduced to define the framework for mining XML association rules.

In Figure 7, there are two tree-structured items, the <PERSON> and <ITEM> elements, extracted from the order.xml example document (Feng et al., 2003), in which the nodes $n_{1,1}$, $n_{2,1}$, $n_{2,2}$, and $n_{2,3}$ are complex, while $n_{1,2}$, $n_{1,3}$, $n_{1,4}$, $n_{2,4}$, $n_{2,5}$, and $n_{2,6}$ are basic. The edges inside the trees are labeled depending on the type of relationship between the nodes. There are two types of labels attached to edges: *ad* (ancestor-descendant) and *ea* (element-attribute). In Figure 7, the edge that connects the PERSON with the Profession node is labeled *ea* because

Figure 7. Example of two tree-structured items in the framework for mining XML association rules as proposed by Feng et al. (2003)

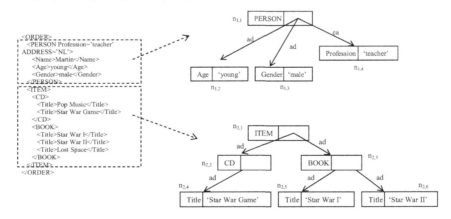

Profession is an attribute of the PERSON in the XML document. All the other edges are labeled *ad* as they represent connections between a parent node and a child node.

There are three types of constraints that can be imposed on nodes and edges, as follows.

1. Level constraints: If *e* is an *ad* relationship $n_{source} \rightarrow n_{target}$, Level (e)=m (m integer) means that n_{target} is the *m*th descendant of the n_{source}.

2. Adhesion constraints: If *e* is an *ea* relationship $n_{source} \rightarrow n_{target}$, Adhesion(e)=strong means that n_{target} is a compulsory attribute of n_{source}, while Adhesion(e)=weak means that n_{target} is an optional attribute of the n_{source}.

3. Position constraints: They refer to the actual contextual position of the node among all the nodes sharing the same parent. For example, in Figure 7, Posi($n_{2,4}$)=last() means the Title node with the Star War Game content is the title of the last ordered CD.

In this framework, a well-formed tree is a tree that observes three conditions: (a) It has a unique root node, (b) for any chosen edge in the tree, if it is labelled *ad*, it will link a complex node with a basic node, while if it is labeled *ea*, the source node needs to be a complex node, and (c) all the constraints are correctly applied, that is, a level constraint can be applied only on an *ad* edge, while an adhesion constraint can be applied only on an *ea* edge. Using the above described concepts, the subtree concept (subitem) is defined based on the definition of the subtree relationship. A tree *T* with root *r* is a subtree of the tree *T'* with root *r'* (noted $T \leq_{tree} T'$) if and only if there is a node *n'* in *T'* such that *r* is a part of *n'* (noted $r \leq_{node} n'$). We refer the reader to the original paper (Feng et al., 2003) for more details and explanations on these concepts.

Finally, the association rule is defined as an implication $T_1 \rightarrow T_2$ that satisfies two conditions.

1. $X \subset T, Y \subset T$ and $X \cap Y = \varnothing$, where *T* is the set of tree-structured items and

2. For any T_m and $T_n \in (X \cup Y)$, there is no tree T_p that can satisfy the conditions $T_p \leq_{tree} T_m$ and $T_p \leq_{tree} T_n$.

An example of the association rule in terms of tree-structured items (named XML-enabled association rules by the authors) is presented in Figure 8.

Figure 8. An example of the XML-enabled association rule (Feng et al., 2003)

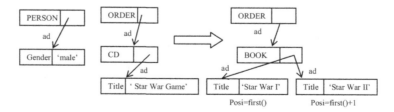

The rule exemplified in Figure 8 tells that if a male person orders a CD with the title Star War Game, he will also order two books, that is, *Star War I* and *Star War II*, in this order. Though an algorithm to implement the above described framework is still under development, the obtained association rules are powerful as they address the specific format of the XML documents; the associated items are hierarchical structures, not simple nodes. Furthermore, they carry the notion of order, as exemplified by rule in Figure 8.

Summary of Association Rule Mining Techniques for Static XML Documents

To conclude this section, we make some comments on the major differences between the above discussed XML association rule techniques and the degree of the possible generalization of them, considering both the number of XML documents mined at once and the structure of these documents, together with some experimental results of the authors.

The main difference between the Apriori-based approaches and the non-Apriori-based framework presented in this chapter consists of the way they perceive the notion of *item*, which they consider in their mining algorithms. While the former ones extract the items to be mined as a list of nodes by querying the XML document for a specific path, for the last one, each subtree (substructure) in the XML document tree representation is an item and the framework actually looks to discover association rules between the substructures of the document.

Another significant difference resides in the number of XML documents allowed by the algorithms and the degree of the complexity of the documents (levels of nesting). Sometimes we may want to find association rules from a single XML document (e.g., books in a library) or from two or more XML documents (e.g., documents containing books in a library, one containing personal details of the authors and the third containing sales of the books for a period of time). If we have a collection of XML documents, it is probable that we will get more interesting information by analysing all the documents together instead of one at a time.

The simple (one-step) XML association rule mining techniques (Wan & Dobbie, 2003, 2004) are considering one single document, with a simple structure (see Figure 2a), for example, an XML document containing transactions in a superstore, with the corresponding purchased items. The authors state that their proposed algorithm "works with any XML document, as long as the structure of it is known in advance" (p. 94), but they consider that applying their algorithm to an XML document with a more complex structure is still an open issue from the performance point of view.

The three-step approaches (Braga et al., 2003; Braga, Campi, Ceri et al., 2002; Braga, Campi, Klemettinen et al., 2002) are designed to work with more complex-structured XML documents (see the example in Figure 3 with five levels of nesting). Still, the structure of the document needs to be known in advance as the context, body, and head of the association rules should be defined at the beginning of the algorithm. The authors acknowledge that, even if the experiments were done without considering efficiency as a main concern, the results proved excellent performance when using the Xalan (2005). Also, the experimental results showed that only a small percentage of time was spent for preprocessing and postprocessing the XML document, while the actual mining was the slowest phase. The authors reckon that any future step in the XQuery development to allow more complex conditions in filtering XML documents will determine a substantial improvement of the mining step's efficiency and speed.

Discovering Association Rules
from Dynamic XML Documents

As specified in the background section, this section details some of the work done for dynamic XML document versioning and mining. A dynamic XML document is one that is continually changing its content and/or structure in time depending on the data requested to be stored at a certain moment. An example could be the content of an online bookstore, where any change in the number of existing books, their prices, and/or availability will affect the content of the XML document that stores this information. The possible user (e.g., the online store manager) might decide to store each new version of the XML document, which results after each change, so he or she would be able to refer to the history of the store's content at any time in the future for business purposes. In this case, a high degree of redundancy might appear, and the user will end up with a large collection of XML documents in which a large amount of information is repeated.

The issue for researchers was how to efficiently store all these versions so the user will be able to get a historic version of the document with as less redundancy of information as possible. Moreover, a new question was raised about what kind of knowledge can be discovered from the multiple versions of an XML document; the goal in the case of mining dynamic XML documents would be to find a different type of knowledge than can be obtained from snapshots of data. For example, some parts of the XML document representing the online store could change more often, and some other parts could change together; for instance, deletions could appear more often than updates, and so on. All this information could be usefully utilised by the end user in making business decisions related to the online store's content.

In this section, we will first refer to the work done for versioning XML documents, that is, methodologies that efficiently store the changing XML documents in a way that allows the fast retrieval of the historic versions. They will include our own proposed solution to the issue of versioning dynamic XML documents to collect all the changes between versions in a single XML document, named consolidated delta. Finally, we will describe our proposed solution for mining association rules from changes supported by the dynamic XML documents.

Most of the methodologies addressing the issue of versioning XML documents are based on the concept of the *delta* document (Cobena, Abiteboul, & Marian, 2005; Marian, Abiteboul, Cobena, & Mignet, 2001). This is calculated and built by comparing two consecutive versions of the XML document and recording the changes that have been taking place.

XML versioning techniques come to solve two main issues (Zhao, 2004), as follows:

1.   The querying time can be improved by limiting the amount of data that need to be queried if the result of the same query in the previous state of the document is already known.

2.   Storing historical structural deltas (the actual changes) of the XML documents can help to find knowledge (e.g., association rules) not just for snapshot data (as in mining static XML documents), but also considering their evolution in time.

For a better understanding of the differences between the XML versioning techniques, we will exemplify them on two versions of an XML document (catalog.xml), which contains data about some products in an online store (Figure 9).

A change-centric management of versions in an XML warehouse was first introduced by Marian et al. (2001). They consider a sequence of snapshots of XML documents and, for each pair of consecutive versions, the algorithm calculates a delta document as the difference between them. Delta Δ_i is a sequence of *update*, *delete*, and *insert* operations capable to transform the initial version of the document (D_i) into the final version (D_{i+1}). Furthermore, based on the observation that the delta Δ_i is not enough to transform D_{i+1} back into D_i, the

Figure 9. Two consecutive versions of the same XML document, catalog.xml, with corresponding IDs, in both XML document format and trees

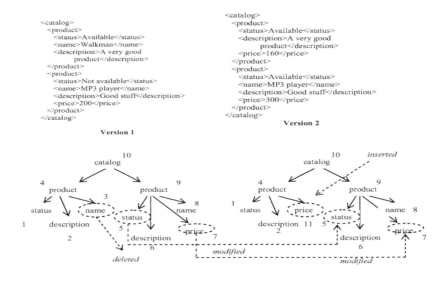

Figure 10. Examples of forward, backward, and completed deltas

Forward delta:	Backward delta:	Completed delta:
Delete (3)	Insert (4,3, T_2)	Delete (4,3,T_2)
Update (5,"Available"	Update (5, "Not available")	Update (5, "Available", "Not available")
Update (7,300)	Update (7, 200)	Update (7,300,200)
Insert (4,3, T_1)	Delete (11)	Insert (4,3,T_1)

authors introduce the notion of *completed delta*. This is a delta that contains more information and works both forward and backward, being able to obtain D_i or D_{i+1} when the other version is available.

In our working example (Figure 9), the forward, backward, and completed deltas are shown in Figure 10.

In the example in Figure 10, T_1 is the tree rooted at node 11, that is, the <price> node, while T_2 is the tree rooted at node 3, the <name> node. These two trees will be included in the completed delta XML document. In the delete and insert sequences, the first parameters are the parent node, the second parameters are the affected node positions, and the third parameters are the trees rooted at the affected nodes. In the update sequences, the first parameters are the affected nodes, the second ones are the new values, while the third parameters are the old values.

In this approach (Marian et al., 2001), a presumptive XML warehouse will need to store the initial version of an XML document together with all the completed deltas calculated in time so the model will be able to successfully solve different versioning requests. At the same time, the authors acknowledge that one of the most important issues in their approach is the storage of the redundant information (e.g., both the old version and new version of elements consecutively updated will be stored in the completed deltas).

Another change detection algorithm, X-Diff, was proposed by Wang, DeWitt, and Cai (2003), focusing on unordered XML document trees (where the left-to-right order among siblings is not important). They argue that an unordered tree model is more appropriate for most applications than the ordered model (where both the ancestor-descendant and the left-to-right order among siblings are important) and propose a methodology that detects changes in XML documents by integrating specific XML structure characteristics with standard tree-to-tree correction techniques. We do not detail here the X-Diff algorithm, but mainly, it performs the followings steps to determine the minimum-cost edit sequence that is able to transform document D_1 into document D_2. (a) It parses the D_1 and D_2 documents and builds the associated T_1 and T_2 trees while at the same time, it computes an XHash value for every node used to represent the entire subtree rooted at the node. (b) It compares the XHash values for the roots and decides if the trees are equivalent (when the XHash values are equal); otherwise, it calculates $\min(T_1, T_2)$ as a minimum-cost matching between trees. (c) It determines the generated minimum-cost edit script E based on the min (T_1, T_2) found at step b.

For our working example, the minimum edit script generated by X-Diff would be:

E= {delete (3), update (5, "Available"), update (7,300), insert (4, (Price, 160)}.

As it can be noticed, the insert operation does not include the position of the new inserted node because the X-Diff technique is focused on the unordered XML trees, and the position of the node is not considered important for the algorithm.

A novel way of storing changes in time with less overhead was proposed by Rusu, Rahayu, and Taniar (2005b). In this approach, earlier versions of the documents can be easily queried and the degree of redundancy is very small. Our algorithm replaces the way of storing differences between two versions of an XML document in deltas and keeping all the deltas in the warehouse with a new concept of *consolidated delta*, in which changes between versions are recorded in a new XML document, modified any time a new version appears. The main idea is to build a single (consolidated) XML delta document containing all the changes supported by the versioned XML document in the T_1–T_n period of time by introducing a new temporal element (namely, <stamp>) to store the changes at each time stamp for each altered element. Each <stamp> element has two attributes: *time* to store the time stamp and *delta* to store the type of change (delta can take one of the values inserted, modified, or deleted).

To exemplify the consolidated delta approach, Figure 11 shows another set of changes that have been applied to the document in Figure 9. The changes between Version 1 and Version 2 are recorded in the first consolidated delta (left), which is built starting from the initial version (Version 1), adding the <stamp> elements as explained before. Similarly, after another set of changes happen at time T_3 (Version 3), new <stamp> elements are added and the consolidated delta is updated to reflect these (right). Every time the consolidated delta is modified to reflect new changes, there are rules to be observed in order to increase the efficiency of the algorithm and eliminate the redundancy as much as possible; we list them here, as follows. (a) If all the children are unchanged, the parent is unchanged. If a parent is unchanged at the time *Ti*, its children are not marked (stamped) for that particular time stamp; they will be easily rebuilt from the existing previous versions of their parents. (b) If any of the children are modified, deleted, or inserted, the parent is modified. If a parent is modified at the time *Ti*, all its children will be stamped, each with their own status, that is, modified, inserted, deleted, or unchanged. (c) If a parent is deleted at the time *Ti*, all its children will be deleted so they will not appear in the consolidated delta for that particular time stamp or for any time stamp after that.

To get a high speed in building the consolidated delta, we assign unique identifiers to elements in the initial XML document and store the maximum ID value. When new elements are inserted in a following version, they will receive IDs based on the existing maximum ID so at any time, one element will be uniquely identified and we will be able to track its changes.

The two big advantages of the consolidated approach are the following: (a) There is a very small degree of redundancy of the stored data as unchanged data between versions will not be repeated, and (b) it is enough for the user to store the calculated consolidated delta to be able to get an earlier version of the document at any time. We have tested the algorithm of building the consolidated delta and it has excellent results for various dimensions of XML documents.

Figure 11. Example of the consolidated delta after two series of changes applied to the initial XML document catalog.xml

Versioning Dynamic XML Documents Using the Consolidated Delta Approach

The consolidated delta is a very efficient tool when the user wants to retrieve an old version of the document. Suppose the latest version of the document is at the moment T_n in time (see Figure 12), and the user wants to determine the effective look (structure and content) for the XML document at a moment Ti, where i<n (i=3 in the example in Figure 12). Using the consolidated delta, he or she does not need to re-create the entire set of intermediate documents from T_n to T_i ($T_n \rightarrow T_{n-1}$, $T_{n-1} \rightarrow T_{n-2}$....$T_{i+1} \rightarrow T_i$). Instead, the consolidated delta can be directly queried to get the elements that have <stamp> elements with a T_i value of the time attribute. This query will not return at once the entire structure and content of the XML document at the moment T_i— this would be an ideal output. We still have to query backward in the history of certain elements, but only for a limited number, that is, the unchanged ones as the modified or inserted elements will contain the actual values at the time T_i.

Figure 12. Using consolidated delta to get an earlier version of an XML document

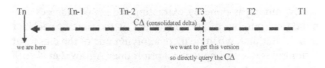

When an earlier version is required, the consolidated delta document is scanned starting from the root, and for each element, the algorithm determines if the delta attribute has one of the *modified, deleted, added,* or *unchanged* values, building, at the same time, the required D_i version of the document as follows. (a) When the delta has the *modified* value, if the element is a complex one (it has children), we analyse the changes for each of its children elements; they may have a *modified, deleted, added,* or *unchanged* value as well. If the element is not a complex one, we take its value. (b) When the delta has the *inserted* value, if it is a complex element, all its children were inserted, too; so, we take their values as they are returned for the T_i time stamp. If the element is not a complex one, we take its value. (c) When the delta has the *deleted* value, if the parent element was deleted (together with its children) at the time T_i, the consolidated delta will contain the *deleted* value for the delta and no children details; consequently, the element will not appear in the built version document. (d) When the delta has the *unchanged* value, we know a complex unchanged element does not include its unchanged children; so if we find an unchanged element, we will query backward for each of the T_{i-1}, T_{i-2}, and so forth, and earlier time-stamp changes until we get to a version without an unchanged delta attribute or until we get to the initial D_1 version of the document (included in the consolidated delta as a starting point).

Mining the Changes Extracted from Dynamic XML Documents

In our view, there are two different ways to approach the task of mining dynamic XML documents. Supposing there is a collection of versions of *n* dynamic XML documents stored in an XML data warehouse, composed by using one of the above presented methods, the user might be interested in discovering either of the following:

a. Interesting knowledge (in our case, association rules) that can be found in the collection of historic versions of the document(s)

b. Association rules extracted from the actual changes between versions, that is, from the differences recorded in delta documents

There was some work done to discover frequently changing structures in versions of XML documents (Chen et al., 2004; Zhao, Bhowmick, Mohania, & Kambayashi, 2004; Zhao, Bhowmick, & Mandria, 2004) applicable more to discovering the first type of knowledge (Case a above). We do not detail them here; instead, we will propose a novel method of mining changes extracted from dynamic XML documents (applicable for the second type of knowledge, Case b above) by using the consolidated delta described earlier in the previous subsection. Mainly, mining is done by extracting the set of changes for each time T_i ($2<i<n$, where n is the total number of versions and T_i is the time of each set of changes) as a set of transactions. After that, we mine them applying one of the classic algorithms for discovering association rules, for example, the a priori one (Agrawal et al., 1993). Because the implementation of the actual algorithm is still under review, we will give only a general description of the technique using an example.

We consider again the consolidated delta example in Figure 10. If we extract only the changes from the consolidated delta for each of the times T_2 and T_3, we get the following two transactions:

At time T2 → <catalog> modified & <product> modified & <name> deleted & <price> inserted value="160" & <status> modified value="Available" & <price> modified value=300;

At time T3 → <catalog> modified & <product> modified & <description> modified value="A new stuff" & <price> modified value="150" & <price> modified value="400" & <product> inserted & <status> inserted value="Not available" & <description> inserted value="good book" & <price> inserted value="25";

In a generalized Apriori-based algorithm, the set of items I will be the list of all distinct elements from the initial XML document. In our example, $I = \{$<catalog>, <product>, <status>, <name>, <description>, <price>$\}$. The extracted changes will form the set of transactions D, where each transaction T from D is a set of items from I represented by one set of changes extracted for one time stamp T_i, $2<i<n$. A possible association rule will be an implication $X \rightarrow Y$ where $X, Y \subset I$ and $X \cap Y = \varnothing$. The rule's support and confidence will be calculated with regard to the total number of changes extracted. Dynamic association rules discovered in this way could give precious information about the relationship between changes affecting specific parts of the initial XML document. For example, it could be found that the insertion of new products determine a fall in the availability of certain products. We are currently working on implementing and proving the efficacy of this mining algorithm.

Summary of Association Rule Mining Techniques for Dynamic XML Documents

In this section, we have presented some of the state-of-the-art work in the area of recording changes between versions of dynamic XML documents, detailing more on the consolidated delta approach, which is an effective way to store successive changes of the documents in a single document. Then, we have presented an algorithm for extracting a historic version of the document at any time where its versions are stored by using the consolidated delta approach. Finally, we presented our view on mining the set of changes extracted for a given period of time.

The methods presented for storing the changes between versions of the XML documents are all using the concept of *delta* as a difference between two consecutive versions of the

XML document, but each approach comes with its own definition and implementation as the target is to find the most efficient representation that is easy to interrogate and mine later on. While the work of Marian et al. (2001) proposes building a consolidated delta as a set of instructions able to reverse the initial version of the document to the final one and vice versa for ordered XML documents, the technique introduced by Wang et al. (2003) is similar but focuses on unordered XML documents. A different approach is given by Rusu, Rahayu, and Taniar (2005), in which the proposal is to record the historic changes in one single document, named consolidated delta, that is easy to be queried when the user needs to extract an old version of the document. The same consolidated delta approach can be used to perform the mining of association rules out of the set of changes applied to the initial document, returning possible interesting information about the relationships between changes and their influences on the XML document's behaviour in the future.

Future Trends

In this section, we present our view on the future trends in the area of mining XML documents, considering how the existing work answers possible user needs.

- **Mining association rules from static XML documents** (i.e., documents that are not changing their content in time): In this area, the majority of the research work has been focused not so much on determining generic association rules (what type of knowledge can be extracted from a certain XML document or from a collection of XML documents), but more on seeking a confirmation of possible association rules between elements or parts of the document. For example, the majority of the presented algorithms for mining static XML documents need to know from the beginning which are the specific areas they need to look at to find either the antecedent or the consequent of the association rule. In this context, future work is needed to improve the existing methodologies in terms of generalization (Buchner, Baumgarten, Mulvenna, Bohm, & Anand, 2000; Garofalakis, Rastogi, Seshadri, & Shim, 1999). Finding algorithms with a high degree of generalization is imperative as scalability is a priority for the current and future XML-driven applications.

- **Mining association rules from dynamic XML documents** (i.e., documents that change their content in time to allow different formats of data): Dynamic mining is still a very young area in which a lot of research has been undertaken. From our perspective, intense activity in this field will be noticed soon as Web applications are used on a large scale and manipulate dynamic data. Besides association rules, researchers are looking to find other types of patterns in dynamic XML documents, that is, structural changes from an XML document version to another, and content changes. Our next research work is to implement and evaluate a mining algorithm able to discover association rules and other types of knowledge from the sequence of actual changes of dynamic XML documents. The outcome of this work will be very useful in finding not only what the patterns are in the changing documents, but also how they relate to one another and how they could affect the future behaviour of the initial XML document.

Conclusion

This chapter is a systematic analysis of some of the existing techniques for mining association rules out of XML documents in the context of rapid changes and discoveries in the Web knowledge area. The XML format is more and more used to store data that now exist in the traditional relational-database format, and also to exchange them between various applications over the Internet.

In this context, we presented the latest discoveries in the area of mining association rules from XML documents, both static and dynamic, in a well-structured manner, with examples and explanations so the reader will be able to easily identify the appropriate technique for his or her needs and replicate the algorithm in a development environment. At the same time, we have included in this chapter only the research work with a high level of usability in which concepts and models are easy to be applied in real situations without imposing knowledge of any high-level mathematics concepts.

The overall conclusion is that this chapter is a well-structured tool very useful for understanding the concepts behind discovering association rules out of collections of XML documents. It is addressed not only to the students and other academics studying the mining area, but to the real end users as a guide in creating powerful XML mining applications.

References

Agrawal, R., Imielinski, T., & Swami, A. N. (1993). Mining association rules between sets of items in large databases. *Proceedings of the ACM International Conference on Management of Data (SIGMOD 1993)* (pp. 207-216).

Agrawal, R., & Srikant, R. (1998). Fast algorithms for mining association rules. In *Readings in database systems* (3rd ed., pp. 580-592). San Francisco: Morgan Kaufmann Publishers Inc.

Ashrafi, M. Z., Taniar, D., & Smith, K. A. (2004a). A new approach of eliminating redundant association rules. In *Database and expert systems applications* (LNCS 3180, pp. 465-474). Heidelberg, Germany: Springer-Verlag.

Ashrafi, M. Z., Taniar, D. & Smith, K. A. (2004b). ODAM: An optimized distributed association rule mining algorithm. *IEEE Distributed Systems Online, 5*(3).

Ashrafi, M. Z., Taniar, D., & Smith, K. (2005). An efficient compression technique for frequent itemset generation in association rule mining. In *Proceedings of International Conference in Advances in Knowledge Discovery and Data Mining (PAKDD 2005)* (LNCS 3518, pp. 125-135). Heidelberg, Germany: Springer-Verlag.

Braga, D., Campi, A., & Ceri, S. (2003). Discovering interesting information in XML with association rules. *Proceedings of 2003 ACM Symposium on Applied Computing (SAC'03)* (pp. 450-454).

Braga, D., Campi, A., Ceri, S., Klemettinen, M., & Lanzi, P. L. (2002). A tool for extracting XML association rules. *Proceedings of the 14th International Conference on Tools with Artificial Intelligence (ICTAI '02)* (p. 57).

Braga, D., Campi, A., Klemettinen, M., & Lanzi, P. L. (2002). Mining association rules from XML data. In *Proceedings of International Conference on Data Warehousing and Knowledge Discovery (DaWak 2002)* (LNCS 2454, pp. 21-30). Heidelberg, Germany: Springer-Verlag.

Buchner, A. G., Baumgarten, M., Mulvenna, M. D., Bohm, R., & Anand, S. S. (2000). Data mining and XML: Current and future issues. *Proceedings of 1st International Conference on Web Information System Engineering (WISE 2000)* (pp. 127-131).

Chen, L., Browmick, S. S., & Chia, L. T. (2004). Mining association rules from structural deltas of historical XML documents. In *Proceedings of International Conference in Advances in Knowledge Discovery and Data Mining (PAKDD 2004)* (LNCS 3056, pp. 452-457). Heidelberg, Germany: Springer-Verlag.

Cobena, G., Abiteboul, S., & Marian, A. (2005). *XyDiff tools: Detecting changes in XML documents.* Retrieved February 2006, from http://www.rocq.inria.fr/gemo

Daly, O., & Taniar, D. (2004). Exception rules mining based on negative association rules. In *Computational science and applications* (LNCS 3046, pp. 543-552). Heidelberg, Germany: Springer-Verlag.

Ding, O., Ricords, K., & Lumpkin, J. (2003). Deriving general association rules from XML data. *Proceedings of the ACIS 4th International Conference on Software Engineering, Artificial Intelligence, Networking and Parallel/Distributed Computing (SNPD'03)* (pp. 348-352).

Feng, L., Dillon, T., Wiegand, H., & Chang, E. (2003). An XML-enabled association rules framework. In *Proceedings of International Conference on Database and Expert Systems Applications (DEXA 2003)* (LNCS 2736, pp. 88-97). Heidelberg, Germany: Springer-Verlag.

Garofalakis, M. N., Rastogi, R., Seshadri, S., & Shim, K. (1999). Data mining and the Web: Past, present and future. *Proceedings of the 2nd Workshop on Web Information and Data Management (WIDM 1999)* (pp. 43-47).

Laurent, M., Denilson, B., & Pierangelo, V. (2003). The XML Web: A first study. *Proceedings of the International WWW Conference* (pp. 500-510).

Marian, A., Abiteboul, S., Cobena, G., & Mignet, L. (2001). Change-centric management of versions in an XML warehouse. *VLDB Journal*, 581-590.

Nayak, R. (2005). Discovering knowledge from XML documents. In J. Wong (Ed.), *Encyclopedia of data warehousing and mining* (pp. 372-376). Hershey, PA: Idea Group Reference.

Nayak, R., Witt, R., & Tonev, A. (2002). Data mining and XML documents. *Proceedings of the 2002 International Conference on Internet Computing* (pp. 660-666).

Rusu, L. I., Rahayu, W., & Taniar, D. (2005a). Maintaining versions of dynamic XML documents. In *Proceedings of the 6ᵗʰ International Conference on Web Information System Engineering (WISE 2005)* (LNCS 3806, pp. 536-543). Heidelberg, Germany: Springer-Verlag.

Rusu, L. I., Rahayu, W., & Taniar, D. (2005b). A methodology for building XML data warehouses. *International Journal of Data Warehousing and Mining, 1*(2), 67-92.

Tjioe, H. C., & Taniar, D. (2005). Mining association rules in data warehouses. *International Journal of Data Warehousing and Mining, 1*(3), 28-62.

Wan, J. W., & Dobbie, G. (2003). Extracting association rules from XML documents using XQuery. *Proceedings of the 5ᵗʰ ACM International Workshop on Web Information and Data Management (WIDM'03)* (pp. 94-97).

Wan, J. W., & Dobbie, G. (2004). Mining association rules from XML data using XQuery. *Proceedings of International Conference on Research and Practice in Information Technology (CRPIT 2004)* (pp. 169-174).

Wang, Y., DeWitt, D. J., & Cai, J. Y. (2003). X-Diff: An effective change detection algorithm for XML documents. *Proceedings of the 19ᵗʰ International Conference on Data Engineering (ICDE 2003)* (pp. 519-530).

World Wide Web Consortium (W3C). (n.d.). Retrieved February 2006, from http://www.w3c.org

Xalan. (2005). *The Apache Software Foundation: Apache XML project.* Retrieved December 2005, from http://xml.apache.org/xalan-j/

XQuery. (2005). Retrieved February 2006, from http://www.w3.org/TR/2005/WD-xquery-20050915/

Zhao, Q., Bhowmick, S. S., & Mandria, S. (2004). Discovering pattern-based dynamic structures from versions of unordered XML documents. In *Proceedings of International Conference on Data Warehousing and Knowledge Discovery (DaWaK 2004)* (LNCS 3181, pp. 77-86). Heidelberg, Germany: Springer-Verlag.

Zhao, Q., Bhowmick, S. S., Mohania, M., & Kambayashi, Y. (2004). Discovering frequently changing structures from historical structural deltas of unordered XML. *Proceedings of ACM International Conference on Information and Knowledge Management (CIKM'04)* (pp. 188-197). Heidelberg, Germany: Springer Berlin.

Section II

Content Management
on the Web

Chapter V

Dynamically Generated Web Content:
Research and Technology Practices

Stavros Papastavrou, University of Cyprus, Cyprus

George Samaras, University of Cyprus, Cyprus

Paraskevas Evripidou, University of Cyprus, Cyprus

Panos K. Chrysanthis, University of Pittsburgh, USA

Abstract

This chapter takes a tutorial approach to present the Web-related technologies and content middleware that attempt to accelerate the generation and optimize the delivery of dynamic content. It covers the historical aspects of dynamic content and presents the reasoning behind its introduction while discussing early content middleware such as the CGI and FastCGI. It then presents the evolution of content middleware along the lines of contacted research. The discussion focuses on popular techniques that mostly include content caching and content fragmentation. It also discusses a variety of other research efforts such as hardware and low-level acceleration techniques, active caching, and delta encoding. Finally, the authors hope that this chapter will serve as an introductory tutorial to students and researchers in the field of dynamic Web content technology.

Introduction

The personalization and customization of Web services that increase user satisfaction require the delivery of dynamic rather than static Web documents or pages. This means that the content of such Web pages is generated on demand and tailored to a particular Web user (e.g., e-banking) or group of users (e.g., the delivery of local online sport results). Specifically, the term *dynamically generated Web content*, otherwise known as dynamic Web content or simply dynamic content, refers to chunks of HTML (hypertext markup language) or XML (extensible markup language) code or media that are generated and combined on the fly to build a requested Web page.

Currently, dynamic content constitutes more than 40% of Internet traffic despite the fact that generating Web pages on the fly incurs a major overhead on server resources and increases the response time of the Web servers (Feldmann, Caceres, Douglis, Glass, & Rabinovich, 1999). This percentage of Internet traffic associated with dynamic content is expected to keep increasing, especially with the improvement of dynamic-content technologies and content middleware such as application servers, client-side proxies, and server-side caches.

In this chapter, we take a tutorial approach to present the Web-related technologies and content middleware that attempt to accelerate the generation and optimize the delivery of dynamic content. We begin the chapter by covering the historical aspects of dynamic content and presenting the reasoning behind its introduction while discussing early content middleware such as the CGI (common gateway interface) and FastCGI that enable the execution of external programs and scripts. We then present the evolution of content middleware along the lines of contacted research. Our discussion focuses on popular techniques that mostly include content caching and content fragmentation at different levels along the communication path from the Web client, through any intermediate proxies, and to the Web server and back-end database servers. We also discuss a variety of other research efforts such as hardware and low-level acceleration techniques, active caching, and delta encoding.

We conclude the chapter with a discussion on the interplay between the quality of service (QoS), such as the response time or user-perceived latency, and the quality of data (QoD), such as freshness. We consider various proposals that attempt to strike a balance between user-perceived latency and the freshness of delivered documents, which can be broadly classified as client driven or data driven. Finally, motivated by growing Web user needs, we discuss future trends of dynamic-content technology.

Historical Aspects

In order to better understand the semantics of dynamic content, we first review the basics of static content. Static content emerged along with the introduction of the World Wide Web

(WWW or simply Web) back in the early '90s. The Web is a vast network of servers linked together by a common protocol called the hypertext transfer protocol (HTTP), allowing access to various forms of content uniquely identified by global addresses called uniform resource locators or URLs. Static content refers to preexisting files with extensions such as .html and .jpg that denote their content and purpose. HTML files contain tags that define the logical and visual structure of a Web document. Text content is laid within those tags. HTML files may also contain references, hyperlinks, or URLs to other documents, or links to graphic and multimedia content such as image and audio files.

Web users or clients request a static document by pointing their browsers to it either indirectly via hyperlinks found inside other documents, or directly by explicitly specifying the location and name of the document. Those requests are better known as HTTP GET requests and cause the Web server on the other side to issue an HTTP response that is immediately followed by the requested static file. The control text of both HTTP requests and responses are hidden from the user. Once a browser downloads a static document, it parses and renders it according to the HTML tags found inside it. References to static graphic content of the form *<img src=image1.jpg>* trigger a new HTTP request without any extra effort by the user.

Later on, the need to embed basic dynamic information into Web documents, such as the time at the server side or the last date the document was modified, initiated server-side includes (SSI) as a first step toward dynamic Web content. HTML documents written according to SSI included tags of the form *<!--#echo var="DATE_LOCAL" -->* and carried the file extension of .shtml instead of the traditional .html. An HTTP request for a document with that file extension triggered the Web server to behave differently. Instead of submitting the actual contents of the document (as stored on the file system), the Web server parses the document and substitutes the SSI tags with the corresponding dynamic information. In addition to tag substitution, SSI introduced another breakthrough for Web development by providing support for an HTML document to include another one by simply using an SSI tag of the form *<!--#include file="top_menu.html" -->*, pointing the way for modular Web development.

The quick adoption of the Web, first by the academic community and then by the business community, led to a whole new class of Web-based applications. The key element in the popularity and success of this new class of Web applications was the ability to serve Web users with customizable content. The key requirement was that an HTTP request for a document, for example, http://www.stocks.com/mystocks.cgi, produced different content for each Web user under certain situations.

The evolution came along with the introduction of the common gateway interface. According to CGI, a Web server was able to execute programs and return their output to Web users. In this case, the Web server was more like a mediator or a gateway between the Web users and the executable programs rather than being a simple file dispenser. Nonetheless, the big question was how a CGI program could distinguish between different users.

A Web user causes a CGI program, for example, mystocks.cgi, to execute by issuing an HTTP GET request for it that triggers the gateway functionality on the Web server. The latter will then fork a new process to execute that file. However, in order to make that call meaningful, extra client-related parameters must be provided to the CGI program, such as the ID of the user and the stock quote. One way to achieve this is by appending a list of variable names and values next to the file name of the CGI program. For example, for a user with ID=123 and a stock quote for Intel, the target file of the HTTP GET request would target the URL http://www.stocks.com/mystocks.cgi?id=123&stock=Intel. The given variables and values in this case are called URL parameters and are passed as input to the CGI program by the Web server. The CGI program queries one or more local (or remote) application databases to retrieve data concerning the user with ID=123 and his or her stock preferences for stock=Intel. It then dynamically constructs HTML code enriched with the retrieved data. Finally, the complete result is sent to the Web user via the Web server (our gateway).

Another popular way of passing parameters to a CGI program is by submitting the contents of HTML forms to the Web server. Similar to our previous example, the Web user uses two text boxes inside an HTML form and fills in the ID and the stock symbol. Upon submission of the form, the parameters are not placed next to the file name of the CGI program as URL parameters. Instead, they are appended at the end of the HTTP request, which in this case is called an HTTP POST request.

Both HTTP-based request approaches — the HTTP GET, which uses URL parameters, and the HTTP POST, which uses HTML form input — are still very popular mechanisms for modern Web applications to distinguish between individual users and situations. In the rest of this chapter, we will refer back to these mechanisms while describing more recent content middleware.

From CGI to FASTCGI

CGI suffered from one major drawback that surfaced soon after its introduction. Every client HTTP request for a dynamic page required the forking of a new process on the middleware by the Web server. In the case of having to serve multiple concurrent requests, this approach led to decreased performance since the server system spent more time between context switching, and forking and terminating processes rather than actually serving the client requests (a phenomenon better known in the literature as thrashing).

Besides scalability problems, this nonpersistent nature of the CGI processes introduces a number of other inefficiencies. The most important, in our belief, is the inability to keep open (persistent) database connections to the application database(s). Persistent database connections accelerate the processing of client requests since they are immediately available to the middleware processes for submitting a series of queries. As we discuss later on, it is a common practice for modern content middleware to assign an open database connection to each running process.

Another major shortcoming of CGI is that consecutive client requests each have to be reconnected to a different middleware process. This practice, however, does not enable the use of a single network connection between a client and a middleware process for the complete duration of the client session.

To address the shortcomings of CGI, FastCGI was introduced. Its revolutionary design allowed for middleware processes to be persistent and execute in a different context than that of the Web server. According to the FastCGI approach, the Web server tunnels a client request for dynamic content to a content middleware system that is already up and running. Under a commonly used practice, a content middleware maintains a small number of preforked processes or threads, typically between 5 and 20, to handle client requests. Thus, FastCGI introduced a completely new architecture for developing content middleware systems that was quickly adopted by major software vendors.

Modern Content Middleware and Scripting Languages

FastCGI reshaped the architecture of content middleware systems. According to this new approach, the Web server runs completely in isolation from any content middleware and performs the following two tasks. First, it delivers static content to clients, such as images, static HTML files, and cascading style sheets.[1] Second, it redirects client requests for dynamic content to running content middleware in its vicinity. This procedure of dynamic-content generation and delivery is illustrated in Figure 1.

A client request for a dynamic page is redirected to the appropriate content middleware according to the extension of the requested file that reveals the scripting language inside that file. The file extension .asp stands for active server pages, a technology from Microsoft that uses visual-basic scripts along with HTML. Files with the .cfm extension use a tag-based scripting language, a technology by Macromedia called Cold Fusion. Files with the .php extension use a C-like scripting language, a project of the Apache Group. Files with these extensions are better known in the literature as script files.

Figure 1. The procedure of generating dynamic content

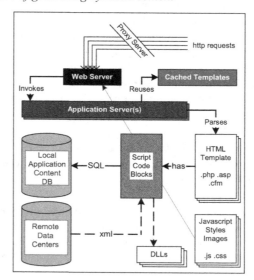

Upon receipt of a request for a script file, the corresponding content middleware assigns the request to one if its own running processes (or threads). The process parses the requested file and executes the script code included. During this procedure, it substitutes the execution outcome of the script-code blocks inside the script file, and the final outcome is sent to the client always via the Web server. Some script code may contain heavy computational tasks such as lengthy database transactions, dynamic image generation such as stock charts, session handling, shopping-card validation, or external data retrieval and processing.

Script files contain both static HTML and script code arranged in such a way that the static HTML defines the arrangement or layout of the dynamic page to be generated, while the script parts generate the missing dynamic information. Therefore, we call the script files *templates*, and the notion that isolates dynamic-content parts *fragmentation*. We discuss fragmentation in more detail later on when we explore methods for accelerating dynamic Web content.

Finally, it is a common practice for Web administrators to support and run more than one content middleware in an attempt to attract a wider range of Web developers that use different scripting languages. Content middleware that handle template files are also known in the literature and industry as application servers since they are used to process templates encapsulating the business or application logic of a Web application.

Issues and Practices in
Accelerating Dynamic Web Content

Performance has always been a key concern in generating dynamic Web content. This can be clearly realized by the fact that the generation of a single dynamic Web document involves the coordination of at least four middleware: a cache server, a Web server, an application server, and a database server. Amza et al. (2002) identify potential bottlenecks in this *n*-tier architecture by simulating typical dynamic-content Web applications. The findings indicate that e-commence and catalog-related Web applications create bottlenecks at the Web server and the database server. For less processing-intensive applications, such as regional news and those that are media related, the bottleneck shifts toward the proxy side.

The literature contains a plethora of proposed approaches and techniques toward accelerating the generation and delivery of dynamic Web content. Many of the proposed approaches are implemented in commercial products, proving in this way the importance and applicability of dynamic Web content technology. Here we summarize the most interesting approaches by classifying them according to their underlying methodologies and their locations: server side, proxy side, or client side.

Early Server-Side Practices

As we have already discussed, a first attempt toward accelerating the generation of dynamic Web content is the introduction of persistent processes with FastCGI. Both the Web server and the application servers maintain a pool of running processes (or threads) that handle, possibly in round-robin order, consecutive client requests. In addition, each application process can keep a number of open connections to the database server(s) (Liu, Dantzig, Wu, Challenger, & Ni, 1996). This multiprocess or multithreaded paradigm of FastCGI has been the pioneer system for almost all the modern content middleware.

Performance depends heavily on the implementation of a middleware. Current studies compare various heterogeneous middleware and reach the conclusion that systems written in the C programming language outperform others that are written in Java (Cecchet, Chanda, Elnikety, Marguerite, & Zwaenepoel, 2003). The Apache Web server and the PHP application server are examples of the former case, while Cold Fusion, Servlets, and JSP application servers are examples of the latter case. However, the latter examples are very popular to the developer community due to their programmability and openness. A complete study on the programmability and performance of all the Java-based middleware for dynamic-content generation can be found in Papastavrou, Chrysanthis, Samaras, and Pitoura (2001).

Beyond the dominant multiprocess-multithreaded architecture of content middleware, there have been significant efforts for the development of more efficient architectures to boost content generation. A classic example is the Flash Web server (Pai, Druschel, & Zwaenepoel, 1999). Flash is a portable, event-driven Web server that has been demonstrated to outperform industry-strength multiprocess servers such as Apache and Zeus. Its portability lies on the fact that it uses standard APIs found in any modern operating system. Flash, however, was originally designed to accelerate the delivery of static content, and there has been no adaptation of it for delivering dynamic content as yet.

Other studies also propose the use of an event-driven Web server and introduce the notion of a stage. According to Welsh, Culler, and Brewer (2001), a content middleware, for example, a Web server, is built as a network of explicit computation stages connected by explicit queues aiming at supporting massive concurrency and simplifying the construction of Web applications. Another similar proposal by Larus and Parkes (2001) introduces staged computation for Web servers, which replaces threads and introduces a more sophisticated task scheduling mechanism. To the best of our knowledge, there is no system that facilitates either event-driven or stage-based architectures for the generation and delivery of dynamic Web content since the current focus is on multiprocess systems.

Content Fragmentation at the Server Side

As the popularity of dynamic content evolved, its supporting technology could not keep up with its pace. That was because a dynamic page produced by the execution of a single script (like CGI) could not be easily fine-tuned to include the heterogeneity of content that popular Web applications demanded. This problem can be successfully addressed with a methodology called fragmentation, which isolates the different dynamic-content parts of a page. As an example, let us consider the popular Web site of the Amazon retailer, which has five different dynamic-content components.

The content of Amazon's book-search dynamic page is split into fragments as follows: a top fragment with the search box and the sections, left and right fragments with book suggestions relevant to the search criteria, a main fragment with the three most favorite relevant books, a center fragment with search results showing 10 books, and a bottom fragment that changes the search result page.

As already discussed, an early form of a dynamic Web content middleware is the SSI, which injects dynamic information into static documents at the Web-server side. One can assume that SSI is also an early form of content fragmentation since it isolates the dynamic parts of a document and generates them on demand.

Surprisingly, SSI is still a popular alternative for generating dynamic content. We believe that its simplistic design and the limited amount of processing resources required have helped SSI to survive over the last 10 years. SSI is an ideal solution for simple Web applications that require basic dynamic features such as including templates or simple dynamic information such as the time at the server or the network address of the client.

Challenger, Iyengar, Witting, Ferstat, and Reed (2000) take SSI one step further by proposing a more general form: a content fragmentation that allows the dissection of a dynamic page into distinct parts (fragments) that are assembled according to a template file. A fresh version of a fragment is generated using database triggers every time its underlying data objects are modified. With the fresh fragments in place, a dynamic page can be either immediately delivered or cached (as discussed next). This method is ideal for sites with content that changes very frequently such as a sport Web site.

A recent proposal suggests the processing of the dynamic fragments of a template in a concurrent fashion using additional processes or threads (Papastavrou, Samaras, Evripidou, & Chrysanthis, 2003). Instead of utilizing only one server process per request, as already seen in multiprocess servers, this approach requires that a new process (or thread) be spawned per content fragment. This approach, however, achieves increased performance when the workload is moderate since it dramatically increases the number of running processes (or threads).

Content Caching at the Server Side

The quick adoption of content fragmentation introduced additional processing overhead at the server side. In order to save valuable processing resources, a methodology from accelerating static content is borrowed. Server-side content caching (Holmedahl, Smith, & Yang, 1998; Iyengar & Challenger, 1997) boosts the generation and delivery of dynamic Web content by eliminating redundant server-side processing. Let us consider once again the Amazon Web site. If there are currently 1,000 online users who search for books with the keyword *Java*, then it would be wise for the application server that implements the bookstore to periodically save to and retrieve from the cache the content related to that search criteria. There are many interesting approaches for server-side caching that vary mostly on the granularity of caching. We begin by discussing page-level caching.

Similar to caching complete static documents, the caching of dynamic documents at the granularity of a page is proposed for early content middleware such as CGI and FastCGI. Smith, Acharya, Yang, and Zhu (1999) propose the dynamic content caching protocol (DCCP), which can be implemented as an extension to HTTP. This protocol allows for content middleware to specify full or partial equivalence between different dynamic documents (HTTP GET requests). The equivalence information is inserted by the content middleware into the HTTP response header of a dynamically generated page, and stored at the caching module along with the cached page. For example, the HTTP request http://www.server.com/LAdriveTo.php?DestCity=newyork instructs the content middleware to generate a page with driving directions from Los Angeles to New York. Prior to transmitting the result page, the middleware inserts the *cache-control: equivalent_result=Dest=queens* attribute in the HTTP response header. The caching module will cache the page, transmit it to the client, and store the cache-control directive for future use. A subsequent client request for the same URL but for a different DestinationCity value will be evaluated by the cache module for a possible match with the value of *queens* or *newyork*. If a match is found, then the cached page is transmitted to the client. This sort of coarse-grained dynamic-content caching (that applies to whole pages) was very popular when CGI and FastCGI variants dominated the scenery back in the '90s. However, emerging Web applications and increasing user needs were about to change technology from scratch as we explore in while.

Caching Content at Finer Granularities

In order to achieve greater reuse of cached content across time and multiple users, caching at finer granularities is proposed. Yagoub, Florescu, Issamy, and Valduriez (2000) suggests the caching of only specific content such as static HTML fragments, XML fragments, and database query results. This approach, however, applies to Web applications that follow a strict declarative definition and follow a certain implementation only. In addition, caching cannot be applied to random parts inside a dynamic page and, in extent, does not allow for arbitrary fragmentation.

Later on, Datta (2001) introduces a more general and easier-to-use approach for fragment caching. According to Datta (2001), caching can be applied to an arbitrary fragment of a template by first wrapping it with the appropriate tags (explicit tagging). XCache is a commercial product that installs as a plug-in popular dynamic-content middleware and supports fragment caching of any type using explicit tagging. Also, the Java-based Cold Fusion application server provides tags for explicitly defining the page fragment to be cached. For example, the coding *<cf_cache refresh-rate=60> ...some script code...</cf_cache>* caches an arbitrary fragment that refreshes every 60 seconds.

Proxy Caching of Dynamic Web Content

The rising demand of users for more responsive applications pushes researchers to borrow again from the technology of accelerating static content. Traditional proxy caching implemented by proxy servers[2] (Wang, 1999), better known as edge caching for the case of dynamic content (Yuan, Chen, & Zhang, 2003), is the most popular approach for faster delivery of reusable static content such as static HTML pages and media files. A proxy server reduces bandwidth consumption by eliminating unnecessary traffic between clients and servers by being strategically located. Spring and Wetherall (2000) and Wang show that the usual hit ratio for proxy caches is around 40% while another 40% of the traffic is redundant when proxies are employed.

Despite the location of cached content, server-side and proxy-side caching differ on how data consistency between the cached content and the underlying database objects is achieved. For server-side caching, cache consistency is easier to be enforced since the caching module is local to the application server. For proxy-side caching, efficient cache invalidation techniques are required as discussed later on.

DCCP at the granularity of a page, previously proposed for server-side caching, can be used for proxy-based caching as well. It works by allowing the manipulation of the HTTP header information and URL query-string parameters (GET variables) at a proxy server.

Another interesting approach for caching complete dynamic pages suggests that the proxy server is allowed to examine the HTTP POST variables that are submitted as part of a client HTTP request from within an HTML form (Luo & Naughton, 2001). In brief, the proxy server attempts to reuse cached SQL query results by looking them up on a predefined mapping. This mapping relates the HTML form fields that are submitted with a URI (uniform resource identifier) request to the SQL query that uses those form fields as input. Two strong points of this work are, first, that the proxy can extract and reuse portions of cached query results if necessary to satisfy future requests, and second, it can aggregate a cached query result on demand by negotiating with the Web server. Since the HTTP POST variables are generated from HTML form fields, this approach is called form based. Similar to server-side caching, the proxy caching of whole dynamic pages only worked for as long as CGI and its variants were the only means of producing dynamic content.

Fine-Grained Proxy Caching

Following proxy caching and content fragmentation, caching at the granularity of a fragment was proposed for proxy caches. According to this fine-grained proxy caching, the template file can be cached at the proxy server whereas its dynamic fragments are either reused from the proxy cache or fetched fresh from the Web server.

This approach was realized with the successor of SSI: the edge-side includes (ESI). ESI is introduced by Akamai and Oracle Corp as a standard scripting language for caching page templates along with their fragments on proxy servers. According to ESI, the dynamic fragments of a page are explicitly marked using tag-based macro commands inside the page's template file. An ESI-compliant proxy server must provide support for parsing the cached template file and executing macros that dictate whether a fragment should also be retrieved from cache or pulled from the original server. ESI macros have access to a client's HTTP request attributes (cookies, URL string, browser used) in order to choose between fragment alternatives. An example of that would be the identification of the client's browser version or vendor in order to pick the appropriate fragment that meets the browser capabilities.

ESI is a key component for content distribution networks (CDNs), a popular caching approach that supports the leasing of cache space on a service-based network of interconnected proxy servers. A typical CDN employs a set of proxy servers strategically arranged by geographical or network location. It is noteworthy to mention that for a Web site to be registered and served by a CDN network, an off-line procedure of updating the templates of the Web site is required. Krishnamurthy, Wills, and Zhang (2001) compile a thorough study on CDNs.

More recently, Ramaswamy, Iyengar, Liu, and Douglis (2005) proposed a different approach to content fragmentation and its caching. Instead of using explicit fragmentation techniques such as tagging (ESI, Cold Fusion), it proposes an automatic fragment-detection framework that isolates the most beneficial content in terms of caching. More specifically, the fragmentation is based on the nature and the pattern of the changes occurring in dynamic Web pages and their potential reuse across consecutive accesses.

Polymorphism: A Second Dimension of Content Dynamism

As discussed earlier, caching at the fragment level requires the existence of a page layout or template that dictates a strict arrangement for cached content fragments. If this restriction is removed by allowing for arbitrary arrangements of fragments, this leads to the notion of polymorphism (in Greek, it means the ability for something to show different phases or morphs) in content caching. Live examples of polymorphism are found in the Yahoo! and Google News Web sites.

Datta, Dutta, Thomas, VanderMeer, Suresha, and Ramamritham (2002) suggest proxy-side arbitrary polymorphism by switching between a set of available templates for a specific dynamic page. A client request for a dynamic page (for example, http://www.server.com/page1.php?id=2) is always routed to the origin Web server and causes the execution of the original script (in this case, homepage.php). This execution is necessary for determining the desired template for page1.php at runtime. The selected template is then pushed to the proxy server (if not cached there) and parsed for identifying which fragments should be reused from cache and which ones should be requested fresh from the server. Performance tests demonstrated solid bandwidth reductions when applying fragment caching; however, performance analysis for other critical metrics, such as scalability and responsiveness, remains to be seen. Both the necessary routing of each request to the origin content server and the invocation of the original script can hurt client response time and server scalability, respectively. Nevertheless, the proposed techniques introduced are an excellent starting point for further research.

We also find limited support for polymorphism in ESI. Instead of choosing between a set of templates, basic ESI branching commands can reorganize parts of the layout inside a template according to client preferences. Fine-grained proxy caching and polymorphism are still the most popular techniques for accelerating dynamic content for a wide range of modern Web applications.

Fine-Grained Caching at the Client Side

Interestingly, the notion of assembling a dynamic page away from the original content middleware was first introduced by Douglis, Haro, and Rabinovich (1997) not for proxy caches, but for client browsers. The proposed technique, called HPP (HTML preprocessing), requires from the client browsers the extra functionality of caching and processing a template file, containing blocks of macro commands, prior to rendering a dynamic page. Each macro command block generates from scratch a page fragment by manipulating local variables and strings. This idea can be viewed as the client-side equivalent to SSI discussed earlier.

As an extension, Rabinovich, Xiao, Douglis, and Kalmanek (2003) proposes the client-side includes (CSI) by merging HPP and ESI. In order to provide support for CSI in the Internet Explorer Web browser, the approach requires a generic downloadable wrapper (plug-in) that uses JavaScript and ActiveX. The wrapper pulls and caches at the client side the template and fragments that are associated with a requested DWP, assembles them together according to the ESI directives in the template, and finally renders the page. According to the authors, CSI is suitable for "addressing the last mile," and it better suits low-bandwidth dial-up users.

Caching with Delta Encoding

Delta encoding is a popular technique for efficiently compressing a file relatively to another one called the base file (Hunt, Vo, & Tichy, 1998). This is achieved by computing the difference (delta) between the file being compressed and the base file. Streaming-media compression, displaying differences between files (the UNIX diff command), and backing up data are common applications of delta encoding.

Under the assumption that consecutive client requests for a specific URI would generate a sequence of slightly different dynamic pages, delta encoding can be exploited as an alternative for caching dynamic content. To this extent, a proposal by Psounis (2002) requires the caching of a base file for each group (also called class) of correlated documents, that is, pages that share a common layout. With the base file cached, the next client request would force the content middleware to compute the delta between the new dynamic page that the client would normally receive and the base file. The computed delta is then transmitted from the content middleware to the site where the base file is cached for computation of the new dynamic page. Eventually, the result is transmitted to the client. An interesting feature of this class-based delta-encoding approach is that the base file can be cached either at the server side, proxy side, or even at the client browser itself as long as the required infrastructure exists. In the latter case, delta encoding could benefit low-bandwidth users.

We believe that an adaptation of delta encoding that employs fragmentation would make the approach much more appealing to Web developers since its current coarse-grained form does not meet the requirements of modern Web applications.

Active Caching and Active XML

The notion of active caching refers to the built-in functionality of a caching middleware to manipulate cached content instead of requesting fresh versions of it from the server. A popular approach piggybacks a Java object into a dynamically generated document, which is then cached at the proxy (Cao, Zhang, & Beach, 1999). The proxy provides a Java runtime environment in which the object executes in order to modify the dynamic parts of the cached document according to a client's preferences. Examples of document modifications include advertising banner rotation, logging user requests, SSI execution, and even delta compression. Besides these general types of modification, the Java object can personalize cached documents by retrieving personal information from the application database at the server side. Data chunks of personal information are kept by the object for future reuse.

Luo (2002) proposes a more general approach for dynamic-content caching that employs active caching. Similar to the form-based approach discussed earlier, Luo provides support for the cached Java object to manipulate the HTTP POST variables (the user form input) in order to generate the dynamic parts of the cached document. However, active caching relates more to SSI and CSI rather than fragmentation since it does not decouple the content fragments from the templates.

An approach similar to active caching is active XML (AXML; Abiteboul, Benjelloun, Manolescu, Milo, & Weber, 2002). A cacheable template designed according to AXML employs calls or references to Web services, which look like <sc>rentdvd.com/getPopularDvdList()</sc>, and refers to the dynamic parts of the template. A run-time environment is required at the location where the templates are cached in order to parse the templates and trigger the calls to the referred Web services. We can say that AXML is an alternative form of arbitrary fragmentation in which the template of the dynamic page is cached at the proxy, but the fragments themselves are substituted by function calls that can be reused by other templates. The active caching and active XML approaches have not yet gained enough attention due to the fact that they require a trusted run-time environment at the proxies, a situation that raises many security issues.

Taking active caching a step further, Akamai has recently introduced EdgeComputing, a proxy-based platform that allows the execution of Java-based code for generating dynamic content (Davis, Parikh, & Weihl, 2004). According to EdgeComputing, the execution code of a Web application is split into two groups. The first group executes on the server while the second group, called the edge layer, is allowed to execute only on the secured proxies of Akamai. The edge-layer code is employed for frequently changing information such as product catalogs. There is no support, however, for content that relies on transactional databases such as online banking and e-commerce. In this case, the Web application is split into to parts as mentioned before.

Multicasting of Dynamic Content

It has been observed in early studies on workload characterization that the request distribution of documents in a Web site is Zipf like with parameter α less than 1 (Arlitt & Williamson, 1997; Breslau, 1998). Most recently, Krishnan, Raz, and Shavitt (2000) and Padmanabhan and Qui (2000) placed the parameter α between 1.4 and 1.6, which implies that fewer documents (about 2%) account for the most accesses (about 90%). These observations have motivated researchers to suggest the multicasting of hot pages, and several studies have proven the advantage of multicasting hot content in terms of bandwidth consumption and user-perceived latency (Azar, Feder, Lubetzky, Rajwan, & Shulman, 2001; Beaver, 2004). Dolev, Mokryn, Shavitt, and Sukhov (2002) introduces the HTTPM protocol for the transfer of hot dynamically generated documents over multicasting channels in conjunction with the use of HTTP for the unicasting (sent via HTTP requests) of less popular pages. Recently, a data-dissemination middleware that supports multicast push channels for hot documents, multicast pull channels for warm documents, and unicast channels has been developed (Chrysanthis, Pruhs, & Liberatore, 2003; Li, 2003). However, none of these approaches consider the fact that modern Web applications use content fragments and hence none of them propose the multicasting of hot content fragments.

Clustered Servers and Cooperative Proxies

The duplication of resources, either hardware or software, is a prevalent method for accelerating content generation and delivery. Clustered Web, database, and application servers are examples of server-side acceleration, whereas cooperative caches relate to proxy-side acceleration. While a cooperative caching approach for dynamic content has not yet emerged (possibly due to the complex caching characteristics of dynamic content), clustering is a popular practice for server-side acceleration. Amongst the three examples of server-side clustering mentioned above, the most challenging, and performance accelerating, is the replication of the application database. According to database clustering, an HTTP request that requires the read access of a data object can be served by any database in the cluster. However, a write access on a database object, triggered, for example, by a purchase order, must be performed on all databases at the expense of performance and service availability. Amza, Cox, and Zwaenepoel (2003) propose an interesting solution to this problem by using distributed versioning.

Quality of Service and Quality of Data

Quality of service is used to characterize the behavior or performance of an interactive system, whereas the quality of data (QoD) is used to characterize its goodness or functionality. An example of QoS that can be used to measure scalability is server throughput, which refers to the average number of requests that the server (or proxy) can handle within a period of (typically) a second. An example of QoD is the consistency between the data in the database and in a cache.

In the case of dynamic content, the two dominant metrics are user centric, namely, client-perceived latency for QoS and freshness for QoD. The client-perceived latency refers to the average response time from a client perspective and can be measured at the client side as well as safely at the proxy or server side (Adali, Candan, Papakonstantinou, & Subrahmanian, 1996; Gruser, Raschid, Zadorozhny, & Zhan, 2000).

The metric of freshness measures the relation between a cached dynamic object (page or fragment) and the underlying data objects involved in its generation. As a general rule, a chunk of dynamic content is considered fresh as long as its related data objects remain unmodified. Otherwise, a number of approaches have been proposed in the literature that estimates the degree of freshness or staleness in different ways (Cho & Garcia-Molina, 2000; Gal, 1999). One approach considers the time elapsed from the moment the underlying data objects are modified, whereas another considers the number of operations (or transactions) performed on the data objects such as insertions, updates, and deletions. Finally, another approach considers the degree of value divergence of the data objects, such as the amount of increase or decrease on a customer's balance. Nevertheless, the selection of an appropriate metric depends heavily on the application semantics.

Research on Performance vs. Freshness

A number of interesting approaches that deal with the problem of balancing dynamic-content performance and freshness are found in the literature. Labrinidis (2004) proposes the use of a server-side run-time component responsible for pregenerating (materializing) and caching selected content fragments. In addition, an importance weight is assigned to each fragment, which is then used by the runtime in order to compute the overall freshness of the Web application's content at any given time. The runtime also computes at any given time the current overall performance of the system in terms of average client response time. Performance and freshness thresholds are defined so that the runtime can modify the frequency of fragment materialization. Increased fragment materialization enhances server performance at the expense of content freshness.

Similarly, Li (2003) proposes a freshness-driven adaptive dynamic-content caching technique that attempts to coordinate the client request frequency with the synchronization cycle[3] of the cached documents in order to maintain the best possible content freshness for clients at the lowest overhead.

Finally, an approach called recency-latency employs a proxy-based run-time component that computes a combined score of content freshness and expected latency for a cached object (Bright & Raschid, 2002). This score is then compared against the preferences defined by the client's profile so that the runtime can select whether to reuse the cached version of the object or request a fresh version from the server.

The first two approaches are considered data driven in the sense that the generation of dynamic content is triggered by updates on the underlying data objects. In a nutshell, the idea is to maintain cached-content freshness to the highest possible degree toward meeting a certain performance goal. The third discussed approach is rather user driven because the decision to reuse the cached version or request a fresh version of a dynamic object is initiated by the clients through their HTTP requests. Consequently, the former two approaches are suitable for Web applications that do not interact much with their users by means of user input preferences. The content served in this case targets groups of clients of applications such as news sites, portals, and sport results sites. The latter approach is more suitable for interactive Web applications such as e-banking, online retailers, stock trading, and Web-based e-mail. The content served in this case is considered personalized (i.e., targets a single user based on her or his preferences or input submission), and the possibilities for content reuse across other clients are limited.

What's Next? Future Trends

Over the past 10 years, technology around dynamic content has mainly evolved across the two dimensions of caching and fragmentation. At the early stages, the need for increased response times and reduced network utilization motivated the evolution of caching strategies, while the diversity of modern Web applications stimulated the research around fragmentation and content polymorphism. Modern Web applications, however, are always in need for more efficient and sophisticated means of dynamic-content delivery. We finally discuss two open challenges that can stimulate further research.

The procedure of user authentication is a typical application of dynamic Web content technology. The problem with it is that it suffers from the overhead of (secured) server-side communication and computation. A possible migration of the authentication procedure from the server side closer to the client side would alleviate this network and computational overhead and enhance the browsing experience. Still, it requires the secure shipping and hosting of vendor code and application data from the server to, for example, a proxy. As we have seen earlier, a number of approaches, such as active caching, are a few steps away from achieving this. Nevertheless, a general-purpose content middleware that migrates both code and data at proxies, or even the client itself, remains a challenge.

Since data replication at the proxy side is still for read-only purposes (as seen in EdgeComputing by Akamai), client requests for data updates (i.e., an order placement or a message post) require all three of server-side processing, proxy cache invalidation, and update. The open challenge of supporting Web transactions without the immediate intervention of the server extends the user authentication example by requiring that (a) the cached data be writable and (b) the cached vendor code implement the appropriate database consistency model between cached and server-side data. Potential solutions must challenge important issues such as limited service availability imposed by a strong consistency model between the cached data and the original database server. In this respect, the issues of QoD in terms of freshness and the consistency of fragments in a page are still unresolved.

Conclusion

Dynamic Web content technology is definitely one the most exciting and applicable topics in the world of computer science and information technology. The literature encloses a large number of approaches and methodologies that attempt to accelerate the generation and delivery of dynamic content given that client needs are always on the rise. In this chapter, we have presented a summary of the most important of these approaches and methodologies that can serve as a starting point for further research and that could lead to the next evolution of dynamic-content middleware.

References

Abiteboul, S., Benjelloun, O., Manolescu, I., Milo, T., & Weber, R. (2002, August). *Active XML: Peer-to-peer data and Web services integration.* Paper presented at the Very Large Databases Conference, Hong Kong, China.

Adali, S., Candan, K. S., Papakonstantinou, Y., & Subrahmanian, V. S. (1996, June). *Query caching and optimization in distributed mediator systems.* Paper presented at the Special Interest Group on Management of Data Conference, Montreal, Canada.

Amza, C., Cecchet, E., Chanda, A., Cox, A., Elnikety, S., Gil, R., et al. (2002, November). *Specification and implementation of dynamic Web site benchmarks.* Paper presented at the IEEE Fifth Annual Workshop on Workload Characterization, Austin, TX.

Amza, C., Cox, A., & Zwaenepoel, W. (2003, June). *Distributed versioning: Consistent replication for scaling back-end databases of dynamic content Web sites.* Paper presented at the ACM/IFIP/Usenix Middleware Conference, Rio de Janeiro, Brazil.

Arlitt, M. F., & Williamson, C. L. (1997, October). Internet Web servers: Workload characterization and performance implications. *IEEE/ACM Transactions on Networking, 5*(1), 631-645.

Azar, Y., Feder, M., Lubetzky, E., Rajwan, E., & Shulman, N. (2001, November). *The multicast bandwidth advantage in serving a Web site.* Paper presented at the Third International Workshop on Networked Group Communication, London.

Beaver, J., Morsillo, N. W., Pruhs, K., Chrysanthis, P. K., & Liberatore, V. (2004, June). *Scalable dissemination: What's hot and what's not.* Paper presented at the Seventh International Workshop on the Web and Databases, ACM SIGMOD 2004 Conference, Paris.

Beaver, J., Pruhs, K., Chrysanthis, P. K., & Liberatore, V. (2004, July). *The multicast pull advantage in dissemination-based data delivery.* Third Hellenic Data Management Symposium.

Breslau, L., Cao, P., Fan, L., Phillips, G., & Shenker, S. (1999, March). *Web caching and zipf-like distributions: Evidence and implications.* Paper presented at the International Conference on Computer Communications, New York.

Bright, L., & Raschid, L. (2002, August). *Using latency-recency profiles for data delivery on the Web.* Paper presented at the Very Large Databases Conference, Hong Kong, China.

Cao, P., Zhang, J., & Beach, K. (1999, March). Active cache: Caching dynamic contents on the Web. *Distributed Systems Engineering, 6*(1), 43-50.

Cecchet, E., Chanda, A., Elnikety, S., Marguerite, J., & Zwaenepoel, W. (2003, June). *Performance comparison of middleware architectures for generating dynamic Web content.* Paper presented at the ACM/IFIP/Usenix Middleware Conference, Rio de Janeiro, Brazil.

Challenger, J., Iyengar, A., Witting, W., Ferstat, C., & Reed, P. (2000, March). *A publishing system for efficiently creating dynamic Web content.* Paper presented at the International Conference on Computer Communications, Tel-Aviv, Israel.

Cho, J., & Garcia-Molina, H. (2000, May). *Synchronizing a database to improve freshness.* Paper presented at the Special Interest Group on Management of Data Conference, Dallas, TX.

Chrysanthis, P. K., Pruhs, K., & Liberatore, V. (2003, January). *Middleware support for multicast-based data dissemination: A working reality.* Paper presented at the Eighth IEEE International Workshop on Object-Oriented Real-Time Dependable Systems, Guadalajara, Mexico.

Datta, A., Dutta, K., Ramamritham, K., Thomas, H. M., & VanderMeer, D. E. (2001, May). *Dynamic content acceleration: A caching solution to enable scalable dynamic Web page generation.* Paper presented at the Special Interest Group on Management of Data Conference, Santa Barbara, CA.

Datta, A., Dutta, K., Thomas, H. M., VanderMeer, D. E., Ramamritham, K., & Fishman, D. (2001, September). *A comparative study of alternative middle tier caching solutions to support dynamic Web content acceleration.* Paper presented at the Very Large Databases Conference, Rome.

Datta, A., Dutta, K., Thomas, H. M., VanderMeer, D. E., Suresha, & Ramamritham, K. (2002, June). *Proxy-based acceleration of dynamically generated content on the World Wide Web: An approach and implementation.* Paper presented at the Special Interest Group on Management of Data Conference, Madison, WI.

Davis, A., Parikh, J., & Weihl, W. E. (2004, May). *Edgecomputing: Extending enterprise applications to the edge of the Internet.* Paper presented at the International Word Wide Web Conference, New York.

Dolev, D., Mokryn, O., Shavitt, Y., & Sukhov, I. (2002, July). *An integrated architecture for the scalable delivery of semi-dynamic Web content.* Paper presented at the Seventh IEEE Symposium on Computers and Communications, Taormina, Italy.

Douglis, F., Haro, A., & Rabinovich, M. (1997, December). *HPP: HTML macro-preprocessing to support dynamic document caching.* Paper presented at the USENIX Symposium on Internet Technologies and Systems, CA.

Feldmann, A., Caceres, R., Douglis, F., Glass, G., & Rabinovich, M. (1999, March). *Performance of Web proxy caching in heterogeneous bandwidth environments.* Paper presented at the International Conference on Computer Communications, New York.

Gal, A. (1999, November). *Obsolescent materialized views in query processing of enterprise information systems.* Paper presented at the ACM International Conference on Information and Knowledge Management, Kansas City, MI.

Gruser, J.-R., Raschid, L., Zadorozhny, V., & Zhan, T. (2000, March). Learning response time for Web sources using query feedback and application in query optimization. *The International Journal on Very Large Data Bases, 9*(1), 18-37.

Holmedahl, V., Smith, B., & Yang, T. (1998, July). *Cooperative caching of dynamic content on a distributed Web server.* Paper presented at the IEEE International Symposium on High Performance Distributed Computing, Chicago.

Hunt, J. J., Vo, K. P., & Tichy, W. F. (1998, April). Delta algorithms an empirical analysis. *ACM Transactions on Software Engineering and Methodology, 7*(2), 192-214.

Iyengar, A., & Challenger, J. (1997, December). *Improving Web server performance by caching dynamic data.* Paper presented at the USENIX Symposium on Internet Technologies and Systems, CA.

Krishnamurthy, B., Wills, C. E., & Zhang, Y. (2001, November). *On the use and performance of content distribution networks.* Paper presented at the Internet Measurement Workshop, San Francisco.

Krishnan, P., Raz, D., & Shavitt, Y. (2000, October). The cache location problem. *IEEE/ACM Transactions on Networking, 8*(5), 568-582.

Labrinidis, A., & Roussopoulos, N. (2004, September). Exploring the tradeoff between performance and data freshness in database-driven Web servers. *The International Journal on Very Large Data Bases, 13*(3), 240-255.

Larus, J. R., & Parkes, M. (2001, June). *Using cohort scheduling to enhance server performance (extended abstract).* Paper presented at the Workshop on Languages, Compilers, and Tools for Embedded Systems, Snowbird, UT.

Li, W., Zhang, W., Liberatore, V., Penkrot, V., Beaver, J., Sharaf, M. A., et al. (2003, March). *An optimized multicast-based data dissemination middleware.* Paper presented at the 19th International Conference on Data Engineering, Bangalore, India.

Li, W. S., Po, O., Hsiung, W. P., Candan, K. S., & Agrawal, D. (2003, May). *Engineering and hosting adaptive freshness-sensitive Web applications on data centers.* Paper presented at the International Word Wide Web Conference, Budapest, Hungary.

Liu, Y. H., Dantzig, P., Wu, C.-F. E., Challenger, J., & Ni, L. M. (1996, May). *A distributed scalable Web server and its program visualization in multiple platforms.* Paper presented at the International Conference on Distributed Computing Systems, Hong Kong, China.

Luo, Q., & Naughton, J. F. (2001, September). *Form-based proxy caching for database-backed Web sites.* Paper presented at the International Conference on Very Large Data Bases, Rome.

Luo, Q., Naughton, J. F., Krishnamurthy, R., Cao, P., & Li, Y. (2000, May). *Active query caching for database Web servers.* Paper presented at the WebDB Conference, Dallas, TX.

Padmanabhan, V. N., & Qui, L. (2000, August). *The content and access dynamics of a busy Web site: Findings and implications.* Paper presented at the Conference on Applications, Technologies, Architectures, and Protocols for Computer Communication, Stockholm.

Pai, V. S., Druschel, P., & Zwaenepoel, W. (1999, June). *Flash: An efficient and portable Web server.* Paper presented at the USENIX 1999 Annual Technical Conference, Monterey, CA.

Papastavrou, S., Chrysanthis, P. K., Samaras, G., & Pitoura, E. (2001, March). An evaluation of the Java-based approaches to Web database access. *International Journal of Cooperative Information Systems, 10*(4), 401-422.

Papastavrou, S., Samaras, G., Evripidou, P., & Chrysanthis, P. K. (2003, November). *Fine-grained parallelism in dynamic Web content generation: The parse dispatch and approach.* Paper presented at the International Conference on Cooperative Information Systems, Catania, Sicily.

Psounis, K. (2002, July). *Class-based delta-encoding: A scalable scheme for caching dynamic Web content.* Paper presented at the International Conference on Distributed Computing Systems Workshops, Vienna.

Rabinovich, M., Xiao, Z., Douglis, F., & Kalmanek, C. R. (2003, June). *Moving edge-side includes to the real edge: The clients.* Paper presented at the USENIX Symposium on Internet Technologies and Systems, San Antonio, TX.

Ramaswamy, L., Iyengar, A., Liu, L., & Douglis, F. (2005, June). Automatic fragment detection in dynamic Web pages and its impact on caching. *IEEE Transactions on Knowledge and Data Engineering, 17*(6), 859-874.

Smith, B., Acharya, A., Yang, T., & Zhu, H. (1999, June). *Exploiting result equivalence in caching dynamic Web content.* Paper presented at the USENIX Symposium on Internet Technologies and Systems, Monterey, CA.

Spring, N. T., & Wetherall, D. (2000, August). *A protocol-independent technique for eliminating redundant network traffic.* Paper presented at the Conference on Applications, Technologies, Architectures, and Protocols for Computer Communication, Stockholm.

Wang, J. (1999). A survey of Web caching schemes for the Internet. *ACM Computer Communication Review, 25*(9), 36-46.

Welsh, M., Culler, D. E., & Brewer, E. A. (2001, October). *SEDA: An architecture for well-conditioned, scalable Internet services.* Paper presented at the ACM Symposium on Operating Systems Principles, Alberta, Canada.

Wolman, A., Voelker, G. M., Sharma, N., Cardwell, N., Karlin, A. R., & Levy, H. M. (1999, December). *On the scale and performance of cooperative Web proxy caching.* Paper presented at the ACM Symposium on Operating Systems Principles, Kiawah Island Resort, SC.

Yagoub, K., Florescu, D., Issarny, V., & Valduriez, P. (2000, September). *Caching strategies for data-intensive Web sites.* Paper presented at the Very Large Databases Conference, Cairo, Egypt.

Yuan, C., Chen, Y., & Zhang, Z. (2003, May). *Evaluation of edge caching/offloading for dynamic content delivery.* Paper presented at the International Word Wide Web Conference, Budapest, Hungary.

Chapter VI

Caching on the Web

Mehregan Mahdavi, The University of New South Wales, Australia

Boualem Benatallah, The University of New South Wales, Australia

Abstract

The World Wide Web provides a means for sharing data and applications among users. However, its performance, in particular providing fast response time, is still an issue. Caching is a key technique that addresses some of the performance issues in today's Web-enabled applications. Deploying dynamic data, especially in an emerging class of Web applications, called Web portals, makes caching even more interesting. In this chapter, we study Web caching techniques with focus on dynamic content. We also discuss the limitations of caching in Web portals and study a solution that addresses these limitations. The solution is based on the collaboration between the portal and its providers.

Introduction

The World Wide Web has influenced many aspects of life such as communication, education, business, shopping, and entertainment. There are many resources on the Internet; some provide data for being used and shared among users, while others are designed to provide services. For example, some Web sites such as Web sites of universities, people's home pages, and yellow and white pages provide data. Examples of Web sites that provide services include those used for online shopping, booking and buying flight tickets, and banking. Users find and access appropriate data or services through Web browsers.

Performance is one of the major issues in today's Web-enabled applications. Previous research has shown that the abandonment of Web sites dramatically increases with an increase in response time (Zona Research Inc., 2001), resulting in loss of revenue by businesses. In other words, providing fast response time is one of the critical issues that today's Web applications must deal with. Nowadays, many Web sites employ dynamic Web pages by accessing a back-end database and formatting the result into HTML (hypertext markup language) pages. Accessing the database and assembling the final result on the fly is an expensive process and a contributive factor to the performance issue. Server workload or failure, and network traffic are some other contributing factors for slow response times.

Caching is a key technique that addresses some of the performance issues of Web-enabled applications. Caching can improve the response time. As a result, customer satisfaction is increased and better revenue for the business is generated. In addition, network traffic and the workload on the providers' servers are considerably reduced. This in turn improves throughput and scalability, and reduces hardware and software costs.

In this chapter, we study caching solutions for Web applications with focus on dynamic content. We discuss the limitations of existing caching solutions in Web portals as an emerging class of Web applications, and we introduce a caching strategy based on the collaboration between the portal and its providers. Providers trace their logs, extract information to identify good candidates for caching, and notify the portal. Caching at the portal is decided based on the scores calculated by providers and is associated with objects. We also address the issue of heterogeneous scoring policies by different providers and introduce mechanisms to regulate them.

Web Caching Overview

A Web cache is located somewhere between the Web browser and the origin content provider and stores Web objects for future requests. Candidate Web objects for caching include HTML (Hyper Text Markup Language) pages, images, audio and video files, XML (eXtensible Markup Language) pages or fragments, query results (e.g., SQL [Stuctured Query Language]), results of dynamic Web pages (e.g., JSP [Java Server Pages] or Servlet, ASP [Active Server Pages], PHP [Personal Home Page Hypertext Preprocessor]), and programs (e.g., Java applets). When the cache server receives a request, it checks the cache to see whether the request can be answered locally or not. If it can, then the result is sent to the client. Otherwise, the request will be forwarded to the content provider. A Web cache can result in one or more of the following.

- Reducing network traffic and therefore reducing network costs for both content providers and consumers
- Reducing user-perceived delay

- Reducing load on the Web or application server and the database server for dynamically generated Web pages from back-end databases
- Increasing reliability and availability of Web and application servers
- Reducing hardware and support costs

Deploying cache servers close to clients (e.g., browser or proxy cache) reduces the network traffic. When a hit is detected, the content can be served to the user using the cached copy. This eliminates the need for receiving the content from the original server, which in turn reduces additional network traffic.

One of the important aspects of caching is that it can improve user-perceived delay. When the content is served from a shorter distance, users experience less delay. In other words, by answering requests locally, caches hide or reduce network latency. This is a very important aspect of caching for today's Web applications, and is directly relevant to the problems of losing e-commerce customers under the "8-second rule" according to Zona Research Inc (2001).

Caching can also improve performance by decreasing the load on the Web or application server or the database server. Caching the result of dynamic Web pages, such as JSP, ASP, or PHP pages, on the Web or application server reduces the computation cost for generating these pages from the back-end database each time the page is requested. Moreover, caching the result of parameterized queries, such as the result of SQL queries, on the database server and using them for subsequent requests reduces the computation cost. It improves performance when the query execution time is a major cost and when page generation requires access to the database through expensive SQL statements (Florescu, Yagoub, Valduriez, & Issamy, 2000; Labrinidis & Roussopoulos, 2000, 2001; Tan, Goh, & Ooi, 2001; Yagoub, Florescu, Valduriez, & Issamy, 2000).

Using local caches can hide temporary unavailability of network during network outages, making the network appear to be more reliable. This is especially important for the delivery of multimedia objects, such as video or audio, where consistent bandwidth and response times are important (Barish & Obraczka, 2000). Moreover, Web server availability can be improved by deploying cache servers in a reverse fashion. A reverse proxy is managed by or on behalf of content providers and improves the scalability of their site. In this case, cache servers improve the availability and fault tolerance of Web servers and the network seems more reliable. During Web server downtime, requests can be replied by cached copies even though the cached copy is not fresh. Research shows that most users prefer to be given stale data than being shown an error message if the server is down (Barish & Obraczka, 2000). The reverse proxy server can also act as a load balancer if a farm of Web or application servers is being used.

Finally, caching data on remote machines reduces the load on the origin server. When a hit occurs, the request can be answered using the cached copy, which otherwise should have been requested from the origin server. This results in lightening the load on the origin server, which in turn results in reducing the hardware and support costs.

Cache Hierarchy

Data items can be cached within the following nodes: the Web browser, proxy server, Web or application server, server accelerator, database server, database accelerator, transparent proxy, content delivery or distribution network (CDN) services, and application program. Caching a particular data item among eligible nodes depends both on the behavioral information (e.g., access and update pattern of original data) and on the processing capability of the given node (Yagoub et al., 2000).

Browser. Caching is a feature supported by nearly all traditional Web browsers in use on PCs (personal computers) today. Most browsers can store static objects, such as images that a user has accessed on the Web, to a directory on the user's hard drive. The browser is configured to allocate a certain amount of hard-drive space for this purpose. Browser caching can speed up the rendering of pages that contain cached objects. When a URL (uniform resource locator) is requested, the browser will first look at its cache. Depending on the browser's configuration, if it finds the object, the browser will load it from the cache rather than connecting to the origin server to get a new one. If the object is not available in the cache, then the browser retrieves it from the origin Web server and saves it to its local cache for future requests. A browser cache may help speed up the delivery of some static page elements, such as images, but does little to off-load the computation required to construct dynamic pages on the origin Web servers. Another reason browser caching is not very effective is that content providers tend to mark their statically generated content with special HTTP (hypertext transfer protocol) headers, such as a *Pragma: no-cache* header or an expiration in the past, that render the content not cacheable. Content providers do this because they want to maintain control over their content, which is especially important when that content is changing frequently. It is impossible for content providers to retrieve or check the freshness of cached objects at Web browsers once those objects have been delivered, so content providers are careful about which objects they allow the browser to cache (Oracle Corporation, 2001).

Proxy Server. Proxy servers are located between a large number of client machines such as an ISP (Internet service provider) or intranet users and the Internet. Similar to a browser cache, when a request is received, the proxy server checks its cache. If the object is available, it sends the object to the client. If the object is not available or if it has expired, it will request the object from the origin server and send it to the client. The object will be stored in the proxy's local cache for future requests. Squid Web Proxy Cache (http://www.squid-cache. org) is an example. Web browsers need to be configured to refer to proxy servers. Unlike the browser cache which deals with only one user, a proxy cache deals with a large number of users. The main problem of browser and proxy caches is that they only deal with static Web pages and do little or nothing about dynamic Web pages. Despite this, proxy caches are still the most common caching strategy for Web pages (Florescu et al., 2000; Yagoub et al., 2000). With emerging personalized Web pages and Web databases, Web pages are no longer static. Specifically, in e-business applications, Web pages are highly dynamic and personalized, which prevents them to be easily cached in proxy. Caching dynamic Web pages at a proxy server can be enabled by sending and caching some programs to the proxy server, such as Java applets. These programs generate the dynamic part of some Web pages while the static part can be directly provided from the cache (Li, Cao, & Dahlin, 2001; Luo, 2000; Luo, Naughton, Krishnamurthy, Cao, & Li, 2000).

Web or Application Server. The Web or application server is more likely to be able to cache dynamic Web pages. Generating dynamic Web pages (e.g., JSPs or Servlets) puts a lot of workload on Web or application servers and database servers due to processing and generating the dynamic content. Caching the result of such pages can reduce the workload on the Web or application server and back-end database (Candan, Li, Luo, Hsiung, & Agrawal, 2001). Under a hit, the Web or application server answers the request using the cache if it is still valid. Changes in the back-end database invalidate relevant Web pages that use the modified data. For this purpose, the Web or application server creates an entry for each cached page in a table called the cache validation table. Changes in the back-end database invalidate relevant entries in the table. When the Web or application server detects a hit, it will check the relevant entry to see whether the page is still valid or not. Current application servers such as BEA WebLogic (http://www.bea.com), IBM WebSphere Application Server (http://www.ibm.com), and Oracle Application Server (http://www.oracle.com) support caching dynamic Web pages. To provide more scalability, the application can be distributed over different Web or application servers.

Server Accelerator. Cache servers can be deployed in front of the Web or application server. This type of caching solution is known as reverse proxy or server acceleration. Unlike a proxy server that caches content from an infinite number of sources, a server accelerator caches content for one or a small number of origin servers. It intercepts requests to the Web or application server and either answers the request (if the result is cached) or forwards the request to the origin server. After a cache miss, the server accelerator caches any cacheable result returned by the origin server and forwards the reply back to the requester. It can be used to cache dynamic Web pages as well. Some examples include IBM WebSphere Cache Manager (http://www.ibm.com) and Oracle 9i AS Web Cache (http://www.oracle.com). They promise caching dynamic and personalized Web pages. They can decrease the processing overhead on the origin Web or application server and the back-end database server. Due to decreasing such overheads, they increase the throughput of the Web or application server. They also increase the reliability of the application server when the server is down or a crash occurs by serving the request from the cache. In this case, they can even answer the request with outdated cached copies. Some traces of research show that many applications (such as e-business applications) are better off serving outdated results than not answering the request at all.

Figure 1

- User requests content from origin server
- Accelerator receives the request and checks the cache. Two cases may occur.

Figure 1. Server acceleration

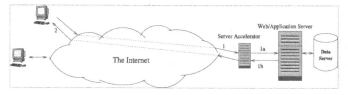

Miss:

- Cache server asks the origin server for the result or missing fragments
- Origin server sends the result
- Result is sent back to the user and a copy is stored in the cache

Hit:

- The copy in cache is fresh (by checking *Expires* in HTTP header) and is sent to user

Or:

- Accelerator asks the server for the freshness (using *If-Modified-Since* request)
- Server validates the freshness or sends the fresh result to the accelerator
- Result is sent back to the user and a copy is stored in the cache

Database Server. When dynamic Web pages are generated by querying a back-end database, the result of such queries can be cached at the database server. For example, caching the result of SQL queries on the database server as materialized views and using them for future requests can reduce computational cost on the database server. Similarly, the result of XML queries can be stored in an XML database.

Database Accelerator. Unlike the database cache, which is deployed at the data server, the database accelerator is deployed at the application server. It accelerates the processing of database queries by caching common data sets. This kind of caching is also known as middle-tier caching. A database accelerator increases the performance by reducing the communication between the application server and the database server. It also reduces the load on the back-end database resulting in more scalability. Products such as Oracle Application Server Database Cache (http://www.oracle.com) and TimesTen (http://www.timesten.com) provide this kind of caching.

Transparent Proxy. Transparent proxy caching eliminates one of the big drawbacks of the proxy-server approach: the requirement to configure Web browsers to refer to a specific proxy. Transparent caches work by intercepting HTTP requests and redirecting them to Web cache servers or cache clusters. This style of caching establishes a point at which different kinds of administrative control are possible, for example, deciding how to load balance requests across multiple caches (Barish & Obraczka, 2000).

Content Delivery or Distribution Network. Caching Web objects has already created a multimillion-dollar business: content delivery or distribution networks. Companies such as Akamai (http://www.akamai.com) have been providing CDN services for several years. CDN services are designed to deploy cache or replication servers at different geographical locations. The first generation of such services aimed at caching or replicating static Web pages or fragments such as HTML pages, images, and audio and video files at special servers called edge servers. These servers are deployed at different geographical areas all around the world and serve the requests or part of them. Static content is not likely to change frequently and will most likely be requested by other users in the same geographic area. In theory, moving content closer to the end users reduces the network traffic and also shortens response times. By caching frequently accessed content closer to end users, the number of router hops is reduced and data will reach its destination more quickly. Lightening the traffic to and from Web or application servers and database servers leaves more power for them to process and generate dynamic Web pages (Markatos, 2001; Oracle Corporation, 2001). Examples of edge servers include Akamai EdgeSuite (http://www.akamai.com) and IBM WebSphere Edge Server (http://www.ibm.com). They can be used in a reverse or forward set-up. In a reverse setup, the host name is used for the edge server. Therefore, it can intercept the request and make a decision to answer the request with its cache or forward the request to the origin server. In a forward setup, the request first goes to the Web or application server and a decision is made to serve the request based on the cache at the edge server(s). Using Edge Side Includes (ESI; http://www.esi.org), the origin server returns a template (rather than the actual Web page) with references to the fragments, such as image files, that exist in the edge server. ESI enables the definition of different cacheability for different fragments of an object. Processing ESI at these servers enables the dynamic assembly of objects at edge servers, which otherwise may be done at the server accelerator, proxy server, or browser. Detecting fragments for caching might also be done automatically (Ramaswamy, Iyengar, Liu, & Douglis, 2005). Typical customers of CDNs are large Web sites like cnn.com, yahoo.com, and microsoft.com. Note that the caches are not necessarily filled with the most popular content but rather by the content of the Web sites buying the service.

Figure 2

- User requests content from origin server
- Edge server receives the request and checks the cache. Two cases may occur.

Miss:

  ○ Edge server asks the origin server for the result or missing fragments
  ○ Origin server sends the result
  ○ Result is sent back to the user and a copy is stored in the cache

Hit:

  ○ The copy in cache is fresh (by checking *Expires* in HTTP header) and is sent to user

Or:

  ○ Edge server asks the server for the freshness (using *If-Modified-Since*)
  ○ Server validates the freshness or sends the fresh result to the edge server
  ○ Result is sent back to the user and a copy is stored in the cache

Application Program. Some applications may need a customized caching technique. Therefore, the existing caching solutions might be insufficient. Application-level caching is normally

Figure 2. Edge servers (reverse setup)

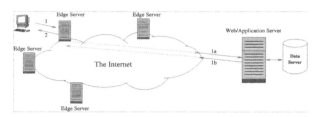

enabled by providing a cache API (application program interface), allowing application writers to explicitly manage the cache to add, delete, and modify cached objects. A system that provides a generic application-level cache is presented in Degenaro, Iyengar, and Ruvellou (2001). Object Caching Service for Java (OCS4J) is a caching system used in Oracle9i that enables caching static and nonstatic Java objects (Bortvedt, 2004). OCS4J is also referred to as JSR-107. JSRs (Java specification requests) are the specifications of caching such caching systems for the Java platform (Sun Microsystems, 2004). JCache Open Source is an effort to make an open-source version of JSR-107 (http://www.jcache.sourceforge.net). JCS (Java Caching System) is an attempt by Apache (http://www.apache.org) to build a system close to JCache based on JSR-107 (Apache Software Foundation, 2004).

Figure 3

- User requests content from origin server
- Server replies to the request with in-line references to fragments included in edge server
- Client machine asks the edge server for the fragments
- Fragments are sent to the client machine and assembled at client's machine

Figure 3. Edge servers (forward setup)

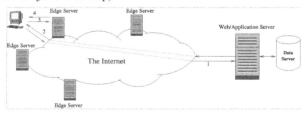

Caching Issues

Despite the advantages of caching, there are some issues that should be considered when applying caching techniques.

- **Misleading Statistics:** Many e-commerce Web sites need to know the number of hits they get because their businesses are valued by the number of hits they receive. If the content is delivered by cache without notifying the origin server, the user statistics collected on the origin server will be misleadingly low. This is one reason for many content providers to make their content noncacheable, for example, by specifying a *Pragma: no-cache* header or an expiration date in the past (Oracle Corporation, 2001).

- **Copyright Protection:** Providers of copyrighted material want to make their material available only to those who have arranged to pay a fee, such as through prepayment for an access code, by credit card, or in some cases through direct electronic payment via e-cash. A potentially serious problem with caching is that copyrighted materials residing in a cache are available for further access, either from the original end user or other end users. There is no mechanism to enable payment to the copyright holder for such secondary access. Given that proxy cache servers relabel requests for information from the end user to the server, it becomes difficult for such payment mechanisms to work. There is also a legal issue of whether caching without the explicit permission of the copyright owner results in infringement, even in the case that no payment is demanded. At present, the only way of dealing with this situation is for the copyright holder to tag the material as noncacheable. This prevents it from being served to secondary users, but also effectively prevents it from being cached. As more sites choose to enforce copyright in such a manner, the effectiveness of existing caching schemes will be severely impaired.

- **Privacy:** A cache implicitly contains records of an individual's Web-browsing activities. This is more of an issue with local caches since an ownership relationship exists between cache files and the end user. At the level of a proxy cache server, such information is lost due to the multiple-access nature that is its reason for existence. Whether the access trail in a local cache is more easily examined than network activity logs or direct packet-level traces is open to some question; however, insofar as caching may facilitate snooping on an end user's habits and activities, it holds great potential for abuse.

- **Security:** Security issues regarding the use of the Internet for secure data transfer such as for personal information or financial transactions are challenging. For example, in a university database, some data can be only accessed by academics. If these data are cached in a proxy and a student is going to access these data, there should be mechanisms to prevent him or her from accessing these data. It should be possible to efficiently impose the security policy of data sources on cached data. However, if some data are cached outside the data source, imposing access policy to cached data by data sources will be a challenging issue. Clearly, the caching of pages exchanged in a secure transaction should be protected from secondary unauthorized access. However, simply preventing secure transactions from being cached forces the end user to re-request the data from the content provider. As more transactions are made in a secure manner, caching will lose its effectiveness. One of the solutions to security issues is the use of encrypted sessions using, for example, the secure socket-layer (SSL) protocol for Web transactions.

Cache Replacement Strategy

Traditional cache replacement strategies such as first in, first out (FIFO) and least recently used (LRU) were developed to solve the page-level caching problem and thus may not be suitable for Web objects. Page-level caching was developed in the context of executing programs in virtual memory and involves maintaining a cache of fixed-size objects and exploiting the working-set behavior of programs. Web caching differs from this in dealing with objects that are heterogeneous in type and size and whose access patterns do not necessarily follow a working-set model. Surveys of Web cache replacement strategies are presented in Podlipnig and Boszormenyi (2003) and Balamash and Krunz (2004). Some of the cache replacement strategies targeted at Web objects include the following:

- The recency of Web objects is considered in the replacement strategy of Cao and Irani (1997). It indicates that the probability of access to Web objects dramatically decreases as the time since the last access increases.

- Least likely to be used (LLU) evicts objects that are less likely to be used in future (Datta, Dutta, Thomas, VanderMeer, & Ramamritham, 2002). This is achieved by mining access logs and extracting association rules between objects.

- LRUMIN favors smaller sized objects to minimize the number of objects replaced (Aggrawal, Wolf, & Yu, 1999). If there is no space in the cache for the newly arrived object of size S, an object of at least size S is removed from the cache. Among such objects, the least recently used one is evicted. Otherwise, objects of at least size $S / 2$ are removed in LRU order. Otherwise, the same thing is done for objects of at least size $S / 4$ and so forth until enough space is made.

- The size strategy (Aggrawal et al., 1999) assigns larger objects a higher priority for removal. If there are two objects with the same size, the least recently accessed one is removed first. This uses the idea that removing a large object leaves more space for a number of small objects, which are also believed to be accessed more frequently on the Web (traces of Web access logs show that most requests are for small objects; Williams & Abrams, 1996).

- Size-adjusted LRU (SLRU; Aggrawal, 1996) chooses the objects with the best cost-to-size ratio, which is defined as $1(S_i.\Delta T_k)$. S_i is the size of object i and ΔT_k is the number of accesses since the last time object i was accessed. In other words, it sorts the objects in order of nondescending values of $S_i.\Delta T_k$, and then greedily picks up the objects with the highest values and purges them one by one from the cache until enough space for the incoming object is created.

- Size-adjusted and popularity-aware LRU (LRU-SP; Cheng & Kambayashi, 2000) addresses the missing part of SLRU where objects with similar size are treated equally regardless of their popularity. LRU-SP uses both the size and popularity of Web objects in the context of LRU. Given that f_i is the number of accesses to object i since it was cached, LRU-SP uses the following cost-to size ratio: $f_i/(S_i.\Delta T_k)$. In other words, LRU-SP sorts the objects in order of nondescending values of $\Delta T_k/f_i$, and then greedily picks up the objects with the highest values.

- GreedyDual (Young, 1994) takes into account the different costs of fetching objects into the cache. The original GreedyDual algorithm only considers the situation where all the objects have the same size, but the costs of fetching them into the cache is different. According to this algorithm, each cached page p is associated with a non-negative value H. This is initially set to the cost of bringing the object into the cache. When a replacement is needed, the object with the lowest H value (H_{min}) is removed and the H value of all the objects in the cache is reduced by H_{min}. Upon accessing a page, its H value is restored to the initial value. Through this way of reducing H values of objects and restoring them when they are accessed, this algorithm integrates the locality of accesses and replacement cost.

- To incorporate different-sized objects, GreedyDual-Size (P. Cao & Irani, 1997) extends the GreedyDual algorithm by setting H to the cost-per-size ratio *Cost / Size* of objects. *Cost* is the cost of bringing the object into cache, and *Size* is the size of the object in bytes. Depending on the goal of the replacement algorithm, the cost will have different definitions. If the goal is to maximize the hit ratio, *Cost* is set to 1. However, it is set to the download time if minimizing the user-perceived delay is considered. In the general case, the total network cost should be considered. A good implementation of GreedyDual-Size avoids k subtractions when an object is replaced, where k is the number of objects in the cache. This is achieved by using an inflation value of H_{min} and offsetting all future settings of H by H_{min}.

- Site-based LRU uses the name of Web sites for the cache replacement strategy (Wong & Yeung, 2001). When a user requests an object from a site, the site name is inserted at the top of a list rather than the object name, and the object is stored under the newly inserted site. In this approach, only a limited amount of a site's objects are cached, which is specified by *Max_Ob*. When an object arrives from a site that already has *Max_Ob* objects in the cache, the least recently used object from the site will be removed and the newly arrived object will be inserted in the cache. This prevents caching the unpopular objects of a popular Web site. Each time an object is requested, its site name moves to top of the site list and the least recently accessed sites migrate to the bottom of the list. When a replacement is required, the system chooses the last sites in the list and their related objects.

Cache Coherency

Changes on original data sources should be effectively propagated to cached copies. In other words, the cached copies should be consistent with the original data. This can be achieved either by invalidating or refreshing the copy of data in the cache. The decision between these two options should be made using a cost-based approach based on the usefulness of the data item. If the data item is likely to be accessed frequently and will not change in the near future, it is worth refreshing the cache. Otherwise, the copy in the cache should be invalidated. It is desirable also to send only changes (deltas) to the cache instead of resending the whole data set. By receiving the delta, the cache manager updates the data in the cache (Manolescu, Bouganim, Fabret, & Simon, 2001; Marian, Abiteboul, Cobena, & Mignet, 2001; Nguyen, Abiteboul, Cobena, & Preda, 2001; Tatarinov, Ives, & Halvey, 2001).

Basic HTTP provides mechanisms for caching that aim at either eliminating the need to send requests to servers or eliminating the need to send full responses by servers. The former reduces the number of network round-trips while the latter reduces network bandwidth usage. A server or client uses caching directives and includes them in the *Cache-Control* header. The two major mechanisms for caching provided by HTTP are the *Expires* response header and the *If-Modified-Since* (IMS) request header (Fielding et al., 1999).

- The *Expires* response header is the simplest mechanism to determine the freshness of a cached object. It simply requires comparing the object's *Expires* response header to the current time (using GMT [Greenwich mean time]). This mechanism is also referred to as time-to-live (TTL). Generally, the cache manager, without disturbing the Web or application server where the object was originated, can serve objects that have not yet expired. If the content providers know the time that the content changes, this approach takes full advantage of caching. Otherwise, they have to set a short expiry time or an expiry time in the past to prevent the object from being cached. This overcomes the benefit of caching. This mechanism aims at eliminating the need to send subsequent requests to the same object before it expires.

- The *If-Modified-Since* request header is another mechanism the cache server uses to manage cache coherency. The cache server serves cache copies to the user after checking with the origin server if a newer version is available. If a newer version exists, the cache server will request it from the origin server and refreshes its cache as it serves the new object. If the object has not changed, the cache server delivers the cached object. This mechanism aims at eliminating the need to send a full response if the object is still valid; that is, only a validation response message indicating a response status of 304 (not modified) is returned by the server.

In applications involving data such as stock-market data or flight information, the requirement for coherency is very strict; in others such as the catalog of a bookshop, the coherency requirement is not so strict and out-of-date data can be tolerated to some extent. The former is said to require a strong coherency mechanism while the latter needs only a weak coherency mechanism. In weak cache coherency, a stale copy of a document might be returned to the user; with strong cache coherency, no stale copy of a modified document will be returned to the user, and the coherence between cached copies and original data is always maintained (L. Y. Cao & Ozsu, 2002). To be more precise, coherency requirements can be distinguished in the following three categories.

- **Strict:** Cached copies must be coherent with the original data at all times.
- **Strong:** It is desirable to have coherency between the cached copies and the original data, but the coherency requirement is not as strict as in the former.
- **Weak:** Stale copies of cached data are acceptable to some extent.

The problem is therefore maintaining the required level of coherency according to the requirements of the application. Maintaining coherency can be achieved either by a pull or push approach.

Pull-Based Coherency Mechanism

In the pull approach, the cache server contacts the source to check the freshness. If the original data have changed, the cache server either refreshes the cache by requesting the data or invalidates the cache copy by removing it from the cache. This is also called client polling. There are two main methods based on which coherency is to be achieved.

- Polling-Every-Time
- Time-to-Refresh (TTR)

In polling-every-time, whenever a cache hit occurs, the cache server sends an IMS message to the origin server to check the freshness. The problem of this mechanism (although it provides a strong cache consistency) is the overhead involved in sending an IMS message each time a cache hit occurs. The overhead includes generating these messages by the cache server and processing these messages by the origin data server. Moreover, the network overhead of these messages results in delays in response messages. Although the cache copy might be fresh when the hit occurs, the user has to experience the delay of sending and receiving IMS messages.

According to TTR, each client periodically checks the data source in a certain time period. A smaller TTR provides stronger coherency but increases the number of refresh messages. A larger TTR decreases the number of refresh messages but provides weaker coherency. Adaptive TTR aims at determining the TTR based on change frequency, coherency requirements, network traffic, and so forth (Deolasee, Katkar, Panchbudhe, Ramamritham, & Shenoy, 2001; Ramamritham, Deolasee, Kathar, Panchbudhe, & Shenoy, 2000).

In a pull-based approach, TTL could be used to decrease the number of IMS messages in polling-every-time or to avoid unnecessary refreshes in TTR. According to TTL, each object (document, image file, etc.) is assigned a TTL. This is a reasonable value normally set by the content provider. This shows approximately when the object will expire. In other words, before this time, a cached copy of the object can be used, but not after this time. If a cache server receives a request after the TTL has expired, the object will be requested from the original server. Selecting an appropriate value for TTL is a challenge. Smaller values provide higher coherency but less effective caching. In this case, objects expire sooner and more requests are sent to the original server. More network bandwidth is used and users will experience more latency. Larger values of TTL provide better performance but lower cache coherency. Adaptive TTL approaches try to overcome the problem by adapting the TTL values based on the update frequency of the object (Gwertzman & Seltzer, 1996). If it has not been modified for a long time, then it tends to stay unchanged for a longer time than an object that has changed frequently. However, all TTL-based approaches fail to provide strong coherency and can only be used when weak cache coherency is acceptable.

In Gwertzman and Seltzer (1996), the notion of an object's age is used to define the time. They define a term called *update threshold* as a percentage of an object's age. If the time since the last validation exceeds the product of the update threshold and the object's age, then the object becomes invalid. In this case, upon invalidation or under the next request, a validation message will be sent to the origin to check the validity of the object. Piggy-back client validation (PCV; Krishnamurthy & Willis, 1997) is an algorithm that checks the validity of objects in advance. Through communication with the data server, the cache checks a list of objects to validate that their TTLs have expired. This method reduces the chance of stale objects being served. Sending a bunch of validation messages reduces the communication overhead as well.

Push-Based Coherency Mechanism

In a push approach, the server takes the responsibility of refreshing or invalidating cached copies. Content providers can achieve this by keeping a list of all cached objects and notifying the client cache manager when the content changes. The invalidation algorithm frees the client manager from the burden of sending IMS messages. To ensure strong consistency, if an object A gets changed on the server, the server must send out an invalidation message right away to all the caches that store a copy of A. In this way, cache managers do not need to worry about object validity. As long as an invalidation message is not received, the object is valid. The invalidation approach requires the server to play a major role in the consistency-control process over cached objects. This might be a significant burden for the Web server because it has to maintain the state of each object that has ever been accessed, as well as a list of the addresses of all the requesters. Such a list is likely to grow very fast, especially for popular objects. The server has to maintain at least a big storage space for keeping the lists. On the other hand, although an object is stored in a cache whose address is kept on the server list, this object might be evicted from the cache later on because it is rarely, if ever, requested again, or because the cache manager needs free space for newly arrived objects. Therefore, it does not make sense for the server to keep the address of that cache on the list. Even worse, if the object is about to be changed, the server has to send invalidation messages to the caches whose addresses are on the list but no longer keep the object, which adds unnecessary traffic to the network.

To enforce a strong cache consistency, all invalidation messages should be acknowledged. The server delays the updates until it receives all the acknowledgements from the cache servers to whom invalidation messages were sent (L. Y. Cao & Ozsu, 2002; Rabinovich & Spatscheck, 2001). However, the unreachability of any cache server causes others to keep waiting, and none of them gets an updated version of the object. This results in stale copies of the object being used (L. Y. Cao & Ozsu, 2002; Yu, Breslau, & Shenker, 1999).

Table 1. A classification of cache coherency mechanisms

	Pull	Push
Strict	Polling-every-time	Invalidation
Strong	TTR	Invalidation, TTR
Weak	TTL, PCV, TTR	PSI, TTR

Multicasting is one of the modifications to the invalidation mechanism that addresses the performance issue faced by the server. As discussed in Krishnamurthy and Willis (1998), a multicast group is assigned to each object. Each multicast group is a list of cache servers and is maintained by routers. When an update occurs, the server sends an invalidation message to the corresponding remulticast group. It is the router's job to send individual invalidation messages to all the caches whose names are included in the list (L. Y. Cao & Ozsu, 2002).

Piggyback server invalidation (PSI; Krishnamurthy & Willis, 1998) is a variation of server invalidation that sends invalidation messages in batches. Sending invalidation messages in batches reduces the server workload compared to sending individual invalidations as it reduces the number of invalidation messages. However, a strong coherency cannot be guaranteed using this mechanism.

Combining Push and Pull

According to Ramamritham et al. (2000), Deolasee et al. (2001), L. Y. Cao and Ozsu (2002), and Liu and Cao (1998), push and pull approaches have complementary properties regarding coherency, overheads (i.e., network, computation, and space), and resilience.

- **Coherency:** In the pull approach based on polling-every-time, strong coherency is guaranteed. In the push approach, when a change happens in the source that affects the freshness of a cached item, the source will either invalidate or refresh the cached copy. In other words, the push approach can offer high coherency. In a TTR-based mechanism either on a pull- or push-based approach, the provided coherency depends on the TTR. A smaller TTR provides stronger consistency but increases the number of refresh messages. A larger TTR decreases the number of refresh messages but provides weaker consistency. Invalidation can provide either a strict or strong coherency depending on how it is implemented and how its parameters are set. Table 1 shows a classification of cache coherency mechanisms.

- **Network Overheads:** A pull-based approach requires two messages per poll: an HTTP request followed by a response. In the TTR-based pull approach, a cache server polls the server based on its estimate of how frequently the data is changing. If the data actually changes at a slower rate, then the cache server might poll more frequently than necessary. Hence, a pull-based approach is liable to impose a large load on the network. In the push-based approach, the number of messages transferred over the network is equal to the number of times the data changes. However, a push-based approach may push to clients who are no longer interested in a piece of information, thereby incurring unnecessary message overheads.

- **Computational Overheads:** Computational overheads for a pull-based approach result from the need to deal with individual pull requests. After getting a pull request from the cache server, the origin server only has to look up the latest data value and respond. On the other hand, when the server has to push changes to the proxy, for each change that occurs, the server has to check if the coherency requirement for any of the caches has been violated. This computation is directly proportional to the rate of arrival of new data values and the number of unique temporal coherency requirements associated with that data value.

- **Space Overheads:** A pull-based approach is stateless, meaning that neither the origin server nor the cache server needs to store any information for coherency purposes. In contrast, in a push-based approach, the server must maintain some information such as the consistency requirement for each client and the latest pushed value, along with the state associated with an open connection. Since this state is maintained throughout the duration of client connectivity, the number of clients that the origin server can handle may be limited when the space overhead becomes large (resulting in scalability problems).

- **Resilience:** By virtue of being stateless, a pull-based server is resilient to failures. In contrast, a push server maintains crucial state information about the needs of its clients; this state is lost when the server fails. Consequently, the client's coherency requirements will not be met until the cache server detects the failure and reregisters the coherency requirements with the server. Failures can be classified in three groups, each of which has different implications on the behavior of the system.

    o **Origin Server:** In case of server failures, the state at the server is lost. Most of the push algorithms require the state to be maintained at the server and hence their correctness may get compromised in such cases. Cache coherency is not guaranteed until the state is reconstructed at the server

    o **Cache Server:** The cache server may also fail. An origin server has to allocate resources to each cache server. As resources are valuable, in case of unreachable clients, these resources must be reclaimed.

    o **Communication:** Communication failures occur either due to socket failures at any one of the ends, network congestion, or network partition. Push-based techniques must employ special mechanisms to deal with such errors. Otherwise, the state information kept by the server will be incorrect.

- **Scalability:** Pull servers are generally stateless and hence scalable. Cache servers deployed all over the world are pull based and stateless. A user sends a request and waits for the response. The primary consideration has been to make Web servers scalable. This works for many normal applications, but for data that is changing rapidly, it will not be so effective. When data at a source are changing very fast, the cache server will generate a large number of requests to keep its cache synchronized with the source. Thus, there will be a large overhead in opening and closing the connections. Also, the computational load on the server becomes high because it has to respond to far more requests. Push servers have complementary characteristics. The server has to keep network connections open and allocate enough buffers to handle each client. With a large number of clients, state space and network resources can soon become bottlenecks and the server may start dropping requests. In short, scalability issues may arise because of the excessive server computation and network traffic, or the state space maintained at the server and resources allocated (such as sockets), and there is a clear trade-off between these two constraints.

In summary, the pull approach does not offer high coherency when the data change rapidly and strong consistency is required. Achieving high coherency needs a small TTR, which in turn increases network traffic and incurs extra workload on the origin server to process

Table 2. Comparison of push and pull

	Resilience	Coherency	Overhead		
			Network	Computation	State Space
Push	Low	High	Low	High	High
Pull	High or low	Low	High	Low	Low

messages. This workload will be significant if the number of clients is large. On the other hand, the push approach is more likely to offer high coherency for rapidly changing data and/or strict coherency requirements. However, it increases the overhead on the origin data server to produce and send push messages. Moreover, the approach is less resilient to failures as it has to store state information for clients.

These properties indicate that a push-based approach is suitable when a client expects its coherency requirements to be satisfied with high fidelity, or when the communication overheads are a bottleneck. A pull-based approach is better suited to less frequently changing data or for less stringent coherency requirements, and when resilience to failures is important. As is clear from the discussion, neither push nor pull alone is sufficient for the efficient dissemination of dynamic data. The complementary properties of the two approaches indicate the need for having an approach that combines the advantages of both while not suffering from any of their disadvantages. The comparison between push and pull is summarized in Table 2

A lease is one attempt to combine push and pull. Leases are like contracts given to lease holders over some property. Whenever some client sends a request to a server for a certain document, the server returns that document along with a lease. In other words, a server takes the responsibility of informing the client about any changes during the lease period. Once a lease expires, the client must contact the server and renew the lease. The client can use the cached copy while it has a valid lease over the data item. During the valid lease period, the client remains in push mode and is switched back to pull mode after the lease expires. Thus, the client is alternatively served in push and pull modes. When the lease expires, upon the next request of the object, the cache manager will send IMS messages to the origin server, and the server either responds with the new version of the object or, if the object has not been changed yet, extends the lease and returns that to the client; then the same rule applies. It is very important to choose a good lease period. For long lease periods, the client remains in push mode for most of the time, and the scalability problem may arise. On the other hand, for small values, the lease renewal cost may be very high. The trade-off between storage space and control messages depends on the duration of the leases. By choosing a smaller lease duration, this approach behaves like a pull-based system, and by choosing a larger lease duration, it behaves like a push-based system (Duvuri, Shenoy, & Tewari, 2000).

The lease algorithm can maintain strong cache coherency while keeping servers from indefinitely waiting due to a client failure. If a server cannot contact a client, it delays updating the object until the unreachable client's lease expires, and from then on it becomes the client's responsibility to contact the server for validation. On the other hand, the lease algorithm needs to be implemented both at the client side and on the server.

As with the TTL algorithm, the lease duration affects the efficiency of the algorithm itself. If the lease value is shorter than the interval between two requests, every subsequent request comes when the current lease has already expired. In this case, leasing becomes polling-every-time, which is far from desirable. However, this does not mean that a long lease is better. Having a very long lease forces the server to delay object updates until that lease expires. This problem can be solved by introducing the idea of a volume lease in addition to leases on individual objects (Yin, Alvisi, Dahlin, & Lin, 1999). In this approach, each volume lease is assigned to a set of related objects on the same server. In order to use a cached object, a client must hold the leases on both the object and the volume it belongs to. The cache manager cannot respond to a user request with a cached object unless both the object and volume lease on that object are valid. The server is free to update an object as soon as either the volume or object lease on the object has expired. By making object leases long and volume leases short, the server can make object updates without long delays. Meanwhile, long object leases prevent the cache manager from having to validate individual objects frequently.

Adaptive leases determine the lease duration based on current information such as access and update frequencies, the amount of available storage space for keeping state information, and the workload on the original server (Duvuri et al., 2000).

To combine push and pull, the proxy can operate in pull mode using some TTR algorithm while the server is in push mode knowing the coherency requirement (Ramamritham et al., 2000). Using this requirement and proxy access patterns, the server tries to predict when a client is going to poll next. If it determines that within this predicted time the client is likely to miss a relevant change, it pushes that change to the client. For predicting the client connection times, the server may run the TTR algorithm in parallel with the client, or use some simpler approximation of it. In the ideal case, the coherency offered will be 100%, but due to synchronization problems and other factors, it will be slightly less. However, it will always be much greater than pull. Because of the pull component, the resilience of the system will be high. Also, due to the push component, communication overheads will be low. This algorithm has parameters, such as window size for pushing the changes to the client, that swing it toward more push or more pull, and thus its performance in terms of fidelity and coherency can be controlled.

Another possibility is to divide incoming clients at the server into either push or pull clients and dynamically switch them to one or the other mode (Ramamritham et al., 2000). If resources are plentiful, every client is given a push connection irrespective of its coherency requirements. This ensures that the best coherency is offered. As more and more clients start requesting the service, resource contention may arise at the server, leading to performance problems. Some clients are then shifted to pull mode. Thus, valuable resources are freed and the system scales properly. When resources again become available, high-priority clients can be switched back to push mode, thus ensuring high coherency. The most important issue is how to assign priorities to different clients. Some of the possible parameters are the access frequency of each client, the temporal coherency requirement, and the network bandwidth available. Clearly, no single criterion suffices, but collectively they have the potential to offer high average coherency while keeping the system scalable.

Dynamic-Content Caching

While static Web pages were sufficient for the first generation of Web sites, they cannot support the requirements of many of today's Web applications such as e-businesses (Oracle Corporation, 2001). Dynamic Web pages are automatically generated by querying a back-end database and wrapping the result in HTML format. A JSP or Servlet, ASP, or PHP page is usually used to query the database and produce an appropriate HTML file. Regenerating a Web page, even with the same input parameters, may result in a different HTML page as the underling data may have changed since the last time the database was queried. While the static part of such a Web page can be cached, the dynamic part may not be easily cached. Thus, the resulting Web page can be assembled by requesting the dynamic part (Aberdeen Group, 2001; Chidlovskii & Borgho, 2000; Datta, Dutta, Ramamritham, Thomas, & VanderMeer, 2002). To enable caching dynamic parts, the changes on the back-end database should be effectively detected. These changes should then invalidate or refresh cached copies (Anton, Jacobs, Liu, Parker, Zeng, & Zhong, 2002; Candan et al., 2001; Challenger, Iyengar, & Dantzig, 1999; Oracle Corporation). In what follows, we refer to such content as dynamic Web pages or dynamic objects. Dynamic content can be categorized into two groups.

- The first group includes pages that are assembled on the fly based on the user request preference. These include personalized Web pages for users or user groups containing different images, news pages, and so forth, such as My Yahoo.

- The second group includes pages that are generated dynamically by a program running on a Web server, typically with access to a back-end database (e.g., through JDBC [Java Database Connectivity]) and formatting the results into HTML or some other format for presentation. Such dynamic pages clearly depend on the current values in the underlying data store. When such underlying data are modified (e.g., the price of a product has changed), a number of pages are typically affected.

The latter is more complicated from the coherency point of view. Determining the relevant objects based on the changes in the back-end database is more challenging.

Dynamic Web pages (e.g., those produced by JSPs or Servlets) can be cached at a cache server. Web or application servers or server accelerators are more capable of caching such content. For this purpose, a lookup table is kept at the Web or application server or server accelerator, which stores the URI (unified resource identifier) of the cached page. When a change (e.g., in the back-end database) affects the freshness of the page, the relevant entry in the lookup table will be invalidated. When a cache hit occurs at the Web or application server, the lookup table is probed to see if the page is still fresh or not. If it is fresh, then the request can be answered by cache. Similarly, if a hit occurs at a server accelerator, a validation request message is sent to the Web or application server to validate the cache. The Web or application server sends a reply indicating a positive or negative reply. If positive, the object can be served by the accelerator from its cache. Otherwise, the Web or application server sends the object to the accelerator.

There are different solutions to relating changes in the back-end database to the freshness of a page in the cache. Triggers are one option that the content provider can use to cause changes on the base data to validate (refresh) or invalidate the cached copy. When a limited number of cache servers is involved, it is feasible to make use of such triggers. However, managing and handling triggers involves overhead on the data server, and this overhead increases significantly as the number of cache servers increases.

Using materialized views is another option for queries submitted on base data. When the data are generated by the data server, they are cached as materialized views either on the data server or the Web or application server, and triggers can then be defined on these materialized views. The difference with the previous approach is that in this approach, the views can be managed by the application (if it runs the same DBMS [database management system] as the data server or a DBMS that can collaborate with the data server for view management). It provides a more expressive way for defining and using triggers, but also incurs a significant workload for view and trigger management on the database server (Anton et al., 2002).

An alternative approach (to using database mechanisms) for invalidation is to use the URLs that invoke access to the back-end database. Fine-grained invalidation (e.g., by an exact URL resulting from an HTML form with the *GET* method) incurs a lot of workload, but the result is more accurate. Coarse-grained invalidation (e.g., invalidation of all cache copies by a similar URI prefix) incurs less workload on the data server but is less accurate. An example of coarse-grained invalidation is when something changes in a table, all queries on this table are invalidated regardless of whether the change affects the query result or not. By using a combination of fine-grained and coarse-grained invalidation, it is possible to reach a trade-off between the workload and the invalidation quality (Candan, Agrawal, Li, Po, & Hsiug, 2002).

Another option is using server logs to detect changes and invalidate relevant entries, as proposed in CachePortal (Candan et al., 2001). CachePortal intercepts and analyzes three kinds of system logs to detect changes on base data and invalidate the relevant entries: HTTP request and delivery logs, which determine the requested page; query-instance request and delivery logs, which determine the query issued on the database based on the user query; and database update logs. A sniffer module finds the map between the query instances and URLs based on HTTP and query-instance logs and generates a QI (query instance) to URL map table. An invalidator module uses the database update logs and invalidates cached copies based on the updates and the QI or URL map table. This approach needs to keep a state space for all cached data. Moreover, it cannot guarantee 100% freshness of cached data as the invalidator module may not be able to process logs and invalidate cached copies in real time. In order to guarantee 100% fresh data, if required, it is necessary to use a pull-based approach or a combination of pull with this approach, which can adapt itself based on the current server load, storage space, and required coherency.

The DUP (data update propagation) algorithm (Challenger et al., 1999; Challenger, Iyengar, Witting, Ferstat, & Reed, 2000; Degenaro et al., 2001) uses an object dependence graph (ODG) for the dependence between cached objects and the underlying data. The cache architecture is based on a cache manager that manages one or more caches. Application programs use an API to explicitly access caches to add, delete, and update cached objects.

Table 3. Summary of ESI tags

Tag	Purpose
<esi:include>	Include a separately cacheable fragment.
<esi:choose>	It is a conditional execution: Choose among several different alternatives based on, for example, a cookie value or user agent.
<esi:try>	Specify alternative processing when a request fails (e.g., the origin server is not accessible).
<esi:vars>	Permit variable substitution (for environment variables).
<esi:remove>	Specify alternative content to be stripped by ESI but displayed by the browser if ESI processing is not done.
<!--esi ... -->	Specify content to be processed by ESI but that is hidden from the browser.
<esi:inline>	Include a separately cacheable fragment whose body is included in the template.

Case Studies

There are a number of systems and products on the market that support dynamic-content caching in one way or another. We study the most important ones here.

Oracle 9iAS Web Cache

Oracle 9iAS WebCache is a product that is used as a server accelerator with the capability of caching dynamic Web pages (Oracle Corporation, 2001). It enables system administrators to specify cacheability rules using regular expressions. These rules specify whether a particular URL or a group of URLs should or should not be cached. Supported objects include static contents such as GIF (graphic interchange format) and JPEG (Joint Photographic Experts Group) as well as dynamic content from server-side languages such as JSP or Servlets, ASP, PL / SQL (Procedural Language SQL) server pages (PSPs), and CGI (common gateway interface). There are a number of cases where content should be declared as noncacheable. Some examples include update transactions, shopping-cart views, and personal-account views. If no cacheability rules are specified, then Oracle Web Cache behaves like a traditional proxy server and uses HTTP header information for caching purposes. It also enables caching personalized Web pages, such as greeting pages:

"Welcome <name>."

For this purpose, special SGML (standard generalized markup language) comments called Web cache tags are used to identify the personalized attribute information within a page, for example,

```
<HTML>
...
Welcome to our store,
<!-- WEBCACHETAG="person_name"-->
John Citizen
<!--WEBCACHEEND-->
...
<\HTML>.
```

Oracle AS Web Cache parses the HTML and caches a generic version of the page, leaving a placeholder for the personalized attributes placed between the Web cache tags.

Some applications such as e-commerce or portal applications need a fine-grained caching solution. Oracle AS Web Cache can break the content down into its building elements and cache elements separately. It takes advantage of ESI (http://www.esi.org) to identify content fragments for caching. For cache coherency purposes, Oracle AS Web Cache supports expiration and message-based invalidation.

In the expiration method, an expiration policy can be assigned to the cache content. When an object expires, Oracle AS Web Cache marks it as invalid.

In the invalidation method, an XML or HTTP invalidation message is sent to the Oracle AS Web Cache host machine. Invalidation messages are HTTP *POST* requests that carry an XML payload. The contents of the XML message body tells the cache which URLs to mark as invalid.

Edge Side Includes

The Edge Side Includes *(*ESI) markup language defined by Oracle and Akamai allows applications to identify content fragments for caching and assembly at the network edges, either at the application edge (i.e., application server or server accelerator) or the Internet edge (i.e., CDNs). Assembling dynamic pages from individual page fragments means that only expired or noncacheable fragments need to be fetched from the origin server, which results in better performance.

A server-side include is a variable value that a server can include in an HTML file before sending it to the requester. For example, *LAST-MODIFIED* is one of several environment variables that an operating system can keep track of and that can be accessible to a server program. When writing a Web page, an include statement can be inserted in the file that looks like:

```
<!--#echo var="LAST-MODIFIED"-->.
```

In this case, the server will obtain the last modified date for the file and insert it before the HTML file is sent to requesters. A server-side include can be considered a limited form of a CGI application. The server simply searches the server-side include file for CGI environ-

Table 4. Summary of JESI tags

Tag	Purpose
<jesi:include>	It is used in a template page to indicate to the ESI processor how the fragments are to be assembled (the tag generates the <esi:include> tag).
<jesi:control>	Assign an attribute (e.g., expiration) to templates and fragments.
<jesi:template>	It is used to contain the entire content of a JSP container page within its body.
<jesi:fragment>	Encapsulate individual content fragments within a JSP page.
<jesi:codeblock>	Specify that a particular piece of code needs to be executed before any other fragment is executed (a database connection is established, user ID computed, etc.).
<jesi:invalidate>	Explicitly remove and/or expire selected objects cached in an ESI processor.
<jesi: personalize>	Insert personalized content into a page where the content is placed in cookies and inserted into the page by the ESI processor.

ment variables and inserts the variable information in the places in the file where the include statements have been inserted. Table 3 shows a summary of ESI tags.

Oracle and Akamai have also defined an adaptation of ESI for Java, called Java Edge Side Includes (JESI), which can be used in JSP pages. In other words, it is a specification and custom JSP tag library that can be used by developers to automatically generate ESI code. Table 4 summarizes the JESI tags.

JSP Cache Tag Library in BEA WebLogic

One of the JSP tags provided by BEA is cache tag that is packaged in the weblogic-tags.jar tag library file. By copying this file to the WEB-INF/lib directory of the Web application, cache tags can be used in JSP files. Using cache tags enables caching the body of the tag, that is, the fragment within the tag. The following XML fragment in web.xml enables a Web application to refer to this library.

```
<taglib>
   <taglib-uri>weblogic-tags.tld</taglib-uri>
   <taglib-location>
      /WEB-ING/lib/weblogic-tags.jar
   </taglib-location>
</taglib>
```

Referencing the tag library in JSP files is done using the *taglib* directive.

```
<%@ taglib uri="weblogic-tags.tld" prefix="w1" %>
```

Table 5. Supported cache-tag attributes in BEA WebLogic

Attribute	Description
timeout	Specifies the amount of time after which the body of the cache tag is refreshed
scope	Specifies the scope in which data are cached. Valid scopes include page, request, session, and application.
key	Specifies additional values for evaluating the condition based on which caching is decided on
async	A *true* value for this attribute denotes updating the cache asynchronously, if possible.
name	This attribute specifies a unique name for the cache. This allows a cache to be shared between different JSP files.
size	Specifies the maximum number of entries in the cache
vars	This attribute is used for input caching, that is, caching calculated values.
flush	A *true* value for this attribute causes the cache to be flushed.

Table 5 summarizes the supported cache-tag attributes in BEA WebLogic.

Invalidation Mechanism in Dynamai

Dynamai (http://www.persistence.com) from Persistence Software acts as a server accelerator and caches the result of requests for dynamic Web pages. Such pages will become invalid when the data on which they were based change in the underlying database. Two kinds of events may cause this to happen.

*   A database update by the application through the Web interface
*   A database update by an external event such as a system administrator or another application

In the first case, incoming requests are monitored, and if they cause an update on the database, the affected pages will be invalidated.

In the second case, the invalidation mechanism will need to be programmed in a script file and executed by the administrator to invalidate appropriate Web pages.

Cache Directives and API in ASP.NET

ASP.NET provides both page-level caching and fragment caching. It also provides application-level caching by providing cache API to be used in the application to manually manage the cache (Smith, 2003). To incorporate page-level output caching, an *OutputCache* directive could be added to the page as follows:

Table 6. Supported cache directive attributes in ASP.NET

Attribute	Required	Description
Duration	Yes	The time, in seconds, the page should be cached. Must be a positive integer.
Location	No	The location to which the output should be cached. It must be one of *Any*, *Client*, *Downstream*, *None*, *Server*, or *ServerAndClient*, if specified.
VaryByParam	Yes	The names of the variables in the request, which should result in separate cache entries. *None* can be used to specify no variation. The symbol * can be used to create new cache entries for every different set of variables. Variables are separated with a semicolon.
VaryByHeader	No	It varies cache entries based on variations in a specified header.
VaryByCustom	No	It allows custom variations to be specified in the global.asax (for example, *browser*).

```
<%@ OutputCache Duration="60" VaryByParam="*" %>
```

This directive appears at the top of the ASPX page before any output. Five attributes are supported by this directive, two of which are required and the others are optional, as shown in Table 6.

Most situations can be handled with a combination of the required *Duration* and *VaryBy-Param* options. For instance, we consider a product catalog that allows the user to view pages of the catalog based on a *categoryID* and a *page* variable. The page could be cached for some period of time (probably an hour would be acceptable unless the products change all the time) with a *VaryByParam* of *categoryID;page*. This would create separate cache entries for every page of the catalog for each category. Each entry would persist for one hour from its first request.

VaryByHeader and *VaryByCustom* are primarily used to allow caching customization of the page's look or content based on the client that is accessing it. For example, the same URL that generates output for both Web browsers and mobile-phone clients has to cache separate versions for each. Also, the page might be optimized for Internet Explorer but needs to be rendered for Netscape or Mozilla, perhaps with degraded quality. In order to enable separate cache entries for each browser, *VaryByCustom* can be set to a value of *browser*. This functionality will insert separate cached versions of the page for each browser name and major version.

```
<%@ OutputCache Duration="60" VaryByParam="None"
                      VaryByCustom="browser" %>
```

ASP.Net also enables caching different fragments within a Web page using the same syntax as in full-page caching. In ASP.NET, a Web page is referred to as a Web form (.aspx file), and a fragment within a page is referred to as a user control (.ascx file). The same syntax may be used for caching user controls. All the attributes supported by the *OutputCache* directive on a Web form are also supported for user controls except for the *Location* attribute. There is, however, an extra attribute for user controls called *VaryByControl*, which caches a separate copy of the user control based on the value of a member of that control, such as a *DropDownList*. *VaryByParam* may be omitted if *VaryByControl* is specified. If a user control is used among different pages with the same name, the *Shared="true"* parameter enables using the cached version(s) of the user control for all the pages containing that control. However, by default, each user control on each page is cached separately.

The cache directive:

```
<%@ OutputCache Duration="60" VaryByParam="*" %>
```

caches the user control for 60 seconds and creates a separate cache entry for every variation of input parameters.

Using the directive:

```
<%@ OutputCache Duration="60" VaryByParam="none"
                VaryByControl="CategoryDropDownList" %>
```

causes the user control be cached for 60 seconds. It creates a separate cache entry for each different value of the *CategoryDropDownList* control and for each page that contains this control.

```
<%@ OutputCache Duration="60" VaryByParam="none"
                VaryByCustom="browser" Shared="true" %>
```

The above cache directive caches the user control for 60 seconds and creates separate cache entries for each browser name and major version. All pages containing a reference to this user control can share such entries in the cache.

ASP.NET also provides a more flexible means for caching through the *Cache* object. Using the *Cache* object, any object that can be serialized can be placed in a cache and its expiration can be controlled using one or more dependencies. Examples of dependencies include the time elapsed since caching the object, time elapsed since the last access to the object, changes on files and folders, and so forth.

Objects are inserted in the cache in a *key, value* pair, similar to a *HashTable*. To store an object in the cache, the following assignment may be used, which stores the item in the cache without any dependencies. In this case, the object will stay in the cache and will not expire unless the cache engine removes it as a result of running a cache replacement strategy.

Cache["key"] = "value";

Some APIs may be used to include specific cache dependencies, such as the *Add()* or *Insert()* methods.

PreLoader from Chutney Technologies

Chutney's PreLoader (http://www.chutneytech.com) may be deployed as a server accelerator that sits next to an application-server farm and caches Web pages or individual components of Web pages (Aberdeen Group, 2001).

It enables page-level dynamic-content caching, including personalized Web pages such as those that contain personal greetings, for example, "Welcome to our store, John Citizen!" The cache stores a generic page for such pages with a placeholder for personalized information that can be changed on the fly by the cache to represent different personalized pages.

Moreover, it enables component-level caching by breaking the content down into its components and caching them separately. It automatically assembles such components when a request is made.

Finally, it provides a variety of invalidation mechanisms, such as TTL settings and database triggers.

Future Trends

Web portals are emerging Web-based applications enabling access to different providers through a single interface. The idea is to save time and effort for users who only need to access the portal's Web interface instead of having to navigate through many providers' Web sites.

Caching dynamic objects at Web portals introduces new problems to which existing techniques cannot be easily adapted and used. Available systems such as Oracle Web Cache, IBM WebSphere Edge Server, and Dynamai enable system administrators to specify caching policies. This is done primarily by including or excluding objects or object groups (e.g., objects with a common prefix in the URI) to be cached, determining expiry dates for cached objects or object groups, and so forth. Server logs (i.e., Web server access logs and database update logs) are also used to identify objects that are good candidates for caching.

In a portal-enabled environment, the portal and providers are managed by different organizations and administrators. Therefore, the administrator of a portal does not normally have enough information to determine caching policies for individual providers. Moreover, since the portal may be dealing with a (large) number of providers, determining the best objects for caching manually or by processing logs is impractical. On the one hand, an administrator cannot identify candidate objects in a dynamic environment where providers may join and leave the portal frequently. On the other hand, keeping and processing access logs in the portal is impractical due to high storage-space and processing-time requirements. Also, database update logs are not normally accessible by the portal.

In current systems, caching policies are defined and tuned by parameters that are set by system administrators based on the previous history of available resources, and access and update patterns. A more useful infrastructure should be able to provide more powerful means to define and deploy caching policies, preferably with minimal manual intervention. As the owners of objects, providers are deemed more eligible for and capable of deciding objects for caching purposes.

Both portal and providers can contribute information that allows an effective caching strategy to evolve automatically on the portal as proposed in Mahdavi, Benatallah, and Shepherd (2004), Mahdavi and Shepherd (2004), Mahdavi, Benatallah, and Rabhi (2003). Providers trace their logs, extract information to identify good candidates for caching, and notify the portal. A caching score (called cache-worthiness) is associated to each object by the provider. The decision of whether to cache an object or not is made by the portal based on the cache-worthiness scores along with other parameters such as the recency of objects, the utility of the providers, and the correlation of objects.

Calculating Cache-Worthiness

As mentioned earlier, due to the potentially large number of providers and dynamicity of the environment, in terms of joining and leaving providers, it is not feasible to identify cache-worthy objects on the portal either by a system administrator or by mining server logs. A human administrator cannot handle frequent changes to the collection of providers, maintaining and processing access logs in the portal imposes too much storage and processing overhead, and database update logs from the providers are typically not accessible by the portal. Providers, as the owners of the objects, are more capable of deciding which objects should be selected. In order to provide effective caching in a distributed, dynamic portal environment, we propose a strategy based on the collaboration between the providers and the portal.

The best candidates for caching are objects that are (a) requested frequently, (b) not changed frequently, and (c) expensive to compute or deliver (Yagoub et al., 2000). For other objects, the caching overheads may outweigh the caching benefits. We use server logs at provider sites to calculate a score for cache-worthiness. In the rest of this chapter, we use $O_{i,m}$ to denote an object i from a provider m. Four important parameters are identified.

- **Access frequency** is denoted by $A(O_{i,m}, k)$ and indicates the access frequency of $O_{i,m}$ through portal k during the time the log has been recorded or since the last time the access frequency of objects was calculated. It is calculated by processing the Web-application-server access log and counting the accesses being made to each object $O_{i,m}$. More frequently accessed objects are better choices for caching.

- **Update frequency** is denoted by $U(O_{i,m})$ and indicates the number of times $O_{i,m}$ has been invalidated during the time the calculation was being done (i.e., the time the log has been recorded or since the last time the update frequency was calculated). It is calculated by processing the update log. Objects with lower update frequency are better for caching.

- **Computation or construction cost** is denoted by $C(O_{i,m})$ and indicates the cost of generating $O_{i,m}$ in terms of database accesses and formatting the results. It is calculated by processing the server logs and calculating the time elapsed between the request being sent to the database until the result of the request being ready to be delivered. Objects with more computation cost are better for caching.

- **Delivery cost** is represented by the size of the object and is denoted by $S(O_{i,m})$. Larger objects are more expensive to deliver in terms of network bandwidth consumption and also the elapsed time for delivering the object, and therefore they are more appropriate for caching.

The cache-worthiness score is calculated as the aggregation of the above-mentioned parameters. As can be noticed, each of the above-mentioned parameters could have a different range of values and/or have different units. To make these parameters comparable and therefore able to be aggregated, we standardize each parameter X using the following formula:

$$Z_X = \frac{1}{n} \sum_{i=1}^{n} (X - \overline{X})^2 = \frac{1}{n} \sum_{i=1}^{n} X^2 - \overline{X}^2$$

The second version of the formula can be used in order to use a single pass over the input.

The corresponding standard variables will be Z_A for access, Z_U for update, Z_C for computation cost, and Z_S for size. The resulting standard variables will have an average ($\overline{Z}$) equal to 0 and a standard deviation ($d(Z)$) equal to 1.

The above parameters are finally aggregated to generate the value for cache-worthiness. The resulting value is denoted by $CW(O_{i,m}, k)$. It indicates how useful caching $O_{i,m}$ at portal k is.

There are other parameters that may be used in conjunction with cache-worthiness scores in order to provide a more efficient caching strategy. These parameters include the following.

- **Recency:** The recency of an object is defined as a value in [0, 1]. The oldest object in the cache has a recency equal to 0, and the recency of the newest object is defined as 1. More recent objects are more likely to stay in the cache, and older objects are more likely to be removed when the cache replacement strategy is run. The following formula shows how the recency of an object can be calculated using the time stamps (TSs) assigned to each object:

$$R(O_i) = (TS(O_i) - TS(O_E)) / (TS(O_K) - TS(O_E)),$$

where:

O_E is the oldest object in the cache and

O_K is the most recent object.

- **Utility of Providers:** It should be noted that the throughput of the portal is bounded by the throughput of the provider(s) with least performance. This is when the result of such a provider cannot be ignored; for example, the portal is keen to do business with the provider, the provider normally offers good deals for the customers, commission is paid to the portal, or the provider satisfies a composite service when there is no other option. Boosting the performance of such providers can result in increasing the performance of the portal as a whole. Therefore, such providers might be given higher utility.

$$T \leq \min(T_1, T_2, T_3, ...)$$

Each provider can be given a weight in advance, and this weight can be used to favor some providers against others for caching. This weight can be used in conjunction with cache-worthiness scores to boost the performance of some particular providers.

- **Correlation of Objects:** In a Web application, some objects are normally requested in order. For example, in a travel portal, a browse session for accommodation in a particular region might be followed by a browse session for car rental in the same region. Therefore, it would be worth caching the result of the car-rental browsing session if the result of the accommodation browsing session is already cached. The correlation between O_i and O_j shows the rate by which O_j is accessed after O_i and can be calculated by processing access logs as follows:

$$r(O_i, O_j) = (f(O_j : O_i \rightarrow O_j) / (f(O_i)),$$

where:

$f(O_j : O_i \rightarrow O_j)$ is the access frequency of O_j when it is accessed after O_i and

$f(O_i)$ is the access frequency of O_i.

The results of the processing will be maintained in a correlation matrix, where every cell stores $r(O_i, O_j)$. Please note that the calculation of correlation we use is different from the one used in statistics books. However, the idea of correlation follows the same concept.

These parameters can be used in conjunction with cache-worthiness scores to provide a more effective caching strategy.

Heterogeneous Caching Scores

The fact that it is up to providers to calculate cache-worthiness scores may lead to inconsistencies between them. Although, all providers may use the same overall strategy to score their objects, the scores may not be consistent. In the absence of any regulation of cache-worthiness scores, objects from providers who give higher scores will have more chance to be cached, and such providers will get more cache space than others. This leads to unfair treatment of providers. As a result, those who give lower scores get comparatively less cache space, and their performance improvements are expected to be less than those who score higher. It may also result in less effective cache performance as a whole. The following factors contribute to causing inconsistencies in caching scores among providers.

- Each provider uses a limited number of log entries to extract the required information, and the available log entries may vary from one to another.
- The value of the computation cost ($C(O_{i,m})$) depends on the provider's hardware and software platform, workload, and so forth.
- Providers may use other mechanisms to score the objects (they are not required to use the above approach).
- Malicious providers may claim that all of their own objects should be cached in the hope of getting more cache space.

To achieve a fair and effective caching strategy, the portal should detect these inconsistencies and regulate the scores given by different providers. For this purpose, the portal uses a regulating factor $\lambda(m)$ for each provider and applies it to the cache-worthiness scores, using the result in the calculation of the overall caching scores received from provider m. This factor has a neutral value in the beginning and is adapted dynamically by monitoring the cache behavior. This is done by tracing false hits and true hits.

A false hit is a cache hit occurring at the portal when the object is already invalidated. False hits degrade the performance and increase the overheads both at the portal and provider sites without any outcome.

A true hit is a cache hit occurring at the portal when the object is still fresh and can be served by the cache. The performance of the cache can only be judged by true hits.

The portal monitors the performance of the cache in terms of tracing false and true hits and dynamically adapts $\lambda(m)$ for each provider. For those providers with higher ratios of false hits, all the cache-worthiness scores from that provider are treated as lower scores, that is, $\lambda(m) \rightarrow \lambda^-(m)$. For those providers with higher ratios of true hits, the portal upgrades $\lambda(m)$, that is, $I(m) \rightarrow I^+(m)$. Therefore, all the cache-worthiness scores from that provider are treated as being higher than before.

A high false-hit ratio for a provider m indicates that the cache space for that particular provider is not utilized. That is because the cached objects for that provider are not as worthy as they should be. In other words, the provider has given higher cache-worthiness scores to its objects. This can be resolved by downgrading the scores from that provider and treating them as if they were lower.

Although unlikely, a high true-hit ratio for a provider m indicates that the cache performance for this provider is good. Therefore, provider m is taking good advantage of the cache space. Upgrading the cache-worthiness scores of provider m results in more cache space being assigned to this provider. This ensures fairness in cache usage based on how the cache is utilized by providers. The fair distribution of cache space among providers will also result in better cache performance.

Conclusion

In this chapter, we studied existing solutions for caching Web data. We considered Web portals as a growing class of Web applications and addressed the problem of providing fast response times via caching. There are limitations with existing solutions to be applied to Web portals in terms of defining caching policies for the objects. In existing solutions, system administrators can include or exclude objects or object groups for caching. In such systems, caching policies are defined and tuned by parameters that are set by the system administrator based on the previous history of available resources, and the access and update patterns. As already mentioned, this is implausible in portal environments where the portal and providers are normally managed by different organizations, and the administrator of the portal does not normally have enough information to determine such policies for individual providers. A caching strategy based on collaboration between the portal and providers addresses these limitations. According to this strategy, caching policies are dynamically defined and tuned based on the cache-worthiness scores associated with objects by the providers.

References

Aberdeen Group. (2001). *Cutting the costs of personalization with dynamic content caching.* Retrieved June 2004 from http://www.chutneytech.com/tech/aberdeen.cfm

Aggrawal, C., Wolf, J. L., & Yu, P. S. (1999). Caching on the World Wide Web. *IEEE Transactions on Knowledge and Data Engineering, 11*(1), 94-107.

Anton, J., Jacobs, L., Liu, X., Parker, J., Zeng, Z., & Zhong, T. (2002). Web caching for database applications with Oracle Web Cache. *Proceedings of the 2002 ACM SIGMOD International Conference on Management of Data* (pp. 594-599).

Apache Software Foundation. (2004). *JCS and JCACHE (JSR-107)*. Retrieved June 2004 from http://jakarta.apache.org/turbine/jcs/index.html

Balamash, A., & Krunz, M. (2004). An overview of Web caching replacement algorithms. *IEEE Communications Surveys and Tutorials, 6*(2), 44-56.

Barish, G., & Obraczka, K. (2000). World Wide Web caching: Trends and techniques. *ACM Communications, 38*(5), 178-185.

Bortvedt, J. (2004). *Functional specification for object caching service for Java (OCS4J), 2.0*. Retrieved June 2004 from http://jcp.org/aboutJava/communityprocess/jsr/cacheFS.pdf

Candan, K. S., Agrawal, D., Li, W., Po, O., & Hsiug, W. (2002). View invalidation for dynamic content caching in multitiered architectures. In *Proceedings of the 28ᵗʰ VLDB Conference* (pp. 562-573).

Candan, K. S., Li, W., Luo, Q., Hsiung, W., & Agrawal, D. (2001). Enabling dynamic content caching for database-driven Web sites. In *Proceedings of the 2001 ACM SIGMOD International Conference on Management of Data* (pp. 532-543).

Cao, L. Y., & Ozsu, M. T. (2002). Evaluation of strong consistency Web caching techniques. In *World Wide Web: Internet and Web Information Systems, 5*(2), 95-124.

Cao, P., & Irani, S. (1997). Cost-aware WWW proxy caching algorithms. In *Proceedings of The USENIX Symposium on Internet Technologies and Systems* (pp. 193-206).

Challenger, J., Iyengar, A., & Dantzig, P. (1999). A scalable system for consistently caching dynamic Web data. In *Proceedings of IEEE INFOCOM* (pp. 294-303).

Challenger, J., Iyengar, A., Witting, K., Ferstat, K., & Reed, P. (2000). A publishing system for efficiently creating dynamic Web content. In *Proceedings of IEEE INFOCOM* (pp. 844-853).

Cheng, K., & Kambayashi, Y. (2000). LRU-SP: A size-adjusted and popularity aware LRU replacement algorithm for Web caching. *IEEE Compsac*, 48-53.

Chidlovskii, B., & Borgho, U. (2000). Semantic caching of Web queries. *VLDB Journal, 9*(1), 2-17.

Datta, A., Dutta, K., Thomas, H. M., VanderMeer, D. E., & Ramamritham, K. (2002). Accelerating dynamic Web content generation. *IEEE Internet Computing, 6*(5), 27-36.

Degenaro, L., Iyengar, A., & Rouvellou, I. (2001). Improving performance with application-level caching. *International Conference on Advances in Infrastructure for Electronic Business, Science, and Education on the Internet (SSGRR)*.

Deolasee, P., Katkar, A., Panchbudhe, A., Ramamritham, K., & Shenoy, P. (2001). Adaptive push-pull: Disseminating dynamic Web data. *The 10ᵗʰ World Wide Web Conference (WWW-10)* (pp. 265-274).

Duvuri, V., Shenoy, P., & Tewari, R. (2000). Adaptive leases: A strong consistency mechanism for the World Wide Web. *Proceedings of IEEE INFOCOM2000* (pp. 834-843).

Fielding, R., Gettys, J., Mogul, J., Frystyk, H., Masinter, L., Leach, P., et al. (1999). *Hypertext transfer protocol: Http/1.1*. Retrieved June 2004 from http://www.cis.ohio-state.edu/cgi-bin/rfc/rfc2616.html

Florescu, D., Yagoub, K., Valduriez, P., & Issarny, V. (2000). WEAVE: A data-intensive Web site management system. *The Conference on Extending Database Technology (EDBT)*.

Gwertzman, J., & Seltzer, M. (1996). World Wide Web cache consistency. *Proceedings of the USENIX Technical Conference* (pp. 141-152).

Krishnamurthy, B., & Willis, C. E. (1997). Study of piggyback cache validation for proxy caches in the World Wide Web. *Proceedings of the USENIX Symposium on Internet Technologies and Systems* (pp. 413-424).

Krishnamurthy, B., & Willis, C. E. (1998). Piggyback server invalidation for proxy cache coherency. *Computer Networks and ISDN Systems, 30*(1-7), 185-193.

Labrinidis, A., & Roussopoulos, N. (2000). On the materialization of Web views. *Proceedings of the 2000 ACM SIGMOD International Conference on Management of Data* (pp. 367-378).

Labrinidis, A., & Roussopoulos, N. (2001). Adaptive Webview materialization. *WebDB Workshop* (pp. 85-90).

Li, D., Cao, P., & Dahlin, M. (2001). *WCIP: Web cache invalidation protocol.* Retrieved June 2004 from http://www.ietf.org/internet-drafts/draft-danli-wrec-wcip-01.txt

Liu, C., & Cao, P. (1998). Maintaining strong cache consistency in the World-Wide Web. *International Conference on Distributed Computing Systems* (pp. 12-210).

Luo, Q., & Naughton, J. F. (2001). Form-based proxy caching for database-backed Web sites. *Proceedings of the 27th International Conference on Very Large Data Bases* (pp. 191-200).

Luo, Q., Naughton, J. F., Krishnamurthy, R., Cao, P., & Li, Y. (2000). Active query caching for database Web servers. *WebDB Workshop* (pp. 29-34).

Mahdavi, M., Benatallah, B., & Rabhi, F. (2003). Caching dynamic data for e-business applications. *International Conference on Intelligent Information Systems (IIS'03): New Trends in Intelligent Information Processing and Web Mining (IIPWM)* (pp. 459-466).

Mahdavi, M., & Shepherd, J. (2004). Enabling dynamic content caching in Web portals. *14th International Workshop on Research Issues on Data Engineering (RIDE'04)* (pp. 129-136).

Mahdavi, M., Shepherd, J., & Benatallah, B. (2004). A collaborative approach for caching dynamic data in portal applications. *The 15th Australasian Database Conference (ADC'04)* (pp. 181-188).

Manolescu, I., Bouganim, L., Fabret, F., & Simon, E. (2001). *Efficient data and program integration using binding patterns* (Tech. Rep. 4239). France: Inria.

Marian, A., Abiteboul, S., Cobena, G., & Mignet, L. (2001). Change-centric management of versions in an XML warehouse. *Proceedings of the 27th International Conference on Very Large Data Bases* (pp. 581-590).

Markatos, E. P. (2001). On caching search engine query results. *Computer Communications, 24*(2), 137-143.

Nguyen, B., Abiteboul, S., Cobena, G., & Preda, M. (2001). Monitoring XML data on the Web. *Proceedings of the 2001 ACM SIGMOD International Conference on Management of Data* (pp. 437-448).

Oracle Corporation. (2001). *Oracle9iAS Web Cache.* Retrieved June 2004 from http://www.oracle.com

Podlipnig, S., & Boszormenyi, I. L. (2003). A survey of Web cache replacement strategies. *ACM Computing Surveys, 35*(4), 374-398.

Rabinovich, M., & Spatscheck, O. (2001). *Web caching and replication.* Boston: Addison-Wesley.

Ramamritham, K., Deolasee, P., Kathar, A., Panchbudhe, A., & Shenoy, P. (2000). Dissemination of dynamic data on the Internet. *Proceedings of the International Workshop on Databases in Networked Information Systems* (pp. 173-178).

Ramaswamy, L., Iyengar, A., Liu, L., & Douglis, F. (2005). Automatic fragment detection in dynamic Web pages and its impact on caching. *IEEE Transactions on Knowledge and Data Engineering, 17*(6), 859-874.

Smith, S. A. (2003). *ASP.NET caching: Techniques and best practices.* Retrieved June 2004 from http://msdn.microsoft.com/library/default.asp?url=/library/en-us/dnaspp/html/aspnet-cachingtechniquesbestpract.asp

Sun Microsystems. (2004). *JSRs: Java specification requests.* Retrieved June 2004 from http://www.jcp.org/en/jsr/overview

Tatarinov, I., Ives, Z. G., & Halvey, A. Y. (2001). Updating XML. *Proceedings of the 2000 ACM SIGMOD International Conference on Management of Data.*

Williams, S., & Abrams, M. (1996). Removal policies in network caches for World-Wide Web documents. *ACM SIGCOMM Computer Communication Review, 26*(4), 293-305.

Wong, K. Y., & Yeung, K. H. (2001). Site-based approach to Web cache design. *IEEE Internet Computing, 5*(5), 28-34.

Yagoub, K., Florescu, D., Valduriez, P., & Issarny, V. (2000). Caching strategies for data-intensive Web sites. *Proceedings of the 27th International Conference on Very Large Data Bases* (pp. 188-199).

Yin, J., Alvisi, L., Dahlin, M., & Lin, C. (1999). Volume leases for consistency in large-scale systems. *IEEE Transactions on Knowledge and Data Engineering, 11*(4), 563-576.

Young, N. E. (1994). The k-server dual and loose competitiveness for paging. *Algorithmica, 11*(6), 525-541.

Yu, H., Breslau, L., & Shenker, S. (1999). A scalable Web cache consistency architecture. *Proceedings of the Conference on Applications, Technologies, Architectures, and Protocols for Computer Communication, 163-174.*

Zona Research Inc. (2001). *Zona Research releases Need for Speed II.* Retrieved June 2004 from http://www.zonaresearch.com/info/press/01-may03.htm

Chapter VII

Information-Theoretic Methods for Prediction in the Wireless and Wired Web

Dimitrios Katsaros, Aristotle University of Thessaloniki, Greece

Abstract

Discrete sequence modeling and prediction is an important goal and challenge for Web environments, both wired and wireless. Web clients' data-request forecasting and mobile location tracking in wireless cellular networks are characteristic application areas of sequence prediction in such environments. Accurate data-request prediction results in effective data prefetching, which combined with a caching mechanism can reduce user-perceived latencies as well as server and network loads. Also, effective solutions to the mobility tracking and prediction problem can reduce the update and paging costs, freeing the network from excessive signaling traffic. Therefore, sequence prediction comprises a very important study and development area. This chapter presents information-theoretic techniques for discrete sequence prediction. It surveys, classifies, and compares the state-of-the-art solutions, suggesting routes for further research by discussing the critical issues and challenges of prediction in wired and wireless networks.

Introduction

The proliferation of wireless cellular networks and the penetration of Internet services are changing many aspects of Web computing. Constantly increasing client populations utilize diverse devices to access the wired and wireless medium, and various heterogeneous applications (e.g., traffic- and weather-condition broadcasting, streaming video) are being developed to satisfy the eager requirements of the clients. In this environment, seamless and ubiquitous connectivity as well as low client-perceived latencies are two fundamental goals. The first goal calls for smart techniques for determining the current and future location of a mobile node, and the second goal calls for efficient and effective techniques for deducing future client requests for information pieces.

Both of the aforementioned problems are related to the ability of the underlying network to record, learn, and subsequently predict the mobile user's behavior, that is, its movements or its information needs. The success of the prediction is presupposed and is boosted by the fact that mobile users exhibit some degree of regularity in their movement and/or in their access patterns (Bhattacharya & Das, 2002; Nanopoulos, Katsaros, & Manolopoulos, 2003). This regularity may be apparent in the behavior of each individual client or in client groups. The detection of regularity patterns can lead to drastic improvements on the underlying wireless network's performance. Accurate data-request prediction results in effective data prefetching (Nanopoulos et al., 2003) combined with a caching mechanism (Katsaros & Manolopoulos, 2004; Vakali, 2001) can reduce user-perceived latencies as well as server and network loads. Also, effective solutions to the mobility tracking and prediction problem can reduce the update and paging costs, freeing the network from excessive signaling traffic (Bhattacharya & Das, 2002).

These issues had been treated in isolation, but pioneering works (Bhattacharya & Das, 2002; Vitter & Krishnan, 1996) are paving the way for treating both problems in a homogeneous fashion. They exhibited the possibility of using methods that have traditionally been used for data compression (thus characterized as information-theoretic) in carrying out prediction. The unifying principle is that they model the respective state space as finite alphabets comprised of discrete symbols. In the mobility tracking scenario, the alphabet consists of all possible sites (cells) where the client has ever visited or might visit (assuming that the number of cells in the coverage area is finite). In the request-prediction scenario, the alphabet consists of all the data objects requested by the client plus the objects that might be requested in the future (assuming that the objects come from a database and thus their number is finite).

A smart network can record the movement (request) history and then construct a mobility (data-access) model for its clients. The history refers to the past, but the model is probabilistic and extends to the future. As uncertainty is inherent in mobile movements or requests, we can consider the requests to be the outcome of an underlying stochastic process, which can be modeled using established information-theoretic concepts and tools (Misra, Roy, & Das, 2004; Vitter & Krishnan, 1996).

In our earlier work, reported in Nanopoulos et al. (2003), we described a framework that was able to embrace some algorithms that had been presented in the context of Web prefetching. That framework was able to present those algorithms as variations of the standard PPM (prediction by partial match) technique. The emphasis of the framework was on differentiating between the techniques based on whether they record contiguous subsequences or noncontiguous subsequences. From that work, it was clear that the discovery of noncontiguous subsequences required considerable computational effort and could be realized only through off-line algorithms.

Extending this work, this chapter provides a unifying framework for all the methods, which deal with the issues of location tracking and prediction and request forecasting using known information-theoretic structures, not only the PPM structures; the framework treats them as (variable or fixed-length) Markov chains and presents the different families of methods, categorizing the state-of-the-art algorithms into their respective families. It mainly deals with the discovery of contiguous subsequences, although it can relatively easily be extended to include noncontiguous subsequences. An important objective of the chapter is to include in the presentation not only the algorithms that are familiar in the wireless-communications community, but also techniques that have been developed in other disciplines, like computational biology, machine learning, and the World Wide Web, in order to achieve cross-discipline understanding and the proliferation of ideas. The purpose of the categorization is to reveal the shortcomings and advantages of each method and to identify routes for further research. Closely related to our work is that reported in Begleiter, El-Yaniv, and Yolan (2004), which, although it has a more narrow scope, examining only online prediction methods, it gives a completely different notion for the variable-length Markov chain, defining it as a combination of various Markov chains that are of different length.

The rest of the chapter is organized as follows. The next section describes in mathematical terminology the problem of discrete sequence prediction. Then the chapter surveys the different families of Markov predictors, and then provides a qualitative comparison of them. Next, we present a new online prediction algorithm that does not belong to any of the families, though it combines many of the merits presented by each family. Finally, we discuss some fields for further research, and then conclude the chapter.

The Discrete Sequence Prediction Problem

In quantifying the utility of the past in predicting the future, a formal definition of the problem is needed, which we provide in the following lines (Feder, Merhav, & Gutman, 1992; Merhav & Feder, 1998). Let Σ be an alphabet consisting of a finite number of symbols s_1, s_2, ..., $s_{|\Sigma|}$, where $|\cdot|$ stands for the length or cardinality of its argument. A predictor, which is an algorithm used to generate prediction models, accumulates sequences of the type $\alpha_i = \alpha_i^1$, α_i^2, ..., α_i^{ni}, where $\alpha_i^j \in \Sigma$ for all i, j and n_i denotes the number of symbols comprising α_i. Without loss of generality, we can assume that all the knowledge of the predictor consists of a single sequence $\boldsymbol{\alpha} = \alpha^1, \alpha^2, ..., \alpha^n$. Based on $\boldsymbol{\alpha}_i$, the predictor's goal is to construct a model that assigns probabilities for any future outcome given some past information. Using the characterization of the mobility or request model as a stochastic process $(X_t)_{t \in N}$, we can formulate the aforementioned goal as follows.

Definition 1 (Discrete Sequence Prediction Problem). At any given time instance t (meaning that t symbols x_t, x_{t-1}, ..., x_1 have appeared, in reverse order), calculate the conditional probability:

$$\overline{P}[X_{t+1} = x_{t+1} \mid X_t = x_t, X_{t-1} = x_{t-1},...],$$

where $x_i \in \Sigma$ for all $x_{t+1} \in \Sigma$. This model introduces a stationary Markov chain since the probabilities are not time dependent. The outcome of the predictor is a ranking of the symbols according to their $\overline{P}$. The predictors that use such kind of prediction models are termed Markov predictors.

Depending on the application, the predictor may return only the symbol(s) with the highest probability, that is, implementing a most-probable prediction policy, or it may return the symbols with the m highest probabilities, that is, implementing a top-m prediction policy, where m is an administratively set parameter. In any case, the selection of the policy is a minor issue and will not be considered in this chapter, which is only concerned with methods for inferring the ranking.

The history x_t, x_{t-1}, ... used in the above definition is called the context of the predictor, and it refers to the portion of the past that influences the next outcome. The history's length (also, called the length, memory, or order of the Markov chain or predictor) will be denoted by l. Therefore, a predictor that exploits l past symbol will calculate conditional probabilities of the form:

$$\overline{P}[X_{t+1} = x_{t+1} \mid X_t = x_t, X_{t-1} = x_{t-1},...,X_{t-l+1} = x_{t-l+1}].$$

Some Markov predictors fix, in advance of the model creation, the value of l, presetting it in a constant k in order to reduce the size and complexity of the prediction model. These predictors and the respective Markov chains are termed fixed-length Markov chains or predictors of order k. Therefore, they compute probabilities of the form:

$$\overline{P}[X_{t+1} = x_{t+1} \mid X_t = x_t, X_{t-1} = x_{t-1},...,X_{t-k+1} = x_{t-k+1}].$$

where k is a constant. Although it is a nice model from a probabilistic point of view, these Markov chains are not very appropriate from the estimation point of view. Their main limitation is related to their structural poverty since there is no means to set an optimized value for k.

Other Markov predictors deviate from the fixed-memory assumption (Buhlmann & Wyner, 1999) and allow the order of the predictor to be of variable length, that is, to be a function of the values from the past.

$$\overline{P}[X_{t+1} = x_{t+1} \mid X_t = x_t, X_{t-1} = x_{t-1},...,X_{t-l+1} = x_{t-l+1}],$$

where $l = l(x_t, x_{t-1},...)$.

These predictors are termed variable-length Markov chains; the length l might range from 1 to t. If $l=l(x_t, x_{t-1}, \ldots) \equiv k$ for all x_t, x_{t-1}, ..., then we obtain the fixed-length Markov chain. The variable-length Markov predictors may or may not impose an upper bound on the considered length. The concept of variable memory offers richness in the prediction model and the ability to adjust itself to the data distribution. If we can choose in a data-driven way the function $l=l(\cdot)$, then we can only gain with respect to the ordinary fixed-length Markov chains, but this is not a straightforward problem.

The Markov predictors (fixed or variable length) base their probability calculations $\overline{P}$ on counts of the number of appearances of symbols after contexts. They also take special care to deal with the cases of unobserved symbols (i.e., symbols with zero appearance counts after contexts), assigning to them some minimum probability mass, which is acquired from the respective mass of the symbols already seen. For the location-tracking and request-prediction applications, though, the predictors usually adopt a nonprediction approach for the unobserved events and do not apply any smoothing mechanism because the possible alternative symbols may be quite large. Therefore, for the rest of the chapter, we will not deal with the zero-frequency problem and will not adopt smoothing in the presented examples.

Families of Markov Predictors

We explained earlier how Markov predictors create probabilistic models for their input sequence(s). To realize these models, they need a data structure, a dictionary to keep track of the contexts of interest, and some counts used in the calculation of the conditional probabilities $\overline{P}$. The preferred choice for this task is the use of digital search trees (trees). The root node of the tree corresponds to the null event or symbol, whereas every other node of the tree corresponds to a sequence of events; the sequence is used to label the node. An invariant for the trees is that no two children of a father node may have the same label. In the rest of the chapter, we will consider a Markov predictor to be equivalent to its respective tree. Each node is accompanied by a counter, which depicts how many times this event has appeared after the sequence of events corresponding to the path from the root to the node's father that has been observed.

For our convenience, we present some definitions useful for the sequel of the chapter. We use the sample sequence of events $\boldsymbol{\alpha}$=aabacbbabbacbbc. The length of $\boldsymbol{\alpha}$ is the number of symbols it contains, that is, $|\boldsymbol{\alpha}|=15$. We term that the maximal prefix of a (sub)sequence, say, acb, is the (sub)sequence without its rightmost symbol, that is, ac; the maximal suffix of the (sub)sequence acb is the (sub)sequence without its leftmost symbol, that is, cb, whereas a *suffix* of the acb comes out of acb by removing 0, 1, ..., |abc| symbols from the left of acb. The null sequence denoted as R is a suffix of any sequence and it holds that $|R|=0$.

The appearance count of subsequence $\mathbf{s}$=ab is $E(\mathbf{s})=E(ab)=2$, and the normalized appearance count of $\mathbf{s}$ is equal to $E(\mathbf{s})$ divided by the maximum number of (possibly overlapping) occurrences a subsequence of the same length could have, considering $\mathbf{a}$'s length, that is, $E_n(\mathbf{s}) = E(\mathbf{s})/(|\mathbf{a}|-|\mathbf{s}|+1)$. The conditional probability of observing a symbol after a given subsequence is defined as the number of times that symbol has shown up right after the given subsequence divided by the total number of times that the subsequence has shown up at all, followed by any symbol. Therefore, the conditional probability of observing the symbol b after the subsequence a will be denoted as $\bar{p}$ (b|a) and is equal to $\bar{p}$ (b|a)= E(ab)/E(a)=0.4.

The generic procedure for deciding which subsequences will be inserted into the tree is specific to each family of Markov predictors and will be described in the next subsections. For purposes related to the clarity of presentation and comparison, we will build the respective tree of each family considering as input the sequence aabacbbabbacbbc. We will present the construction of each family's tree as simple as possible, omitting any optimizations, and we will assume that the input is given beforehand, although some predictors, that is, the online ones, do not demand the whole input to be known in advance.

The Prediction-by-Partial-Match Scheme

The prediction-by-partial-match scheme is based on the universal compression algorithm reported in Cleary and Witten (1984) and constructs a prediction model for an input sequence as follows. It assumes a predetermined maximal order, say, k, for the generated model. Then, for every possible subsequence of length of 1 up to k+1, if it has never been encountered before, we determine the node whose label is the maximal prefix of the considered subsequence. We create a new node under that node. The label of the new node is the length-1 suffix of the considered subsequence, and the new node's counter is initialized to the value of 1. If the considered subsequence has been encountered before, then the counter of the respective node is incremented by 1. Although this description implies that the whole input sequence is known in advance, the method works in an online fashion by exploiting a sliding window of size k+1 over the sequence as it grows symbol by symbol. The PPM predictor for the sample sequence aabacbbabbacbbc is depicted in Figure 1.

Upon completion of the construction phase, we can compute the probability of a symbol σ to appear after a context s by detecting the sequence sσ as a path in the tree emanating from the root, provided that |sσ| ≤ k. The conditional probability of sσ is computed as the ratio of the node counter corresponding to sσ divided by the counter corresponding to σ. Therefore, having built the predictor of Figure 1, we can use it to carry out symbol prediction for a progressing sequence of events as follows: We determine the maximum context with length less than or equal to k that appears as a path in the tree, and compute the conditional probabilities of all symbols to appear after this context. For instance, adopting a most-probable prediction policy, the predicted symbol for the test context ab is a or b, and its conditional probability is 0.50 for either of them (see the gray-shaded nodes in Figure 1).

Figure 1. A PPM Markov predictor for the sequence aabacbbabbacbbc

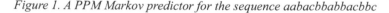

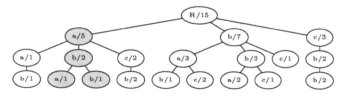

The maximum context that the PPM predictor can exploit in carrying out predictions is k, though all intermediate contexts with length from 1 to k-1 can be used since they have already been stored into the tree. This model is also referred as the all-kth-order PPM model because it encodes a set of PPM predictors whose order ranges from 1 to k. The interleaving of various-length contexts does not mean that this scheme is a variable-length Markov predictor (although sometimes it is referred to as such) because the decision on the context length is made beforehand and not in a data-driven way.

Apart from this basic scheme, a number of variations have been proposed that attempt to reduce the size of the tree by pruning some of its paths or suffixes of some paths based on statistical information derived from the input data. They set lower bounds for the normalized appearance count and for the conditional probabilities of subsequences, and then prune any branch that does not exceed these bounds. Characteristic works adopting such an approach are reported in Chen and Zhang (2003), Nanopoulos et al. (2003), and Deshpande and Karypis (2004). Their basic motivation stems from the assumption that the pruned states add very little to the prediction capability of the original model, and thus they could be eliminated without sacrificing significantly its effectiveness. The validity of this assumption cannot be justified and, in any case, it strongly depends on the input data distribution. Apparently, these schemes are off line, making one or multiple passes over the input sequence in order to gather the required statistical information.

Application Fields

The PPM scheme was the first compression algorithm that was used in carrying out prediction in wired networks (Fan, Cao, Lin, & Jacobson, 1999; Palpanas & Mendelzon, 1999). Earlier, it had been exploited for the same task in databases (Curewitz, Krishnan, & Vitter, 1993). Although the currently implemented approaches, for example, in the Mozilla browser, implement link prefetching, the sophisticated procedure of the PPM could provide significant benefits.

The Lempel-Ziv-78 Scheme

The Lempel-Ziv-78 Markov predictor, LZ78 for short, is the second scheme whose virtues in carrying out predictions were investigated very early in the literature (Bhattacharya & Das, 2002; Krishnan & Vitter, 1998; Vitter & Krishnan, 1996). The algorithm LZ78 (Lempel & Ziv, 1978) arose from a need for finding a universal variable to the fixed-length coding method and constructs a prediction model for an input sequence as follows. It makes no assumptions about the maximal order for the generated model. Then, it parses the input sequence into a number of distinct subsequences, say, $s_1, s_2, ..., s_x$, such that for all j, $1 \leq j \leq x$, the prefix of subsequence s_j (i.e., all but the last character of s_j) is equal to some s_i, for some $1 \leq i \leq j$. The discovered subsequences are inserted into a tree in a manner identical to that of the PPM scheme. In addition, the statistics regarding the number of appearances of each subsequence are stored into the nodes of the tree.

As the process of incremental parsing progresses, larger and larger subsequences are inserted into the tree, allowing the computation of conditional probabilities of increasingly larger

Figure 2. (Left) An LZ78 Markov predictor for the sequence aabacbbabbacbbc. (Right) An LZ78 predictor enhanced according to Bhattacharya and Das (2002)

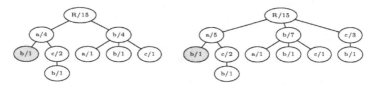

subsequences, thus exploiting larger contexts. The LZ78 predictor for the sample sequence aabacbbabbacbbc is depicted in the left part of Figure 2. The computation of conditional probabilities takes place in a manner completely analogous to that of PPM. However, LZ78 for this example is not able to produce a prediction for the test context ab (i.e., there is no subtree under the gray-shaded node).

Apparently, the LZ78 Markov predictor is an online scheme, it lacks administratively tuned parameters like lower bounds on appearance counts, and it is a characteristic paradigm of a variable-length Markov predictor. Although results do exist that prove its asymptotic optimality and its superiority over any fixed-length PPM predictor, in practice, various studies contradict this result because of the finite length of the input sequence. Nevertheless, the LZ78 predictor remains a very popular prediction method. The original LZ78 prediction scheme was enhanced in Bhattacharya and Das (2002), and Misra et al. (2004) in a way such that apart from a considered subsequence that is going to be inserted into the tree, all its suffixes are inserted as well (see right part of Figure 2).

Application Fields

Apart from the traditional use of the LZ78 algorithm in data-compression areas, recently it has found important application in problems related to location management in mobile networks. It has been proposed as a tool to reduce the communication overhead of the messages that are exchanged between the network and the roaming client (Misra et al., 2004; Roy, Das, & Misra, 2004). However, the applicability of the prediction algorithm is not confined to situations in which the alphabet is easily recognized; in the case of the wireless network, the alphabet consists of the cell IDs. We can have more general situations in which the application defines the symbols of the alphabet. The LZ78 algorithm has been used to track and predict the position of the inhabitants in smart-home applications (Das, Cook, Bhattacharya, Heierman, & Lin, 2002) in order to provide control over home devices. In this context, the house is modeled as a collection of nonoverlapping areas, which are later mapped into a symbolic map corresponding to the neighborhood information for each area. These notions are depicted in Figure 3 and Figure 4. Once we have done this mapping, the application of the prediction algorithm is straightforward.

Figure 3. The areas of a smart home

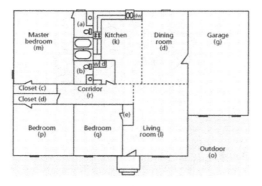

Figure 4. The symbolic representation of the example smart home

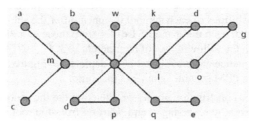

The Probabilistic Suffix Tree Scheme

The probabilistic suffix tree predictor, PST for short, was introduced in Ron, Singer, and Tishby (1996), and it presents some similarities to LZ78 and PPM. Although it specifies a maximum order for the contexts it will consider, it is actually a variable-length Markov predictor and constructs its tree for an input sequence as follows. The construction procedure uses five administratively set parameters: k, the maximum context length; a P_{min} minimum normalized appearance count for any subsequence in order to be considered for insertion into the tree; r, which is a simple measure of the difference between the prediction capability of the subsequence at hand and its direct father node; and γ_{min} and α, which together define the significance threshold for a conditional appearance of a symbol. Then, for every subsequence of length of 1 up to k, if it has never been encountered before, a new node is added to the tree, labeled by this subsequence in reverse symbol order provided that a set of three conditions hold. To exhibit the conditions, suppose that the subsequence at hand is abcd. Then, this subsequence will be inserted into the tree of the PST if

1. $E_n(abcd) \geq P_{min}$, and
2.   there exists some symbol, say, x, for which the following relations hold:

Figure 5. A PST Markov predictor for the sequence aabacbbabbacbbc

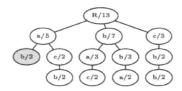

a. $\dfrac{E(abcdx)}{E(abcd)} \geq (1+a)g_{min}$, and

b. $\dfrac{\tilde{P}(x|abcd)}{\tilde{P}(x|abc)} \geq r$ or $\leq 1/r \equiv \dfrac{E(abc)}{E(abcd)} * \dfrac{E(abcdx)}{E(abcx)} \geq r$ or $\leq 1/r$

In addition, the node corresponding to the considered subsequence stores the (nonzero only) conditional probabilities of each symbol to appear after the subsequence. Obviously, the labels and statistics of each node of a PST differ from those of a PPM or LZ78 scheme. The PST predictor with the following set of parameters k=3, P_{min}=2/14, r=1.05, γ_{mim}=0.001, a=0 for the sample sequence aabacbbabbacbbc is depicted in Figure 5. Apparently, PST is a subset of the baseline PPM scheme when k is the same.

Upon completion of the construction phase, we can compute the probability of a symbol σ to appear after a context s by reversing s, and, starting from the root, can detect either the node whose label equals the reversed sequence or the deepest node whose label is a prefix of the reversed sequence. However, PST for this example is not able to produce a prediction for the test context ab (i.e., there is no subtree under the gray-shaded node).

Application Fields

Apart from this basic scheme, a number of variations have been developed, the most important reported in Apostolico and Bejerano (2000), which provided improved algorithms, that is, linear algorithms for the procedures of learning the input sequence and making predictions. Other approaches adapt the technique to specialized contexts, such as computational biology (Bejerano & Yona, 2001; Largeron-Leteno, 2003). Currently, this scheme has not been applied in online problems such as location prediction, but it could be effectively employed in the request-prediction scenario under the assumption that the request pattern of the application does not change dramatically. It is relatively stable for large time intervals.

The Context-Tree Weighting Scheme

The context-tree weighting Markov predictor (Willems, Shtarkov, & Tjalkens, 1995), CTW for short, is based on a clever idea of combining exponentially many Markov chains of bounded order. The original proposition dealt with binary alphabets only, and its later extensions for multialphabets (Volf, 2002) maintained this binary nature. For this reason, we will first describe the CTW Markov predictor for binary {0,1} alphabets and then give the most interesting and practical extension.

The CTW assumes a predetermined maximal order, say, k, for the generated model, and constructs a complete binary tree T of height k, that is, a binary tree in which every non-leaf node has two children and all leaves are at the same height k. An outgoing edge to the left-side children of T is labeled 0, and an outgoing edge to the right-side children of T is labeled 1. Each node s in T is associated with the sequence corresponding to the path from this node to the root. This sequence is also denoted as s. We can find to which input subsequence it corresponds by reversing it. The left and right children of node s are denoted as 0s and 1s, respectively.

Each node s maintains two counters, a_s and b_s, that count the number of 0s and 1s, respectively, that followed context s in the input sequence so far. Initially, all counters are set to 0. Then, we scan the input sequence by considering all subsequences of length k and for each subsequence, we update the counters of the nodes along the path defined by this subsequence. Additionally, each context (node) s maintains, apart from the pair (a_s, b_s), two probabilities, P_e^s and P_w^s. The former, P_e^s, is the Krichevsky-Trofimov estimator for a sequence to have exactly a_s 0s and b_s 1s, and it is computed as

$$\frac{\frac{1}{2}*\frac{3}{2}*\cdots\frac{2a_s-1}{2}*\frac{1}{2}*\frac{3}{2}*\cdots\frac{2b_s-1}{2}}{1*2*3*\cdots*(a_s+b_s)},$$

with $P_e^s(0,0)=1$, $P_e^s(1,0)=1/2$ and $P_e^s(0,1)=1/2$. The latter probability, P_w^s, is the weighted sum of some values of P_e, and it is computed with the following recursive formula:

$$P_w^s = \begin{cases} P_e^s & \text{for } |s| = k, \\ \frac{1}{2}P_e^s + \frac{1}{2}P_w^{0s}P_w^{1s} & \text{for } 0 \leq |s| < k. \end{cases}$$

With P_e^R and P_w^R, we denote the Krichevsky-Trofimov estimate and the CTW estimate of the root, respectively. We can predict the next symbol with the aid of a CTW as follows. We make the working hypothesis that the next symbol is a 1, and we update the T accordingly, obtaining a new estimate for the root $P_e^{'R}$. Then, the ratio $P_w^{'R}/P_w^R$ is the conditional probability that the next symbol is a 1. If the next event is indeed a 1, we need not do any update to T; otherwise, we restore the previous values of the tree and perform the update that corresponds to appending a 0 to the input sequence. The CTW predictor for the sample binary sequence 010|11010100011 is depicted in Figure 6. The first three binary digits (at the left of |) are used to create a context for the sequence.

For the case of nonbinary alphabets, Volf (2002) proposed various extensions. We present the decomposed CTW, DeCTW for short, as the best compromise between method efficiency and simplicity. First, we assume that the symbols belong to an alphabet Σ with cardinality $|\Sigma|$. We consider a full binary tree with $|\Sigma|$ leaves. Each leaf is uniquely associated with a

Figure 6. A CTW Markov predictor for the binary sequence 010|11010100011

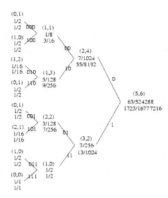

Figure 7. A sketch of the DeCTW Markov predictor for the sequence aabacbbabbacbbc

predictor	sequence it models
CTW$_1$	aaxaxxxaxxaxxxx
CTW$_2$	bcbbbbcbbc

symbol in $|\Sigma|$. Each internal node v defines the binary problem of predicting whether the next symbol is a leaf on v's left subtree or a leaf on v's right subtree. Then, we attach a binary CTW predictor to each internal node. We project the training sequence over the relevant symbols (i.e., corresponding to the subtree rooted by v) and translate the symbols on v's left (respectively, right) subtree to 0s (respectively, 1s). After training, we predict the next symbol σ by assigning each symbol a probability that is the product of binary predictions along the path from the root of the binary tree to the leaf labeled by σ. A diagram of the DeCTW is depicted in Figure 7.

Application Fields

The inherent binary nature of the CTW prohibits its wider applicability. However, it has been successfully applied to some problems related to improving the performance of computer architecture. In particular, Federovsky, Feder, and Weiss (1998) described a direct application of the CTW method to the branch-prediction problem, which is the problem of assessing whether the program under execution will follow a branch or not. They looked at the program as a binary source that generates a binary sequence in which 1s correspond to taken branches and 0s correspond to not-taken branches. Furthermore, they model this binary symbol source using the CTW and perform branch prediction by blending the individual prediction models. Several efforts have been done toward alleviating the binary nature of the CTW and extending it for multialphabets. Of particular importance is the work by Sadakane, Okazaki, and Imai (2000), which provided a very simple and practical implementation along with a technique for combining the prediction strength of PPM and CTW (Okazaki, Sadakane, & Imai, 2002).

Comparison of Prediction Schemes

In the preceding section, we surveyed a number of Markov predictors. Implicitly or explicitly, they are all based on the short-memory principle, which, simply stated, says that the (empirical) probability distribution of the next symbol, given the preceding sequence, can be quite accurately approximated by observing no more than the last k symbols in that sequence.

Although this principle appears to be simple, the complications it introduces for the prediction algorithms are far from being simple. The algorithms are faced with the problems of selecting an appropriate value for k, which in general depends on the actual values of these most recent symbols. In absence of any other information, some methods fixed in advance the value of k (e.g., PPM, CTW). Such policies mainly suffer from the following drawback. If the value of k is too low and thus too general to capture all the dependencies between symbols, then the prediction efficiency of the respective model will not be satisfactory. On the other hand, if the value of k is too large, then the model will overfit the training sequence. Therefore, variable-length Markov predictors (e.g., LZ78, PST) are most appropriate from this point of view. This was the motivation for subsequent enhancements to PPM and CTW so as to consider unbounded-length contexts, for example, the PPM* algorithm (Cleary & Teahan, 1997).

On the other hand, variable-length predictors face the problem of which sequences and of what length should be considered. PST attempts to estimate the predictive capability of each subsequence in order to store it in the tree, which results in deploying many tunable parameters. LZ78 employs a prefix-based decorrelation process, which results in some recurrent structures being excluded from the tree, at least at the first stages. This characteristic is not very important for infinite-length sequences, but may incur severe performance penalty for short sequences or for sequences in which the patterns appear only a limited number of times; for instance, the pattern bba is missing in both variants of LZ78 of Figure 2.

Despite its superior prediction performance (for instance, see Effros, 2000), PPM is far less commonly applied than algorithms like LZ78. In practice, the LZ78 schemes are favored over PPM algorithms for their relative efficiencies in memory and computational complexity. While the LZ78 predictors can be implemented with O(n) memory and complexity, straightforward implementations of some PPM variants require worst case $O(n^2)$ memory and complexity to process a data sequence of length n (Cleary & Teahan, 1997). The high computational complexity of PPM algorithms remains an impediment for their more widespread use.

Finally, particular features encountered in each algorithm may make them less appealing for some applications. For instance, the CTW, due to its coupling with binary alphabets, is not the preferred choice for applications regarding multialphabets. Off-line schemes, for example, those in Deshpande and Karypis (2004) and Ron et al. (1996), are not appropriate when request prefetching must be performed by mobile clients.

Table 1. Qualitative comparison of discrete sequence-prediction models

Prediction Method		Overhead			Drawback
Family	Markov Class	Training	Parameterization	Storage	
LZ78	variable	online	moderate	moderate	misses patterns
PPM	fixed	online	moderate	large	fixed length high complexity
PST	variable	Off line	heavy	low	parameterization
CTW	fixed	online	moderate	large	binary nature

Table 1 summarizes the Markov-predictor families and their main limitations and advantages. While the considered features and metrics provide a general guideline for algorithm evaluation, the choice and performance of a specific model largely depends on the application.

A Suffix-Tree-Based Prediction Scheme

The suffix-tree-based prediction scheme, STP for short, is a new prediction algorithm not belonging to any of the aforementioned families, and it is described in Katsaros and Manolopoulos (2005). It works as follows. It finds the largest suffix of the input sequence s_i^n—let us call it ss_i^n—whose copy appears somewhere inside s_i^n. Then, it takes a suffix of ss_i^n (the length of this suffix is a parameter of the algorithm) and locates its appearances inside s_i^n. The symbols that appear after the appearances of it are the candidate predictions of the algorithm. The final outcome of the prediction algorithms is the symbol that appears the most times. In pseudocode language, the algorithms are presented in Figure 8.

To explain how the STP algorithm works, we present a simple example.

Example. Suppose that the sequence of symbols seen so far is the following:

s_i^{24}=abcdefgabcdklmabcdexabcd. The largest suffix of s_i^{24} that appears somewhere in s_i^{24} is ss_i^4=abcd. Let α=0.5. Then, sss_i^2= cd. The appearances of cd inside s_i^{24} are located at the positions 3, 10, 17, and 23. Therefore, the marked positions are 5, 12, 19, and 25. Obviously, the last one is not null since it contains the symbol we want to predict. In the general case, all marked positions will contain some valid symbol. Thus, the sequence of candidate predicted symbols is e, k, e. Since the symbol that appears most of the time in this sequence is e, the output of the STP algorithm, that is, the predicted symbol at this stage, is e.

The implementation of the algorithm requires an appropriate data structure to support its basic operations, which are the following: (a) the determination of the maximal suffix (at Step 1), and (b) substring matching (at Steps 1 and 2). These two operations can be optimally supported by a suffix tree. The suffix tree of a string $x_1, x_2, ..., x_n$ is a tree built from all suffixes of $x_1, x_2, ..., x_n\$$, where \$ is a special symbol not belonging to the alphabet. External nodes of a suffix tree contain information about the suffix positions in the original string

Figure 8. The STP algorithm

```
Algorithm STP
// Current sequence is s₁ⁿ = s₁, s₂,..., sₙ.
// Predict the symbol after sₙ.
begin
STEP 1.
        Find the largest suffix of s₁ⁿ, whose copy appears somewhere inside s₁ⁿ.
                Let this suffix be named ss₁ˡ. Its length is l and starts at
                        the position i in s₁ⁿ, i.e.,
                        ss₁ˡ = (s_{n−l+1}, s_{n−l+2},..., sₙ) = (s_{n−i−l+1}, s_{n−i−l+2},..., s_{n−i}).
STEP 2.
        Take a suffix of ss₁ˡ of length k with k = ⌈α ∗ l⌉, where α is a parameter.
                Let this suffix be named sss₁ᵏ, where sss₁ᵏ = (s_{n−k+1}, s_{n−k+2},..., sₙ).
        Suppose that ss₁ˡ appears m times inside s₁ⁿ.
        Each such occurence defines a marker and the m positions after
                each market are called marked positions.
STEP 3.
        The predicted symbol is the symbol that appears
                the most times in the marked positions.
                (In case of ties, the prediction consists of multiple symbols.)
end
```

and the substring itself that leads to that node (or a pair of indexes to the original string in order to keep the storage requirement linear in the string length). It is a well-known result that the suffix tree can be built in linear (optimal) time (in the string length), and can support substring finding in this string also in linear (optimal) time (in the length of the substring). Therefore, the substring searching operation of our algorithm can optimally be implemented. As for the maximal suffix determination operation, if we keep pointers to those external nodes that contain suffixes ending with the $ symbol (since one of them will be the longest suffix we are looking for), then we can very efficiently support this operation as well. From the above discussion, we conclude the following: (a) The STP algorithm is online, which means it needs no training or preprocessing of the historical data, (b) the storage overhead of the algorithm is low since it is implemented upon the suffix tree, and (c) the algorithm has only one tunable parameter α, which fine-tunes the algorithm's accuracy.

Further Research

This section presents a couple of directions that we feel would be significant to explore in future research. The first suggestion concerns the development of a new prediction model, and the second proposes to remove one of the assumptions that lead to the development of the current models.

The classical result about the duality between lossless compression (Feder & Merhav, 1994) and prediction implies that any universal lossless compression algorithm can be used to carry out prediction. Although quite a lot of theoretical lossless compression schemes do exist in the literature, only a few of them have been implemented for practical purposes.

This is due to the need for effectively combining prediction efficiency, computational complexity, and low implementation effort. These three dimensions limit the range of possible alternative, practical prediction models. Toward this direction, the Burrows-Wheeler (BW) lossless compression scheme offers significant opportunities (Effros, 2000) for combining the excellent prediction ratios of PPM and the low complexity of schemes based on LZ78. So far, no practical prediction scheme is based on the BW scheme, and a plethora of issues have yet to be considered to propose a practical model based on the BW method.

The cornerstone for building the Markov predictors described in this chapter is the "stationarity" assumption, which implied time-homogeneous transition probabilities. Under this assumption, the tree of each predictor grows node by node, increasing the respective node counters; that is, identical subsequences are aggregated (mapped) into the same node of the tree. If we remove the stationarity assumption, this technique is no longer appropriate. In the simplest case, for a mobile client whose roaming patterns change gradually, the predictors will tend to favor the old habits of the client and will adapt to the changing conditions at a very slow rate. Therefore, the assumption of non-time-homogeneous transition probabilities makes the current predictors inefficient and raises some design challenges for any new scheme that will be designed to address this assumption. As we mentioned, full aggregation is not helpful; partial (controlled) or no aggregation could be considered as well, but in any case, novel prediction algorithms should be designed. The technique reported in Ehrenfeucht and Mycielski (1992) could open some directions for research.

Conclusion

Discrete sequence prediction is an effective means to reduce access latencies and location uncertainty in networking applications. Due to the importance of the problem in various scientific fields, for example, machine learning, the Web, and bioinformatics, various methods have been reported in the literature. This chapter serves as a survey in this field, promoting the cross-discipline proliferation of ideas, although it by no means covers all proposed techniques. Important research issues have yet to be addressed, such as predictions for nonstationary sequences. We envision predictive model design as a fertile research area with both theoretical and practical solutions.

Acknowledgment

This research was supported by a Γ.Γ.Ε.Τ. grant in the context of the project Data Management in Mobile Ad Hoc Networks funded by the ΠΥΘΑΓΟΡΑΣ national research program.

References

Apostolico, A., & Bejerano, G. (2000). Optimal amnesic probabilistic automata or how to learn and classify proteins in linear time and space. *Journal of Computational Biology, 7*(3-4), 381-393.

Begleiter, R., El-Yaniv, R., & Yolan, G. (2004). On prediction using variable order Markov models. *Journal of Artificial Intelligence Research, 22*, 385-421.

Bejerano, G., & Yona, G. (2001). Variations on probabilistic suffix trees: Statistical modeling and prediction of protein families. *Bioinformatics, 17*(1), 23-43.

Bhattacharya, A., & Das, S. K. (2002). LeZi-update: An information-theoretic framework for personal mobility tracking in PCS networks. *ACM/Kluwer Wireless Networks, 8*(2-3), 121-135.

Buhlmann, P., & Wyner, A. J. (1999). Variable length Markov chains. *The Annals of Statistics, 27*(2), 480-513.

Chen, X., & Zhang, X. (2003). A popularity-based prediction model for Web prefetching. *IEEE Computer, 36*(3), 63-70.

Cleary, J. G., & Teahan, W. J. (1997). Unbounded length contexts for PPM. *The Computer Journal, 40*(2-3), 67-75.

Cleary, J. G., & Witten, I. H. (1984). Data compression using adaptive coding and partial string matching. *IEEE Transactions on Communications, 32*(4), 396-402.

Curewitz, K., Krishnan, P., & Vitter, J. S. (1993). Practical prefetching via data compression. *Proceedings of the ACM International Conference on Management of Data (SIGMOD)* (pp. 257-266).

Das, S. K., Cook, D., Bhattacharya, A., Heierman, E., & Lin, T. Y. (2002). The role of prediction algorithms in the MavHome smart home architecture. *IEEE Wireless Communications Magazine, 9*(6), 77-84.

Deshpande, M., & Karypis, G. (2004). Selective Markov models for predicting Web page accesses. *ACM Transactions on Internet Technology, 4*(2), 163-184.

Effros, M. (2000). PPM performance with BWT complexity: A fast and effective data compression algorithm. *Proceedings of the IEEE, 88*(11), 1703-1712.

Ehrenfeucht, A., & Mycielski, J. (1992). A pseudorandom sequence: How random is it? *The American Mathematical Monthly, 99*(4), 373-375.

Fan, L., Cao, P., Lin, W., & Jacobson, Q. (1999). Web prefetching between low-bandwidth clients and proxies: Potential and performance. *Proceedings of ACM International Conference on Measurement and Modeling of Computer Systems (SIGMETRICS)* (pp. 178-187).

Feder, M., & Merhav, N. (1994). Relations between entropy and error probability. *IEEE Transactions on Information Theory, 40*(1), 259-266.

Feder, M., Merhav, N., & Gutman, M. (1992). Universal prediction of individual sequences. *IEEE Transactions on Information Theory, 38*(4), 1258-1270.

Federovsky, E., Feder, M., & Weiss, S. (1998). Branch prediction based on universal data compression algorithms. *Proceedings of the International Symposium on Computer Architecture (ISCA)* (pp. 62-71).

Katsaros, D., & Manolopoulos, Y. (2004). Web caching in broadcast mobile wireless environments. *IEEE Internet Computing, 8*(3), 37-45.

Katsaros, D., & Manolopoulos, Y. (2005). A suffix tree based prediction scheme for pervasive computing environments. In *Lecture notes in computer science* (LNCS 3746, pp. 267-277). Volos, Greece: Springer-Verlag.

Krishnan, P., & Vitter, J. S. (1998). Optimal prediction for prefetching in the worst case. *SIAM Journal on Computing, 27*(6), 1617-1636.

Largeron-Leteno, C. (2003). Prediction suffix trees for supervised classification of sequences. *Pattern Recognition Letters, 24*, 3153-3164.

Merhav, N., & Feder, M. (1998). Universal prediction. *IEEE Transactions on Information Theory, 44*(6), 2124-2147.

Misra, A., Roy, A., & Das, S. K. (2004). An information-theoretic framework for optimal location tracking in multi-system 4G wireless networks. *Proceedings of the IEEE International Conference on Computer Communications (INFOCOM)* (pp. 286-297).

Nanopoulos, A., Katsaros, D., & Manolopoulos, Y. (2003). A data mining algorithm for generalized Web prefetching. *IEEE Transactions on Knowledge and Data Engineering, 15*(5), 1155-1169.

Okazaki, T., Sadakane, K., & Imai, H. (2002). Data compression method combining properties of PPM and CTW. In S. Arikawa & A. Shinohara (Eds.), *Progress in Discovery Science* (LNCS 2281, pp. 268-283).

Palpanas, T., & Mendelzon, A. (1999). Web prefetching using partial match prediction. *Proceedings of the 4th Web Caching Workshop (WCW)*.

Pitkow, J., & Pirolli, P. (1999). Mining longest repeating subsequences to predict World Wide Web surfing. *Proceedings of the USENIX Symposium on Internet Technologies and Systems (USITS)* (pp. 139-150).

Ron, D., Singer, Y., & Tishby, N. (1996). The power of amnesia: Learning probabilistic automata with variable memory length. *Machine Learning, 25*(2-3), 117-149.

Roy, A., Das, S. K., & Misra, A. (2004). Exploiting information theory for adaptive mobility and resource management in future wireless networks. *IEEE Wireless Communications Magazine, 11*(4), 59-65.

Sadakane, K., Okazaki, T., & Imai, H. (2000). Implementing the context tree weighting method for text compression. *Proceedings of the Data Compression Conference (DCC)* (pp. 123-132).

Vakali, A. (2001). Proxy cache replacement algorithms: A history-based approach. *World Wide Web Journal, 4*(4), 277-297.

Vitter, J. S., & Krishnan, P. (1996). Optimal prefetching via data compression. *Journal of the ACM, 43*(5), 771-793.

Volf, P. (2002). *Weighting techniques in data compression: Theory and algorithms.* Unpublished doctoral dissertation, Technische Universiteit Eindhoven, Eindhoven, The Netherlands.

Willems, F. J., Shtarkov, Y. M., & Tjalkens, T. J. (1995). The context-tree weighting method: Basic properties. *IEEE Transactions on Information Theory, 41*(3), 653-664.

Ziv, J., & Lempel, A. (1978). Compression of individual sequences via variable-rate coding. *IEEE Transactions on Information Theory, 24*(5), 530-536.

Section III

Web Information Integration and Applications

Chapter VIII

Designing and Mining Web Applications:
A Conceptual Modeling Approach

Rosa Meo, Università di Torino, Italy

Maristella Matera, Politecnico di Milano, Italy

Abstract

In this chapter, we present the usage of a modeling language, WebML, for the design and the management of dynamic Web applications. WebML also makes easier the analysis of the usage of the application contents by the users, even if applications are dynamic. In fact, it makes use of some special-purpose logs, called conceptual logs, generated by the application runtime engine. In this chapter, we report on a case study about the analysis of conceptual logs for testifying to the effectiveness of WebML and its conceptual modeling methods. The methodology of the analysis of the Web logs is based on the data-mining paradigm of item sets and frequent patterns, and makes full use of constraints on the conceptual logs' content. As a consequence, we could obtain many interesting patterns for application management such as recurrent navigation paths, the most frequently visited page's contents, and anomalies.

Introduction

In recent years, the World Wide Web has become the preferred platform for developing Internet applications thanks to its powerful communication paradigm based on multimedia content and browsing, and to its open architectural standards that facilitate the integration of different types of content and systems (Fraternali, 1999).

Current Web applications are very complex, and the quality, as perceived by users, of highly sophisticated software products can heavily determine their success or failure. A number of methods has been proposed for evaluating their effectiveness in content delivery. Content personalization, for instance, aims at tailoring Web contents to the final recipients according to their profiles. Another approach is the adoption of Web usage-mining techniques for the analysis of the navigational behaviour of Web users by means of the discovery of patterns in the Web server log.

Traditionally, to be effective, Web usage mining requires some additional preprocessing, such as the application of methods of page annotation for the extraction of metadata about page semantics or for the construction of a Web site ontology.

In this chapter, we propose a novel approach to Web usage mining. It has the advantage of integrating Web usage mining goals directly into the Web application development process. Thanks to the adoption of a conceptual modeling method for Web application design and its supporting case tool, the generated Web applications embed a logging mechanism that, by means of a synchronization tool, is able to produce semantically enriched Web log files. This log, that we call a conceptual log (Fraternali, Matera, & Maurino, 2003), contains additional information with respect to standard (ECLF [extended comon log format]) Web server logs, and some of this information is useful to the Web mining process. It refers not only to the composition of Web pages in terms of atomic units of contents and to the conceptual entities Web pages deal with, but also to the identifier of the user crawling session and to the specific data instances that are published within dynamic pages, as well as to some data concerning the topology of the hypertext. Therefore, no extra effort is needed during or after the application development to collect the data that are necessary for reconstructing and analyzing usage behaviour.

The main contribution of this chapter comes from the integration of two existing frameworks. The first one is the model-based design and development of Web applications based on the Web Modeling Language (WebML; Ceri, Fraternali, & Bongio, 2000; Ceri, Fraternali, Bongio, et al., 2002) and its supporting CASE (computer aided software engineering) tool WebRatio (Ceri et al., 2003). The second one is an evaluation of the applications based on data-mining analytics that had started by collecting the application data based both on the static (i.e., compile-time) analysis of conceptual schemas and on the dynamic (i.e., runtime) collection of usage data. The evaluation of the application is aimed at studying its suitability to respond to users' needs by observing their most frequent paths or by observing the application response in different contexts, often difficult due to the network traffic conditions, the users themselves (such as their browsers), or even security attacks.

The distinctive merit of WebML and WebRatio in this collection of application-specific data lies in the ease with which relevant data are retrieved, automatically organized, and stored. However, the illustrated results are of general validity and apply to any application that has been designed using a model-driven approach, provided that the conceptual schema is available and the application runtime architecture permits the collection of customized log data.

This chapter presents a case study on the analysis of conceptual Web log files of the Web site of a university department. Our objective is to testify to the power and versatility of the conceptual modeling of data-intensive Web applications. The aim of our study is manifold: (a) analyzing the Web logs and extracting interesting, usable, and actionable patterns, (b) evaluating the usability (in practical cases) and the expressive power of the conceptual Web logs, and (c) verifying the suitability of some KDD scenarios. In particular, KDD (knowledge discovery in databases) scenarios have been produced as a set of characteristic data-mining requests, a sort of templates, to be filled in with specific parameter values. KDD scenarios should be able to solve some frequently asked questions (mining problems) by users or analysts (Web site administrators and/or information-system designers) in order to recover from frequently occurring problems. Some KDD scenarios for some applications, such as Web mining and financial stock-market analysis, have been studied already in Meo, Lanzi, Matera, Careggio, and Esposito (2005).

Background

The majority of the public and shareware tools for the analysis of Web application usage are traffic analyzers (see, for example, Analog, AWSD-WebLog, and CAPE WebLogs). Their functionality is limited to producing reports about site traffic, (e.g., number of visits, number of hits, page view time, etc.), diagnostic statistics (such as server errors and pages not found), referrer statistics (such as search engines accessing the application), and user and client statistics (such as user geographical region, Web browser and operating systems, etc.). Only few of them also track user sessions and present specific statistics about individual users' accesses.

A number of methods have been proposed for evaluating also Web applications' quality. In particular, Web usage mining methods are employed to analyze how users exploit the information provided by a Web site. For instance, they highlight those navigation patterns that correspond to high Web usage, or those that correspond to early leaving (Kohavi & Parekh, 2003). However, Web usage mining approaches rely heavily on the pre-processing of log data as a way to obtain high level information regarding user navigation patterns and to ground such information into the actual data underlying the Web application (Cooley, 2002; Facca & Lanzi, 2005; Srivastava, Cooley, Deshpande, & Tan, 2000).

Preprocessing generally includes four main steps: data cleaning, the identification of user sessions, content and structure information retrieval (for mapping users' requests into the actual information of visited pages), and data formatting. Notwithstanding the preprocessing efforts, in most cases, the information extracted is usually insufficient and there is much loss of the knowledge that is embedded in the application design. Futhermore, such approaches, mostly based on Web structure mining, are ineffective on applications that dynamically create Web pages.

In Dai and Mobasher (2002), the authors propose the use of ontologies to go beyond the classification of pages on the basis of the mere discovery of associations between pages and keywords. The approach uses complex structured objects to represent items associated with the pages.

Some efforts have been recently undertaken for enriching Web log files using semantic Web techniques. In Oberle, Berendt, Hotho, and Gonzales (2003), the authors exploit RDF (resource description framework) annotations of static pages for mapping page URLs (uniform resource locators) into a set of ontological entities. Within dynamic applications, the same mapping is achieved by analyzing the query strings enclosed within page URLs.

In Jin, Zhou, and Mobasher (2004), the authors have observed that standard mining approaches, such as clustering user sessions and discovering association rules or frequent navigational paths, do not generally provide the ability to automatically characterize or quantify the unobservable factors that lead to common navigational patterns. The reason is that the semantic relationships among users as well as between users and Web objects are generally hidden, that is, not available in currently generated Web logs. The authors therefore propose a probabilistic latent semantic analysis (PLSA) with the aim of uncovering latent semantic associations among users and pages based on the co-occurrence patterns of these pages in user sessions.

With respect to the previous works, the approach we present in this chapter has the advantage of integrating Web usage mining goals directly into the Web application development process. In conceptual modeling, the semantic models of the Web applications allow the specification of the application and of related data in an increased level of abstraction. The fundamental issues in the adopted methodology, as we will see better through this chapter, are the separation of the distinct tasks of the specification of a Web application; the structure of the information, designed in terms of the data entities and their logical relationships; the composition of pages in terms of content units; and their final presentation and collocation in the flow of the hypertext crawling by the user. This neat separation of roles of the various components of a Web application architecture and the clear reference to the actual objects to which the information content of each page refers to gives an enriched semantics to the obtained logs, which can be used immediately for mining, thus improving the overall application quality, its maintenance, and the experience of users on the Web site. Therefore, no extra effort is needed for Web mining during or after the application development. This is instead required by other methods for page annotation, the extraction of metadata about page semantics, or even for the construction of a Web site ontology.

The WebML Method for Web Application Development

In this section, we will shortly illustrate the main features of the adopted design model, WebML, and the rich logs that WebML-based applications are able to produce.

WebML is a conceptual model that provides a set of visual primitives for specifying the design of the information content and the hypertext of data-intensive Web applications (Ceri et al., 2002). It is also complemented by a development methodology that, in line with other model-based development methods (Baresi, Garzotto, & Paolini, 2001; Gomez, Cachero, & Pastor, 2001; Rossi, Schwabe, Esmeraldo, & Lyardet, 2001), consists of different phases centred on the definition and/or the refinement of the application's conceptual design. Thanks to the use of a CASE tool enabling automatic code generation (Ceri et al., 2003), at each iteration the conceptual design can be automatically transformed into a running prototype. This greatly facilitates the evaluation activities from the early phases of development.

WebML consists of a data model and a hypertext model for specifying respectively the content structure of a Web application and the organization and presentation of content in one or more hypertexts.

The WebML data model allows designers to express the organization of data through well-known notations (namely, the entity-relationship [E/R] and UML [Unified Modeling Language] -class diagrams). For simplicity, in this chapter, we will refer to the E/R model, which mainly consists of entities, defined as containers of data elements, and relationships, defined as semantic connections between entities.

The WebML hypertext model allows describing how contents, whose organization is specified in the data model, are published through elementary units called content units, whose composition makes up pages. It also specifies how content units and pages are interconnected by links to constitute site views, that is, the front-end hypertexts.

The WebML hypertext model includes the following:

- The composition model, concerning the definition of pages and their internal organization in terms of elementary pieces of publishable content: the content units. Content units offer alternative ways of arranging content dynamically extracted from entities and relationships of the data schema. The binding between the hypertext and the data schema is represented by the source entity and the selector of the content units. The source entity specifies the type of objects published by a content unit by referencing an entity of the E/R schema. The selector is a filter condition over the instances of the source entity, which determines the actual objects published by the unit.

- The navigation model, describing links between pages and content units that support information location and hypertext browsing. Links are represented as oriented arcs and have the double role of enabling user navigation and transporting parameters needed for unit computation.

- The content-management model, consisting of a set of operation units specifying the creation, updating, and deletion of content, and the interaction with external services.

Figure 1a shows the visual specification for the page Research Area taken from the WebML schema of the application we will analyze later on in this chapter. The page publishes the description of a university department's research area and the list of the current research topics covered by the area.

Figure 1. A simplified WebML schema for the Research Area page *in the DEI (Department of Electronics and Information, Politecnico di Milano) Web application*

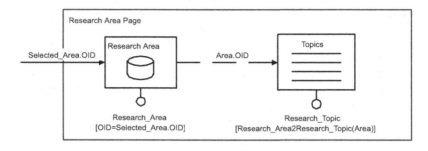

a)

```
01 <PAGE id="page3" name="Research Area">
02 <CONTENTUNITS>
03    <DATAUNIT id="dau84" name="Research Area"
04        entity="ent4" entity_name="Research_Area">
05        <DISPLAYATTRIBUTE attribute="att51" name="Area Title"/>
06        <DISPLAYATTRIBUTE attribute="att57" name="Area Description"/>
07        <SELECTOR>
08          <SELECTORCONDITION attributes="att58" att_name="OID"
09              id="cond90" sel_name="Area Selection"
10              predicate="eq" value="Selected_Area.OID"/>
11        </SELECTOR>
12        <LINK id="ln42" name="To_Area_Topics" newWindow="no" to="inu9"
13                        type="transport" parameter="Area.OID"/>
14    </DATAUNIT>
15    <INDEXUNIT id="inu9" name="Area Topics"
16        entity="ent19" entity_name="Topic" >
17        <SORTATTRIBUTE attribute="att60" name="Topic Title"
18            order="ascending"/>
19        <DISPLAYATTRIBUTE attribute="att60" name="Topic Title"/>
20        <SELECTOR>
21          <SELECTORCONDITION relationship="rel7"
22                          id="cond40" sel_name="Topics_Selection"
23                          rel_name="Research_Area2Research_Topic"
24            predicate="in"/>
25        </SELECTOR>
26    </INDEXUNIT>
27    ... ...
28 </PAGE>
```
b)

Among others (we report here a simplified schema), the page includes two content units. The first one is a data unit, publishing some attributes (e.g., the title and the textual description) of a single instance of the Research_Area entity. The instance is retrieved from the database according to a selector condition that allows selecting an area based on the equality of its OID with the OID of the area previously selected by a user (in a previous page). Such a parameter is transported by the input link of the unit. The second content unit is an index unit. It receives as input a parameter carried by a transport link coming from the data unit; such a parameter represents the OID of the area displayed by the data unit. The index unit thus lists some instances of the entity Research_Topic extracted from the database according to a condition based on the data relationship Research_Area2Research_Field, which associates each research area with a set of correlated research fields.

Besides the visual representation, WebML primitives are also provided with an XML-based representation suitable to specify additional detailed properties that would not be conveniently expressed by a graphical notation. Figure 1b reports a simplified XML specification of the Research Area page.

For further details on WebML, the reader is referred to Ceri et al. (2002).

Implementation and Deployment of WebML Applications

The XML representation of WebML schemas enables automatic code generation by means of CASE tools. In particular, WebML is supported by the WebRatio CASE tool (Ceri et al., 2003), which translates the XML specifications into concrete implementations.

WebRatio offers a visual environment for drawing the data and hypertext conceptual schemas, and an interface to the data layer that assists designers in automatically mapping the conceptual-level entities, attributes, and relationships to physical data structures in the data sources, where the actual data will be stored. The core of WebRatio is a code generator, based on XML and XSL (eXtensible Stylesheet Language) technologies, that is able to generate automatically the application code to be deployed on the J2EE (Java 2 Enterprise Edition) or .NET platforms. More specifically, the code generator produces the queries for data extraction from the application-data sources, the code for managing the application business logic, and the page templates for the automatic generation of the application front end. The generated applications run in a framework implemented on top of an application server. The runtime framework has a flexible, service-based architecture that allows the customization of components. In particular, the logging service can be extended with user-

Figure 2. Conceptual logs generation (Fraternali, Lanzi, Matera, & Maurino, 2004; Fraternali et al., 2003).

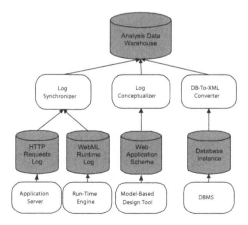

defined modules so as to log the desired data. As better clarified in the following section, this service has been used for gathering the conceptual data needed for the enrichment of the conceptual logs.

WebML Conceptual Logs

Conceptual logs (Fraternali et al., 2004; Fraternali et al., 2003) are obtained by enriching standard log files with information available in the WebML conceptual schema of the Web application, and with knowledge of accessed data. As reported in Figure 2, they are generated thanks to some modules, developed as extensions to the WebML-WebRatio framework, that are responsible for extracting and integrating logs from the application server, the WebML application runtime, and the application conceptual schema. The XML dump of the application-data source is also used for deriving detailed information about data accessed within pages. The conceptual logs indeed just include indications about OIDs of data instances.

Figure 3 reports an excerpt from a conceptual log referring to an access to the Research Area page previously described. Requests are sorted by user session.[1] Each request is then extended with the corresponding events and data coded in the runtime log.

Figure 3. An extract from a conceptual log that refers to an access to the Research Area page specified in Figure 1

```
01  <Request Request_Id="3178">
02      <LocalTime>
03      <DD>29</DD>  <Month>Mar</Month>  <YY>2003</YY>
04      <hh>02</hh><mm>03</mm><ss>34</ss>
05      <Timestamp>+0100</Timestamp>
06      </LocalTime>
07      <User>
08      <IPaddress>XXX.XXX.XXX.XXX</IPaddress>
09      <jSessionID>acbTwnzgkSz6</jSessionID>
10      <Browser>MSIE</Browser>
11      <Version>6.0</Version>
12      <Platform>compatible</Platform>
13      <OS>Windows NT 5.0</OS>
14      <CountryName/>
15      </User>
16      <Page SchemaRef="page3">
17        <PageContent>
18          <Unit SchemaRef="dau84">
20              <Data_Oid>4</Data_Oid>
21          </Unit>
22          <Unit SchemaRef="inu9">
24              <Data_Oid>15</Data_Oid>
25              <Data_Oid>24</Data_Oid>
26              <Data_Oid>10</Data_Oid>
31          </Unit>
32        </PageContent>
33      </Page>
34  </Request>
```

- The identifiers of the units composing the page are delimited by the tag <Unit>.
- The OIDs of the database objects extracted for populating such units are delimited by the <Data OID> tag.

The attribute SchemaRef, defined for pages and units, represents values that univocally identify pages and units within the application's conceptual schema. Therefore, it provides a reference to the definition of such elements, which permits the retrieval of additional properties not traced by the logging mechanism but represented in the conceptual schema, and the integration of them in the conceptual log if needed.

Main Thrust of the Chapter

The data-mining analysis of Web logs has exploited the iterative and interactive extraction of data-mining patterns from databases typical of the KDD process (Brachman & Anand, 1996). In this study, we want to extract from the rich semantic content and structured nature of the conceptual Web logs interesting, usable, and actionable patterns. In doing this, we apply constraints on the patterns. Constraints are applied to patterns by means of KDD scenarios. A KDD scenario is a set of characteristic data-mining requests on patterns. It is a sort of template to be filled in with specific parameter values. KDD scenarios should be able to solve some frequently asked questions (mining problems) by users and analysts (Web site administrators and/or information-system designers) in order to recover from frequently occurring problems.

We have identified three main typologies of mining problems for which patterns on frequently observed events could constitute an aid.

1. The identification of frequent crawling paths by the users (Web structure and Web usage analysis)
2. The identification of user communities (set of users requesting similar information)
3. The identification of critical situations (anomalies, security attacks, low performance) in which the information system could be placed

The first task enables the customization and construction of adaptive Web sites and recommendation systems, as well as the quality analysis of Web applications (Demiriz, 2004; Fraternali et al., 2003). The analysis of user crawling paths has been used also in Aggarwal (2004) to model the likelihood that a page belongs to a specific topic. This is a relevant problem in the construction of crawlers' indices and in Web resource discovery. Thus, the mining of collective users' experiences has been applied successfully to find resources on a certain topic, though this issue is typically related to the second task, that is, the identification of user communities. The discovery and management of user communities is an important aim for customer-relationship management and business applications (e.g., e-commerce).

Finally, the identification of critical situations in an information system is essential for the management of an efficient and reliable Web site together with the security of the underlying information-technology system.

Mining Conceptual Logs

The use of conceptual logs introduces many advantages over the approaches usually followed in Web usage mining. First of all, they offer rich information that is not available with most traditional approaches. Also, they eliminate the typical Web usage mining preprocessing phase completely. In fact, we note that according to our approach, the following apply.

- Data cleaning is mainly encapsulated within the procedure that integrates the different log sources (logs from the application server, the WebML application runtime, and the application's conceptual schema).
- The identification of user sessions is done by the WebML runtime through the management of session IDs.
- The retrieval of content and structure information is unnecessary since all these information are available from the WebML conceptual schema.

Finally, since mining methods are applied specifically to a type of rich log files, it is possible to tailor these methods to improve their effectiveness in this particular context.

In the following section, we describe the typology of information contained in the Web logs we processed and analyzed, as well as the KDD scenarios, that is, the templates in a Constraint-Based Mining Language.

DEI Web Application Conceptual Logs

The Web logs of the DEI Web site[2] record accesses on a very large application, collecting one fourth of the overall click stream directed to Politecnico di Milano, Italy. The application manages the publication and storage of the Web pages of professors, and research and administration staff. It publishes also the didactic offerings in terms of courses and their materials, the departments and the research centres each person is affiliated with together with their resources, and finally the list of publications, activities, and projects in which the persons are involved.

We collected the Web logs for the first consecutive 3 months in 2003. The original Web log stored by the Web server (Apache) was 60 MB large and is constituted by a relation that has the following information: RequestID, IPcaller, Date, TimeStamp, Operation, Page Url, Protocol, Return Code, Dimension, Browser, *and* OS.

The additional data, deriving from the WebML application design and from the runtime logging module, include the following items: Jsession (identifier of the user crawling session by an enabled Java browser), PageId (generated dynamically by the application server), UnitId (atomic content unit), OID (the object displayed in a page), and Order (in which content units are presented in the page).

The Web log contained almost 353,000 user sessions for a total of more than 4.2 million page requests. The total number of pages (dynamic, instantiated by means of OIDs) was 38,554. Each user session was constituted by an average of 12 page requests.

KDD Scenarios

In this section, we describe the KDD scenarios we have designed for the discovery of frequent patterns in the DEI Web logs.

A KDD scenario is a template introducing some constraints on data and on patterns to be discovered on that data. A template will be instantiated by the user in a request of frequent patterns by filling the template parameters with specific values. KDD scenarios are described by specifying the following features: grouping features (used to form groups of data in the database from which data-mining patterns will be extracted), pattern features (used to describe any element included in a pattern), mining features (used to apply mining constraints for increasing the relevance of the result), and an evaluation function, that is, one or more aggregate functions used to evaluate the patterns statistically (e.g., count(), sum(), max(), etc.).

The statistics, computed for any pattern, are compared with a parameter (displayed in the template within brackets). A template is instantiated by the user into a mining request in which the template parameters are bound to values. A mining request returns the values of the pattern features observed in groups of data made by the grouping features. The returned patterns satisfy the pattern-feature, mining-feature, and statistical constraints. For instance, the first template we discuss is the following:

Template: UsersRequestingSamePage

grouping features: Page Url

pattern features: {IPcaller}

mining features: IPcaller NOT IN{list-of-IP-of-search-engines}

evaluation function: count(Page Url)> [minValue].

It consists of partitioning the Web log data by the grouping features and the page URL. Then, in each of the groups, patterns are formed by the construction of sets of IPs of callers. In this case, the set of callers requested a same page. For each pattern, the mining features are checked. In this case, the set of IP (Internet protocols) callers is checked to be free of IPs of search engines. Finally, each pattern is evaluated statistically, counting the number of groups in which the pattern is present (i.e., the pages that have been requested by the set of callers). Notice that such a template causes the execution of a process that is essentially a typical frequent-item-set mining algorithm with an evaluation of the constraints on qualifying item-set attributes. Many efficient algorithms for this task exist dealing with different types of constraints, such as those in Srikant, Vu, and Agrawal (1997), Pei and Han (2002), and Gallo, Esposito, Meo, and Botta (2005).

We implemented KDD scenarios and related templates as mining requests in a Constraint-Based Mining Language for frequent patterns and association rules. The language is similar to the mine rule   (Meo, Psaila, & Ceri, 1998), an SQL-like extension to mine association rules from relational content. The description of the implemented prototype, the relevant algorithms, and the optimizations that exploit the properties of the constraints on patterns are beyond the scope of this chapter. However, a detailed description can be found in Meo, Botta, Esposito, and Gallo (2005). At the end of this section, we show an experimental report on the execution times that were necessary to execute with our prototype an instantiation of each of the templates.

In the following, we report some of the most relevant templates we instantiated in our experimentation on the conceptual logs, and we comment on them. In addition, when possible (for privacy reasons), we report some of the most interesting patterns retrieved and their statistics.

As the reader will be aware of, all of the templates have an immediate and practical impact on the daily activities of the administration and tuning of a Web application and its Web front end. The discovered patterns help the designer to design an adaptive application that is context and user aware, and adapts its presentation layer according to the information requested and to whom is requesting it.

Analysis of Users that Visit the Same Pages. The goal of this analysis is to discover Web communities of users on the basis of the pages they frequently visited. When this template is instantiated, the sets of IPcallers are returned who visited the same sets of a sufficiently large number of pages (>minValue).

Template: UsersVisitingCommonPages

grouping features: Page Url

pattern features: {IPcaller}

mining features: none (or specific predicates qualifying some
        specific IPcallers).

evaluation function: count(Page Url)> [minValue]

In our experiments, we discovered that the most frequently co-occurring IP addresses belong to Web crawler engines or big entities, such as universities (occurring tens of times). In the immediately lower value of support, we obviously discovered the members of the various research groups in the university. A similar query would occur if we wish to discover user communities that share the same user profile in terms of the usage of the network resources. In this case (as we will see in another example that will follow), we would add constraints (in the mining features) on the volume of the data transferred as a consequence of the user request.

Both these requests would be followed by a postprocessing phase in order to obtain a description of the actual commonalities of the users. For instance, the postprocessing step would perform a crossover query between the users and the requested resources. Examples of discovered patterns are the requests of frequent the download of materials for courses and the documentation provided in personal home pages.

It is an open issue whether the discovered regularities among IP addresses used by users in their visits to the pages occur because these IP addresses have been commonly used by the users. Indeed, this phenomenon could put in evidence the existence of different IP addresses dynamically assigned to the same users, for instance, by the information system of a big institution.

Most Frequent Crawling Paths. The goal of this template is to discover sequences of pages (ordered by the date of visit) frequently visited by the users.

Template: FreqPaths

grouping features: IPcaller

pattern features: {Page Url}

mining features: Page Urls are ordered according to the Date
        feature.

evaluation function: count(IPcaller)> [minValue]

You can notice that in this case, we did the grouping by user (IPcaller) and searched for sets of pages frequently occurring in the visits of a sufficient number of users (evaluation function). Notice also that we used a condition on the mining features to constrain the temporal ordering between pages, thus ensuring the discovery of sequential patterns. In practice, examples of resulting patterns showed that requests of a research-centre page or research-expertise area were later followed by the home page of a professor. This pattern was later used by Web administrators as a hint for restructuring the Web site access paths. Indeed, the hypothesis is that indexes for performing people search at the whole institution level were too slow. As a consequence, visitors, searching for the personal home page of a person, would have preferred to step into that page coming from the research-centre page with which the searched person was affiliated.

Units that Occur Frequently inside User Crawling Sessions. The goal of this request is to discover sets of content units that appeared together in at least a number (minValue) of crawling sessions. Notice how this query is actually possible in virtue of the conceptual logs. In fact, the presence in the log of the session identifier is not common and is a semantic notion that usually requires complicated heuristics to be reconstructed.

Template: CommonUnitsInSessions

grouping features: Jsession

pattern features: {UnitId}

mining features: none (or some specific predicate qualifying
        the particular Units).

evaluation function: count(Jsession)> [minValue]

With this template, we discovered patterns that helped Web designers to redesign the Web application. In fact, we found that the units that most frequently co-occur in visits are the structural components of the Web site (indexes, overview pages, and so on). This finding

192 Meo & Matera

could mean that the hypergraph was designed in such a way that final pages were too distant from the main access point. As a consequence, visitors happened to visit almost always the structural components of the site without reaching their final destination.

Anomalies Detection. The goal of this request is to discover the associations between pages and users who caused authentication errors when accessing those pages. In other words, we wanted to discover those pages that could be effectively used by callers as a way to illegally enter into the information system.

```
Template: Anomalies
grouping features: Date
pattern features: IPcaller, {Page Url}
mining features: IPcaller must have visited in a single Date
          all the Pages
          in the set {Page Url} and the request for
          those Pages is returned with an error = [bad
          authentication error].
evaluation function: count(Date)> [minValue]
```

In this template, we grouped source data by date, thus identifying patterns (association of users to page requests) that are frequent in time. Notice that the mining condition ensures that page requests (Page Url) effectively were originated by the callers associated to them (IPcaller). Examples of most retrieved patterns are attempts to change passwords or download some reserved information. Other queries could be instantiated by this template with the error code bounded to other values, such as "page not found." These could help in identifying the pages whose links are obsolete or erroneous.

Communication-Channel Congestion Control. The goal is to discover the causes of congested traffic over the network. The aim is to retrieve the user IP addresses (with the volume of data requested in KB) that most frequently caused high traffic (the volume must be larger than a given threshold in KB).

```
Template: ChannelCongestion
grouping features: Date
pattern features: IPcaller, {KBytes}
mining features: IPcaller must have requested in a single Date
the delivery of a volume of data (KBytes) > [thresholdDimension]
evaluation function: count(Date)> [minValue]
```

Notice that we grouped the input relation by date, thus identifying the users that requested high-volume pages frequently in time. After this query, we needed a crossover query that discovered those pages causing the high traffic. As examples of discovered patterns, there are the requests of the frequent download of materials for courses and the documentation provided on user home pages.

Application Tuning. This template aims at helping the designer in the debugging and tuning of the Web application. It searches for the (technological) conditions in which errors frequently occurred. For instance, it might return the associations between the operating system and browser at the client side with the error code frequently returned by the server.

Template: ApplicationTuning

grouping features: Date

pattern features: OS, Browser, {Return Code}

     mining features: Return Code = [errorCode]

     the requests, originated from a system

     configured with OS and Browser, ended with an

     error in {Return Code} (whose typology is

     errorCode).

evaluation function: count(Date)> [minValue]

Notice that in this template, we selected only the page requests that result in some errors, determined by the parameter errorCode. This template is similar to one aimed at the discovery of anomalies. Both of them are useful to test the reliability and robustness of a new Web application, taking into account the different configuration settings that could occur at the client side.

Users that Visit Frequently Certain Pages. This template aims at discovering if recurrent requests for a set of pages from a certain IP exist. This puts in evidence the fidelity of the users to the service provided by the Web site.

Table 1. The parameter values used to evaluate the frequent patterns extracted by the instantiated template queries

Template Name	**Evaluation-Function Threshold Value**
UsersVisitingCommonPages	30 (0.001% of the total number of pages)
FreqPaths	8 (IP Callers)
CommonUnitsInSessions	3,530 (0.05% of the total number of sessions)
Anomalies	3 (dates)
ChannelCongestion	3 (dates)
ApplicationTuning	1 (date)
UserFidelityToPages	3 (requests)

Template: UserFidelityToPages

grouping features: RequestId

pattern features: IPcaller, {Page Url}

mining features: requests to the pages in {Page Url} are

originated from IPcaller.

evaluation function: count(requestId)> [minValue]

Examples of patterns we discovered are provided again by the pages that allow the download of material (course slides, research reports).

Notice that this latter template could have been instantiated with UnitId instead of Page Url. In this way, we would have leveraged the presence in the conceptual log of the information of the content unit, and we would have highlighted the association between content and users that is more specific than the usual association between pages and users. One of the main advantages gained by the conceptual Web logs is indeed the knowledge of the information content of the pages. These content units can give us more precise information on the ultimate reasons (e.g., real content) for which certain pages are frequently requested by the users. Patterns resulting from these requests confirm that the most recurrent ones are downloads of materials from the Web site.

Execution Times of Instances of Templates

We conducted a study on the performance and feasibility of instances of the presented templates. The template instances and mining queries were executed by running a prototype of a mining system for the extraction of frequent patterns with constraints.

In Figure 4, we show instead the execution times of the above templates instantiated with the values of the parameters shown in Table 1.

Figure 4. Query execution times in experiments on conceptual logs

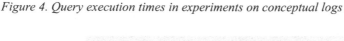

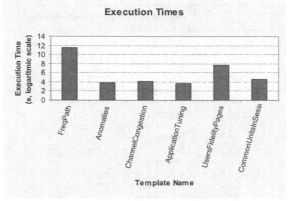

Future Trends

During the last years, several methods and tools for the analysis of Web logs have been proposed with the two emerging goals of calculating statistics about site activities and mining data about user profiles to support personalization. Several data-mining projects have demonstrated the usefulness of a representation of the structure and content organization of a Web application. However, the description of the application structure is considered a critical input to the pattern-discovery algorithms, providing information about expected user behaviours (Cooley, 2003).

Our approach is promising. It is based both on a conceptual modeling of the Web application and on templates for its analysis. Templates can be immediately instantiated according to the specificity of the single cases, and can rely on a great amount of information coming both from the conceptual schemas of the application and from the runtime collection of usage data. This will allow in the future analyzing easily the dynamic applications.

This study points out a new trend in the analysis of Web applications. Conceptual modeling and analysis allow both the improvement of the application quality and efficiency, but also allow a deeper understanding of the users' experience on the Web and help to improve the offered service. In fact, the knowledge about users themselves, their choices, and their preferences allows the construction of an adaptive site, possibly integrated with a recommendation system.

Conclusion

In this chapter, we discussed the advantages of adopting conceptual modeling for the design and maintenance of a data-intensive Web application. We presented a case study to testify to the power and versatility of conceptual modeling in consideration of the analysis of Web logs. Our application was the Web application of the DEI department, designed with WebML. The resulting Web log was a conceptual log, obtained by the integration of standard (ECFL) Web server logs with information on the Web design application and information content of Web pages.

In this case study, we applied and evaluated also the usability and flexibility of KDD scenarios for the analysis of Web logs. This proved the possibility to employ in practice these scenarios, a sort of constraint-based mining templates, to be instantiated with parameter values, resulting in patterns that are frequent in data.

We can draw now some conclusions on the discovered patterns.

In order to be useful, discovered patterns must be interesting for the user or analyst and actionable in the sense that immediate actions or decisions can be taken as a consequence of their observation. In constraint-based mining, the first point is immediately fulfilled by the retrieved patterns because, by definition, extracted patterns satisfy the given constraints. Indeed, constraints are provided by the analyst to the system in order to identify the desired patterns and discard all the remaining ones. Desired patterns could be the interesting ones, first of all, because they occur frequently and therefore refer to a statistically relevant number of events that occurred in the Web application, and secondarily because some user constraints can discriminate the properties of the desired pattern class with respect to some contrasting classes.

The second point is more difficult to establish in an absolute sense. Usually, a postprocessing phase following the proper mining phase is necessary to establish if the retrieved patterns are actionable. Generally, a crossover query that retrieves the original data in which a pattern occurs is sufficient to reveal in which way or which data representing real-life entities are involved in the phenomena described by the patterns themselves. For instance, if patterns are found describing users' attempts to change passwords, or if patterns are found putting in evidence which user configuration settings more frequently are correlated to system errors, identifying which users are causing the problem, those patterns are immediately actionable because they suggest the way in which the problem can be solved. Other patterns, such as the users' most frequent crawling paths, are more difficult to translate immediately because they involve a new design of the hypertext and main content areas that organize the Web site. Furthermore, these patterns could also identify two content areas that are contextually cor-related but do not require the involvement of a new Web site design. In this case, the solution could consist of providing the users with some additional suggestions on the pages where the user could find some correlated contents, as it happens in recommendation systems.

References

Aggarwal, C. C. (2004). On leveraging user access patterns for topic specific crawling. *Data Mining and Knowledge Discovery, 9*(2), 123-145.

Baresi, L., Garzotto, F., & Paolini, P. (2001). Extending UML for modeling Web applications. *Proceedings of HICSS'01* (pp. 1285-1294).

Brachman, R. J., & Anand, T. (1996). The process of knowledge discovery in databases: A human-centered approach. In *Advances in knowledge discovery and data mining* (p. 239). San Francisco: Morgan Kaufmann.

Ceri, S., P., & Bongio, A. (2000). Web Modeling Language (WEBML): A modeling language for designing Web sites. *Proceedings of WWW9 Conference* (pp. 137-157).

Ceri, S., Fraternali, P., Bongio, A., Brambilla, M., Comai, S., & Matera, M. (2002). *Designing data-intensive Web applications.* San Francisco: Morgan Kauffman.

Ceri, S., Fraternali, P., Bongio, A., Butti, S., Acerbis, R., Tagliasacchi, M., et al. (2003). *Architectural issues and solutions in the development of data-intensive Web applications.* Proceedings of CIDR 2003, Asilomar, CA.

Cooley, R. (2000). *Web usage mining: Discovery and application of interesting patterns from Web data.* Unpublished doctoral dissertation, University of Minnesota, Minneapolis.

Cooley, R. (2003). The use of Web structures and content to identify subjectively interesting Web usage patterns. *ACM Transactions on Internet Technology, 3*(2), 93-116.

Dai, H., & Mobasher, B. (2002). Using ontologies to discover domain-level Web usage profiles. *Proceedings of the 2nd Semantic Web Mining Workshop at ECML/PKDD-2002*. Retrieved from http://km.aifb.uni-karlsruhe.de/ws/semwebmine2002/online_html

Demiriz, A. (2004). Enhancing product recommender systems on sparse binary data. *Data Mining and Knowledge Discovery, 9*(2), 147-170.

Facca, F. M., & Lanzi, P. L. (2005). Mining interesting knowledge from Weblogs: A survey. *Data & Knowledge Engineering, 53*(3), 225-241.

Fraternali, P. (1999). Tools and approaches for developing data-intensive Web applications: A survey. *ACM Computing Surveys, 31*(3), 227-263.

Fraternali, P., Lanzi, P. L., Matera, M., & Maurino, A. (2004). Model-driven Web usage analysis for the evaluation of Web application quality. *Journal of Web Engineering, 3*(2), 124-152.

Fraternali, P., Matera, M., & Maurino, A. (2003). *Conceptual-level log analysis for the evaluation of Web application quality.* Proceedings of LA-Web'03, Santiago, Chile.

Gallo, A., Esposito, R., Meo, R., & Botta, M. (2005). Optimization of association rules extraction through exploitation of context dependent constraints. In *Lecture notes in artificial intelligence* (Vol. 3673, p. 258). Berlin; Heidelberg, Germany: Springer Verlag.

Gomez, J., Cachero, C., & Pastor, O. (2001). Conceptual modeling of device-independent Web applications. *IEEE MultiMedia, 8*(2), 26-39.

Jin, X., Zhou, Y., & Mobasher, B. (2004). Web usage mining based on probabilistic latent semantic analysis. *Proceedings of the 10th ACM SIGKDD International Conference on Knowledge Discovery and Data Mining* (pp. 197-205).

Kohavi, R., & Parekh, R. (2003). Ten supplementary analyses to improve e-commerce Web sites. *Proceedings of the 5th WEBKDD Workshop: Web Mining as a Premise to Effective and Intelligent Web Applications, ACM SIGKDD*. Retrieved from http://www.acm.org/sigs/sigkdd/kdd2003/workshops/webkdd03/

Meo, R., Botta, M., Esposito, R., & Gallo, A. (2005). A novel incremental approach to association rules mining in inductive databases. In *Constraint-based mining* (pp. 267-294). Hinterzarten, Germany: Springer Verlag.

Meo, R., Lanzi, P. L., Matera, M., Careggio, D., & Esposito, R. (2005). Employing inductive databases in concrete applications. In *Constraint-based mining* (pp. 295-327). Hinterzarten, Germany: Springer Verlag.

Meo, R., Psaila, G., & Ceri, S. (1998). An extension to SQL for mining association rules. *Journal of Data Mining and Knowledge Discovery, 2*(2), 195-224.

Oberle, D., Berendt, B., Hotho, A., & Gonzales, J. (2003). Conceptual user tracking. In *Lecture notes in artificial intelligence: Vol. 2663. Proceedings of the First International Atlantic Web Intelligence Conference, AWIC 2003* (pp. 142-154). Madrid: Springer Verlag.

Pei, J., & Han, J. (2002). Constrained frequent pattern mining: A pattern-growth view. *SIGKDD Explorations, 4*(1), 31-39.

Rossi, G., Schwabe, D., Esmeraldo, L., & Lyardet, F. (2001). Engineering Web applications for reuse. *IEEE Multimedia, 8*(1), 20-31.

Srikant, R., Vu, Q., & Agrawal, R. (1997). Mining association rules with item constraints. *Proceedings of the 3rd International Conference on Knowledge Discovery and Data Mining: KDD'97* (pp. 67-73).

Srivastava, J., Cooley, R., Deshpande, M., & Tan, P. N. (2000). Web usage mining: Discovery and applications of usage patterns from Web data. *SIGKDD Explorations, 1*(2), 12-23.

Chapter IX

Integrating Heterogeneous Data Sources in the Web

Angelo Brayner, University of Fortaleza, Brazil

Marcelo Meirelles, University of Fortaleza, Brazil

José de Aguiar Moraes Filho, University of Fortaleza, Brazil

Abstract

Integrating data sources published on the Web requires an integration strategy that guarantees the local data sources' autonomy. A multidatabase system (MDBS) has been consolidated as an approach to integrate multiple heterogeneous and distributed data sources in flexible and dynamic environments such as the Web. A key property of MDBSs is to guarantee a higher degree of local autonomy. In order to adopt the MDBS strategy, it is necessary to use a query language, called the MultiDatabase Language (MDL), which provides the necessary constructs for jointly manipulating and accessing data in heterogeneous data sources. In other words, the MDL is responsible for solving integration conflicts. This chapter describes an extension to the XQuery Language, called MXQuery, which supports queries over several data sources and solves such integration problems as semantic heterogeneity and incomplete information.

Introduction

The Web (World Wide Web) can be seen as a wide network consisting of the union of several local area networks (LANs) spread over the entire world. However, the local networks that constitute the Web are autonomous and capable of plugging or unplugging themselves into and from the Web at any time.

Over the last few years, the Web has been used to publish several databases. Of course, databases available on the Web are heterogeneous since they might be defined by using different data models (e.g., relational or object data model), managed by different database systems (DBSs), or running in different computational environments (regarding operating system and hardware). Furthermore, the integration of databases on the Web should be realized without interfering in the management and processing of local data. In other words, databases should be integrated preserving the local autonomy of each database. Despite the fact that heterogeneity and the autonomy of multiple databases on the Web is a reality nowadays, users (and applications) need shared access to those databases. Thus, it is possible to submit queries against several heterogeneous databases located in distinct local networks throughout the Web.

Consequently, integrating databases published on the Web has become a challenge to the database technology. Several approaches for integrating heterogeneous and autonomous data sources have been proposed since the late '80s. In this chapter, we propose a strategy based on the multidatabase approach for integrating heterogeneous databases published on the Web. For that reason, we describe a new MultiDatabase Language (MDL), called MX-Query, since the proposed strategy uses XML (extensible markup language) as the common data model (CDM; conceptual schema) to represent the multiple data sources' schemas. The MXQuery, which is an extension to the XQuery Language, provides constructors and operators for supporting queries over multiple heterogeneous data sources. The MXQuery solves integration problems such as semantic heterogeneity and incomplete information. Furthermore, this chapter presents an architecture to process MXQuery queries.

This chapter is organized as follows. Approaches for integrating heterogeneous data sources are studied next. Then, related work is discussed, followed by a description of the MXQuery MultiDatabase Language. Next we present in detail the features of the proposed integration strategy, and then give an overview of the query-processor architecture for the MXQuery Language. Finally, we conclude the chapter.

Data-Integration Approaches

Federated Databases

Federated database is an approach for integrating heterogeneous databases. In a federation of databases, there is a federated schema global to all local component databases. With a federated schema, users make use of an external schema to submit data queries and updates. The federated schema suffers from the (local to global) schema-evolution drawback. In other words, an evolution (modification) of a local schema demands a corresponding modification of the federated (global) schema and can bring about a consistency-loss risk. Federated schema is static in the sense that its maintenance is up to a database administrator (DBA). In general, the federated schema is stored as part of each component database.

Mediators

Motivated by the Web, several research works (Bougamin, Fabret, Mohan, & Valduriez, 2000; Chen, DeWitt, Tian, & Wang, 2000; Das, Shuster, & Wu, 2002; Goldman & Widom, 2000; Manolescu, Florescu, & Kossman, 2001) have focused on the issue of using mediators for integrating databases available on the Web. Mediators are usually specialized software components (and/or engines) for integrating data. A mediator provides a set of virtual views over different sources, called mediated schema, so that it does not change any local database (LDB) schemas. It provides a service for hiding all data characteristics from its users, allowing them to get data in a uniform way.

With respect to the task of building an integrated view (federated or mediated schema), there are three different strategies. The first is global-as-view (GAV), which is also called the global-schema-centric approach. The global schema is described as a view over the local schemas. In other words, each component of the global schema is defined in terms of the source schemas. Next is local-as-view (LAV), which is also called the source-centric approach. Local schemas are described as views over the global schema. In other words, the mappings may define the components of each source schema in terms of the global schema. Third is generalized local-as-view (GLAV), which is a mixed approach that consists of associating views over the global schema with views over local schemas.

Multidatabase

An approach for integrating databases is the multidatabase technology, whose key feature is to provide interoperability among multiple heterogeneous and autonomous databases without attempting to integrate them by means of a single global schema (Elmagarmid, Rusinkiewicz, & Shethm, 1999). A multidatabase consists of a collection of autonomous databases, called local databases. Systems used to manage multidatabases are called multidatabase systems (MDBSs). An MDBS should provide full database functionality and is built on top of multiple DBSs, called local DBSs (LDBSs), each of which operates autonomously. Local autonomy is a key feature of the multidatabase technology.

In an MDBS, the multidatabase language plays a key role since it guarantees database integration and interoperability. Roughly speaking, an MDL represents simultaneously the DDL and the DML of an MDBS. Notwithstanding, the MDL should provide additional features not presented by existing database languages (e.g., SQL). An example of such a feature is the ability to use logical database names for qualifying data in different databases. This is because the multidatabase approach shifts the integration task from global DBAs to users and local DBAs. Therefore, a global query should contain the necessary information for manipulating local data. This implies that the user knows what information is required and where it can be found. For that reason, it is important that an MDBS offers a tool, for example, an object browser, to help the user to obtain this knowledge. For a detailed discussion about multidatabase languages, the reader is referred to Domenig and Dittrich (2000), Elmagarmid, Bouguettaya, and Benatallah (1998), Grant, Litwin, Roussopoulos, and Sellis (1993), and Özsu and Valduriez (1999).

In a context where the integration should be carried on in flexible and dynamic environments such as the Web and a high degree of autonomy of each local database is critical, the multidatabase approach is quite adequate. On the other hand, XML provides quite a natural way to be used as a common data model for data integration. It is powerful enough to represent structured, unstructured, and semistructured data. Moreover, its related technologies, such as DOM, XML schema, and XQuery, can contribute to the development of a standard mapping language.

Therefore, in order to adopt the MDBS strategy to access data stored in data sources available on the Web, it is necessary to use a multidatabase language that (a) can support the capability to jointly manipulate data in different data sources and (b) can be based on the XML data model since XML is almost a de facto standard for data representation on the Web.

Related Work

Several MDLs have been proposed in order to provide support for accessing distributed and heterogeneous data sources. In Grant et al. (1993) and Litwin, Abdellatif, Zeroual, Nicolas, and Vigier (1989), an MDL called MSQL is proposed. In order to integrate heterogeneous databases by means of MSQL, the relational data model is used as the CDM. Although MSQL is more expressive than SQL, the language is quite limited in its ability to deal with structural incompatibilities. MSQL introduces semantic variables. However, such variables are only responsible for solving name conflicts (synonymous and homonymous). Furthermore, the join operation among databases is limited to domain-compatible operations (Missier & Rusimkiewicz, 1995). Finally, another limitation to MSQL, pointed out by Krishnamurthy, Litwin, and Kent (2001), is having to cope with schematic discrepancies or structural conflicts.

As already mentioned, in order to use MSQL, it is necessary to adopt the relational model as the conceptual data model. In other words, MSQL allows only queries on relational schemas. Mapping a postrelational data model, such as a semistructured data model, in such a rigid data model is a quite complex task. Therefore, MSQL is not efficient for integrating data sources based on the Web.

The work proposed by Missier and Rusimkiewicz (1995) defines global attributes that will represent the integration result from a query. Then, declarative instructions are used to map the attributes of the local databases to these global attributes. After the mapping definition (query context), one can submit queries against the data sources using a language borrowed from SQL. Furthermore, the queries can use implicit joins, which makes these queries more powerful and result oriented.

The IDL language, presented by Krishnamurthy et al. (2001), allows solving the problems addressed by the MSQL language; however, the main contribution of the IDL is coping with structural conflicts, called schematic discrepancies (Krishnamurthy et al.). Although a part of these problems can be solved by the MSQL language, other kinds of problems cannot, for instance, integrating data represented as data in one schema and as metadata in another schema. Both approaches presented by Krishnamurthy et al. and Missier and Rusimkiewicz (1995) are more expressive than the MSQL language. However, they are still limited by the relational data model.

Domenig and Dittrich (2000) present an OQL-like language in which the data can be visualized at different conceptual levels. Such conceptual levels arrange the data from distinct data sources according to similar features. This conceptual-level presentation is called data space, which is used for integrating structured, semistructured, and unstructured data. Since the OQL language presents mechanisms to query data sets, these mechanisms cannot be used to query over unstructured or semistructured data. For that reason, the authors present an extension to the OQL, called SOQL (Domenig & Dittrich, 2000).

The SOQL approach defines two distinct steps for integrating data sources. In the first one, called preintegration, the DBAs identify similarities and conflicts among data sources and then specify correspondence rules among the schemas (query context). In the second step, called integration, the final schema is built from the correspondence rules. Despite the flexibility from that approach, it is necessary to build a (global) schema before submitting queries. Moreover, the schema must be rebuilt each time a new correspondence rule or a new data source comes into the multidatabase community.

The approach proposed by Sattler, Conrad, and Saake (2000), called FRAQL, is similar to the approach presented in Missier and Rusimkiewicz (1995). The FRAQL language uses declarative instructions that make it possible to map objects from a local schema into objects of a global schema (Sattler et al., 2000). Initially, it is defined as a global schema that will be used for the users to submit queries. Then, the local schemas are mapped according to the global schema, where it is possible to use user-defined functions if is necessary. The correspondence between local and global schemas defines the query-execution context. The queries are submitted over the global schema and then are translated into subqueries using the predefined mapping.

Differently from the approach adopted in Domenig and Dittrich (2000), the FRAQL approach does not require one to rebuild the global schema whenever a new data source comes into the community. However, it is necessary to define a mapping between local and global schema before one can submit a query.

The XQuery Language (Boag et al., 2003; Chamberlin, Robie, & Florescu, 2000; Robie, Chamberlin, & Florescu, 2000) has several features that allow querying XML documents and presenting a new XML document as a result. This new XML document can be a subtree from the original XML document or can present a different structure. These features make the XQuery Language quite expressive and powerful. Furthermore, it is possible to submit queries against multiple data sources. Although it is possible to represent union and join operations between these data sources, the XQuery Language does not present any mechanism for solving integration conflicts. Thus, the XQuery queries presume that distinct data sources were created in a single data-source design.

The XQuery Language allows element construction, which makes it possible to repair the absence of mechanisms for conflict resolution. Despite the fact that element constructors present some facilities to solve conflicts, it does not give a formal mapping among attributes from distinct data sources. Therefore, such constructors do not define, in a simple way, the conceptual relationship among these data sources. Consequently, the XQuery queries are quite complex to query data in several data sources on the Web. Moreover, the XQuery Language does not cope with the connection and disconnection of data sources. This feature is essential in dynamic environments such as Web and ad hoc networks.

MXQUERY

The proposed MDL, MXQuery, extends the XQuery Language by introducing constructors and operators for supporting queries over multiple heterogeneous data sources. MXQuery should be used in the MDBS context, where local data sources are viewed as XML documents. MXQuery provides mechanisms for coping with semantic heterogeneity and incomplete information during the execution of queries over heterogeneous data sources.

The XQuery Language is focused on querying semistructured data and, therefore, it presents flexible structures to identify the required information and arrange them according to the user's specification. The MXQuery Language incorporates these features and introduces mapping declarations among distinct data sources to represent the conceptual relationship among those data sources.

The idea behind MXQuery is to use mapping declarations among the data sources to one or more elements of an XML document, which will contain the query result. The mapping process is expressed in the query itself, making the MXQuery Language more flexible than the approaches presented in Missier and Rusimkiewicz (1995) and Sattler et al. (2000). Moreover, it is possible to use result variables, which represent the result XML document, and data-source variables, which represent the data sources, in the WHERE-clause specification. Thus, one may introduce filters (conditions) over data already integrated and/or over local data sources. For that reason, the existing conditions in the query are evaluated in two distinct moments. Conditions over local data sources are inserted in the subqueries submitted to the data sources. Conditions over integrated data are evaluated after the global result construction; that is, it is possible that the query postprocessor excludes elements after a condition evaluation. For instance, the expression "WHERE $p/book/year > '1999'," in which $p represents a result XML document, is evaluated after the data integration. Thus, it could be generated as useless data traffic. <Book> elements with <year> subelements that have values of less than 1999 are sent to the query manager (QM), and only after data integration are these elements discarded. However, in the MXQuery approach, the MDBS architecture tries first to transform the conditions over integrated data to conditions over local data sources. Such kinds of simplification could reduce the data traffic.

Differently from the approaches proposed in Domenig and Dittrich (2000), Missier and Rusimkiewicz (1995), and Sattler et al. (2000), the MXQuery Language does not require a query context definition. Thus, queries expressed by the MXQuery are more dynamic and, consequently, they suffer less from influences of the local schema evolutions, and the connection and disconnection of new data sources. Therefore, when an MXQuery query is submitted, all information about how to integrate the local data sources is represented in the query.

Coping with incomplete information is a great challenge for processing queries that access multiple heterogeneous data sources (Abiteboul, Segoufin, & Vianu, 2001; Tomasic, Raschid, & Valduriez, 1996). To solve this problem, MXQuery makes it possible to identify in a query what information is mandatory for the user. Nonmandatory information is considered as backing information. When such information is not available or even incorrectly defined, it is not returned in the query result. Consequently, the query processor can change the original query to extract any reference to an optional data source when the reference of the original query is unavailable at the moment of the query evaluation.

EFLWOR Expressions

MXQuery introduces the notion of EFLWOR (each FLWOR) expressions, an extension to the concept FLWOR expressions in the XQuery syntax. An EFLWOR expression has the functionality of traversing all elements of trees that represent XML documents. Recall that XML documents represent, in turn, a local data source in an MDBS. It is important to note that in the proposed integration strategy, each data source is viewed as an XML document. The result of an EFLWOR is represented by a tree as well, called a result tree.

The result tree is produced through the union, join, and/or fusion (algebraic) operations over elements belonging to distinct XML documents, each of these representing a distinct local data source. Before defining those operations, it is important to define the concept of equivalence between two XML elements. Two XML elements are said to be equivalent if they have the same value for a given attribute, defined as a matching attribute. The idea behind the concept of XML-element equivalence is to identify elements that represent the same entity of the real world.

The union operation is a binary operation in which the operands are XML documents. The union operation represents the less restrictive way to build a result tree for queries over heterogeneous data sources since it does not require type compatibility (as required in the relational data model, for example) between the operands. The union of two XML documents in MXQuery has the semantic of enclosing the operands as children of the root node of the result tree.

The join operation in an MXQuery expression can be implicit or explicit. An implicit join is specified when the dereference operator is used in a path expression. An explicit join has the same semantic of a theta join of the relational algebra. For that reason, it is necessary to use a WHERE clause to specify the join condition in order to identify whether or not elements belonging to a distinct document satisfy the join condition. It is important to note that it is not possible to use the dereference operator for jointly manipulating distinct data sources. Consequently, only the explicit join can be used to perform joins between elements belonging to distinct data sources.

The fusion operation is similar to the concept of the full outer join of the relational algebra. The result tree produced by a fusion operation encloses all elements belonging to distinct documents (data sources) that satisfy a join condition and the ones that do not satisfy that condition. Query 1 (under "Using MXQuery" later in the chapter) illustrates a fusion operation.

Table 1. EFLWOR-expression syntax

[42]	EFLWORExpr	::=	EachClause (ForClause | LetClause) * WhereClause? OrderByClause? "return" ExprSingle
[144]	EachClause	::=	"each" "$" VarName "full"? ("," "$" VarName "full"?)* DefClause
[145]	DefClause	::=	AliasClause (AliasClause)* (EqualClause)*
[146]	AliasClause	::=	"alias" PathExpr "$" VarName "null"? ("," "$" VarName "null"?)*
[147]	EqualClause	::=	"equal" RelativePathExpr* "is" RelativePathExpr "key"? "hide"?
[43]	ForClause	::=	"for" "$" VarName TypeDeclaration? PositionalVar? "in" ExprSingle ("," "$" VarName TypeDeclaration? PositionalVar? "in" ExprSingle)*
[45]	LetClause	::=	"let" "$" VarName TypeDeclaration? ":=" ExprSingle ("," "$" VarName TypeDeclaration? ":=" ExprSingle)*
[122]	TypeDeclaration	::=	"as" SequenceType
[44]	PositionalVar	::=	"at" "$" VarName
[46]	WhereClause	::=	"where" Expr
[47]	OrderByClause	::=	("order" "by" | "stable" "order" "by") OrderSpecList
[48]	OrderSpecList	::=	OrderSpec ("," OrderSpec)*
[49]	OrderSpec	::=	ExprSingle OrderModifier
[50]	OrderModifier	::=	("ascending" | "descending")? (("empty" "greatest") | ("empty" "least"))? ("collation" StringLiteral)?

Since MXQuery extends XQuery, part of the MXQuery's grammar can be found in Boag et al. (2003). Therefore, Table 1 extends the syntax description of the XQuery Language by introducing the EFLWOR expressions. The first column presents sequential numbers that represent clauses of XQuery's grammar (Boag et al.). In the table, the elements 144 to 147 have been inserted in the original XQuery grammar. The elements 42, 43, 44, 45, 46, 47, and 122 replace the elements from the original grammar.

The EFLWOR expression from the MXQuery Language introduces the following new clauses: EACH, ALIAS, EQUAL, FULL, NULL, HIDE, and KEY. These clauses are used to identify the queried data sources and to specify the mapping between local attributes (from the local data sources) and global attributes (from the result tree).

EACH. The EACH clause binds values to one or more variables, denoted as result variables. Such variables are used to construct the result tree that represents the result of the integrating process of the integration mechanism. For example, the clause "EACH $p" defines that a variable $p will contain the result of a query over multiple heterogeneous data sources. The rules for the integrating process (such as rules for conflict resolution) should be specified in other declarations of an MXQuery expression. A variable bound in an EACH clause is a well-formed XML document. For that reason, such a variable can be used in any other MXQuery clause that accepts a tree as an input parameter.

ALIAS. This clause specifies one or more variables, denoted as source variables, representing an XML tree (document), which in turn represents a data source in the MXQuery integration strategy. Variables specified in an ALIAS clause can be used by any EFLWOR declaration that accepts a tree as an input parameter. In order to illustrate the use of an ALIAS clause, consider the following MXQuery expression: "ALIAS document ('d2.xml')/lib $d2." This expression defines a variable $d2 that represents a data source represented by the document d2.xml. The document function defined in Boag et al. (2003) identifies an XML document that represents one local data source. Moreover, this function indicates the entry point in a forest of nodes of an XML document. The declaration order from ALIAS clauses in an MXQuery expression specifies the priority of the data sources involved in the query. The priority order specified in an ALIAS clause will be used to solve value conflicts (Sattler et al., 2000) in which the values from elements belonging to data sources with a higher order of priority will be considered as valid values. For example, the first ALIAS declaration identifies the data source that has the higher priority.

EQUAL. The optional EQUAL clause specifies rules for integrating elements belonging to distinct documents (data sources). This clause is responsible for resolving most of the integration conflicts. The key idea of an EQUAL clause is to specify semantic relationships among elements of distinct documents. For example, in the MXQuery expression "EQUAL $d1/livro $d2/book IS $p/book," it is specified that the <livro> element of document $d1 and the <book> element of the document $d2 represent the same concept of the real world; that is, they are synonyms. For that reason, the <livro> element and <book> element will appear in the result as the <book> element. The specification of an EQUAL clause can be shortened. For example, in the expression "EQUAL $d1/livro $d2/book IS $p/book," this can be done by omitting the <book> element of document $d2 since it has the same name as the new element (<book> element of $p). The shortened declaration is the following: "EQUAL $d1/livro IS $p/book." In Query 1 (see "Using MXQuery" later in the chapter), one can observe the use of the abbreviation mechanism in an EQUAL clause. Normally, only elements referenced in some EQUAL-clause declaration will compose the variable specified in the EACH clause (see the definition of the FULL clause).

FULL. The optional FULL clause can be used in association with the EACH clause. This clause specifies that all elements from all data sources declared in the ALIAS clauses will compose the result tree even though they are not declared in the EQUAL clause. If one does not specify any type of restriction (filter), then a FULL clause produces the UNION of all documents referenced in the query.

NULL. The optional NULL clause can be used in association with the ALIAS clause. This clause specifies that a document is nonmandatory for the query result. Consequently, if a data source is unavailable or is not correctly declared in the query (e.g., incorrect path expression), then any declaration to this data source (or some element belonging to it) will be ignored. For example, in a query that contains the MXQuery expression "ALIAS document('d2. xml')/lib $d2 NULL," the document d2.xml is defined as nonmandatory for the query result. In this case, despite the fact that the data source corresponding to the document d2.xml is unavailable, the query is still processed. In the same way, elements belonging to d2.xml that appear in other declarations of the same query will be suppressed. For instance, the declaration "EQUAL $d1/livro $d2/book IS $p/book" in the same query would be processed as if the element $d2/book was not part of the expression. This makes it possible that schema evolution in local data sources does not imply aborting a query. This property is important to flexible and dynamic environments such as the Web.

HIDE. The optional HIDE clause can be used in association with the EQUAL clause. This clause indicates that the elements declared in the EQUAL clause will not appear in the result tree. For example, consider the declaration "EQUAL $d2/book/year $d1/livro/ano IS $p/book/year HIDE" in a given query. The element book/year (result from the resolution of a synonyms conflict) can be referenced in other clauses; however, it will not be part of the result tree. The HIDE clause has precedence over the FULL clause; that is, an element that uses the HIDE clause will not compose the result tree presented even though it has been used by the FULL clause.

KEY. The optional KEY clause can be used in association with the EQUAL clause. It indicates that the specified elements represent matching attributes. This is done by matching properties of distinct documents. For example, in "EQUAL $d1/livro/@isbn $d2/book/isbn IS $p/book/isbn KEY," the documents d1.xml and d2.xml produce a new element book/isbn, which behaves as a matching attribute for the elements of the original documents ($d1 and $d2).

NAME(n) Function

The NAME(n) function was also incorporated by the XQuery Language (Boag et al., 2003). However, in the XQuery Language, it is only responsible for identifying a data origin. In other words, that function returns the name of the data assigned for n. The MXQuery also incorporates the NAME(.n) function. This function returns the container from the data specified for n. In a hierarchy, the term container represents the upper object to a specific object. For example, in a relational database, a table behaves as the container of attributes, while the database behaves as a table container. It is also possible to nest the NAME(.n) function. For example, NAME(.NAME(.n)) returns the container of the container of n.

Using MXQuery

In this section, the applicability of the MXQuery Language is illustrated. Consider that two bookstores (B1 in Brazil and B2 in New Zealand) decide to jointly offer their books on the Web. However, they have decided as well that each bookstore manages its own data source. In other words, local autonomy should be preserved. Now, suppose that the data sources belonging to the bookstores are heterogeneous. Therefore, the idea is to integrate hetero-geneous data sources without violating the local autonomy of each data source. For that reason, the bookstores' managers have decided to use the MDBS technology for integrating the heterogeneous data sources. Each local data-source schema should be represented in XML schema (Elmagarmid et al., 1998). The document d1.xml (see Appendix A) represents part of a relational database in which data of the bookstore B1 are stored. The document d2.xml represents data of bookstore B2, which are stored in a data source that cannot be characterized as a database system (for example, HTML documents).

Query 1. A Brazilian customer wants to search for a title, author, and price from all books in the bookstores B1 and B2. For this query, the ISBN should be used as a matching attribute. A possible MXQuery expression is presented in Figure 1.

The execution of Query 1 returns a variable $p that contains <book> elements of documents d1.xml and d2.xml (specified in the ALIAS clauses), each of which contains the <isbn> subelements, <title> subelements, <author> subelements, and <price> subelements. The result of this query is bound to an element with a <library> root element (because of the declaration of the RETURN clause). It is important to note that the expression "EQUAL $d1/livro/titulo $d2/book/title IS $p/book/title" specifies that livro/titulo and book/title are synonyms, representing, therefore, the same concept of the real world. This shows that the MXQuery provides necessary support to users in order to define directives for solving semantic conflicts.

Note that in the expression "EQUAL ($d1/livro/preco / 2.98) IS $p/book/price," a currency conversion is made (in this example, from real to dollar). Therefore, this conversion func-tion solves a domain conflict existing between both data sources specified in Query 1. Other arithmetical operators can be used to produce any kind of conversion functions.

Observe that, the KEY clause is used to specify the matching attribute, in this case, the ISBN. By doing this, it is possible to specify when books that are stored as different objects represent, in fact, the same entity of the real world. In this case, a fusion operation should be applied over those objects. Observe that in Query 1 the equivalence declaration for author

Figure 1. MXQuery expression for Query 1

```
EACH $p
  ALIAS document("d1.xml")/bib $d1
  ALIAS document("d2.xml")/lib $d2
  EQUAL $d1/livro $d2/book IS $p/book
  EQUAL $d1/livro/@isbn $d2/book/isbn IS $p/book/isbn KEY
  EQUAL $d1/livro/titulo $d2/book/title IS $p/book/title
  EQUAL $d1/livro/autor IS $p/book/author          Shorted EQUAL-clause
  EQUAL ($d1/livro/preco / 2.98) IS $p/book/price
RETURN
  <library>
    $p                                    Currency conversion
  </library>
```

and price are in the shortened form. It is important to note that this fact does not cause any impact on the query result. The query result corresponds to an element composed by four <book> subelements.

Query 2. A costumer wants to search titles from all books published after 1999 in the databases of the bookstores B1 and B2. For this query, the ISBN should be used as the matching attribute. The MXQuery expression shown in Figure 2 can be used to express this query.

Query 2 is similar to Query 1; however, the equivalence declaration of the <ano> subelement with the <year> subelement was added, thereby solving a synonyms conflict. Observe that, different from the equivalence declarations of subelements specified in Query 1, the declaration specified in Query 2 does not determine that the <year> subelement composes the result of this query. This is because the HIDE clause was used. The idea is to use the <year> subelement (after the resolution of the synonym conflict) for performing a query filter, which was specified in a WHERE clause.

As in the scenario presented in Appendix A, there is a value conflict between two of the elements that should compose the result tree of this query. Two <book> elements have the same ISBN; however, they have the <year> and <title> subelements with distinct values. In document d1.xml, the <ano> subelement is equal to 2001. On the other hand, in document d2.xml, the same object has a <year> element with a value equal to 1999. Furthermore, the <titulo> subelement is presented in Portuguese in document d1.xml, and the <title> subelement is presented in English in document d2.xml. These value conflicts are solved, indicating the data source whose documents' properties' contents must prevail over the other one. This indication is made through the declarations order of the participant data sources. In Query 2, the data source specified by the variable $d1 is prioritized; that means, in case of value conflict, its content will be preserved. Due to this fact, the integration result between the data sources d1.xml and d2.xml determines that the value of the <year> subelement must be equal to 2001, and the <title> subelement must appear in the query result in Portuguese.

The use of a NULL clause in Query 2 determines that the nonavailability of the document d2.xml during the query execution does not make the result impracticable. Coincidently, the presented result is the same independent of the availability of d2.xml; however, its nonavailability causes an error if the NULL clause was not specified.

Figure 2. MXQuery expression for Query 2

```
EACH $p
  ALIAS document("d1.xml")/bib $d1
  ALIAS document("d2.xml")/lib $d2 NULL
  EQUAL $d1/livro IS $p/book
  EQUAL $d1/livro/@isbn $d2/book/isbn IS $p/book/isbn KEY
  EQUAL $d1/livro/titulo IS $p/book/title
  EQUAL $d1/livro/ano IS $p/book/year HIDE
WHERE $p/book/year > "1999"
RETURN
  <library>
    $p                          Result variable based
  </library>                    filter
```

Integration Strategy

Since we are proposing the use of the MDBS technology as an integration strategy for heterogeneous data sources, in Figure 3 is depicted an abstract model of the proposed architecture for integrating data stored in heterogeneous, distributed, and autonomous data sources.

In Figure 3, the query user interface (QUI) does the mediation between the user and the integration architecture, being responsible for receiving queries and presenting the query results. A user who wishes to access multiple integrated data sources through this architecture must send a query using MXQuery syntax, called global query. After that, global queries are sent to the QM. The main function of this component is to divide a global query into subqueries and to send them to the corresponding data sources.

The query manager is divided into three main components, which are the query processor (QP), location processor (LP), and query postprocessor (QPp). The query processor receives queries expressed in MXQuery syntax, identifies the data sources referenced, simplifies and optimizes the global queries, generates the subqueries, and finally sends these subqueries to the corresponding data sources. The location processor plays an auxiliary role for the query processor since it has to locate the referenced data sources and specify the location errors. Location errors can mean the nonavailability of some referenced data source. Such information is useful in the query-simplification process because the inaccessible data sources must be excluded from the query. The exclusion process of a data source from a query must obey the rules established in the proper query. If it is possible to exclude the data source, then all expressions that refer to the data source excluded should be excluded too. The data sources that can be excluded are identified in the MXQuery syntax using the NULL clause.

Subqueries are sent for XML interfaces, for which they are translated into a native query language and directed to the local data sources corresponding to the XML interfaces. Therefore, a query has an XML interface associated with each local data source. The role played for an XML interface will be argued later.

Figure 3. Integration-mechanism architecture

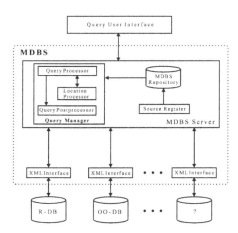

After a local processing, the result of a subquery is sent to the XML interface, where it is translated (for XML format) and directed to the query postprocessor. This component must use the rules established in the original query for conflict resolution. For example, a rule can be established to solve problems of synonyms using the EQUAL expression. Therefore, the user is capable of supplying information to the query postprocessor; thus, the QPp can solve conflict problems using the MXQuery syntax.

After the conflict resolution, the QPp must match the result from the diverse subqueries received using the rules established in the original query for result construction. The combined result of the subqueries is, finally, directed to the query user interface.

The source register (SR) is responsible for controlling the connection and disconnection of the participant data sources from the MDBS. This component receives requests from a local data source for participating in the MDBS, registers the physical location of the data sources (URL, uniform resource location), and publishes the local data sources' schemas. The MDBS repository stores control data of the MDBS, which may include the metadata from the participant data sources, definitions of the MDBS (for example, local data sources or preformatted queries), and the physical location of participant data sources.

An XML interface is responsible for mapping the local data sources' schemas in a common data model (conceptual schema). In the proposed architecture, the conceptual schemas must be represented through XML schemas defined through the XML schema language, a language for the schema definition for XML data (Fallside, 2001). Some proposals for mapping data stored in conventional databases into XML documents have been published and implemented, such as, for example, the XDK for the PL/SQL tool from Oracle (*XDK: Oracle XML Developer's Kit for PL/SQL*, 2003).

Figure 4 presents the XML interface in more detail. Beside the mapping activity, executed by the mapping-definition component, the XML interface must translate queries expressed in the XML data model to the native data model of the local data source. This task is carried out by the query translator. The last component from the XML interface is the result translator, which executes the inverse function of the query translator since it should present the query result in XML format.

Figure 4. XML interface

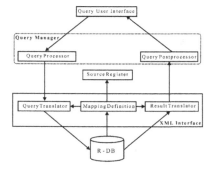

Query Processor

The first step executed by the QP is to check the syntax and semantics of the MXQuery expression, and to generate an expression tree (representing the original query). In Figure 5, one can identify two components responsible for executing this first step. The first one makes the syntax verification, comparing the syntax analysis tree to the MXQuery grammar. If the query is valid, the second component verifies the existence of the objects in the metadata catalog. Finally, if all objects exist and were correctly specified, an expression tree of the global query is generated.

The global optimizer simplifies, to improve performance, the original query by analyzing different logical query plans. Such query plans are obtained by applying transformation rules that were specified by the query language algebra.

In a conventional database, the query processor must define the physical query plan to be executed; however, when integrating multiple databases, data availability is not known before the query execution. Such kind of information could change the physical query plan (Ozcan, Nural, Koksal, & Evrendilek, 1997). Furthermore, the MDBS does not have all the statistical information about the data sources; consequently, choosing a better physical query plan before the partial results is a complex task.

The subquery generator uses the simplified expression tree to generate XQuery subqueries. At least one XQuery subquery will be generated for each data source. Since XQuery expressions can be simplified by using formal specifications proposed in Draper et al. (2003),

Figure 5. QP-generated products

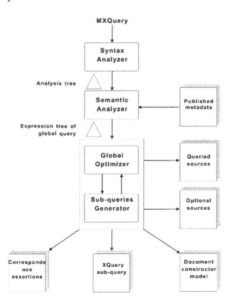

there is a two-way flow between the global optimizer and the subquery generator. Thus, the interaction between these two processes defines the generation of five products.

1. **Queried sources:** This is a list of all data sources that were referenced in the global query. This information will be used by the location processor, the query processor, and query postprocessor.

2. **Optional sources:** The MXQuery Language allows classifying the data sources into two distinct groups: mandatory data sources and nonmandatory (optional) data sources. If an optional data source is unavailable, the query is performed any way. In this case, the result tree could be different. A list of all optional data sources is queried each time when an unavailable data source is detected. If this data source is in the list of optional sources, the query will be performed even though it is unavailable.

3. **XQuery Subquery:** At least one simplified XQuery subquery will be generated for each data source.

4. **Correspondence assertions:** A list of all correspondence assertions is generated (Spaccapietra, Parent, & Dupont, 1992). The correspondence assertions define rules for conflict resolution that were extracted from the XQuery query.

5. **Document-constructor model:** A document is generated that specifies transformations and constructions that should be done in the original elements to obtain the result document.

The idea behind the generation of products from the MXQuery query is permitting the generation of less complex XQuery subqueries. The XML element transformation and integration-conflict resolution are done only by the integration architecture. Thus, the local data sources do not need to execute any effort to present their results. Then, the QPp will use the products originated by the QP to build the expected result.

In order to send subqueries to the corresponding data sources, it is necessary to replace the logical reference used to identify the data source with its physical location. The location processor executes this task. It queries the MDBS repository, extracts the required information, and replaces the logical reference.

Finally, the QP sends the subqueries to the corresponding XML interface and expects an acknowledgment signal. After an interval $\triangle T$, if the acknowledgment signal has not arrived at the QP, the QP resends the query. The QP tries to send the subquery during an interval $\triangle T$'; after that, the QP executes a discard operation or cancels the query execution according to the following criteria. The QP will execute a discard operation if the unavailable data source is part of the optional source list; references to this data source will be excluded. Thus, integration rules and element construction that reference to such data sources are discarded as well. The QP will perform a cancel operation if the unavailable data source is not part of the optional source list. The QP sends an error message to the QPp and abort messages to the rest of the XML interface.

Conclusion

This chapter proposes an extension to the XQuery Language, called MXQuery. The key goal is to use MXQuery as a multidatabase language for integrating heterogeneous data sources on the Web. The proposed language provides the necessary support for integrating a variable number of data sources with different degrees of autonomy. MXQuery solves problems of data integration, such as semantics heterogeneity, and copes with incomplete information. Furthermore, an architecture for processing queries over multiple heterogeneous databases available on the Web is described. The idea is to process MXQuery expressions by means of the proposed architecture.

References

Abiteboul, S., Segoufin, L., & Vianu, V. (2001). Representing and querying XML with incomplete information. *Proceedings of the 20th ACM SIGMOD-SIGACT-SIGART Symposium on Principles of Database Systems*, (pp. 150-161).

Boag, S., Chamberlin, D., Fernadez, M., Florescu, D., Robie, J., Siméon, et al. (2003). *XQuery 1.0: An XML query language-Work in progress.* Retrieved November 12, 2003, from http://www.w3.org/TR/xquery/

Bouganim, L., Fabret, F., Mohan, C., & Valduriez, P. (2000). A dynamic query processing architecture for data integration. *IEEE Data Engineering Bulletin, 23*(2), 42-48.

Bray, T., Paoli, J., Sperberg-McQueen, C., & Maler, E. (2000). *Extensible Markup Language (XML) 1.0* (2nd ed.). Retrieved September 19, 2001, from http://www.w3.org/TR/REC-xml

Brayner, A., & Aguiar Moraes Filho, J. de. (2003). Sharing mobile databases in dynamically configurable environments. In J. Eder & M. Missikoff (Eds.), *Advanced information systems engineering* (pp. 724-737). Klagenfurt, Austria.

Chamberlin, D., Robie, J., & Florescu, D. (2000). Quilt: An XML query language for heterogeneous data sources. *The World Wide Web and Databases: Third International Workshop WebDB2000*, 1-25.

Chen, J., DeWitt, D. J., Tian, F., & Wang, Y. (2000). NiagaraCQ: A scalable continuous query system for Internet databases. *Proceedings of the 2000 ACM SIGMOD International Conference on Management of Data* (pp. 379-390).

Das, S., Shuster, K., & Wu, C. (2002). ACQUIRE: Agent-based complex query and information retrieval engine. *Proceedings of the 1st International Joint Conference on Autonomous Agents and Multiagent Systems* (pp. 631-638).

Domenig, R., & Dittrich, K. (2000). A query based approach for integrating heterogeneous data sources. *Proceedings of the 9th International Conference on Information and Knowledge Management* (pp. 453-460).

Draper, D., Fankhauser, P., Fernández, M., Malhotra, A., Rose, K., Rys, et al. (2003). *XQuery 1.0 and XPath 2.0 formal semantics* (Working draft). Retrieved February 20, 2004, from http://www.w3.org/TR/xquery-semantics/

Elmagarmid, A., Bouguettaya, A., & Benatallah, B. (1998). *Interconnecting heterogeneous information systems.* Norwell, MA: Kluwer Academic Publishers.

Elmagarmid, A., Rusinkiewicz, M., & Shethm, A. (1999). *Management of heterogeneous and autonomous database systems.* San Francisco: Morgan Kaufman Publishers.

Fallside, D. (2001). *XML schema part 0: Primer* (W3C recommendation). Retrieved September 21, 2001, from http://www.w3.org/TR/xmlschema-0/

Goldman, R., & Widom, J. (2000). WSQ/DSQ: A practical approach for combined querying of databases and the Web. *Proceedings of the 2000 ACM SIGMOD International Conference on Management of Data* (pp. 285-296).

Grant, J., Litwin, W., Roussopoulos, N., & Sellis, T. (1993). Query languages for relational multidatabases. *VLDB Journal, 2,* 153-171.

Krishnamurthy, R., Litwin, W., & Kent, W. (2001). Languages features for interoperability of databases with schematic discrepancies. *ACM SIGMOD Record, 20*(2), 40-49.

Litwin, W., Abdellatif, A., Zeroual, A., Nicolas, B., & Vigier, P. (1989). MSQL: A multidatabase language. *Information Sciences, 49,* 59-101.

Manolescu, I., Florescu, D., & Kossman, D. (2001). Answering XML queries over heterogeneous data sources. *Proceedings of the 27th International Conference on Very Large Databases* (pp. 241-250).

Missier, P., & Rusimkiewicz, M. (1995). Extending a multidatabase manipulation language to resolve schema and data conflicts. *Database Applications Semantics: Proceedings of the Sixth IFIP TC-2 Working Conference on Data Semantics* (pp. 93-115).

Ozcan, F., Nural, S., Koksal, P., & Evrendilek, C. (1997). Dynamic query optimization in multidatabases. *Bulletin of the IEEE Computer Society Technical Committee on Data Engineering, 20*(3), 38-45.

Özsu, M., & Valduriez, P. (1999). *Principles of distributed database systems* (2nd ed.). Upper Saddle River, NJ: Prentice-Hall.

Robie, J., Chamberlin, D., & Florescu, D. (2000). Quilt: An XML query language. *Proceedings of the XML Europe 2000.* Retrieved from http://www.gca.org/papers/xmleurope2000/papers/s08-01.html

Sattler, K., Conrad, S., & Saake, G. (2000). Adding conflict resolution features to a query language for database federations. *Proceedings of the 3rd International Workshop on Engineering Federated Information Systems* (pp. 41-52).

Spaccapietra, S., Parent, C., & Dupont, Y. (1992). Model independent assertions for integration of heterogeneous schemas. *VLDB Journal, 1,* 81-126.

Tomasic, A., Raschid, L., & Valduriez, P. (1996). Scaling heterogeneous databases and the design of disco. *Proceedings of the 16th IEEE International Conference on Distributed Computing Systems* (pp. 449-457).

XDK: Oracle XML developer's kit for PL/SQL. (2003). Retrieved October 22, 2003, from http://otn.oracle.com/tech/xml/xdk_plsql/indesx.html

XQuery 1.0 formal semantics. (n.d.). Retrieved from http://www.w3c.org/TR/query-se-mantics/

Appendix A: XML Documents

Document: d1.xml

```
<bib>
 <livro isbn="393">
  <titulo>Princípios de SBDs Distribuídos</titulo>
  <autor>Özsu</autor>
  <autor>Valduriez</autor>
  <ano>1999</ano>
  <preco>89.00</preco> </livro>
 <livro isbn= "352">
  <titulo>Implementação de Sistemas de BDs</titulo>
  <autor>Garcia-Mollina</autor>
  <autor>Ullman</autor>
  <autor>Widom</autor>
  <ano>2001</ano>
  <editora>Campus</editora>
  <preco>110.00</preco> </livro>  </bib>
```

Document: d2.xml

```
<lib>
 <book>
  <isbn>053</isbn>
  <title>Fundamentals of Database Systems</title>
  <author>Elmasri</author>
  <author>Navathe</author>
  <year>1994</year>
  <price>54.00</price> </book>
 <book>
  <isbn>013</isbn>
  <title>A First Course in Database Systems</title>
  <author>Ullman</author>
  <author>Widom</author>
  <year>1997</year>
  <press>Prentice Hall</press>
  <price>45.00</price> </book>
 <book>
```

```
<isbn>352</isbn>
<title>Database System Implementation</title>
<author>Garcia-Mollina</author>
<author>Ullman</author>
<author>Widom</author>
<year>1999</year>
<price>50.00</price> </book>  </lib>
```

Chapter X

E-Mail Mining:
Emerging Techniques for E-Mail Management

Ioannis Katakis, Aristotle University of Thessaloniki, Greece

Grigorios Tsoumakas, Aristotle University of Thessaloniki, Greece

Ioannis Vlahavas, Aristotle University of Thessaloniki, Greece

Abstract

E-mail has met tremendous popularity over the past few years. People are sending and receiving many messages per day, communicating with partners and friends or exchanging files and information. Unfortunately, the phenomenon of e-mail overload has grown over the past years, becoming a personal headache for users and a financial issue for companies. In this chapter, we will discuss how disciplines like machine learning and data mining can contribute to the solution of the problem by constructing intelligent techniques that automate e-mail managing tasks and what advantages they hold over other conventional solutions. We will also discuss the particularity of e-mail data and what special treatment they require. Some interesting e-mail mining applications like mail categorization, summarization, automatic answering, and spam filtering will also be presented.

Introduction

The impact of electronic mail in our daily lives is now more obvious than ever. Each minute, millions of plain text or enriched messages are being sent and received around the globe. Some of them are read with extra care and, at the same time, many of them are deleted with obvious disinterest. As the Internet grows, electronic mail has not only turned into a vital tool for our work, but also into an important means of interpersonal communication.

In professional life, e-mail has invaded everywhere. Team organization, project management, information exchange (Ducheneaut & Belloti, 2001), decision making, and client support are only a few of a company's daily processes for which e-mail has been vital. E-mail also made personal communication significantly easier as it offered instant messaging with minimum cost. People from all over the world can now exchange opinions and information with such ease that it made e-mail the second most popular channel of communications after voice (Miller, 2003).

Features that made e-mail so popular are the rapidity of communication, the minimum cost, and the fact that it is remarkably easy to use. An advantage over voice communication (e.g., phone) is that it is asynchronous, meaning that there is no need for both sides of communication to be online or in front of a computer at the same time.

Unfortunately, e-mail could not escape the curse of information overload. Loads and loads of incoming messages (some extremely important, other simply junk) have turned the handling of electronic mail into a tedious task. Today, an average e-mail user may receive about 100 or 200 messages per day and, in a recent research, IDC[1] predicts that by the year 2006, e-mail traffic will be about 60 billion messages per day worldwide (Johnston, 2002). Nowadays, people struggle to separate important messages that demand immediate attention from the mound, and large companies are investing money in order to maintain e-mail centers with personnel dedicated to answer client requests and queries sent by e-mails. Additionally, the problem of spam messaging has grown at a level that it is now considered an industry problem. It costs billions of dollars (Rockbridge Associates, Inc., 2004) as it takes up bandwidth, clutters inboxes, and occupies employees who are receiving them. Moreover, the content of many spam messages is unsuitable for children (e.g., pornographic).

In this chapter, we will discuss what disciplines like machine learning and data mining have to offer to the solution of this e-mail overload problem; how intelligent techniques, already used before for other text applications, can apply to e-mail data; what difficulties and obstacles have risen; and what are the solutions proposed. Some interesting and novel applications like e-mail answering, classification, and summarization will also be presented.

How E-Mail Works (Terminology)

E-mail does not work so differently than it used to when it first appeared. It relies on two basic communications protocols: SMTP (simple mail transfer protocol), which is used to send messages, and POP3 (post office protocol), which is used to receive messages. A simplified version of the e-mail life cycle can be seen in Figure 1.

Figure 1. Life cycle of an e-mail

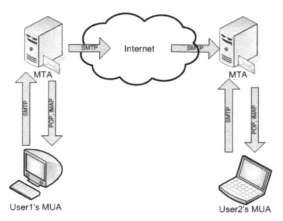

The most important logical elements of the Internet mail system are the following:

1. **Mail User Agent (MUA):** It is responsible for helping the user to read and write e-mail messages. The MUA is usually implemented in software commonly referred to as an e-mail client. Two popular e-mail clients are Microsoft Outlook[2] and Mozilla Thunderbird.[3] These programs transform a text message into the appropriate Internet format in order for the message to reach its destination.

2. **Mail Transfer Agent (MTA):** It accepts a message passed to it by either an MUA or another MTA, and then decides on the appropriate delivery method and the route that the mail should follow. It uses SMTP to send the message to another MTA or a mail delivery agent (MDA).

3. **Mail Delivery Agent:** It receives messages from MTAs and delivers them to the user's mailbox in the user's mail server.

4. **Mail Retrieval Agent (MRA):** It fetches mail messages from the user's mail server to the user's local in-box. MRAs are often embedded in e-mail clients.

An e-mail consists of two parts: headers and a body. The headers form a group of necessary information in order for the mail to reach its destination and be read properly by the recipient. Typical header fields are, for example, the *From*, *To*, or *Subject* fields. Full message headers of an e-mail message can be seen in Figure 2.

E-Mail Mining

E-mail mining can be considered an application of the upcoming research area of text mining (TM, or also known as knowledge discovery from textual data) on e-mail data. Text Mining

Figure 2. Headers of a typical e-mail

```
Received: from Stratos (stratos.csd.auth.gr [155.207.113.238])
          by  hermes.ccf.auth.gr  (8.13.3/8.13.3)  with  ESMTP  id
          j6J7Cq06014460;
          Tue, 19 Jul 2005 10:13:01 +0300 (EEST)
From: "Efstratios Kontopoulos" <skontopo@csd.auth.gr>
To: "Giannis Katakis" <katak@csd.auth.gr>
Cc: "Grigoris Tsoumakas" <greg@csd.auth.gr>
Subject: BasketBall
Date: Tue, 19 Jul 2005 10:12:59 +0300
Message-ID: <001001c58c31$4bd084d0$ee71cf9b@csd.auth.gr>
MIME-Version: 1.0
Content-Type: multipart/alternative;
boundary="----=_NextPart_000_0011_01C58C4A.711DBCD0"
X-Priority: 3 (Normal)
X-MSMail-Priority: Normal
X-Mailer: Microsoft Outlook, Build 10.0.2627
X-MimeOLE: Produced By Microsoft MimeOLE V6.00.2800.1106
Importance: Normal
```

is an emerging field that has attracted the interest of researchers from areas like machine learning, data mining, natural language processing, and computational linguistics.

However, there are some specific characteristics of e-mail data that set a distinctive separating line between e-mail and text mining.

1.   E-mail includes additional information in the headers that can be exploited for various e-mail mining tasks.

2.   Text in e-mail is significantly shorter; therefore, some text-mining techniques might be inefficient for e-mail data.

3.   E-mail is often cursorily written; thus, well-formed linguistics is not guarantied. Spelling and grammar mistakes also appear frequently.

4.   In an e-mail message, different topics may be discussed, a fact that makes, for example, mail classification more difficult.

5.   E-mail is personal and therefore generic techniques are not as effective for individuals.

6.   E-mail is a data stream, and concepts or distributions of target classes may change over time. Algorithms should be incremental in both ways — instance-wise and feature-wise — as new features (e.g., words) may appear.

7.   E-mail will probably have noise. HTML (hypertext markup language) tags and attachments must be removed in order to apply a text-mining technique. In some other cases, noise is intensively inserted. Regarding spam filtering, for example, noisy words and phrases are inserted in order to mislead machine-learning algorithms.

8.   It is rather difficult to have public e-mail data for experiments due to privacy issues. This is a drawback, especially for research, since comparative studies cannot be conducted without publicly available data sets. An exception to the above statement is the Enron Corpus (Klimt & Yang, 2004), which was made public after a legal investigation concerning the Enron Corporation.

E-Mail Preprocessing and Representation

The first step of almost every knowledge discovery task is the preprocessing step of the data, which in the beginning is usually available in what is called raw format. In order to mine raw data and extract knowledge from them, it is necessary to transform them into a format that is more comprehensible to the machine-learning algorithms.

In the last decade, people, with the help of new and advanced e-mail clients, have started to enter HTML code in order to enrich their plain-text messages with different styles of text, different fonts, images, links, and so forth. In fact, this is achieved by sending an HTML page as an attachment, which every contemporary e-mail client with a built-in Web browser is able to present. In an e-mail analysis procedure, HTML is most of the times not exploited to obtain knowledge and is removed using HTML parsers in order to keep the text contained in the HTML document. Some times, though, HTML tags are used as characteristics (attributes) of the e-mail (see the section "Automatic Mail Organization into Folders"). For example, in Corney, Vel, Anderson, and Mohay (2002), the HTML-tag frequency distribution is defined as one of the attributes that describe the e-mail.

In text and e-mail mining, the most prevalent model for representation is the vector-space model (Salton, Wong, & Yang, 1975). In this approach, every message is represented by a single vector. Each element is associated with a token (or a feature in machine-learning terms). In textual data, tokens are usually words or phrases. The elements of the vectors usually have Boolean values (0 or 1) in order to denote the presence or absence of the particular token in the document, or weights (usually numerical values between 0 and 1) to denote the importance of the token for the document (e.g., term frequency). In text classification, the use of single words as tokens is much more common, and it is usually referred to as bag-of-words representation. An alternative would be to pick phrases as tokens, but, maybe contrary to what someone would expect, using phrases instead of single words did not raise the effectiveness of the algorithms (Lewis, 1992). An interesting representation is discussed in Boone (1998), where additional so-called concept features are used. Those features denote the distance between the document and a concept vector. These vectors are constructed after the clustering of all documents and the finding of a representative one for each cluster concept.

So, more formally, we represent an e-mail e_j as a vector $e_j = [w_{1,j}, ..., w_{n,j}]$, where weights $w_{1,j}$ to $w_{n,i}$ are the weights of tokens for the particular document j. In $w_{1,j}$, index i refers to token t_i in our collection of tokens. In case we use words as tokens, then t_i refers to the ith word of our vocabulary, which is basically a set of distinct words.

The vocabulary of each problem is built by analyzing some training documents, if available, and collecting distinct words, or it is incrementally constructed with every new message arrival, with the latter being the most suitable approach taking under consideration the fact that e-mail is a data stream. Of course, either a predefined application-specific or a generic dictionary can be used (local and global lexicon, respectively).

Another decision that has to be made is whether to treat words with common stems as one. In that case, a vocabulary of stems is built, and words like *program*, *programming*, and *programmer* are treated and counted as one. There already exist stemming algorithms, like the Porter stemming algorithm (Porter, 1997). Another common preprocessing step is the removal of commonly used words (like articles, prepositions, etc.), which we call stop words. This could be effective in most applications because these are words that appear in natural language independently of the topic. Hence, they lack discriminative power. On the other hand, in applications like e-mail author identification, the use of stop words might be determinant since the frequency of those terms might reveal the identity of the author (Vel, Anderson, Corney, & Mohay, 2001).

Especially for the e-mail domain, features/words from the e-mail headers can be generated. A word appearing in the subject of the e-mail can be more important than the same word appearing in the body. There is actually related work in the e-mail mining literature that exploits only header information with respectable results (Brutlag & Meek, 2000; Zhang, Zhu, & Yao, 2004).

Thus, in the case when mail headers are also exploited, w_i represents a feature if it appears in the subject, and a different feature if it appears in the body. Therefore, the size of the vector is actually doubled, as it should be in the form shown below (Zhang et al., 2004):

$$E_j = [subject : w_1, body : w_1, \ldots, subject : w_n, body : w_n].$$

Different ways to define the weight of a word in a document have been proposed. Apart from the already mentioned Boolean weights (Androutsopoulos, Koutsias, & Chandrinos, 2000; Sahami, Dumais, Heckerman, & Horvitz, 1998), an alternative approach is to use the TF-IDF (term frequency-invert document frequency; Salton & Buckley, 1988) function for each word to calculate the weights. The TF-IDF function is defined as follows:

$$w_{ij} = TFIDF_i(t_i, e_j) = TF_{i,j} \frac{N}{DF_i},$$

where $TF_{i,j}$ is the number of times token t_i occurs in the document (e-mail) e_j (term frequency), N is the total number of e-mails, and DF_i is the number of e-mails in which t_i occurs (document frequency). The idea behind this metric is the intuition that a word is important for a document if it appears many times in it but is not a common word (a word that appears in many documents). Cosine normalization can be used if there is a need to map the values of the weights into the $[0,1]$ interval (Sebastiani, 2002).

$$w_{ij} = \frac{TFIDF(t_i, e_j)}{\sqrt{\sum_{s=1}^{|V|} (TFIDF(t_s, e_j))^2}},$$

where $|V|$ is the size of the vocabulary in use.

Feature Selection

A typical lexicon of words (e.g., for the English language) may consist of many thousands of words. Those words in a typical bag-of-words approach will constitute the application's feature space. A feature space that large is not only computationally inefficient, but is also misleading for many algorithms as noisy or irrelevant features are taken under consideration and the overfitting phenomena may occur (curse of dimensionality). Therefore, a considerable number of dimensionality-reduction algorithms have been studied in the literature. We usually refer to these algorithms as feature-selection methods because dimensionality reduction is being achieved by trying to select the best features from the whole feature space. In text-classification terms, this means to select words that distinguish one document category from another more efficiently. This is usually being accomplished by calculating a special quality measure for each word, and then selecting to use only the top-N features of the rank.

Typical information-retrieval measures like TF-IDF are still applicable, but now we use them to show the importance of a term for the whole corpus and not only for the specific document, as when we used the TF-IDF function to calculate weights.

$$TFIDF_i = TF_i \log \frac{N}{DF_i},$$

where TF_i is the number of occurrences of the term i in the corpus, and DF_i is the number of different documents in which this term occurs. N is again the total number of documents.

Measures from the information-theory field are more widely used. Most effective in text-mining tasks as noted in Yang and Pedersen (1997), and therefore popular in e-mail applications, are information gain and the chi-squared measure. Another widely used measure is mutual information (Yang & Pedersen, 1997). In general, a measure $M(t_i, c_j)$ indicates how much distinctive power the term t_i has in order to distinguish c_j from other categories. The following is the definition of information gain and Chi-Squared Measure.

Information Gain:

$$IG(t_i, c_j) = P(t_i, c_j) \log \frac{P(t_i, c_j)}{P(c_j)P(t_i)} + P(\bar{t_i}, c_i) \log \frac{P(\bar{t_i}, c_j)}{P(c_j)P(\bar{t_i})}$$

Chi-Squared Measure:

$$x^2(t_i, c_j) = \frac{N[P(t_i, c_j)P(\bar{t_i}, \bar{c_j}) - P(t_i, \bar{c_j})P(\bar{t_i}, c_j)]^2}{P(t_i)P(\bar{t_i})P(c_j)P(\bar{c_j})},$$

where N is the total number of documents, $P(t_i)$ is the number of documents where t_i occurs, $P(\bar{t_i}, c_j)$ is the number of c_j documents where term t_i does not occur, and so forth. Finally, some machine-learning-based methods for feature selection are described in Montanes, Diaz, Ranilla, Combarro, and Fernandez (2005).

E-Mail Classification

Most e-mail mining tasks are being accomplished by using e-mail classification at some point. In general, what e-mail classification confronts is the assignment of an e-mail message to one from a predefined set of categories. Automatic e-mail classification aims at building a model (typically by using machine-learning techniques) that will undertake this task on behalf of the user. Examples of applications are automatic mail categorization into folders, spam filtering, and author identification. However, there are also other applications in which we use classification in the process, like automatic e-mail summarization.

There are actually two kinds of classification. The first and simplest one is the flat classification, in which we have only one level of classes. The other category is known as hierarchical classification, in which we have a hierarchy of classes and subclasses (Bekkerman, McCallum, & Huang, 2004; Itskevitch, 2001).

More formally, and in machine-learning terms, if we have a set of predefined classes $C=\{c_1,...,c_n\}$, we need to construct a function-like model that assigns a mail message (e) to a class, for example, $M(e) \rightarrow C$. These models (also called classifiers) can be built with various machine-learning techniques, such as naïve Bayes (Sahami et al., 1998), support-vector machines (SVMs; Klimt & Yang, 2004), rule learning (Pazzani, 2002), decision–tree- (Quinlan, 1986) based algorithms (Diao, Lu, & Wu, 2000), neural networks (Clark, Koprinska, & Poon, 2003), and inductive logic programming (Crawford, Kay, & McCreath, 2002). Most of the classification algorithms are compatible with the vector-representation model. To build a classifier, a set of training examples is required. An example is a message that has already been categorized, usually by a user or a domain expert. An example is usually a vector $e = [w_1, w_2,...,w_n, c_e]$, where c is the class that example e belongs to. This procedure of building the classifier is called training.

What is important in e-mail classification is the fact that e-mail is a dynamic environment, and messages are constantly arriving. This means that, although there might be a training set in availability, the classifier needs to be able to adapt new knowledge while new examples arrive. Therefore, it is of vital importance for classification algorithms to be characterized by the element of incrementality (Cunningham, Nowlan, Delany, & Haahr, 2003; Katakis, Tsoumakas, & Vlahavas, 2005; Segal & Kephard, 2000).

The Naïve Bayes Classifier. The naïve Bayes classifier (John & Langley, 1995) has been used many times for e-mail classification applications (Rennie, 2000; Sahami et al., 1998). Its simplicity (not only is it computationally cost effective, but it is also easy to implement), flexibility, and considerable performance are the basic characteristics that made it so popular, not only in e-mail applications, but in text classification in general (Lewis, 1998; Li & Jain, 1998; Mladenic, 1998). The naïve Bayes classifier is based on the simplifying assumption that the attribute values (e.g., the TF-IDF values of an e-mail vector) are conditionally independent. The naïve Bayesian classification of an e-mail $e = [w_1, w_2...,w_n]$ into one category from $C = \{c_1, c_2,...,c_n\}$ is calculated as follows (Mitchell, 1997):

$$C_{NB} = \arg \max_{c_j \in C} P(c_j) \prod P(w_i | c_j),$$

where c_{NB} is the classification proposed by the naïve Bayes algorithm. A proposal for probability estimation in text classification that can be found in Mitchell (1997) is displayed next:

$$P(w_i \mid c_j) = \frac{n_i + 1}{n_j + |V|},$$

where n_j is the total number of words (not distinct) in all training examples belonging to the c_j category, n_i is the number of times $word_i$ occurs among these n words, and $|V|$ is the total number of distinct words found within the training data. Of course, there are other alternatives for calculating the probabilities (John & Langley, 1995).

Support-Vector Machines. Since their significantly good performance was confirmed many times in the literature (Sebastiani, 2002), support-vector machines have gained popularity in text and e-mail classification. In their initial and simplest form, support-vector machines are binary classifiers, meaning that they separate objects into only two predefined classes. In that case, the SVM classifier finds a hyperplane that separates a set of positive examples from a set of negative examples with maximum margin (see Figure 3). The margin is defined as the distance of the hyperplane from the nearest positive and negative examples (see Figure 3; these examples are called support vectors). If $\vec{d}$ is the input document and $\vec{v}$ is the normal vector to the hyperplane (margin), then the output (proposed classification for the document $\vec{d}$) of the SVM classifier is calculated as follows:

$$C_{SVM} = sign\{\vec{v}\vec{d} + b\} = \begin{cases} +1, if\ \vec{v} \cdot \vec{d} + b > 0 \\ -1, else \end{cases}.$$

The terminus is to maximize the margin that is represented by the $\vec{v}$ vector. The problem then could be redefined as an optimization problem.

Figure 3. A Support Vector Machine classifier. The hyperplane separating the instances represented by the thick line. Items in grey represent the support vectors. V is the margin to be minimized.

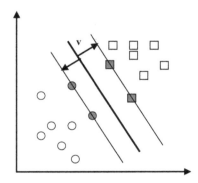

Maximize: $|\vec{v}|$

Subject to: $y_i(\vec{v} \cdot \vec{d}_i + b) \geq 1$,

where vectors $\vec{d}_i$ are all training examples (e-mails), and y_i is the real category (+1 or -1) that document d_i belongs to. Hence, the last constraint requires the correct classification of all training examples. Of course, this applies only if the problem is linearly separable. There are, however, already implemented modifications of this optimization problem that can be applied to nonlinearly separable problems. Its solution usually requires a quadratic optimization method that will calculate the optimal hyperplane and margin. These methods are remarkably slow, especially in high-dimensional feature spaces like e-mail classification. A fast training algorithm, however, developed by Platt (1999), breaks the large QP problem down into a series of smaller ones (known as sequential minimal optimization, SMO); it is already implemented in machine-learning libraries like Weka (Witten & Frank, 2005).

Another advantage of SVMs is that most of the time, there is no need for term selection and no parameters require tuning. On the other hand, support-vector machines can still be computationally cost ineffective, especially for multiclass problems (Joachims, 1998).

E-Mail Clustering

E-mail clustering goes one step further. Subject-based folders can be automatically constructed starting from a set of incoming messages. In this case, the goal is to build automatic organization systems that will analyze an inbox and recognize clusters of messages with the same concept, give an appropriate name to each cluster, and then put all messages into their corresponding folders (Manco, Masciari, & Tagarelli, 2002; Surendran, Platt, & Renshaw, 2005).

The most widely used clustering algorithm in textual data is the k-means algorithm. In order to group some points in k clusters, k-means works in four basic steps.

1. Randomly choose k instances within the data set and assign them as cluster centers.

2. Assign the remaining instances to their closest cluster centers.

3. Find a new center for each cluster.

4. If the new cluster centers are identical to the previous ones, then the algorithm stops. Otherwise, repeat Steps 2 to 4.

The calculation of distances between documents can be achieved by using a vector-space model and a cosine similarity measure. Similarity between messages e_1 and e_2 is defined as:

$$Sim(\vec{e}_1,\vec{e}_2) = \cos(\vec{e}_1,\vec{e}_2) = \frac{\vec{e}_1 \cdot \vec{e}_2}{|\vec{e}_1||\vec{e}_2|}.$$

Other similarity measures are proposed in Baeza-Yates and Ribeiro-Neto (1999) and Strehl, Ghosh, and Mooney (2000).

Applications

While techniques for tasks like document summarization, organization, clustering, and author identification are already explored in the literature, e-mail data with their characteristics, as discussed earlier, raise a new challenge to the community of text mining. Moreover, the domain itself offered the ground for new applications to be created. Such applications are automatic answering, thread summarization, and spam filtering.

Automatic Answering

Large companies usually maintain e-mail centers (in conjunction with call centers) with employees committed to answering incoming messages. Those messages usually come from company clients and partners, and many times address the same problems and queries. Automatic e-mail answering is an effort to build mail centers or personalized software that will be able to analyze an incoming message and then propose or even send an applicable answer. Efforts toward this direction have been made recently in Bickel and Scheffer (2004), Busemann, Schmeier, and Arens (2000), and Scheffer (2004).

Bickel and Scheffer (2004) describe methods for building an automatic answering system utilizing message pairs: questions and answers. Assuming that a respectable number of message pairs is available in a repository $R=\{(q_1, a_1),...,(q_n, a_n)\}$, they have proposed a number of approaches.

The simplest one is to find the question message q_i that is most similar to a new question message e, and then propose the corresponding answer message a_i as the answer to e. Measures and methods to calculate document similarity are described in Baeza-Yates and Ribeiro-Neto (1999).

A more sophisticated approach treats the problem as a classification task. This is accomplished by grouping similar answers into categories (classes) $C_1,..., C_m \in C$, where $m \leq n$. The grouping of answers can be performed either by a human expert, or more efficiently by a clustering algorithm. For each cluster of answers $C_j=\{a_1,...,a_k\}$, where $k \leq n$, a default representative answer is automatically created by selecting the answer $a_i \in C_j$ that is most similar to the centroid of the cluster. Typically, if we have a group of vectors $C_j=\{a_1,...,a_k\}$, the weights of the centroid vector a_c are calculated as $w_{i,c} = \frac{1}{k}\sum_{j=1}^{k} w_{i,j}$. Then, a classifier is trained on the data set $D(\{q_1,C_a\},...,(q_n, C_b\})$ consisting of (*question,classOfAnswer*) pairs. When a new question message e arrives, the classifier outputs the predicted class, and the representative answer of this class is proposed as the answer to e.

In another paper, Scheffer (2004) discusses how automatic e-mail answering could be enhanced by utilizing unlabeled data (a process called semisupervised learning). He experiments with transductive support-vector machines (Joachims, 1999) and co-training (Blum

& Mitchell, 1998). The approach is implemented in an integrated e-mail manager for the Microsoft Outlook e-mail client (Kockelkorn, Luneburg, & Scheffer, 2003).

Automatic Mail Organization into Folders

The growth of e-mail usage has forced users to find ways to organize, archive, and manage their e-mails more efficiently. Many of them are organizing incoming messages into separate folders. Folders can be topic oriented like *work*, *personal*, and *funny*; people specific like *John* and *Mary*, or group-of-people specific like *colleagues*, *family*, and *friends*. Some users are archiving their messages according to importance and thus maintain folders like *Urgent*, *For Future Reference*, *Spam*, and so forth. To achieve this, many users create some so-called rules to classify their mail. These are heuristic rules that search for keywords in the message and then take an action like moving or copying the message to a folder, deleting or forwarding the message, or so forth.

if(sender="John Smith" OR sender="Mary Smith")
then (moveInto FAMILY)

if(body contains "call for papers")
then{(moveInto CFP)
     (forwardTo "COLLEAGUES")}

where FAMILY and CFP are folders, and COLLEAGUES is a group of people (practically a list of addresses the user has created for mass e-mailing). Most e-mail clients today support the creation of such rules.

What machine learning has to offer to this task is the automatic classification of incoming mail by observing past and current classifications made by the user (e.g., analyzing already existing folders or taking a current classification as an example). Thus, the user does not need to create the rules by himself or herself. Furthermore, machine-learning algorithms are able to classify a message, taking under consideration its content not only by searching for specific keywords. This is usually achieved by combining statistical and linguistic techniques. It is extremely convenient for the user since there are some concepts like messages concerning work, interesting messages, or messages that need to be answered today that cannot easily be described with a combination of keywords. In fact, a recent study (Ducheneaut & Belloti, 2001) notes that most users do not use conventional mail filters, not only because they find them difficult to use, but also because they believe that two thirds of their mail volume would be impossible to filter automatically. Moreover, these concepts may change (e.g., the concept of an interesting message) from time to time. On the other hand, a machine-learning algorithm can learn to classify new messages just by silently observing past examples, and can follow drifts of concepts by accepting user feedback.

A lot of research has been recorded in the field (Clark et al., 2003; Cohen, 1996; Klimt & Yang, 2004; Manco, Masciari, Ruffolo, & Tagarelli, 2002), and lots of those ideas have been implemented into useful e-mail tools (Graham-Cumming, 2002; Ho, 2003; Segal & Kephard, 2000).

Popfile (Graham-Cumming, 2002) is a popular online tool for classifying e-mail. It is written by John Graham-Cumming in Perl and is inspired by ifile (Rennie, 2000). It stands between the mail server and the client, retrieves messages from the server, classifies them, and then sends them to the client. Popfile starts its training from point zero, and normally all messages drop to the default in-box folder. If the user creates a bucket in Popfile and then moves some message to it, then Popfile will start to learn how to classify similar messages. Users can create, destroy, or merge buckets at any time. Naturally, Popfile performs poorly in the beginning as it only has few examples to learn from, but reports are showing an average classification accuracy of 98.7% after 500 messages. Popfile implements a naïve Bayesian classifier using a bag-of-words approach, but it has some extra handcrafted features (like the existence of HTML code, the size of images, e-mail addresses in the *To* header field, etc.) mainly to enhance its spam-filtering capabilities. This is because spammers use techniques like entering random text in spam messages in order to mislead the naïve Bayes classifier.

Another e-mail categorization tool, SwiftFile (formerly known as MailCat; Segal & Kephard, 1999), an add-on to Lotus Notes, has been developed by IBM Research (Segal & Kephard, 2000), and it emphasizes the need for incremental learning. With every new message arrival, SwiftFile predicts three destination folders. It places three buttons above the message in order for the user to send them quickly to one of them. SwiftFile uses a TF-IDF type of classifier (basically, a k-nearest-neighbour classifier [Cover & Hart, 1967] using TF-IDF weights; Sebastiani, 2002) that is modified to support incremental learning and a bag-of-words representation, using word frequencies in messages as weights. Each folder F is represented by its centroid vector, calculated from all messages in that folder. Similarity between centroid vectors and the new message is calculated, and the system proposes the three folders with the highest similarity. The centroids of each folder are recalculated after a new classification in order to follow potential concept drift.

Other interesting software applications are EMMA (Ho, 2003), which uses multiple classification ripple-down rules (Kang, Compton, & Preston, 1995), and eMailSift (Aery & Chakravarthy, 2004), which uses a graph-based mining approach for e-mail classification.

There is, however, still some human effort involved in deciding and creating the subject folders for the classification. This step could be avoided by using e-mail clustering. For example, in Surendran et al. (2005), a personal e-mail browser is built by discovering clusters of messages in the user's in-box. The most suitable noun phrase (NP) is then selected by analyzing the messages in order to name the folder with a key phrase that is representative of the folder's content. The authors use TF-IDF vectors to represent the messages, and the k-means algorithm for the clustering. Manco et al. (2002) are exploring the same problem by taking under consideration the similarity of structured and unstructured parts of an e-mail message.

Mail and Thread Summarization

Text summarization has been previously explored in information-technology literature (Hovy & Lin, 1997; Marcu, 1997; Zechner, 1996). The main motivation is again information overload. Large collections of text documents (news, articles, reviews, scientific documents, literature) are available on the World Wide Web and in digital libraries. It is impossible for a reader to find the time to read many documents, and more importantly, to adapt the documents' content. Therefore, new techniques are being developed in order to automatically extract the gist of documents. In particular, some of these techniques embed machine-learning algorithms, building summarizers that at some point of the summarization procedure are able to learn from examples (Neto, Freitas, & Kaestner, 2002).

The same need for summarization appears in electronic mail. There is a certain category of e-mail users that receive hundreds of messages per day. Some of them are newsletters while others are business decision-making messages from colleagues, appointment arrangements, and so forth. It would be extremely useful for them if they could avoid reading all of those messages, and instead read only the most important and necessary parts and then decide if the messages demand immediate attention. From a summary, they could also find out if a newsletter, for example, is interesting or not, and only read the full text if it is. Again, data-mining techniques are explored in order to build trainable tools for summarization.

Muresan, Tzoukerman, and Klavans (2001) describe an e-mail-summarization method that utilizes natural language processing and machine-learning techniques. The basic steps of their method are (a) the extraction of candidate noun phrases from the e-mail message, (b) linguistic filtering of the candidate NPs, such as removing common words and unimportant modifiers, and (c) the induction of a model that will classify the filtered NPs into those that are important, which should be included in the summary, and those that are not.

The last step is accomplished with the aid of machine-learning algorithms. Each candidate NP is described using a vector of features, such as the TF-IDF measure of the head of the candidate NP, the length of the NP (in words and characters), and the position of the NP. To construct a training set, a large number of NPs extracted from several e-mails is manually tagged as important or not. Experimental results with decision-tree, rule–induction, and decision-forest learning algorithms led to several interesting conclusions, including that NPs are better than n-grams (n consecutive words) for the phrase-level representation of e-mail messages, and that linguistic filtering enhances the performance of machine-learning algorithms.

The application of summarizing e-mail threads (conversations among two or more people carried out by the exchange of messages) has also gained interest. E-mail threads might consist of many e-mail messages, and it would be beneficial if a user could avoid reading all of them and instead read just the summary up to that point. In their technical report, Lam, Rohall, Schmandt, and Stern (2002) try to exploit the e-mail structure to improve thread summarization. The basic idea is to identify a message as a part of an e-mail thread, and then try to propose a summary by extracting knowledge from the parent (ancestor) messages as well. Wan and McKeown (2004) are exploring the same problem in business decision-making e-mail threads. They assume that in threads like these, there is always an issue message (containing an issue sentence) that sets the problem or a query to the others. The other messages are supposed to be response messages, each one containing a response sentence. Hence, in order to summarize the thread, all issue and response sentences have to be identified and collected. The method proposed to identify the issue sentence is to take all issue-message sentences and compare them with each response message. Thus, the sentence that is more similar to the response messages is considered the issue sentence. Finally, to extract the response sentences, the authors noticed that simply extracting the first sentence of every response message is an effortless but effective approach.

A system for e-mail summarization for the Spanish language is described in Alonso, Casas, Castellon, and Padro (2004) and is available for demonstration at http://www.lsi.upc.edu/~bcasas/carpanta/demo.html.

Spam Filtering

The main goal of spam filtering is to identify and sort out unsolicited commercial mails (spam) from a user's mail stream. Spam mail (also known as junk or bulk e-mail) has evolved from a small annoyance in the early days of e-mail to become a major industry problem in the last 5 years. The large amount of spam not only causes bandwidth (and therefore financial) problems, but also takes up valuable time from e-mail users who try to separate and delete many unsolicited messages every day. Moreover, many spam messages include pornographic content inappropriate for children.

To defeat spam, the information-technology community began constructing spam filters in order to delete automatically such unwanted incoming messages. There are many different strategies proposed and implemented in the battle against spam. We could organize them into two general groups:

- **Technical or nonstatistical approaches:** These include white and black lists, digital signatures, and handcrafted rules.
- **Machine-learning or statistical approaches:** These include statistical linguistic analysis and machine-learning algorithms.

Spam-filtering techniques can be additionally organized into two other categories:

- **Server-based solutions:** Messages are filtered on the ISP's (Internet service provider's) mail server.
- **Client-based solutions:** Messages are categorized on the user's computer.

While the obvious advantage of the first category is that spam messages never reach the client's computer, server-based filters are not always personalized, and the user must check periodically the junk folder on the server in order to see if there are any misclassified messages. Many different machine-learning classifiers have been tested. An incomplete list follows:

- Naïve Bayes (Sahami et al., 1998)
- Memory-based approaches (Sakkis, Androutsopoulos, Paliouras, Karkaletsis Spyropoulos, & Stamatopoulos, 2003)
- Boosting techniques (Carreras & Marquez, 2001)
- Case-based reasoning (Cunningham et al., 2003)

- Support-vector machines (Drucker, Vapnik, & We, 1999)

- Latent semantic indexing (Gee, 2003)

- Stacking classifiers (Sakkis, Androutsopoulos, Paliouras, Karkaletsis Spyropoulos, & Stamatopoulos, 2001)

A direct comparison of these methods is difficult because of the use of different corpora and optimization of the algorithms. Developers, however, have shown their preference for the naïve Bayes classifier mainly because of its simplicity, flexibility, computational cost, and decent performance.[4,5] Nevertheless, advanced high-accuracy software, like SpamAssasin,[6] usually combines techniques from both categories: statistical and nonstatistical.

To some extent, the task of spam filtering is similar to text and e-mail classification. However, there are some characteristics that distinguish spam filtering from other classification tasks.

In spam filtering, classification mistakes are not all of equal importance. To classify a legitimate e-mail as spam is a much more severe mistake than letting a nonlegitimate message pass the filter. Thus, we should make sure that we mark a message as spam only if the classifier predicts so with high confidence. In naïve Bayes, for example, the classification of an e-mail message e as spam should be made if and only if $P(e{=}SPAM){>}t$, where t is a threshold close to 1 (e.g., 0.98). The same applies in the evaluation of the algorithm. One false-positive mistake should be counted as, for example, 100 false-negative mistakes.

Another distinction is that in spam filtering, we should probably use extra features, like information from headers, morphological characteristics, or punctuation marks, which in fact are great indicators as they exist in abundance in spam messages. Technical approaches like black and white lists are maybe unavoidable as spammers started to input some random "innocent" text in messages in order to mislead the classifier. Additionally, classes in spam filtering are far more heterogeneous in content than in a typical text- or e-mail classification problem, meaning that there are a lot of different types of spam messages and a lot of different types of legitimate messages — a fact that makes the distinction even more difficult. Moreover, spammers tend to change the characteristics of spam messages, and thus the need for incremental learning is more obvious in this case.

Although some of the above-mentioned filters are remarkably accurate (some of them reaching 99% accuracy with only a few false positives), the problem is still remaining. Two conferences take place every year,[7] gathering professionals and academics from all over the world to introduce and discuss new ideas and trends.

Other Interesting Applications

Apart from the applications mentioned before, there are still some others worth mentioning. For example, Lewis and Knowles (1997) mention that there might be a need to identify whether a mail belongs to a thread without the use of structural information inserted by e-mail clients (e.g., the well-known *RE* prefix). Thus, the use of a TF-IDF classifier using similarity measures is proposed in order to find messages belonging to the same thread.

Author identification is another interesting application explored in Vel et al. (2001). E-mail evidence can be central in cases of sexual harassment, racial vilification, threats, blackmailing, and so on. In these cases, the sender will attempt to hide his or her true identity in order to avoid detection. For example, the sender's address can be hidden by using an anonymous mail server, or the e-mail's contents and header information can be modified in an attempt to hide the true identity of the user. Although author identification has been investigated before, e-mail author identification displays again some unique characteristics. The text is significantly shorter, but we could at the same time exploit information from headers, like attachments, time stamps, and so forth. Particularly, the authors of this work use a set of style-marker and structural features like the number of blank lines, the average sentence length, the average word length, vocabulary richness, the existence of a greeting or a farewell acknowledgement, the number of attachments, and so on. Finally, for the identification of the e-mail, an SVM classifier can be used. Some authors have experimented with the identification of the e-mail author's gender (Corney et al., 2002).

Conclusion and Future Trends

E-mail is now extremely important for interpersonal communication and professional life. Therefore, its problems demand immediate attention and efficient solutions. What data mining and machine learning have to offer to the clarification of e-mail overload are intelligent techniques for the automatization of many e-mail management tasks. E-mail categorization into folders, e-mail answering and summarization, and spam filtering are only a few representatives. All of these applications have been explored repeatedly in the literature with very promising results, but spam filtering seems to gather the greater attention of all, probably because of its negative financial impact. It is worth noticing, though, that many of these applications are extremely demanding in terms of accuracy, mainly because information in e-mail data can be significantly important. Therefore, there is still space and need for improvement in performance in many of the applications mentioned above.

E-mail structure is very difficult to be generated from plain text, and therefore we treat e-mail almost always as unstructured text. On the other hand, HTML, which until now was removed in the preprocessing step, could help to give an, at least, semistructured form to the e-mail. Knowledge discovery from structured information is more convenient, and maybe more effort should be made in this direction. For example, we could transform HTML messages into XML (extensible markup language) using XSL-T patterns.

A new idea that seems promising is semantic e-mail. In parallel with the semantic Web, e-mail could be enriched with metatags in order to describe better the information included in the message. As discussed in McDowell, Etzioni, Halevy, and Levy (2004), applications like information dissemination, event planning, report generation, and e-mail auctions and giveaways could be achieved with the use of semantic e-mail.

E-mail mining raised new difficulties and challenges for the text-mining community. New solutions had to be proposed in already discussed areas due to e-mail-data peculiarity. Additionally, domain-specific problems provoked the development of new applications like spam filtering, e-mail answering, and thread summarization.

While effective solutions have been proposed to most e-mail problems, not all of them have been implemented in popular e-mail clients. In fact, with the exception of spam filtering, which is now integrated in most commercial clients, no other applications have been used widely for the average user. There is therefore an obvious need to implement those methods and integrate them into useful and accurate software that will let people take back control of their mailboxes.

References

Aery, M., & Chakravarthy, S. (2004). *eMailSift: Adapting graph mining techniques for email classification* (Tech. Rep. No. CSE-2004-7).

Alonso, L., Casas, B., Castellon, I., & Padro, L. (2004). *Knowledge-intensive automatic e-mail summarization in CARPANTA*. Paper presented at the ACL '04, Barcelona, Spain.

Androutsopoulos, I., Koutsias, J., & Chandrinos, K. V. (2000). *An experimental comparison of naive Bayesian and keyword-based anti-spam filtering with personal e-mail messages*. Paper presented at the 23rd Annual International ACM SIGIR Conference on Research and Development in Information Retrieval, Athens, Greece.

Baeza-Yates, R., & Ribeiro-Neto, B. A. (1999). *Modern information retrieval*. Addison Wesley.

Bekkerman, R., McCallum, A., & Huang, G. (2004). *Automatic categorization of email into folders: Benchmark experiments on Enron and SRI Corpora* (CIIR Tech. Rep. No. IR-418 2004).

Bickel, S., & Scheffer, T. (2004). *Learning from message pairs for automatic email answering*. Paper presented at the ECML 2004, 15th European Conference on Machine Learning, Pisa, Italy.

Blum, A., & Mitchell, T. (1998). *Combining labeled and unlabelled data with co-training*. Paper presented at the Workshop on Computational Learning Theory, Madison, WI.

Boone, G. (1998). *Concept features in Re:Agent, an intelligent email agent*. Paper presented at the International Conference on Autonomous Systems, Minneapolis, MN.

Brutlag, J. D., & Meek, C. (2000). *Challenges of the email domain for text classification*. Paper presented at the 17th International Conference on Machine Learning, Stanford, CA.

Busemann, S., Schmeier, S., & Arens, R. G. (2000). *Message classification in the call center*. Paper presented at the 6th Conference on Applied Natural Language Processing, Seattle, WA.

Carreras, X., & Marquez, L. (2001). *Boosting trees for anti-spam email filtering*. Paper presented at the RANLP-01, 4th International Conference on Recent Advances in Natural Language Processing.

Clark, J., Koprinska, I., & Poon, J. (2003). *A neural network based approach to automated e-mail classification*. Paper presented at the IEEE/WIC International Conference on Web Intelligence (WI'03), Halifax, Canada.

Cohen, W. (1996). *Learning rules that classify e-mail.* Paper presented at the AAAI Spring Symposium on Machine Learning in Information Access, Stanford, CA.

Corney, M., Vel, O. d., Anderson, A., & Mohay, G. (2002). *Gender-preferential text mining of e-mail discourse.* Paper presented at the ACSAC '02: Eighteenth Annual Computer Security Applications Conference, Las Vegas, NV.

Cover, T., & Hart, P. (1967). Nearest neighbor pattern classification. *IEEE Transactions on Information Theory, 13*(1), 21-27.

Crawford, E., Kay, J., & McCreath, E. (2002). *IEMS: The intelligent email sorter.* Paper presented at the International Conference on Machine Learning, Alberta, Canada.

Cunningham, P., Nowlan, N., Delany, S., & Haahr, M. (2003). *A case-based approach to spam filtering that can track concept drift.* Paper presented at the ICCBR'03 Workshop on Long-Lived CBR Systems, Trondheim, Norway.

Diao, Y., Lu, H., & Wu, D. (2000). *A comparative study of classification-based personal e-mail filtering.* Paper presented at the PAKDD-00, 4th Pacific-Asia Conference on Knowledge Discovery and Data Mining, Kyoto, Japan.

Drucker, H., Vapnik, V., & We, D. (1999). Support vector machines for spam categorization. *IEEE Transactions on Neural Networks, 10*(5), 1048-1054.

Ducheneaut, N., & Belloti, V. (2001). E-mail as habitat: An exploration of embedded personal information management. *Interactions, 8*(5), 30-38.

Gee, K. R. (2003). *Using latent semantic indexing to filter spam.* Paper presented at the ACM Symposium on Applied Computing, Data Mining Track, FL.

Graham-Cumming, J. (2002). *PopFile: Automatic email classification.* Retrieved from http://popfile.sourceforge.net

Ho, V. (2003). *EMMA: An e-mail management assistant.* Paper presented at the 2003 IEEE/WIC International Conference on Intelligent Agent Technology (IAT 2003), Halifax, Canada.

Hovy, E., & Lin, C. (1997). Automated text summarization in SUMMARIST. In I. Mani & M. Maybury (Eds.), *Advances in automatic text summarization* (pp. 18-24).

Itskevitch, J. (2001). *Automatic hierarchical e-mail classification using association rules.* Unpublished master's thesis, Simon Fraser University.

Joachims, T. (1998). *Text categorization with support vector machines: Learning with many relevant features.* Paper presented at the ECML-98, 10th European Conference on Machine Learning, Chemnitz, Germany.

Joachims, T. (1999). *Transductive inference for text classification using support vector machines.* Paper presented at the ICML-99, 16th International Conference on Machine Learning, Blend, Slovenia.

John, G. H., & Langley, P. (1995). *Estimating continuous distributions in Bayesian classifiers.* Paper presented at the UAI '95: Eleventh Annual Conference on Uncertainty in Artificial Intelligence, Montreal, Quebec, Canada.

Johnston, G. (2002). We've got mail: 60 billion daily. *PCWorld.* Retrieved from http://www.pcworld.com/news/article/0,aid,105525,00.asp

Kang, B., Compton, P., & Preston, P. (1995). *Multiple classification ripple down rules: Evaluation and possibilities.* Paper presented at the 9th AAAI-Sponsored Banff Knowledge Acquisition for Knowledge-Based Systems Workshop, Canada.

Katakis, I., Tsoumakas, G., & Vlahavas, I. (2005). *On the utility of incremental feature selection for the classification of textual data streams.* Paper presented at the PCI 2005: 10th Panhellenic Conference on Informatics, Volos, Greece.

Klimt, B., & Yang, Y. (2004). *The Enron Corpus: A new dataset for email classification research.* Paper presented at the Machine Learning: ECML 2004, 15th European Conference on Machine Learning, Pisa, Italy.

Kockelkorn, M., Luneburg, A., & Scheffer, T. (2003). *Learning to answer emails.* Paper presented at the International Symposium on Intelligent Data Analysis, Berlin, Germany.

Lam, D., Rohall, S. L., Schmandt, C., & Stern, M. K. (2002). *Exploiting e-mail structure to improve summarization* (Tech. Rep. No. 2002-02). IBM Watson Research Center.

Lewis, D. D. (1992). *An evaluation of phrasal and clustered representations on a text categorization task.* Paper presented at the 15th Annual International ACM SIGIR Conference on Research and Development in Information Retrieval, Copenhagen, Denmark.

Lewis, D. D. (1998). *Naive Bayes at forty: The independence assumption in information retrieval.* Paper presented at the ECML-98, 10th European Conference on Machine Learning, Chemnitz, Germany.

Lewis, D. D., & Knowles, K. A. (1997). Threading electronic mail: A preliminary study. *Information Processing and Management, 33*(2), 209-217.

Li, Y. H., & Jain, A. K. (1998). Classification of text documents. *The Computer Journal, 41*(8), 537-546.

Manco, G., Masciari, E., Ruffolo, M., & Tagarelli, A. (2002). *Towards an adaptive mail classifier.* Paper presented at the AIIA 2002, Sienna, Italy.

Manco, G., Masciari, E., & Tagarelli, A. (2002). *A framework for adaptive mail classification.* Paper presented at the ICTAI'02: Fourteenth IEEE International Conference on Tools with Artificial Intelligence, Washington, DC.

Marcu, D. (1997). *From discourse structures to text summaries.* Paper presented at the 14th National Conference on Artificial Intelligence (AAAI-97), Providence, RI.

McDowell, L., Etzioni, O., Halevy, A. Y., & Levy, H. (2004). *Semantic email.* Paper presented at the 13th International World Wide Web Conference, New York.

Miller, R. (2003). Email: The other content management. *EContent Magazine.* Retrieved from http://www.ecmag.net/?ArticleID=882

Mitchell, T. M. (1997). *Machine learning.* McGraw-Hill.

Mladenic, D. (1998). *Feature subset selection in text learning.* Paper presented at the ECML-98, 10th European Conference on Machine Learning, Chemnitz, Germany.

Montanes, E., Diaz, I., Ranilla, J., Combarro, E. F., & Fernandez, J. (2005). Scoring and selecting terms for text categorization. *IEEE Intelligent Systems, 20*(3), 40-47.

Muresan, S., Tzoukerman, E., & Klavans, J. L. (2001). *Combining linguistic and machine learning techniques for email summarization.* Paper presented at the Proceedings of CoNLL-2001, Toulouse, France.

Neto, J. L., Freitas, A. A., & Kaestner, C. A. A. (2002). *Automatic text summarization using a machine learning approach.* Paper presented at the SBIA '02: Sixteenth Brazilian Symposium on Artificial Intelligence, Porto de Galinhas/Recife, Brazil.

Pazzani, M. J. (2002). *Representation of electronic mail filtering profiles: A user study.* Paper presented at the Intelligent User Interfaces, San Francisco.

Platt, J. C. (1999). Fast training of support vector machines using sequential minimal optimization. In B. Scholkopf, C. Burges, & A. Smola (Eds.), *Advances in kernel methods: Support vector learning* (pp. 185-207). MIT Press.

Porter, M. F. (1997). An algorithm for suffix stripping. In *Readings in information retrieval* (pp. 313-316). Morgan Kaufmann Publishers Inc.

Quinlan, J. R. (1986). Induction of decision trees. *Machine Learning, 1,* 81-106.

Rennie, J. D. M. (2000). *ifile: An application of machine learning to e-mail filtering.* Paper presented at the KDD-2000 Workshop on Text Mining, Boston.

Rockbridge Associates, Inc. (2004). *National technology readiness survey: Summary report.* Retrieved from http://www.rockresearch.com/press_releases/NTRS_2004.pdf

Sahami, M., Dumais, S., Heckerman, D., & Horvitz, E. (1998). A Bayesian approach to filtering junk e-mail (Tech Rep. No. WS-98-05). In *Learning for text categorization: Papers from the 1998 workshop.* Madison, WI: AAAI.

Sakkis, G., Androutsopoulos, I., Paliouras, G., Karkaletsis, V., Spyropoulos, C. D., & Stamatopoulos, P. (2001). *Stacking classifiers for anti-spam filtering of e-mail.* Paper presented at the EMNLP-01, 6th Conference on Empirical Methods in Natural Language Processing, Pittsburgh, PA.

Sakkis, G., Androutsopoulos, I., Paliouras, G., Karkaletsis, V., Spyropoulos, C. D., & Stamatopoulos, P. (2003). A memory-based approach to anti-spam filtering for mailing lists. *Information Retrieval, 6*(1), 49-73.

Salton, G., & Buckley, C. (1988). Term weighting approaches in automatic text retrieval. *Information Processing and Management, 24*(5), 513-523.

Salton, G., Wong, A., & Yang, C. S. (1975). A vector space model for automatic indexing. *Communications of the ACM, 18*(11), 613-620.

Scheffer, T. (2004). Email answering assistance by semi-supervised text classification. *Intelligent Data Analysis, 8*(5), 481-493.

Sebastiani, F. (2002). Machine learning in automated text categorization. *ACM Computing Surveys, 34*(1), 1-47.

Segal, R., & Kephard, J. (1999). *MailCat: An intelligent assistant for organizing e-mail.* Paper presented at the 3rd International Conference on Autonomous Agents, Seattle, WA.

Segal, R., & Kephard, J. O. (2000). *Incremental learning in SwiftFile.* Paper presented at the 7th International Conference on Machine Learning (ICML 2000), Stanford, CA.

Strehl, A., Ghosh, J., & Mooney, R. (2000). *Impact of similarity measures on Web-page clustering.* Paper presented at the 17th National Conference on Artificial Intelligence: Workshop of Artificial Intelligence for Web Search (AAAI 2000), Austin, TX.

Surendran, A. C., Platt, J. C., & Renshaw, E. (2005). *Automatic discovery of personal topics to organize email.* Paper presented at the 2nd Conference on Email and Anti-Spam, Stanford, CA.

Vel, O. d., Anderson, A., Corney, M., & Mohay, G. (2001). Mining e-mail content for author identification forensics. *SIGMOD Record, 30*(4), 55-64.

Wan, S., & McKeown, K. (2004). *Generating overview summaries of ongoing email thread discussions.* Paper presented at the COLING 2004, 20th International Conference on Computational Linguistics, Geneva, Switzerland.

Witten, I. H., & Frank, E. (2005). *Data mining: Practical machine learning tools and techniques* (2nd ed.). San Francisco: Morgan Kaufmann.

Yang, Y., & Pedersen, J. O. (1997). *A comparative study on feature selection in text categorization.* Paper presented at the ICML-97, 14th International Conference on Machine Learning, Nashville, TN.

Zechner, K. (1996). *Fast generation of abstracts from general domain text corpora by extracting relevant sentences.* Paper presented at the 16th Conference on Computational Linguistics, Copenhagen, Denmark.

Zhang, L., Zhu, J., & Yao, T. (2004). An evaluation of statistical spam filtering techniques. *ACM Transactions on Asian Language Information Processing (TALIP), 3*(4), 243-269.

Endnotes

[1]   http://www.idc.com/home.jhtml

[2]   Microsoft Outlook (http://www.microsoft.com/outlook/)

[3]   Mozilla ThunderBird (http://www.mozilla.org/products/thunderbird/)

[4]   Spambayes (http://spambayes.sourceforge.net)

[5]   Popfile (http://popfile.sourceforge.net)

[6]   The Apache Spam Assassin Project (http://spamassasin.sourceforge.net)

[7]   Spam Conference (http://spamconference.org/), Conference on Email and Anti-Spam (http://www.ceas.cc/)

Section IV

Web Services
for Data Accessing

Chapter XI

Web Services:
Technology Issues and Foundations

Bernd Amann, University Paris 6, France

Salima Benbernou, University Lyon 1, France

Benjamin Nguyen, University of Versailles, France

Abstract

Unlike traditional applications, which depend upon a tight interconnection of all program elements, Web-service applications are composed of loosely coupled, autonomous, and independent services published on the Web. In this chapter, we first introduce the concept of service-oriented computing (SOC) on the Web and the current standards enabling the definition and publication of Web services. This technology's next evolution is to facilitate the creation and maintenance of Web applications. This can be achieved by exploiting the self-descriptive nature of Web services combined with more powerful models and languages for composing Web services. A second objective of this chapter is to illustrate the complexity of the Web-service composition problem and to provide a representative overview of the existing approaches. The chapter concludes with a short presentation of two research projects exploiting and extending the Web-service paradigm.

Introduction

The possibility to transform existing software components into services and to combine them in a loosely-coupled and flexible way has transformed service-oriented computing (SOC) into the favorite programming and computing paradigm for the development of complex applications on the Web. Unlike traditional applications, which depend upon a tight interconnection of all program elements, service-oriented applications are compositions of autonomous and independent services obtained by using special methods and tools for their design, development, and deployment.

Intuitively, a Web service (or e-service) is an autodescriptive, software-independent, and hardware-independent application that can be exploited using standard Internet networking technologies. From a more technical point of view, a Web service is a dynamic Web resource with a public programming and communication interface by which clients can interact using structured XML (extensible markup language) -based messages conveyed by Internet protocols. The success of this technology is based on the definition of coherent open standards for encoding (XML) and exchanging messages (SOAP, simple object access protocol), as well as for describing (WSDL, Web service definition language) and publishing (UDDI, Universal Description, Discovery and Integration) service operations. Today, these standards confer interoperability and reusability on individual Web services, and the next important step will be to facilitate the creation and maintenance of complex Web-service applications. This evolution can be achieved by exploiting the self-describing nature of Web services combined with more powerful Web-service composition models and languages. The term powerful can be understood in different ways. From a programmer's point of view, these models and languages should enable the automation of certain programming (e.g., matching service input and output parameters) and administration tasks (e.g., automatically replace a defective service call). Second, they should be able to express and exploit different kinds of static (interface, functionality, and quality) and dynamic (temporal, behavioral) service properties during the design and validation process. One objective of this chapter is to illustrate related technical and scientific issues, their complexity, and a representative overview of the existing solutions.

The rest of this chapter is structured as follows. Next, the chapter shortly presents the industrial and scientific background of the Web-service technology by concentrating on its specificities with respect to other application design and programming infrastructures. Then we describe the problem of building applications with Web services and introduce the main functionalities required for efficient Web-service application development. Next we introduce the general problem of describing a (Web) service and different approaches for service discovery and matchmaking. Web-service composition approaches and languages are studied next, and then the chapter briefly illustrates two research projects exploiting and extending the Web-service paradigm.

Web Services in a Nutshell

Web services are considered a new way of using software components in an information system. Many of the problems that Web services try to solve can be understood by remembering the evolution of distributed information systems through time in a brief history (Alonso, Casati, Kuno, & Machiraju, 2004).

The Industrial Context of Web Services

Consider an institution, such as an international company composed of different departments (research and development, selling, management) and possibly distributed in different locations and countries. In general, each of these departments runs some applications that need to communicate in order to share data and calculations.

Middleware

A first approach to handle distributed applications is to use standard middleware infrastructures such as simple remote procedure calls (RPCs) or more sophisticated object request brokers (ORBs) based on the CORBA (common object request broker) model. Initially, the middleware approach was used to construct new distributed-system environments and to link existing mainframe-based systems together. Later on, it was applied at a more abstract level as a new way to distribute application logics and to integrate applications through three-tier software architectures. However, CORBA and RPC only work well in an environment where all component systems are well defined, stable, and homogeneous concerning their functionalities. Moreover, middleware architectures are generally centralized and need synchronous communications between all the involved processes. With regard to all these restrictions, one can understand that although middleware is successful when used within a well-defined and controlled software environment (inside a department), it fails when building connections between autonomous software applications evolving independently (in different departments) in distributed and heterogeneous environments.

Enterprise Application Integration

Enterprise application integration (EAI) environments can be considered an evolution of middleware technology with the added possibility of sharing program code over multiple departments. This can be referred to as the urbanization of an enterprise's information system, which consists of the enhancement of an existing infrastructure without destroying the underlying architecture. EAI systems are still closely connected and based on a centralized architecture, but they already indicate a trend toward more flexible application integration environments. Inter-EAI technology such as Java 2 Enterprise Edition (J2EE) and Microsoft .NET consists of applying EAI principles for connecting applications of well-known business partners using Internet infrastructures instead of local area networks (LANs). However, this is only a first step to application integration on the Web since it still needs a strongly coupled integration of components.

Service-Oriented Architectures

EAI technology can efficiently be applied to the integration of well-defined, coarse-grained enterprise applications, but it is insufficient in the context of short-term business-to-business (B2B) applications that require more flexible and powerful tools to integrate business data and logics. Service-oriented architecture (SOA; Pilioura & Tsalgotidou, 2002) and SOC resolve business application integration by proposing new integration platforms based on message brokering and work-flow integration. In some sense, SOA can be considered the software industry's attempt to finally align IT with business by transforming coarse-grained business applications into finer grained services that can be delivered to customers, partners, and suppliers. To solve a business integration problem, developers no longer think in terms of applications, but rather in terms of services and how they can be organized according to some well-defined business process. SOA and SOC are by their nature decentralized and aim at offering reusable services (programs) in a loosely coupled environment. For this reason, SOA and SOC have been recognized as the best way to implement B2B collaborations between independent and autonomous business partners.

The Web-service paradigm, which can be seen as the realization of SOC on the Web, constitutes a modular and flexibly integrated approach of application distribution, conception, and development on the Web. It makes use of the Internet as an infrastructure for publishing large collections of software whose potential is not yet fully exploited.

The Web-Service Infrastructure

A Web service is a software system designed to support interoperable machine-to-machine interaction over a network. It has an interface described in a machine-tractable format (specifically WSDL). Other systems interact with the Web service in a manner prescribed by its description using SOAP-messages, typically conveyed using HTTP [hypertext transfer protocol] with an XML serialization in conjunction with other Web-related standards. (World Wide Web Consortium [W3C], 2004)

In the rest of the chapter, we consider Web services to be modular and autonomous applications that can be published, located, and invoked via the Internet through standard interfaces. They are used in a programming-language independent way to overcome the heterogeneous and often incompatible local IT-system layers by providing a common and homogeneous interface to highly heterogeneous local information systems. Table 1 details some functional characteristics of Web services.

Web-service infrastructures can be characterized by an internal and an external architecture as shown in Figure 2. The internal architecture manages the connection of the service with the underlying local system (middleware, databases, or any other kind of software system). It revolves especially around packing and unpacking messages exchanged between the service client and the underlying application system. Message brokering and work-flow management tasks are accomplished by the external (Web service) architecture that relies on public-accessible interfaces and standards for data representation, message-exchange control (protocols), and service publication.

Figure 1. Some functional characteristics of Web services

A Web service is accessible over the Web and communicates using platform-independent and language-neutral Web protocols.

A Web service provides a structured interface with a set of operations that can be called from any type of application client or service. The Web-service interface acts as a liaison between the Web and the actual application logic that implements the service.

A Web service is registered and can be located through a Web-service registry. The registry enables service consumers to find services that match their needs.

Web services support loosely coupled connections between systems. They communicate by passing messages to each other. The Web-service interface adds a layer of abstraction to the environment that makes the connections flexible and adaptable.

Figure 2. Web-service infrastructure

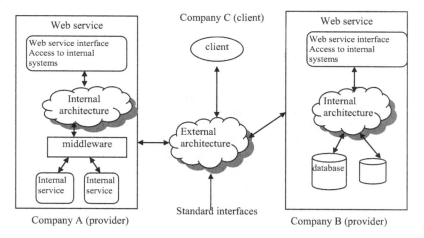

Web-Service Standards

Web services solve the problem of interoperability and reusability by a set of standards developed by international organizations such as the W3C or OASIS (Organization for the Advancement of Structured Information Standards). First of all, Web services use XML as their lingua franca to describe their interfaces and encode their messages. However, XML by itself does not ensure effortless communication, and Web services need additional standard formats and protocols that allow them to properly construct, exchange, and interpret the XML messages.

Figure 3. Some Web-service standards

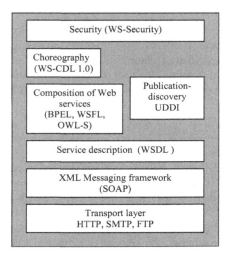

SOC on the Web has rapidly been recognized by industry and research as a future key technology for business and scientific collaborations. Many companies (IBM, Microsoft, Sun, BEA [business enterprise architecure], SAP [systems, applications, and products]) and organizations (W3C, OASIS) have proposed standard models and languages for building the Web-service infrastructure. Obviously, these propositions generally overlap and contradict each other, and their large number has lead to the so-called Web-services acronym hell (WSAH).

Figure 3 shows some established and proposed standards and their role within the Web-service infrastructure. In the rest of this section, we will shortly present three core standards (SOAP, WSDL, UDDI) that are implemented and exploited by today's Web-service infra-structures. Standards for building Web-service applications by service composition will be described later.

SOAP

SOAP is a protocol specification defining a uniform way of passing XML-encoded messages using different kinds of Internet protocols (HTTP, SMTP, XML-RPC). Proposed in 2000 to the W3C by IBM, Microsoft, UserLand, and DevelopMentor, SOAP V1.2 has been a W3C recommendation since June 2003. SOAP is fundamentally a stateless, one-way message-ex-change protocol from which applications can create more complex interaction patterns (see WSDL below). SOAP is an abstract protocol, which means that it is neutral to the semantics of the data it conveys as it is silent on issues such as the routing of messages, reliable data transfer, firewall traversal, and so forth. However, SOAP provides the framework by which it is possible to implement application-specific information transport and to provide a full description of the required actions taken by a SOAP node on receiving a SOAP message.

WSDL

WSDL is a high-level standard for defining all information necessary for using a Web service. WSDL allows service developers to combine structured SOAP messages into operations that can be executed via specified communication endpoints. The structure of these messages (operation interfaces) is defined by XML schemas. Operations can be classified into one-way, request-response (RPC), solicit-response, and notification operations.

UDDI

UDDI is a Web-based distributed directory that enables businesses to list themselves on the Internet and to discover each other. UDDI uses white pages for information such as addresses, contacts, and other known identifiers. It also contains yellow pages for industrial categorizations based on standard taxonomies. Finally, green pages provide technical information about each service exposed by a company. The relatively simple architecture of UDDI consists of duplicating all the Web-service descriptions on many synchronized servers. Implementations of UDDI have already been achieved, and any organization can already register the services they propose or search for some services in UDDI repositories, such as http://uddi.us.com/. Standard-wise, UDDI.org has released UDDI Version 3. This specification extends the vision of UDDI: a meta service for locating Web services by enabling robust queries on rich metadata.

WS-Security

OASIS, BEA, IBM, Microsoft, and SAP propose SOAP Message Security V1.0 (*WS Security*, 2004) as an extension of SOAP v1.1 (and 1.2) that can be used to guarantee message-content integrity, confidentiality, and authentication. As is the case for SOAP, WS Security follows the principle of staying independent of any particular implementation technology and is designed to be used within a wide variety of security models such as public key infrastructure (PKI), Kerberos, and secure socket layer (SSL). WS-Security covers all problems induced by transactional processing, including WS-Policy for defining policies to control individual service behavior, WS-Trust for building trusted relationships between Web services, and WS-Secure Conversation for secure communication.

Building Web-Service Applications

Web services have rapidly been recognized by industrial and scientific communities as a new standard way for data and application integration on the Web. The main Web-service standards (SOAP, WSDL, UDDI) and technologies (Apache extendible interaction system [AXIS], Sun Java Api for XML-based remote procedure call [JAX-RPC], Microsoft .NET) provide a basic infrastructure for publishing and connecting applications by the exchange of structured XML messages. Yet, they are insufficient to build applications integrating existing services in a flexible, open, and dynamic way. Current Web-service technology can be exploited in the form of object-oriented class libraries within standard programming languages like Java and C++. Whereas this kind of deployment is sufficient for using Web-service technology as an extended (object-oriented) form of structured (XML) RPC infrastructure on the Web, it does not exploit the full potential of the Web-service paradigm. Standard programming languages and environments are optimized for the development of complex applications using well-defined classes, objects, and methods that do not evolve (much) in time. On the contrary, the service-oriented computing paradigm promotes the design and validation of new, open, flexible applications via service composition.

Web-service composition denotes the ability to provide added-value services through the composition of existing services, possibly offered by different people and organizations. In order to understand the problem of composing services on the Web, it is useful to remember some basic assumptions about Web services and SOC. First of all, Web services are public interfaces to private software components that are maintained by service providers. In particular, the outside world (other services and users) might only have a partial view of the behavior of a Web service. For example, most service providers only publish WSDL descriptions that define the input and output messages of available service operations and the network protocols that can be used to exchange these messages. These descriptions only provide a partial knowledge about their services, which obviously complicates the composition task and restricts the possibilities of validating logical, temporal, security, and transactional properties of composed services. A second important issue concerns the nature of the Web in general. As any Web resource, an existing Web service might be unavailable for some period of time or disappear forever, and new Web services might appear at any instance of time. This kind of volatility not only concerns atomic Web services, but also composed services that only exist during the short-term collaboration between two business partners. Therefore, Web-service composition is a process that has to take into account a dynamic environment of available services and new services to be defined.

The various properties of Web services (independence, volatility, short-term definition) changes Web-service composition into a complex problem that has to take into account a dynamic environment of available services. It is generally accepted that in order to solve this problem, it has to be solved by a layered software architecture separating the process of service composition into three steps: design, compilation, and validation. The design step consists of the specification of the expected composite service. The result is a service specification (also called service model) written in a given service composition language. Such specifications are often abstract; that is, they do not explicitly define all information needed for executing the composed service. The compilation step consists of the instantiation of the abstract specifications (service grounding). This step often includes the discovery (matchmaking) of services satisfying some (logical, temporal, type) constraints defined in the specification. The result is a composite service that implements the specification. The validation step is optional and consists of validating a composite service according to some given specification. Of course, the possibilities and nature of validation naturally depends on the description model used. Finally, composite services can be deployed in different kinds of infrastructures that might be centralized or distributed.

The efficient combination of these steps can be obtained by defining appropriate models and languages for each layer. The following sections describe current solutions to the Web-service composition problem and a synthetic presentation of representative Web-service description, discovery, and composition models and languages.

Web-Service Discovery and Matchmaking

Describing Web Services

An important preliminary issue in service composition is to discover a coherent set of services that can be composed on the Web. This problem is similar to the problem of finding Web pages relevant to a given user query. The main difference is that the information necessary for using a Web service (WSDL definition) is in general not sufficient to help one decide if it is relevant to a given application. In particular, WSDL definitions do not define service semantics, behavior, or other properties, which are crucial when trying to connect services. Consequently, Web services must provide layers of information to facilitate binding in autonomous and loosely coupled settings. It is necessary to describe the properties and capabilities of the Web services in unambiguous, computer-interpretable form. Web-service properties can be classified according to several dimensions.

Functional or Nonfunctional Properties

Web-service properties can be separated into domain- or application-specific (functional) properties and domain- or application-independent properties, which can be applied to any kind of Web service or task (quality of service, cost, protocols, etc.). Domain-specific properties describe the functionalities of the service (what the service does) and are useful for semantic Web-service discovery and composition. They play an important role in the definition of semantic Web services (McIlraith, Cao, Son, & Zeng, 2002) by exploiting standard semantic Web technology (W3C, n.d.) for the automatic discovery and composition of Web resources. Domain-independent properties define how service functionalities can be used (protocol, quality of service, security) and are useful for validating services according to domain-independent constraints or more general policy descriptions (Verma, Akkiraju, & Goodwin, 2005).

Input and Output Signatures

Service composition includes the detection of services that are compatible with specified input and output specifications called Web-service signatures. Web-service signatures are defined through high-level interface languages describing the available service methods and data at the syntactic (XML) level and the semantic (ontology) level. Syntactic and semantic Web-service signatures are useful for checking if two services can be concatenated by matching the corresponding input-output-type signatures. They may also be used to discover complex and coherent service compositions.

Describing Service Behavior

At a pure conceptual level, the behavior of a service can be described by a simple or complex concept in some domain-specific ontology. For example, it is possible to describe the (functional) behavior of a service and an expected task in the form of complex semantic concepts like "booking service for hotels in Paris." These kinds of conceptual descriptions are useful for discovering Web services that fulfill a specific functionality defined in application-specific (semantic) terms.

At a more structured level, Web services offer a number of operations that clients must invoke in a certain order to achieve their goals. The public external behavior of a single (simple or complex) Web service is called a conversation. Formally speaking, the conversation of a service can be defined as a set of states that can be changed by a set of actions like simple SOAP messages, more complex activities, or external events (Hull & Su, 2004). For example, WSDL publishes the conversation of a Web service as a set of independent (abstract) internal execution states that can be changed by exchanging messages (calling service operations). More powerful languages such as Business Process Execution Language for Web Services (BPEL4WS; BEA, IBM, Microsoft) are based on extended work-flow models in which service operations are considered activities with different execution states (operation x is running, terminated, aborted) that can be changed by exchanging messages. Finally, semantic models such as OWL-S allow publishing service conversations in which each service is considered to perform activities changing the state of an external world defined by some domain-specific ontology. Other variations of conversation languages might take into account other kinds of properties such as temporal, transactional, or security properties. Conversation languages help in defining abstract (business) protocols, and identifying and validating (sets of) services that are expected to behave according to these protocols.

Describing Real-World Semantics

The objective of OWL-S is to supply Web-service providers with a more powerful language for publishing the capabilities of a Web service in terms of real-world concepts and properties defined in rich application- and domain-specific ontologies. Richer semantics support the construction of more powerful tools and methodologies for a greater automation of service selection and invocation, the automated translation of message content between heterogeneous interoperating services, automated or semiautomated approaches to service composition, and more comprehensive approaches to service monitoring and recovery from failure.

Service Discovery with UDDI

Web-service discovery consists of locating Web services that provide a particular service and that adhere to requested properties. For instance, a user might ask for all services that sell airline tickets between Paris and Athens and accept payments by Visa credit card. This kind of query can be answered by a service registry or search engine returning a result in the form of a Web page or XML message that can be processed by a user or an application. UDDI defines a standard language and programming interface for defining and exploiting service registries. On the one hand, it allows service providers (companies) to register their services under different semantic categories, whereas on the other hand, it is used by Web-service application developers to discover a specific service as well as related commercial (service provider) and technical (WSDL file) information (service metadata). UDDI definitions are general enough to be used for services of different kinds that are not necessarily Web services. UDDI registries are typically implemented by standard database systems using a specific data model for publishing and discovering services and their metadata. UDDI directories allow service providers to register new services and allow users to search for and locate services.

Service Discovery vs. Service Matchmaking

Web-service technology has been identified as a favorite infrastructure for deploying ad hoc applications needed for short-term business or scientific collaborations. However, building error-free Web-service applications by choosing and composing coherent sets of existing Web services is still a complex process. UDDI registries facilitate this process by exploiting simple taxonomies for classifying and discovering services on the Web. However, they do not exploit the self-describing nature of Web services at its full potential. In particular, it is not possible to identify services satisfying more complex (behavioral, temporal, transactional, security) constraints with current UDDI registries.

Service matchmaking infrastructures can be considered as a new generation of service registries with more powerful service discovery models and algorithms exploiting a maximum of metadata describing rich service properties. The nature of these properties obviously influences the expressiveness of the matchmaking process, which can be limited to UDDI-like Web-service discovery by matching some simple functional category (e.g., HotelBooking-Service) or the finding of a coherent sets of services satisfying complex temporal, logical, and semantic constraints defined in the desired task (e.g., journey booking service using hotel and flight reservation and booking services and satisfying certain type and transaction constraints). Service matchmaking models and algorithms for comparing (matching) complex service properties will play an increasingly central role in the automation of Web-service design and run-time infrastructures.

Service Matchmaking Approaches

The large choice of properties and the possible combinations of these properties has led to a great number of matchmaking models based on different approaches proposed by different research communities (databases, information retrieval, work-flow management, and knowledge representation). Each of these communities provides a specific complementary view to the service matchmaking problem that will be described in this section.

Database Approaches

The database community has considered the problem of automatically matching database schemas. The work in this area has developed several methods that try to capture clues about the semantics of the database schemas, and suggest matches based on them. Such methods include linguistic analysis, structural analysis, the use of domain knowledge, and previous matching experience. Schema matching is very similar to the matching of service parameter types (signature matchmaking) with some subtle but important differences related to the granularity and complexity of the compared entities (Dong, Halevy, Madhavan, Nemes, & Zhang, 2004). First, signature matchmaking consists of comparing the input and output parameters of some Web-service operation, while schema matching looks for similar components in two schemas that are assumed to be related. Second, operations in a Web service are typically much more loosely related to each other than are tables in a schema (e.g., via foreign key constraints). Finally, each Web service in isolation provides in general much less useful matching information than a database schema.

An interesting matchmaking issue related to database technology concerns data-intensive services, which are defined by structured (XML, relational) parameterized database queries. For example, the Query Set Specification Language (QSSL; Petropoulos, Deutsch, & Papakonstantinou, 2003) service description language can be used for the concise and semantically meaningful description of sets of parameterized (XML) tree-pattern queries. QSSL descriptions can be translated into regular tree languages for solving data-intensive service matchmaking problems like query membership (a service accepts some given query), service inclusion (a service might be replaced by another service), and service overlap (check if there exists a query that is accepted by two given Web services).

An input-output matchmaking issue that has appeared for data-intensive Web services exchanging extended XML documents (ActiveXML, AXML) containing Web-service calls and results (intentional XML data) has been studied in the ActiveXML system by Milo, Abiteboul, Amann, Benjelloun, and Dang-Ngoc (2005). Like standard XML documents, AXML documents can be validated against given AXML schemas. But the possibility to replace a service call by its result also allows adapting invalid documents by the controlled evaluation of service calls. The underlying matchmaking problem can be considered as an input-output matchmaking problem and consists of detecting (for a given source document) a sequence of service calls that have to be evaluated in order to obtain a new document that is valid according to a given target schema.

Information-Retrieval Approaches

By transforming textual information associated with Web services into sets of terms (bag of words, term vectors), it is possible to discover, compare, and rank services using standard information-retrieval techniques. Woogle (Dong et al., 2004) is a Web-service search engine that supports similarity search for Web services. The underlying matchmaking algorithm exploits existing textual service descriptions (WSDL files, UDDI descriptions) in order to determine similarity between pairs of Web-service operations. In particular, it considers similarity between the textual descriptions of the Web-service operations and their parameter names. The key ingredient of the algorithm is a technique that improves the recall and the preciseness of the obtained results by clustering service operation and parameter names into semantically meaningful concepts.

BiAsed Service dIsovery aLgorithm (BASIL; Caverlee, Liu, & Rocco, 2004) provides the discovery and ranking of data-intensive Web services through source-biased probing and source-biased relevance metrics. Matchmaking consists of checking whether a target service is relevant to the given source service by comparing representative sets of terms using standard information-retrieval techniques. The main problem consists of obtaining relevant target terms by probing (calling) the target service with relevant (input) probe terms. Target services can be ranked based on a set of source-biased relevance metrics, and it is possible to identify relationships between source and target services.

Knowledge-Based Approaches

Knowledge representation and reasoning techniques offer the possibility of formally defining and exploiting semantically rich (domain specific and domain independent) Web-service properties. They play an important role in the definition of semantic Web services by using standard semantic Web technologies for the automatic exploitation of Web resources. OWL-S, which is built on top of the OWL knowledge representation language for modeling semantic Web services and domain-specific knowledge (ontology), is the most representative example for this approach. Matchmaking OWL-S service descriptions can be done at two different levels. At the knowledge (OWL) level, it is possible to exploit standard description-logic (DL) techniques for defining and reasoning on conceptual descriptions of services and service parameters. For example, it is possible to compare service operators by their semantic functional description (category; Paolucci, Kawamura, Payne, & Sycara, 2002) and the semantic types of their input-output parameters (Li & Horrocks, 2003). At the more specific service level, OWL-S proposes an activity-based service model that can be represented by situation calculus expressions and Petri nets. This allows the formal description of the behavior of (atomic) services in the form of preconditions and effects, and a check of whether a given collection of services can be combined, using the OWL-S constructors, to form a composite service that accomplishes a stated goal.

Larks (language for advertisement and request for knowledge sharing; Sycara, Widolf, Klush, & Lu, 2002) is an expressive service (agent) publication language combined with a powerful matchmaking process employing techniques from information retrieval (text matching), knowledge processing (concept matching), and logics (constraint matching) to compute the syntactical and semantic similarity among service (agent) descriptions. The matchmaking process can be configured to achieve a desired trade-off between performance and matching quality.

When used for service discovery, service matchmaking often consists of finding the best service with respect to a given input query. This needs the definition of appropriate score measures that allow the choosing of one single service among a set of possible services in the answer. Semantic scores can be obtained by measuring a semantic distance between concepts in an underlying application ontology. An interesting and flexible Web-service matchmaking algorithm based on advanced DL operators is proposed in Benatallah, Hacid, Leger, Rey, and Toumani (2005). This algorithm takes as input a service request Q, an ontology O, and a set of services S and identifies the subset of services $S_0 \subseteq S$ whose descriptions contain as much common information with Q as possible and as little extra information with respect to Q as possible (S_0 is called the best cover of Q). This notion of semantic cover generalizes the standard DL notion of subsumption and results in a more flexible matchmaking process.

Klein and Bernstein (2002) propose the use of a particular process ontology to describe the behavior of services and to query these descriptions with a specific process query language (PQL). Chakraborty, Perich, Avancha, and Joshi (2001) define an ontology based on DARPA Agent Markup L(DAML) to describe and locate mobile devices based on their features (e.g., a type of a printer). The matching mechanism is implemented on top of a Prolog-based system capable of reasoning on the ontology and service features. Bassiliades, Anagnostopoulos, and Vlahavas (2005) describe a knowledge-based Web-service composition system, called SWIM, which is based on the service domain model. Service domains are communities of semantically related Web services. Each such domain can be accessed via a single Web service, called the mediator service. Each SOAP message received by the mediator service is dispatched to one or several domain services. The individual results returned by the domain service are aggregated by the mediator to a single outgoing SOAP message (answer). X-DEVICE, a deductive XML-based rule language, is used for selecting registered Web services, combining the results, and synchronizing the work flow of information among the combined Web services in a declarative way.

An experience in building a matchmaking prototype based on a description logic reasoner that considers DAML+OIL-based (Horrocks, 2002) service descriptions is reported by Gonzàlez-Castillo, Trastour, and Bartolini (2001). The proposed matchmaking algorithm is based on simple subsumption and consistency tests. A more sophisticated matchmaking algorithm between services and requests described in DAML-S is proposed by Paolucci et al. (2002). The algorithm considers various degrees of matching that are determined by the minimal distance between concepts in the concept taxonomy. Based on a similar approach, the Agent Transaction Language for Advertising Services (ATLAS) matchmaker (Payne, Paolucci, & Sycara, 2001) considers DAML-S ontologies and utilizes two separate sets of filters for matching functional attributes (quality of service, etc.) and service functionalities (what the service does). A DAML-based subsumption inference engine is used to compare input and output sets of requests and advertisements.

More details about knowledge-based approaches for semantic service matchmaking can be found in Bernstein and Klein (2002) and Paolucci et al. (2002).

Work-Flow Approaches

Matchmaking services by their behavior is a complex issue related to automatic work-flow design. For example, Gerede, Hull, Ibarra, and Su (2004) represent Web services as activity-based finite-state automata and study the problem of building a mediator that delegates activities of a given target service (also represented as an automaton) to existing Web services. In Beyer, Chakrabarti, and Henzinger (2005), Web services are described by Web-service interfaces that combine signature constraints (input-output parameters), consistency constraints (operation calls and output values that may occur in a Web-service conversation), and protocol constraints on the allowed ordering of method calls. This interface can be used to check, first, if two or more Web services are compatible, and second, if a Web service can safely be replaced by another Web service.

Web Service Composition

The problem of designing, validating, and deploying composite Web services has brought together researchers from different research domains such as work-flow management, databases, program specification and verification, distributed computing, and artificial intelligence. According to their scientific background, members of these communities contribute by making use of specific formal and theoretical languages and models for specifying and validating the behavior of Web services (Hull & Su, 2004). As a result of this, all well-known approaches for the explicit representations of flow control, concurrency, and communication such as Petri nets, process algebra, process calculus, situation calculus, state charts, and so forth have been used when defining formal WS composition languages (Bultan, Fu, Hull, & Su, 2003) or providing formal semantics to existing languages (Brogi, Canal, Pimental, & Vallecillo, 2004; Fu, Bultan, & Su, 2004; Narayanan & McIlraith, 2002; Ouyang, van der Aalst, Breutel, Dumas, ter Hofstede, & Verbeek, 2005). In the rest of this section, we will describe different approaches for Web-service composition.

Choreography and Orchestration

Web-service composition languages are often classified into orchestration languages and choreography languages. This distinction concerns the control flow between individual services participating in a service composition. In the abstract state-action model for Web-service conversations, the state-changing actions have to be synchronized in order to obtain a composite service with a coherent behavior. Orchestration languages compose services by using standard programming or work-flow control structures (condition, loop), whereas choreography languages use constraints that have to be satisfied by the services composing the new service. For example, the control flow in a choreography might be defined by a distributed automaton containing a set of transition rules of the form "If service s is in state x, it can execute action a (which changes the state of another service)."

Choreography and orchestration are often considered as two complementary approaches for composing Web services. At the language level, choreography languages are declarative in the sense that they define what each component service has to do in the composition. Meanwhile, orchestration languages explicitly define how the component services have to collaborate. This distinction is similar to high-level declarative query languages and their lower level physical execution plans. For example, WS-CDL proposes a high-level choreography language for specifying composite services that can be compiled into a lower level orchestration language such as BPEL4WS. At a conceptual level, orchestration languages are better suited for top-down design by decomposing the functionality of a composite service, whereas choreography constructs new services by combing individual functionalities in a bottom-up manner. Finally, choreography languages favor distributed infrastructures, whereas orchestration is often based on centralized deployment engines.

Another dimension for characterizing WS composition languages concerns the level of abstraction used in the specification of a complex service. For example, component services might be referenced by concrete service ports or by more abstract (semantic, syntactic, physical) constraints used for choosing the corresponding service instances at compile or run time.

Web-Service Composition Languages

The Web-service infrastructure has been recently extended with procedural work-flow languages (e.g., Business Process Modeling Language [BPML], BPEL4WS) that enable the specification and the implementation of composite services. Even more recently, new approaches and techniques have been proposed to support dynamic service composition. For example Narayanan and McIlraith (2002) and Hendler, Nau, Parsia, Sirin, and Wu (2003) combine service annotations and planning techniques in order to automate Web-service composition. Given a declarative specification of a service's behavior, one can use a formal framework based on PDL (propositional dynamic logic) to enable the automatic generation of a composite service satisfying the specified behavior. A different approach is proposed in Hull, Benedikt, Christophides, and Su (2003) and Bultan et al. (2003) who focus on the global behavioral properties of composite services (protocols) and their relationship with the local properties of the component services (conversation specifications). Automata theory is used to develop techniques that support the verification and synthesis of global properties from the local ones. In the following, we will describe three representative Web-service composition languages.

BPEL4WS: Extended Work-Flow Approach

BPEL4WS (Andrews et al., 2003) is a recent XML-based standard for the composition of Web services obtained by the fusion of Microsoft's XLANG (Web services for business process design) and IBM's WSFL service composition languages. It is based on the WSDL standard for publishing Web-service compositions, defining data and message types, and referencing external services required by the process. There already exists a number of implementations that can be used on top of standard Web-service infrastructures (see, for example, Oracle BPEL Process Manager and IBM's BPWS4J).

Business Proces Execution Language for Web Services Java™ Run Time (BPEL4WS) has two language components for implementing private executable work flows (orchestrations) and describing abstract (nonexecutable) business protocols (choreographies). The first component allows the specification of business processes (orchestrations) that are interpreted and executed by a centralized orchestration engine. This process can be represented as a graph of activities connected by service links. There are three kinds of activities for invoking external services, publishing the behavior of the composed service, and controlling the flow of execution. The first kind of activity is called invoke and corresponds to the invocation of an external Web-service operation. The second kind of activity is receive and reply, such as waiting for one of the operations defined in the service's interface to be invoked by someone externally, and then generating the response of an input-output operation. Primitive execution-control activities allow the composed process to wait for some time (wait), copy data from one place to another (assign), indicate that something went wrong (throw), terminate the entire service instance (terminate), or do nothing (empty). Activities can be combined using any of the structure activities to define an ordered sequence of steps (sequence), the ability to have branching using the now common case-statement approach (switch), the ability to define a loop (while), the ability to execute one of several alternative paths (pick), and finally the ability to indicate that a collection of steps should be executed in parallel (flow). Within activities executed in parallel, one can indicate execution-order constraints by using the links.

The second language component is implemented via the definition of service link types that specify abstract relationships between partners. This kind of specification is especially useful when the interactions are based on asynchronous messaging rather than on remote procedure calls. It also favors peer-to-peer (P2P) relationships (choreographies). A service link type defines a collection of roles, where each role indicates a list of WSDL port types. The idea is that a service link type essentially defines what each partner has to offer in order to be able to interact with each other. A partner is then defined by a name, a service link type, and the role that the partner will play. These kinds of business protocols are defined by using receive, reply, and invoke activities, where the partner name is used instead of specific, concrete Web-service instances. It is important to note that the BPEL4WS specification concerning choreographies is still evolving.

BPEL4WS also provides transactions and exception handling on top of the WS-Coordination and WS-Transaction specifications. For example, sets of activities can be grouped in a single atomic transaction through the scope tag. Compensation handlers can be invoked if one activity fails. The transactional mechanisms within BPEL work hand in hand with exception handling through the use of throw and catch clauses.

WS-CDL: Web-Services Choreography Description Language

WS-CDL (Kavantzas, Burdett, Ritzinger, Fletcher, & Lafont, 2004) is an XML-based language proposed by the W3C for describing peer-to-peer collaborations (choreographies) of parties by defining, from a global viewpoint, their common and complementary observable behavior.

WS-CDL and its model are based on the synchronized exchange of messages (XML documents) between services via some communication channel. Services can play different roles (buyer, seller, etc.) and send a restricted set of documents in each role. The fact that a service playing some role can send a specific document is called a state. An interaction (activity) is a synchronized exchange of documents between services. A choreography (behavioral unit) is a set of interactions between services. Guard conditions (reactions) allow the definition of global conditions for triggering activities: When the corresponding states are available and a guard condition evaluates to true, the enclosed activities are triggered. Additional control structures (sequence, parallel, choice) introduce an explicit control flow (orchestration) into WS-CDL specifications.

One of the objectives is to define a high-level language for specifying (not executing) choreographies that can be compiled into (executable) private business processes (BPEL orchestrations). In this sense, WS-CDL has been defined as a high-level language for designing and analyzing Web-service composition.

OWL-S: Semantic Service Composition

OWL-S defines an ontology of concepts and roles that facilitates service choreography and orchestrations at a purely semantic level through the use of concepts. Service choreography is facilitated by defining service conversations in the form of service profiles (class ServiceProfile), whereas orchestration work flows can be defined by instances of the class Process, which provides the necessary control structures. OWL-S uses a well-defined fragment of OWL (OWL DL) for modeling services. This fragment is equivalent to some particular description logic and allows efficient reasoning on complex concept definitions (subsumption). In particular, it is possible to define and analyze OWL-S service compositions using the whole range of reasoning tools for description-logic terminologies. Situation calculus (McCarthy, 1986) provides another formal foundation of OWL-S.

Web Services: Some Research Issues

SOC on the Web has raised a number of interesting research problems and led up to new scientific activities and collaborations between different research communities. In this section, we will describe two research activities exploiting and extending the Web-service paradigm.

The ActiveXML Approach for Data-Centric Web Services

We first start with AXML, which is a declarative framework using Web-service standards for distributed data management. ActiveXML is an open-source project that was designed in the Institut de Recherche en Informatique et Automatique (INRIA)-Futurs GEMO Group and has already been used in different research projects by various other research groups. The principle idea of AXML is to extend standard XML documents with intentional XML data defined in the form of Web service calls. AXML finds applications in many different areas, such as data integration, by enabling the simple construction of mediators or warehouses, cooperative work, grid computing, digital libraries, or electronic commerce. All these applications have in common the act of manipulating large quantities of sometimes heterogeneous information. The goal of AXML is to construct a framework providing uniform access to all this information.

So What is ActiveXML?

Simply put, ActiveXML is two things:

- A declarative language (AXML) for defining distributed information and services and

- An infrastructure (AXML system) to manage this data in a P2P framework.

Indeed, the system is supported by a Web-based platform on which to execute the function calls. AXML strongly builds on standard XML and Web-service technologies, such as XML schema, XPath and XQuery, SOAP, WSDL, and UDDI. The basic idea is to combine these technologies in a new data model where XML data might be defined extensionally (as a document fragment) and intentionally (as the result of a service call). The result is an active XML document that contains service calls. The activity of the document can be viewed in three different ways: intentionally, dynamically, and flexibly. In the first case, the document contains, rather than data, the means to obtain data (intension). For instance, if we are writing a document on countries, rather than storing the capital of each country, we might instead store a call to a Web site that can provide us with the capital of each county given the name of the country. In the second case, the information in the document may be changing through time; therefore the same document viewed at different moments might provide different information. For instance, if we are seeking the temperature of each capital, we might call a Web service that could instantly compute the temperature and return it. In the last case, let us imagine that we are listing the countries in the European Union. We may know of some countries at a given point in time (the moment we are writing the document) and have knowledge that this will evolve in the future. AXML gives us the means to exploit an answer that may be completed in the future.

AXML Architecture

The architecture of the AXML system is based on P2P as illustrated in Figure 4. Each AXML peer is an autonomous system containing a repository to store the data, a Web client to call other Web services and process their results, and finally a Web server in order to provide services, usually queries on the data contained in the repository. AXML peers exchange AXML (thus, XML) information. Let us stress that an AXML document is of course platform independent; the peer needs only to know how to run AXML in order to work. There are currently implementations of AXML on both PCs (personal computers) and smaller PDAs (personal digital assistants).

Figure 4. AXML architecture

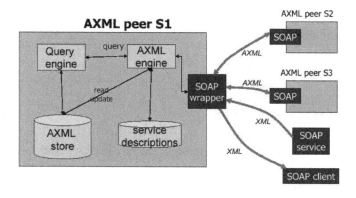

Technical Issues in Web-Service-Based Data Management

We stress in this paragraph the four most important technical and scientific issues that were raised by AXML.

- **Data Exchange:** When calling a service, parameters need to be passed. As we have shown, this is a complex issue, especially when services need to be composed one with the other. However, in the case of AXML, there are many other problems. Since an AXML document may contain several service calls, in which order must these services be activated? Is there a way to guarantee that an answer will be obtained? Should the results of service calls be materialized in order to improve performance? How do we deal with trust?

- **Query Optimization:** When querying a document, the goal is to obtain an answer as fast as possible. This will generally equate to making as less service calls as possible. This is called lazy evaluation: only calling a service when necessary. The problem is quite complex for many reasons. First of all, when should the decision to call or not to call be made? If this is done at query time, this will cost precious time by blocking the query processor. If this is done off line, before query evaluation, finding all the calls triggered by a giving query is difficult since a service call can contain other service calls.

- **Distribution and Replication:** AXML works on mobile devices, that is, devices with limited capacities concerning storage, computational power, and bandwidth. Therefore, documents need to distribute the work among devices (this may be done by calling external services or by distributing documents across several peers) and replicate both information and services in order to improve parallelism.

- **Security and Access Control:** There are many techniques and standards (issued by W3C) around the encryption of documents sent over the Web, and enabling the AXML support of key encryption is not a trivial problem.

More Information on AXML

For a more detailed and complete view of AXML, we refer the reader to Abiteboul, Benjelloun, Manolescu et al. (2004). We provide other references for the specific problems of data exchange (Milo et al., 2005), lazy service calls and query optimization (Abiteboul, Benjelloun, Manolescu et al., 2004), document distribution and replication (Abiteboul, Bonifati, Cobena, Manolescu, & Milo, 2003), and finally security (Abiteboul, Benjelloun, Manolescu et al., 2004).

A Knowledge-Based Approach for Semantic WS Discovery

The objective of semantic Web-service discovery is to use semantic knowledge to find services that can be composed to form an appropriate answer to a query. In this section, we present the author's research work (Benbernou & Hacid, 2005) using a knowledge-based approach to Web-service discovery. Services are described by means of terminological axioms and constraints. The work concentrates on applying specific resolution and constraint propagation mechanisms for the automatic discovery of Web services (finding Web services with a given functionality). We use a hybrid approach for describing Web services and enhance a Web service through the addition of two parts:

- A structural part, describing in terms of a set of axioms the semantic of concepts (unary relations) and roles (binary relations) used to specify services, and
- A constraint part, which consists of Datalog-like rules for capturing constraints that cannot be represented in the structural part. The clauses are assumed to be range restricted.

In this setting, the problem of Web-services discovery can be stated as follows: Given an ontology containing Web-services descriptions and a query, find a combination of Web services that can form a candidate solution to the query. This process can be seen as a rewriting by constraint propagation and resolution. The ontology of Web services is assumed to be structured. This means that every constraint is either purely relational or purely structural. The approach to using both structural and constraint parts for Web services rests on inference rules, namely, constrained resolution and constraint propagation (Baader, Calvanese, MacGuiness, Nardi, & Patel-Shneider, 2003). A query is evaluated by modifying the query using the structural part of the ontology during a process called propagation. In this step, useful information (for the purpose of discovering services) is extracted from the structural part of the ontology. Afterward, the relation part (constraint part) is used to filter services by removing those that do not satisfy the additional relational constraints.

Conclusion

The importance of Web services has been recognized and widely accepted by industry and academic research. Both worlds have proposed solutions that progress along different directions. Academic research has been mostly concerned with the expressiveness of service descriptions, while industry has focused on the modularization of service layers for usability in the short term.

Bringing Web-service technology to its full potential for service-oriented computing on the Web still requires an important research and development effort. Among the open issues, we can mention the problem of automatically composing and validating Web services from high-level (semantic) service specifications including security policies, temporal and transactional constraints, service quality, and so forth. Each of these issues involves many complementary technologies, and a main challenge for the future will be the exchange and integration of theoretical and practical tools and solutions produced by different research and development communities.

This work has been partially supported by the French national research grant ACI Masses de Données SemWeb.

References

Abiteboul, S., Benjelloun, O., Manolescu, I., Milo, T., & Weber, R. (2004). Active XML: A data-centric perspective on Web services. In M. Levene & A. Poulovassilis (Eds.), *Web dynamics* (pp. 275-300). Springer.

Abiteboul, S., Bonifati, A., Cobena, G., Manolescu, I., & Milo, T. (2003). Dynamic XML documents with distribution and replication. *Proceedings of the International ACM Special Interest Group for the Management of Data (SIGMOD) Conference* (pp. 527-538).

Active XML Web site. (n.d.). Retrieved October 2005, from http://activexml.net

Alonso, G., Casati, F., Kuno, H., & Machiraju, V. (2004). Web services: Concepts, architectures and applications. In *Data-centric systems and applications.* Springer Verlag.

Andrews, T., Curbera, F., Dholakia, H., Goland, Y., Klein, J., Leymann, F., et al. (2003). *Business process execution language for Web services version 1.1* (Tech. Rep.). BEA, IBM, Microsoft, SAP, Siebel. Retrieved October 2005, from http://www128.ibm.com/developerworks/library/specification/ws-bpel/

Baader, F., Calvanese, D., MacGuiness, D., Nardi, D., & Patel-Shneider, P. (2003). *The description logic handbook.* Cambridge University Press.

Bassiliades, N., Anagnostopoulos, D., & Vlahavas, I. (2005). Web service composition using a deductive XML rule language. *Distributed and Parallel Databases, 17*, 135-178.

Benatallah, B., Hacid, M.-S., Leger, A., Rey, C., & Toumani, F. (2005). On automating Web services discovery. *The International Journal on Very Large Databases, 14*(1), 84-96.

Benbernou, S., & Hacid, M. S. (2005). Resolution and constraint propagation for semantic Web services discovery. *Distributed and Parallel Database Journal, 18*(1), 61-85.

Bernstein, A., & Klein, M. (2002). Discovering services: Towards high-precision service retrieval. In *Proceedings of the Web Services, E-Business, and the Semantic Web CAiSE 2002 International Workshop* (LNCS 2512, pp. 260-276). Toronto, CA: Springer.

Beyer, D., Chakrabarti, A., & Henzinger, T. A. (2005). Web service interfaces. *WWW '05: Proceedings of the 14th International Conference on World Wide Web* (pp. 148-159).

Brogi, A., Canal, C., Pimentel, E., & Vallecillo, A. (2004). Formalizing Web service choreographies. *Electronic Notes in Theoretical Computer Science, 105*, 73-94.

Bultan, T., Fu, X., Hull, R., & Su, J. (2003). Conversation specification: A new approach to design and analysis of e-service composition. *WWW '03: Proceedings of the 12th International Conference on World Wide Web* (pp. 403-410).

Caverlee, J., Liu, L., & Rocco, D. (2004). Discovering and ranking Web services with basil: A personalized approach with biased focus. *ICSOC '04: Proceedings of the 2nd International Conference on Service Oriented Computing* (pp. 153-162).

Chakraborty, D., Perich, F., Avancha, S., & Joshi, A. D. (2001, October 28-31). *Semantic service discovery for m-commerce applications.* DReggie: Semantic Service Discovery for M-Commerce Applications Workshop on Reliable and Secure Applications in Mobile Environment, in Conjunction with 20th Symposium on Reliable Distributed Systems (SRDS), New Orleans.

DAML Services Coalition. (2002). DAML-S: Web service description for the semantic Web. *Proceedings of the 1st International Semantic Web Conference (ISWC)*, 348-363.

DARPA Agent Markup Language (DAML). (n.d.). Retrieved October 2005, from http://daml. org/services/owl-s/

Dong, X., Halevy, A., Madhavan, J., Nemes, E., & Zhang, J. (2004). Similarity search for Web services. *Proceedings of the Very Large Databases Conference (VLDB)* (pp. 372-383).

Fu, X., Bultan, T., & Su, J. (2004). Analysis of interacting BPEL Web services. *WWW '04: Proceedings of the 13th International Conference on World Wide Web* (pp. 621-630).

Gerede, C. E., Hull, R., Ibarra, O. H., & Su, J. (2004). Automated composition of e-services: Lookaheads. *ICSOC '04: Proceedings of the 2nd International Conference on Service Oriented Computing* (pp. 252-262).

Gonzàlez-Castillo, J., Trastour, D., & Bartolini, C. (2001). Description logics for matchmaking of services. *Proceedings of the KI-2001 Workshop on Applications of Description Logics Vienna, 44.*

Hendler, J., Nau, D., Parsia, B., Sirin, E., & Wu, D. (2003). Automating DAML-S Web services composition using SHOP2. *Proceedings of the International Semantic Web Conference (ISWC)* (pp. 195-210).

Horrocks, I. (2002). DAML+OIL: A reason-able Web ontology language. In *Lecture notes in computer science: Vol. 2287. Proceedings of the Advances in Database Technology: EDBT 2002, 8th International Conference on Extending Database Technology* (pp. 2-13). Springer.

Hull, R., Benedikt, M., Christophides, V., & Su, J. (2003). E-services: A look behind the curtain. *ACM Principles of Database Systems (PODS '03)*, 1-14.

Hull, R., & Su, J. (2004). Tools for design of composite Web services. *Proceedings of the ACM SIGMOD International Conference on Management of Data* (pp. 958-961).

Kavantzas, N., Burdett, D., Ritzinger, G., Fletcher, T., & Lafont, Y. (Eds.). (2004). *Web services choreography description language version 1.0 (working draft)* (Tech. Rep.). W3C. Retrieved from http://www.w3.org/TR/2004/WD-ws-cdl-10-20041012/

Klein, M., & Bernstein, A. (2002). Searching for services on the semantic Web using process ontologies. *The Emerging Semantic Web: Selected Papers from the 1st Semantic Web Working Symposium*, 159-172.

Li, L., & Horrocks, I. (2003). A software framework for matchmaking based on semantic Web technology. *WWW '03: Proceedings of the 12th International Conference on World Wide Web* (pp. 331-339).

McCarthy, J. (1986). Applications of circumscription to formalizing common sense knowledge. *Artificial Intelligence, 28,* 89-116.

McIlraith, S., Cao Son, T., & Zeng, H. (2002). Semantic Web services. *IEEE Intelligent Systems*, 46-53.

Milo, T., Abiteboul, S., Amann, B., Benjelloun, O., & Dang-Ngoc, F. (2005). Exchanging intentional XML data. *ACM Transactions on Database Systems, 30*(1), 1-40.

Narayanan, S., & McIlraith, S. A. (2002). Simulation, verification and automated composition of Web services. *WWW '02: Proceedings of the 11th International Conference on World Wide Web* (pp. 77-88).

Ouyang, C., van der Aalst, W., Breutel, S., Dumas, M., ter Hofstede, A., & Verbeek, H. (2005). *Formal semantics and analysis of control flow in WS-BPEL* (Rep. No. BPM-05-13). BPM Center.

Paolucci, M., Kawamura, T., Payne, T. R., & Sycara, K. P. (2002). Semantic matching of Web services capabilities. *Proceedings of the International Semantic Web Conference (ISWC)* (pp. 333-347).

Payne, T. R., Paolucci, M., & Sycara, K. P. (2001). Advertising and matching DAML-S service descriptions (Position paper). *Proceedings of the International Semantic Web Working Symposium* (pp. 76-78).

Petropoulos, M., Deutsch, A., & Papakonstantinou, Y. (2003). Query set specification language (QSSL). *International Workshop on the Web and Databases (WebDB)* (pp. 99-104).

Pilioura, T., & Tsalgotidou, A. (2002). E-services current technology and open issues. *International Workshop on Technologies for E-Services (TES)*, Rome, Italy, (pp. 1-15).

Sycara, K., Widolf, S., Klush, M., & Lu, J. (2002). Larks: Dynamic matchmaking among heterogeneous software agents in cyberspace. *Autonomous Agents and Multi-Agent Systems, 5*(2), 173-203.

Universal Description, Discovery and Integration (UDDI). (n.d.). Retrieved October 2005, from http://www.uddi.org/

Verma, K., Akkiraju, R., & Goodwin, R. (2005). Semantic matching of Web service policies. *Second International Workshop on Semantic and Dynamic Web Processes (SDWP)* (pp. 79-90).

World Wide Web Consortium (W3C). (n.d.). *W3C semantic Web activity.* Retrieved October 2005, from http://www.w3.org/2001/sw/ & http://www.w3.org/2002/ws/desc/

World Wide Web Consortium (W3C). (2003). *Simple object access protocol (SOAP), version 1.2, W3C recommendation.* Retrieved October 2005, from http://www.w3.org/TR/soap/

World Wide Web Consortium (W3C). (2004). Web services glossary, W3C Working Group note. Retrieved October 2005, from http://www.w3.org/TR/ws-gloss/

WS security. (2004). Retrieved October 2005, from http://oasis.org/

Chapter XII

Web Services Management:
Toward Efficient
Web Data Access

Farhana H. Zulkernine, Queen's University, Canada

Pat Martin, Queen's University, Canada

Abstract

The widespread use and expansion of the World Wide Web has revolutionized the discovery, access, and retrieval of information. The Internet has become the doorway to a vast information base and has leveraged the access to information through standard protocols and technologies like HyperText Markup Language (HTML), active server pages (ASP), Java server pages (JSP), Web databases, and Web services. Web services are software applications that are accessible over the World Wide Web through standard communication protocols. A Web service typically has a Web-accessible interface for its clients at the front end, and is connected to a database system and other related application suites at the back end. Thus, Web services can render efficient Web access to an information base in a secured and selective manner. The true success of this technology, however, largely depends on the efficient management of the various components forming the backbone of a Web service system. This chapter presents an overview and the state of the art of various management approaches, models, and architectures for Web services systems toward achieving quality of service (QoS) in Web data access. Finally, it discusses the importance of autonomic or self-managing systems and provides an outline of our current research on autonomic Web services.

Introduction

The Internet and the World Wide Web have gradually become the main source of information with regard to extent, versatility, and accessibility. Products and services are being traded over the Internet more than ever before. Due to the cost of building and maintaining functionality in a service, outsourcing and acquiring services from other service providers are becoming increasingly popular. Web services are a leading Internet-based technology and a perfect implementation of service-oriented computing (SOC; Casati, Shan, Dayal, & Shan, 2003; Curbera, Khalaf, Mukhi, Tai, & Weerawarana, 2003). It has great potential for being an effective gateway to information accessible on the Web. Web services follow specific standards to ensure interoperability and are accessible on the World Wide Web. In a service-based system, all applications are considered as services in a large distributed network. Web services, which have features like fine-grained functionality, interoperability, and Web accessibility, hold great potential for Web data access and business-to-business (B2B) communication (Hogg, Chilcott, Nolan, & Srinivasan, 2004; Seth, 2002) via cross-vendor service composition.

Efficient management is indispensable to provide good service quality, especially for complex Web service hosting systems that provide services around the clock over the Internet. Quality of service (QoS) is an increasingly important feature of Web data access. It is generally represented by a statistical metric of the system performance, such as the average response time for queries or the level of availability of a service that symbolizes a certain quality of system performance. In order to guarantee the QoS for business and legal aspects, the service provider and consumer should first agree upon a specific service level. This contractual agreement, which is called a service-level agreement (SLA), is a primary economic aspect of Web services management in a corporate environment.

Researchers are working on the architecture, policies, specifications, and enhancement of different standards to facilitate the development of Web services management systems (Farrell & Kreger, 2002). Some of the main management goals are ensuring QoS (Sheth, Cardoso, Miller, Kochut, & Kang, 2002), negotiating SLAs (Liu, Jha, & Ray, 2003), load balancing or resource provisioning (Chung & Hollingsworth, 2004), dynamic reconfiguration (Anzböck, Dustdar, & Gall, 2002), error detection (Sahai, Machiraju, Ouyang, & Wurster, 2001), recovery from failure (Birman, Renesse, & Vogels, 2004), and security (Chou & Yurov, 2005). Most of the management-related research conducted by industry contributes to areas like the architecture and implementation of a management infrastructure for Web services (Catania, Kumar, Murray, Pourhedari, Vambenepe, & Wurster, 2003), the specification of event subscription and notification (*WS-Eventing*, 2004), security and trust relationships (WS-Trust, 2005) in a federated Web services architecture, and the automation of ensuring

SLA negotiation (Dan et al., 2004) among coordinating Web services. There are yet many open problems in the area of Web services management that need to be addressed.

This chapter surveys the state of the art of Web services management to facilitate efficient Web data access. It specifically focuses on the importance of an effective management framework for providing reliable, efficient, and secure data access on the Web. The rest of the chapter is organized as follows. The next section provides background information about the architecture and basic standards of Web services. Then the chapter presents an overview and comparison of Web service management frameworks. It explains the criteria used to compare the frameworks, describes frameworks found in the research literature, and then gives a comparison of the frameworks. Finally, it discusses the open problems in Web service management, summarizes the chapter, and draws some conclusions.

Background

Web Services

Web services are software applications that offer specific services to client applications and have Web-based interfaces to provide user access over the Internet through standard communication protocols. Information about accessibility, protocols, and the functionality of a Web service is advertised in standard-based registry services like Universal Description, Discovery, and Integration (UDDI; Organization for the Advancement of Structured Information Standards [OASIS] UDDI, 2005) hosted by well-known organizations. Client applications and users can look for required services in the UDDI. If a desired service is found, an SLA (Sahai, Machiraju, Sayal, Van Moorsel, & Casati, 2002) can be negotiated between the client and the Web service, if necessary, and then the service can be invoked (as shown in Figure 1). Client applications communicate with Web services by passing messages over the Internet using standard protocols.

Web services technology is based on standards and specifications in order to ensure interoperability. Two main consortiums, OASIS and the World Wide Web Consortium (W3C), work on standardizing various specifications for Web services. The eXtensible Markup Language

Figure 1. Web service life cycle

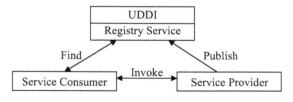

(XML; W3C, 2004a) is the basis of all languages used for the communications or specifications of Web services. An XML schema describes data types used in an XML representation. The most frequently used message-passing protocol for Web services is the simple object access protocol (SOAP; W3C, 2003) over the hypertext transport protocol (HTTP). Web services are published in the UDDI using the Web Services Description Language (WSDL; W3C, 2005), which is an XML-based specification language for service interfaces and accessibility. XML, SOAP, and WSDL are required for publishing, discovering, and invoking Web services. Numerous other standards and specifications have been published and are still being worked on for Web services in order to enable automated service discovery, composition, and management.

Several components are needed to host a Web service on the Internet. Management of the Web service system implies managing all these components to ensure satisfactory performance. The components are typically HTTP or the Web server, application server, SOAP engine, Web-service interfaces (WS1 and WS2 in Figure 2), and associated back-end applications. The back-end applications may in turn include database systems and legacy systems (as shown in Figure 2). These components can reside on the same server machine or be distributed among multiple interconnected servers.

SOAP messages to Web services are received by the Web server. There can be one or more instances of the application server acting as containers to host single or multiple Web services. Messages received by the Web server are forwarded to the application servers. These messages are basically XML data bounded by headers and footers containing the messaging protocol. In most cases, the protocol is SOAP and the interpreter used is called the SOAP engine. The engine translates the envelope of the message and, after necessary preprocessing, passes the message to the appropriate Web service. Web services are applications built with technologies such as Java Servlets (Sun, 2004) that process the messages and compose replies to send back to the client. A more complex service can require connections to back-end applications, or legacy or database systems. These back-end applications may reside on separate servers connected to the HTTP server via a local area network (LAN).

Figure 2. Components of a Web service hosting system

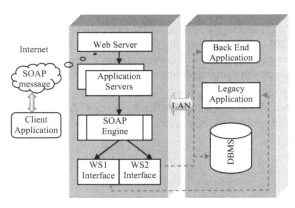

In a more complex setup, the Web service may invoke other Web services provided by multiple enterprises and thus create a chain process constituting a large cross-vendor distributed, composite system. The client invoking a service may be a user using a Web browser, a client application, or another service. The services in a composite system can be selected and bound either before execution of the system (static composition) or on the fly (dynamic composition), in which case the system is built gradually with each service call. In either case, the structure is based on messages communicated over the Internet between the service requester and the service provider. A Web service can be a service requester and a service provider at the same time. The final response can reach the root or initiator of the call through intermediate service providers or via direct messaging.

Web Service Managment Frameworks

The management of Web services in its simplest form refers to monitoring, configuring, and maintaining Web services. Web service management is a specific case of network and systems management, which considers issues such as performance, configuration, accounting, fault detection and correction, and security (Cisco Systems, 2005). The various systems management tools and software perform monitoring, reconfiguration, updating, access control, error reporting, and repair. Web services have largely evolved during the last few years from standard-based, loosely coupled, cross-vendor compatible service components to an industry-wide technology having the potential for constructing complex, multivendor composite systems. It is important to the continued growth and acceptance of this technology that the service providers ensure the QoS desired by the customers. This calls for the specification of the desired level of service through an SLA on the customer's side (Jin, Machiraju, & Sahai, 2002), and efficient management of the Web service system (Farrell & Kreger, 2002) to ensure the required service level on the service provider's side.

The unpredictable nature of the workloads of Web media and the need for high levels of interoperability and accessibility make the management of Web service systems a difficult and challenging task. Web services are also hosted and supported by a number of components, and these components must be managed harmoniously to render a desired service level. This obviously is far more challenging than managing a single application. Moreover, composite Web services can be created by a collaboration of multivendor Web services. The management of such systems, therefore, requires a collaborative service management framework (Lipton, 2004). For Web services, the management system particularly needs to address issues such as the Web media, varying workloads, distributed and heterogeneous clients and system components, and dynamic service composition.

In this section, we first discuss the criteria used to compare Web service management frameworks. A number of management frameworks are then described using a categorization based on their implementation infrastructure. The frameworks are then analyzed based on the given criteria.

Evaluation Criteria

Most of the proposed management approaches by the researchers focus on one or more specific aspects, such as maintaining QoS, SLAs, providing secure and controlled access, ensuring automatic recovery, and provisioning the system resources. These are the most important aspects as they directly influence the business and revenue. They are, therefore, used as criteria for analyzing the various management approaches discussed below.

We also identify two additional criteria for comparing the management frameworks, namely, support for service composition and the implementation model used to develop the framework. The support for service composition can basically be classified as either static or dynamic, where static composition means that Web services are composed prior to run time, and dynamic composition means that Web services can be composed at run time. The implementation model is the main paradigm used to develop the framework, for example, agents, middleware, or reflective programming.

QoS and SLAs

The SLA specifies the required service properties as demanded by the service consumers, while QoS indicates how well a service is functioning. The most common QoS parameter is response time. Depending on the type of the system, other parameters such as memory usage, network delay, and queuing time can be monitored. A statistical QoS data set can also serve as a valuable guide for automatic service selection in a dynamic service composition (Zeng, Benatallah, Ngu, Dumas, Kalagnanam, & Chang, 2004). In most cases, the process of ensuring QoS is carried out by monitoring and analyzing performance data to build a predictive or reactive QoS model. The values of the configuration parameters are then determined to achieve a desired QoS based on the model, and those parameters are modified accordingly to reconfigure the system (Cardoso, Miller, Sheth, & Arnold, 2002; Liu et al., 2003; Sheth et al., 2002). Predictive models are becoming more important from the research perspective than reactive models. Ludwig (2003) discusses the challenges in delivering QoS as specified by SLAs for Web services because of the heterogeneity and network QoS, particularly in the case of composite services.

An SLA may typically define the purpose of the service, authorized parties or customers, the period of validity, the scope, restrictions, penalties, and service-level objectives like availability, performance, and reliability (Jin et al., 2002). The service provider is legally bound to provide the QoS as agreed through the SLA. Monitoring applications are deployed as part of the management application suite usually at both the customer's and service provider's ends to ensure the validity of the SLA throughout the service duration. Automating the process of creating and maintaining the SLA, especially for composite Web service systems, is one of the most challenging problems in the area of Web service management and dynamic service composition.

Recovery

An efficient management system should implement mechanisms to recover from minor and possibly major pitfalls in the least amount of time. Depending on the nature of the failure, the recovery can require a simple restart of the failed resource, or a complex error-tracking process (Sahai, Machiraju, Ouyang, et al., 2001) to identify and replace the failed resource. In a composite Web service system, the detection and replacement of a failed service with a similar service using automated service discovery and selection offers an interesting research problem. Resource provisioning also provides quick recovery from failure using replication with automatic resource replacement.

Security

Security is a major issue for Web services because of the nature of the network and interoperability (Chou & Yurov, 2005). However, currently, no standard security framework ensures all the security features such as authorized access, integrity, authenticity, and confidentiality of the information content. Some of the common approaches to implement security features are the use of access-control lists, security tokens, XML signatures, and message encryption and decryption techniques (Coetzee & Eloff, 2004; Wang, Huang, Qu, & Xie, 2004). New standards to support Web service security are being worked on such as the Security Assertion Markup Language (SAML; OASIS SAML, 2005), eXtensible Access Control Markup Language (XACML; OASIS XACML, 2005), and Web services security (WSS; OASIS WSS, 2004). SAML leverages core Web services standards like XML, SOAP, transport layer security (TLS), XML signatures, and XML encryption. It enables the secure exchange of authentication, attribute, and authorization information between disparate security domains, making vendor-independent, single sign-on, secure e-business transactions possible within federated networks on the Web. XACML is an XML-based language for expressing well-established ideas in the field of access-control policy. It provides profiles for SAML 2.0, XML digital signatures, privacy policies, hierarchical or multiple resources, and role-based access control (RBAC). WS-Security provides an industry standard framework for secure Web service message exchanges.

Security policies may be defined and managed at a higher level as part of the management framework. Communicating parties can use these policies to establish and maintain a trust relationship. Furthermore, for specific business partners, a federation can be created and maintained (Wang et al., 2004) where members can share and distribute trust relationships.

Resource Provisioning

The typical "bursty" and varied nature of client requests to a Web service means that the optimum allocation of resources to a Web service is difficult to predict and will vary over time. As a result, without a resource sharing and provisioning strategy, resources can either remain underutilized or may be insufficient to handle user requests at the peak hours. The effective use of resource management techniques has been shown to improve performance in cluster-based Web service environments (Chung & Hollingsworth, 2004). Much research is going on about automatic resource management these days. The automatic replacement of failed resources can also contribute to efficient service recovery.

Management Frameworks

Researchers have proposed many different strategies and approaches to address the various management aspects. There is also considerable activity on Web management in consortiums and standards organizations such as OASIS and W3C. We categorize a number of management approaches based on the infrastructure used in the approach, that is, whether it is centralized, distributed, or autonomic, and describe their main features. Finally, we present self-managing or autonomic management approaches, and thereby describe our research on autonomic Web service systems. Most of the management frameworks have been implemented as models, and therefore the comparative analysis presented in the last section highlights the main features of the models against the evaluation criteria.

Centralized Management

Centralized management schemes employ a single central unit to carry out the management activities. Cibrán, Verheecke, Suvee, Vanderperren, and Jonckers (2004) present the Web service management layer (WSML), a middleware shown in Figure 3, which facilitates the development and management of integrated service applications. WSML supports client-side service management and criteria-based service selection for dynamic service composition. The rich run-time environment of JAsCo, an Aspect-Oriented Programming

Figure 3. General architecture of the WSML (Cibrán, Verheecke, Suvee et al., 2004)

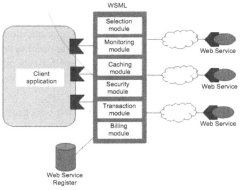

Figure 4. Web Services Management Network (WSMN; Sahai, Machiraju, Sayal et al, 2002)

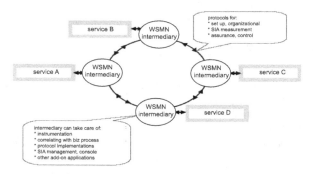

(AOP) Language, is used to modularize the implementation of the management functionality within WSML (Verheecke, Cibrán, Vanderperren, Suvee, & Jonckers, 2004). WSML lies between the client application and the Web services, and receives client requests for specific service types. A new JAsCo aspect bean is defined dynamically as required holding specific policies for each management aspect like service selection and binding, service swapping, automated billing, caching, and monitoring. JAsCo connectors are also created dynamically to bind the client application with a specific Web service based on the policies defined in the aspect bean. Client-side management is implemented using AOP in client applications. By isolating the management tasks in WSML, the replication and maintenance of similar management-related code in the applications is avoided.

Sahai, Machiraju, and Wurster (2001) suggested a management service provider (MSP) model for the remote or outsourced monitoring and controlling of e-services on the Internet. An automated and distributed SLA monitoring engine using the Web service management network (WSMN) agent, as shown in Figure 4 (Sahai et al., 2002), was proposed in a later publication. A specification language for SLAs was also proposed to be used with WSMN. The framework uses a network of cooperating intermediaries as proxy components in between a service and the outside world to enable message tracking. Each intermediary is attached to the SOAP tool kits at each Web service site of a composite process and communicates with each other through a set of protocols specifically defined for this purpose. WSMN agents monitor the process flow defined using WSFL (Web Service Flow Language) to ensure SLA compliance for managing service relationships.

The concept of workflow and process QoS is investigated by a group of researchers at the Large Scale Distributed Information Systems lab (LSDIS) at the University of Georgia. Typically, Web services are composed in a workflow, and it is necessary to manage the QoS metrics for all the services in the composition. Sheth et al. (2002) describe an agent-based service-oriented middleware (SoM) that provides an upper level middleware over Web services-based middleware and leverages the development of multiorganizational applications. SoM uses a process QoS model (Cardoso et al., 2002) that can be used to automatically compute the QoS of a composite Web service workflow process from the QoS metrics of the component Web services.

Fuente, Alonso, Martínez, and Aguilar (2004) propose the reflective and adaptable Web service (RAWS), which is a Web service design model that is based on the concept of reflective programming. It allows the administrators to dynamically modify the definition, behavior, and implementation structure of a Web service during its execution without requiring a shutdown of the service. Technically, the design implements behavioral and structural reflection in a two-level architecture, made of the base level and meta level, to allow the modification of one level to be reflected in the other level.

The Web-services management framework (WSMF) version 2.0 (Catania et al., 2003) defines a general framework for managing different types of resources including Web services and was later published by OASIS as Web-services distributed management (OASIS WSDM, 2005). The framework defines and uses three main concepts: WSMF-Foundation specifies the basic mechanisms for management using Web services, WS-Events introduces a Web-services-based event subsystem, and WSMF-WSM (WSMF-Web service management) describes the management of Web services using WSMF. However, it only allows generic security measures such as the use of HTTPS (secure HTTP), SSL (secure sockets layer) certificates, and access-control mechanisms at the API (application programming interface) level to be implemented.

Tosic, Pagurek, Patel, Esfandiari, and Ma (2004) define the Web Service Offering Language (WSOL) to allow the formal specification of important management information such as classes of service, functional and accessibility constraints, price, penalties, and other management responsibilities. The Web service offering infrastructure (WSOI), in turn, demonstrates the usability of WSOL in the management and composition of Web services (Tosic, Ma, Pagurek, & Esfandiari, 2004).

Dobson, Hall, and Sommerville (2005) propose a container-based fault-tolerant system for a general service-oriented architecture (SOA). It implements proxies to pass each incoming service call to the proper service replica as selected by a set of prespecified XML policies, and thus increases the availability and reliability for outsourced services of different types.

Distributed Management

Web service management systems with a distributed framework contain multiple, distributed management components that cooperate to perform the management functions. Researchers at IBM (Levy, Nagarajarao, Pacifici, Spreitzer, Tantawi, & Youssef, 2003) propose an architecture and prototype implementation of a performance-management system for cluster-based Web services as shown in Figure 5. The system supports SLA and performs dynamic resource allocation, load balancing, and server overload protection for multiple classes of Web services traffic. It uses inner level management for the queuing and scheduling of request messages. Outer level management implements a feedback control loop to periodically adjust the scheduling weights and server allocations of the inner level. The

Figure 5. Performance management system for cluster-based Web services (Levy et al., 2003)

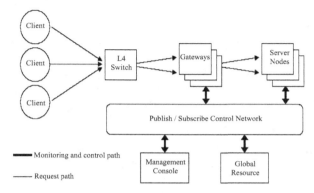

average response time is used as the performance metric for a given cluster utility function. The system supports multiple classes of Web-services traffic and allocates server resources dynamically to maximize the expected value of the utility function. However, it requires users to use a subscription interface to register with the system and subscribe to services.

Dan et al. (2004) define a framework that includes the Web Service Level Agreement (WSLA) Language, a system to provision resources based on SLAs, a workload-management system that prioritizes requests according to the associated SLAs, and a system to monitor compliance with the SLAs. The customers are billed differentially according to their agreed service levels.

Aggarwal, Verma, Miller, and Milnor (2004) present a Web service composition framework called METEOR-S (managing end-to-end operations for semantic Web services) to create and manage service composition. The framework allows automatic service selection, which facilitates the recovery and maintenance of composite Web service systems.

Coetzee and Eloff (2004) propose a logic-based access-control framework for single Web service-based systems. The framework implements authentication through identity verification and defines access-control policies to grant authorized access with the help of an authorization manager.

Autonomic Management

Manual management, especially the reconfiguration of numerous tunable system parameters of large heterogeneous complex systems, is becoming a nightmare for system administrators. Researchers are, therefore, seeking solutions to automate various tasks at different levels of system management. The autonomic-computing paradigm promises a completely new era of systems management (Ganek & Corbi, 2003).

Autonomic systems are self-managing systems that are characterized by the following four properties.

- **Self-configuring:** Systems have the ability to define themselves on the fly to adapt to a dynamically changing environment.

- **Self-healing:** Systems have the ability to identify and fix failed components without introducing apparent disruption.

- **Self-optimizing:** Systems have the ability to provide optimal performance by automatically monitoring and tuning the resources.

- **Self-protecting:** Systems have the ability to protect themselves from attacks by managing user access, detecting intrusions, and providing recovery capabilities.

Autonomic systems are envisioned as imperative for next-generation highly distributed systems. Web services, in particular, can greatly benefit from autonomic computing because of their dynamic workloads and highly accessible communication media like the Internet (Birman et al., 2004). However, many problems need to be addressed in order to materialize the concept of autonomic Web services, rendering it as an interesting research topic. The approaches discussed below can also be categorized under centralized or distributed approaches according to their framework. However, for the self-management feature, they are described under this category.

The core part of an autonomic system is a *controller*, which is designed using either a performance feedback loop in a reactive manner or a feed-forward loop in predictive manner. Researchers propose different methodologies and frameworks to implement the controllers. Different search algorithms are proposed to search for the optimal values of the tunable configuration parameters. Various prediction logics are also followed by different approaches in case of predictive controllers. Typically, a controller can dynamically manipulate the control switches, modify configuration parameters, or implement additional queues based on the performance data to provide optimal throughput.

An automated, cluster-based Web service performance-tuning infrastructure, which is shown in Figure 6, performs adaptive tuning with one or more active harmony servers using

Figure 6. Active harmony automated tuning system (Chung & Hollingsworth, 2004)

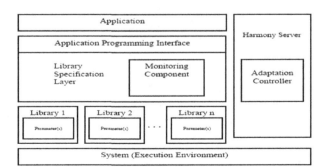

parameter replication and partitioning (Chung & Hollingsworth, 2004). The infrastructure contains a technique for resource sharing and distribution that allows active harmony to reconfigure the roles of specific nodes in the cluster during execution to further boost up the performance. In the active harmony framework, applications and services reveal tunable sets of parameters through API that are dynamically tuned based on the workload, past performance history as recorded in a database, and the current performance level. The core part of the server is a controller that implements optimization algorithms for determining the proper value of the tuning parameters.

We also propose an architecture for an autonomic Web-services environment that supports automatic tuning and reconfiguration in order to ensure that the predefined SLAs are met in Tian, Zebedee, Zulkernine, Powley, and Martin (2005). Each component in the system is assumed to be an autonomic element, as shown in Figure 7, that is managed by an autonomic manager (AM). The framework is based on a hierarchy of autonomic managers that coordinate with each other to provide an organized autonomic environment for Web services.

The autonomic manager consists of four functional modules that perform the following tasks: periodically monitor performance data; analyze the data based on past, current, and targeted performance; plan which parameters to tune in order to achieve the performance goal; and finally execute the action plan. We propose using reflection-based feedback controllers for our autonomic managers. A reflective system is one that can inspect and adapt its internal behavior in response to changing conditions. Typically, a reflective system maintains a model of self-representation, and changes to the self-representation are automatically reflected in the underlying system.

Control-theoretic approaches have been proposed by some researchers to implement the controllers. ControlWare is a middleware that embodies a control-theoretical methodology for QoS provisioning for software services (Abdelzaher, Stankovic, Lu, Zhang, & Lu, 2003). The feedback control mechanism guarantees QoS through the optimized allocation of system resources like various queues and cache sizes to different processes.

Bennani and Menascé (2004) create self-managing computer systems by incorporating mechanisms for self-adjusting the configuration parameters so that the QoS requirements of the system are constantly met. Their approach combines analytical performance models with combinatorial search techniques to develop controllers that run periodically to determine the best possible configuration for the system given its workload.

Birman et al. (2004) extend the general architecture of Web service systems to add high availability, fault tolerance, and autonomous behavior. The authors refer to the standards for Web services like WS-Events, WS-Transaction, and WS-Reliability while discussing failure protection, speedy recovery, and reliable messaging. The architecture includes server- and client-side monitoring, a consistent and reliable messaging system using information replication, a data-dissemination mechanism using multicasting, and an event notification system using WS-Events standards.

A framework for the deployment and subsequent autonomic management of component-based distributed applications is proposed by Dearle, Kirby, and McCarthy (2004). In their work, deployment goals are defined by specifying constraints over available resources, component mappings, and the interconnection topology. An autonomic deployment and management engine (ADME) is used to find a configuration that satisfies the goal, and the configuration is deployed automatically using the Cingal infrastructure (Dearle, Kirby, McCarthy, &

Figure 7. Autonomic element

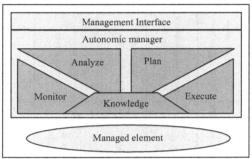

Diaz y Carballo, 2004*)*. If a deviation or change in the goal is detected, the configuration finder and deployment cycle is repeated automatically to generate a revised deployment. The proposed framework mainly addresses the self-configuration and self-healing aspects of autonomic management.

Comparative Analysis of the Management Approaches

The various approaches discussed above address one or more of the management aspects but not all of them. The QoS aspect has been addressed by several researchers in different ways. Sheth et al. (2002) introduce an additional agent-based middleware for computing the QoS of individual Web services and use the model proposed by Cardoso et al. (2002) to compute and thereby monitor the process QoS of a composite service system. Dan et al. (2004) present a more comprehensive distributed framework that contains a service-offering unit, WSLA-based QoS monitoring and differentiated service provisioning using a workload-management unit, and a resource-provisioning unit. Sahai et al. (2002) propose a less comprehensive agent-based WSMN using intermediaries as proxies that enables message tracking to monitor SLA compliance. However, it requires additional protocols for the intermediaries to communicate within themselves securely. WSOI mainly focuses on the application and manipulation of WSOL, a language for the formal specification of service offerings, and hence does not serve as a complete infrastructure for Web service management (Tosic, Pagurek, Patel et al., 2004). The framework by Levy et al. (2003) uses a feedback controller for weighted scheduling, message queuing, and server allocation in a cluster-based system. However, the clients need to subscribe to the service prior to using it.

The recovery aspect is addressed by Dobson et al. (2005), Aggarwal et al. (2004), and Fuente et al. (2004) in different ways. Dobson et al. designed a fault-tolerant system. However, it is difficult to apply rollback or other fault-tolerance mechanisms in case of Web services, especially in composite systems. Aggarwal et al. suggest dynamic service selection and composition in a workflow process using the METEOR-S framework to allow quick recovery. The bi-level architecture by Fuente et al. implements reflective programming to enable dynamic source-code update for Web services and thus facilitates deployment and recovery.

Table 1.

Reference	Type*	QoS/SLA	Security	Recovery	Service Composition	Resource Provisioning	Implementation Model
Cardoso et al., 2002	Cent.	Computes work-flow QoS	N/A	N/A	Static	N/A	Mathematical model
Sheth et al., 2002	Cent.	Computes QoS of composite service	N/A	N/A	Static	N/A	Agent-based middleware
Dan et al., 2004	Dist.	WSLA-based differentiated QoS provisioning	N/A	By component replacement	Static with service-offering unit	Separate unit for dynamic provisioning	Distributed-unit-based framework
Sahai et al., 2002	Cent.	WSFL-based monitoring for SLA compliance	N/A	N/A	Static	N/A	Agent-based network of intermediaries
Tosic et al., 2004	Cent.	WSOL for service offering and SLA	Usual security measures	N/A	Static or dynamic	N/A	WSOI for implementation of WSOL
Levy et al., 2003	Dist.	Differentiated reactive weighted message scheduling	N/A	Resource replacement and overload protection	Static	Dynamic server allocation & load balancing	Two-level management
Dobson et al., in press	Cent.	Higher availability & quick recovery	N/A	Service replication	Unsuitable for composite systems	Policy-based replica selection	Fault-tolerant system
Aggarwal et al., 2004	Cent.	Work-flow QoS	N/A	Dynamic service selection and replacement	Static or dynamic	N/A	METEOR-S framework

* Cent.- Centralized, Dist.- Distributed, Auto. – Automonic

Table 1. Continued

Reference	Type*	QoS/SLA	Security	Recovery	Service Composition	Resource Provisioning	Implementation Model
Fuente et al., 2004	Cent.	Undisturbed during update	N/A	Source-code modification	Static or dynamic	N/A	Bi-level reflective programming
Verheecke et al., 2004	Cent.	Both client- and server-side management	Access control	Dynamic service selection and replacement	Static or dynamic	N/A	Middleware (WSML) using AOP
Coetzee & Eloff, 2004	Cent.	N/A	Policy-based access control	N/A	Not supported	N/A	Authentication and authorization verification
Abdelzaher et al., 2003	Auto.	Dynamic tuning using feedback control	N/A	Parameter tuning and reconfiguration	Static or dynamic	Message queuing and scheduling	Control-theory-based ControlWare
Bennani & Menascé, 2004	Auto.	Dynamic tuning using analytical model	N/A	Parameter tuning and reconfiguration	Static with service-offering unit	None	Uses a performance evaluation model
Chung & Hollingsworth, 2004	Dist. & auto.	Dynamic tuning of only registered parameters	N/A	Reconfiguration, resource sharing and distribution	Static or dynamic	Message queuing and scheduling, resource sharing	Active harmony for cluster-based systems
Tian et al., in press	Auto.	Management of SLA and QoS	N/A	Dynamic parameter tuning and reconfiguration	Static or dynamic	N/A	Reflective-programming-based hierarchy of AMs

* Cent. – Centralized, Dist. – Distributed, Auto. - Autonomic

The WSML middleware implements each management aspect using separate aspect beans in AOP (Verheecke et al., 2004). It facilitates the modular implementation of various management aspects such as dynamic service selection, monitoring, and access control, and enables client-side management. Coetzee and Eloff (2004) propose a policy-based access-control framework for only single Web service based systems. Abdelzaher et al. (2003), Bennani and Menascé (2004), Chung and Hollingsworth (2004), and Tian et al. (2005) propose autonomic management approaches that perform parameter tuning and reconfigurations to maintain QoS. Abdelzaher et al. use control theory to design the feedback control framework augmented by elements of scheduling and queuing theory for resource provisioning. Bennani and Menascé implement a performance evaluation model to search for the best configuration parameters to use with the controller, but the approach does not support resource provisioning. Chung and Hollingsworth use the active-harmony server to tune only the parameters that are registered with the server by the applications and services. In a cluster environment, it also performs resource sharing and distribution, and thereby supports quick recovery. Tian et al. use reflective programming with a hierarchy of autonomic managers to maintain QoS in a varying workload. However, none of the above approaches provide access control.

Conclusion

Open Problems

The above survey demonstrates that none of the proposed management frameworks addresses all the management aspects such as QoS, SLA negotiation, dynamic reconfiguration, security, recovery, and resource provisioning for dynamically composed systems. There has been considerable work done in the field of QoS and SLAs for Web services, but more research is needed to resolve the issues related to service dependency and providing differential services to different clients based on the SLA. The monitoring and maintenance of QoS and SLA for a composite service system is a challenging problem, especially when the QoS of the network is considered. The ranking of services based on specific service selection criteria is necessary to make automatic and run-time service selection. The publication and verification of QoS information that may be used as service selection criteria offer other interesting open problems.

Automatic service discovery and binding implemented by a management system can provide effective failure protection and recovery. However, this requires the use of well-defined semantics and specifications to enable automatic search and replacement of similar services.

Due to the nature and usage of Web media, they are vulnerable to malicious attacks. A good management framework should protect the system from such hazards. Standard specifications have been published for Web service security, but further research is needed to provide application-level security for Web services and to construct a secure management framework. End-user privacy is another important research area for Web services that is yet to be explored. The W3C is working on the Platform for Privacy Preferences Project (P3P) to provide a simple, automated way for users to gain more control over the use of personal information on Web sites they visit (W3C, 2004b). Privacy policies can be defined by service providers, which can be matched by service consumers before subscribing to a service. However, the monitoring of policy agreements at the provider's side is another problem.

Researchers are working on various policy specifications that may be incorporated into the management frameworks to implement policy-based management. The policies defined by service users need to be translated into system-usable formats. Further research is required to define strategies and implementation models to perform this translation effectively for different Web-services-based systems. SLA specification and QoS management for Web service systems have gained a lot of attention because of the wide range of user types and requirements. Resource provisioning for cluster-based Web services (Chung & Hollingsworth, 2004) is another important research problem.

With the rapid growth in the size and complexity of software systems, researchers are working toward designing autonomic systems featuring self-configuring, self-healing, self-optimizing, and self-protecting properties to reduce human intervention. Currently, fully autonomic systems do not exist. Researchers are now working on achieving partial autonomic behavior through various control mechanisms. Regardless of the additional system components and increased management overhead, autonomic computing promises huge potential benefits as a systems-management solution. The existing solutions, in most cases, do not consider composite systems. New specifications and standards can be used to update the existing frameworks to provide enhanced management functionality.

Summary

The World Wide Web is currently perceived as an indispensable resource of information. Different search engines and Web sites provide us with tools to search, select, and retrieve necessary information from the Internet. Most of these tools have an application at the back end that processes user requests and generates the responses to be sent back to the user. Web services are independent software applications that provide specific services to users or client applications on the Web through standard protocols and user interfaces. Thus, a Web service can be designed to effectively provide customized Web data management and powerful information-retrieval services over the Internet. Web services are also an effective implementation of SOC. The immense potential of composing Web services over multiple enterprises and building platform-independent, complex, interacting software systems has elevated the importance of Web services as a research area.

The management frameworks described are mostly research models and do not yet have any practical implementations. Some of the large companies are working together on standardizing various protocols like WS-Eventing, WS-Transfer, and WS-Management for Web-services management. WSMF by HP was later published as WSDM by OASIS. Currently, only a few Web service management software are available in the market. Managed Methods has released a Web service management software called JaxView to monitor availability, throughput, response time, faults, policies, and messages to assist service management. Mike Lehmann (2004), in an article in Oracle Magazine, presents new Web-services management capabilities in Oracle Application Server. AmberPoint Express is another management software that assists Web service developers to incrementally measure, debug, and fine-tune the performance and functionality of their Web services.

During the last few years, Web service technology has rapidly grown to become a part of our everyday lives. Many popular Web sites like Amazon.com are using Web services to serve customer enquiries. The success of this interactive Web technology largely depends on customer satisfaction. An efficient and reliable management framework is indispensable to ensure around-the-clock availability and service quality of Web service systems. This chapter provides an introduction and background on Web service management and outlines some of the challenging research problems in the area. It presents the state of the art of various management approaches for Web-services management. Newer and more interesting management problems will continue to arise from the growing complexity and expansion of this technology. The ongoing research on service management is focused toward achieving automated solutions requiring minimum human intervention. We envision autonomic computing as the most efficient technique for the continuous monitoring and management of large, heterogeneous, and complex systems such as composite Web service based systems.

References

Abdelzaher, T. F., Stankovic, J. A., Lu, C., Zhang, R., & Lu, Y. (2003). Feedback performance control in software services. *IEEE Control Systems Magazine, 23*(3), 74-90.

Aggarwal, R., Verma, K., Miller, J., & Milnor, W. (2004). Constraint driven Web service composition in METEOR-S, services computing. *Proceedings of the IEEE International Conference on Services Computing SCC'04* (pp. 23-30).

Anzböck, R., Dustdar, S., & Gall, H. (2002). Software configuration, distribution, and deployment of Web-services. *ACM International Conference Proceeding Series: Vol. 27. Proceedings of the 14th International Conference on Software Engineering and Knowledge Engineering (SEKE'02): Web-Based Tools, Systems and Environments* (pp. 649-656).

Bennani, M., & Menascé, D. (2004). Assessing the robustness of self-managing computer systems under highly variable workloads. *Proceedings of the International Conference on Autonomic Computing (ICAC'04)*, 62-69.

Birman, K., Renesse, R. V., & Vogels, W. (2004). Adding high availability and autonomic behavior to Web services. *Proceedings of the 26th Annual International Conference on Software Engineering (ICSE'04)* (pp. 17-26).

Cardoso, J., Miller, J., Sheth, A., & Arnold, J. (2002). *Modeling quality of service for workflows and Web service processes* (Tech. Rep. No. 02-002 v2). University of Georgia, Department of Computer Science, LSDIS Lab, Athens.

Casati, F., Shan, E., Dayal, U., & Shan, M. (2003). Service-oriented computing: Business-oriented management of Web services. *Communications of the ACM, 46*(10), 55-60.

Catania, N., Kumar, P., Murray, B., Pourhedari, H., Vambenepe, W., & Wurster, K. (2003). *Overview: Web services management framework.* Hewlett-Packard Company. Retrieved June 20, 2006, from http://devresource.hp.com/drc/specifications/wsmf/WSMF-Overview.jsp

Chou, D. C., & Yurov, K. (2005). Security development in Web services environment. *Computer Standards & Interfaces, 27*(3), 233-240.

Chung, I., & Hollingsworth, J. K. (2004). Automated cluster-based Web service performance tuning. *Proceedings of IEEE Conference on High Performance Distributed Computing (HPDC'04)*, (pp. 36-44).

Cibrán, M. A., Verheecke, B., Suvee, D., Vanderperren, W., & Jonckers, V. (2004). Automatic service discovery and integration using semantic descriptions in the Web services management layer. *Journal of Mathematical Modelling in Physics, Engineering and Cognitive Studies, 11*, 79-89.

Cisco Systems. (2005). Network management basics. In *Internetworking technologies handbook* (ch. VI). Retrieved June 20, 2006, from http://www.cisco.com/univercd/cc/td/doc/cisintwk/ito_doc/nmbasics.pdf

Coetzee, M., & Eloff, J. H. P. (2004). Towards Web service access control. *Computers & Security, 23*(7), 559-570.

Curbera, F., Khalaf, R., Mukhi, N., Tai, S., & Weerawarana, S. (2003). Service-oriented computing: The next step in Web services. *Communications of the ACM, 46*(10), 29-34.

Dan, A., Davis, D., Kearney, R., Keller, A., King, R., Kuebler, D., et al. (2004). Web services on demand: WSLA-driven automated management. *IBM Systems Journal, 43*(1), 136-158.

Dearle, A., Kirby, G., & McCarthy, A. (2004). A framework for constraint-based deployment and autonomic management of distributed applications. *International Conference on Autonomic Computing (ICAC'04)*, 300-301.

Dearle, A., Kirby, G. N. C., McCarthy, A., & Diaz y Carballo, J. C. (2004). A flexible and secure deployment framework for distributed applications. In W. Emmerich & A. L. Wolf (Eds.), *Proceedings of 2nd International Working Conference on Component Deployment* (LNCS 3083, pp. 219-233). Edinburgh, UK: Springer.

Dobson, G., Hall, S., & Sommerville, I. (2005, May). A container-based approach to fault tolerance in service-oriented architectures. *Proceedings of International Conference of Software Engineering (ICSE),* St. Louis, Missouri. Retrieved June 20, 2006, from http://digs.sourceforge.net/papers/2005-icse-paper.pdf

Farrell, J. A., & Kreger, H. (2002). Web services management approaches. *IBM Systems Journal, 41*(2), 212-227.

Fuente, J., Alonso, S., *Martínez,* O., & Aguilar, L. (2004). RAWS: Reflective engineering for Web services. *Proceedings of IEEE International Conference on Web Services (ICWS'04)*, (p. 488).

Ganek, A. G., & Corbi, T. A. (2003). The dawning of the autonomic computing era. *IBM System Journal, 42*(1), 5-18.

Hogg, K., Chilcott, P., Nolan, M., & Srinivasan, B. (2004). An evaluation of Web services in the design of a B2B application. *Proceedings of the 27ʰ Conference on Australasian Computer Science,* (vol. 26, pp. 331-340).

Jin, L., Machiraju, V., & Sahai, A. (2002). *Analysis on service level agreement of Web services.* Software Technology Laboratory, HP Laboratories. Retrieved June 20, 2006, from http://www.hpl.hp.com/techreports/2002/HPL-2002-180.pdf

Lehmann, M. *(2004).* Web services management arrives. *Oracle Magazine.* Retrieved June 20, 2006, from http://www.oracle.com/technology/oramag/oracle/04-nov/o64web.html

Levy, R., Nagarajarao, J., Pacifici, G., Spreitzer, M., Tantawi, A., & Youssef, A. (2003, March). *Performance management for cluster based Web services* (IBM Tech. Rep.). In *Proceedings of the IFIP/IEEE 8ʰ International Symposium on Integrated Network Management (IM 2003),* (pp. 247-261). Norwell, MA: Kluwer.

Lipton, P. (2004). Composition and management of Web services. In *Service-oriented architecture* (White paper). Retrieved June 20, 2006, from http://webservices.sys-con.com/read/43567.htm

Liu, B., Jha, S., & Ray, P. (2003). Mapping distributed application SLA to network QoS parameters. *Proceedings of ICT,* (pp. 1230-1235).

Ludwig, H. (2003). *Web services QoS: External SLAs and internal policies or: How do we deliver what we promise?* Proceedings of the 1ˢᵗ Web Services Quality Workshop, Rome.

Organization for the Advancement of Structured Information Standards Extensible Access Control Markup Language (OASIS XACML). (2005). *OASIS Extensible Access Control Markup Language (XACML) technical committee specification, v2.0.* Retrieved June 20, 2006, from http://www.oasis-open.org/committees/tc_home.php?wg_abbrev=xacml

Organization for the Advancement of Structured Information Standards Security Assertion Markup Language (OASIS SAML). (2005). *OASIS security services specification, v2.0, 2005.* Retrieved June 20, 2006, from http://www.oasis-open.org/committees/tc_home.php?wg_abbrev=security

Organization for the Advancement of Structured Information Standards Universal Description, Discovery and Integration (OASIS UDDI). (2005). *OASIS universal description, discovery and integration technical committee specification, v3.0.2.* Retrieved June 20, 2006, from http://www.uddi.org/specification.html

Organization for the Advancement of Structured Information Standards Web Services Distributed Management (OASIS WSDM). (2005). *Web services distributed management (WSDM), v1.0.* Retrieved June 20, 2006, from http://www.oasis-open.org/committees/tc_home.php?wg_abbrev=wsdm

Organization for the Advancement of Structured Information Standards Web Services Reliability (OASIS WS-Reliability). (2004). *OASIS Web services reliable messaging technical committee specification, v1.1.* Retrieved June 20, 2006, from http://www.oasis-open.org/committees/tc_home.php?wg_abbrev=wsrm

Organization for the Advancement of Structured Information Standards Web Services Security (OASIS WSS). (2004). *OASIS Web services security (WSS) technical committee specification, v1.0.* Retrieved June 20, 2006, from http://www.oasis-open.org/committees/tc_home.php?wg_abbrev=wss

Sahai, A., Machiraju, V., Ouyang, J., & Wurster, K. (2001). *Message tracking in SOAP-based Web services* (Tech. Rep.). HP Labs. Retrieved June 20, 2006, from http://www.hpl.hp.com/techreports/2001/HPL-2001-199.pdf

Sahai, A., Machiraju, V., Sayal, M., Van Moorsel, A., & Casati, F. (2002, October). Automated SLA monitoring for Web services. In *Proceedings of the 13th IFIP/IEEE International Workshop on Distributed Systems: Operations and Management (DSOM'02)* (LNCS 2506, pp. 28-41), Montreal, Canada. Springer-Verlag.

Sahai, A., Machiraju, V., & Wurster, K. (2001). Monitoring and controlling Internet based e-services. *Proceedings of the 2nd IEEE Workshop on Internet Applications (WI-APP'01)*, 41.

Seth, M. (2002). *Web services: A fit for EAI* (White paper). Retrieved June 20, 2006, from http://www.developer.com/tech/article.php/10923_1489501_2

Sheth, A., Cardoso, J., Miller, J., Kochut, K., & Kang, M. (2002). QoS for service-oriented middleware. *Proceedings of the 6th World Multiconference on Systemics, Cybernetics and Informatics (SCI'02)*, 528-534.

Sun. (2004). *J2EE, Java Servlet technology.* Retrieved June 20, 2006, from http://java.sun.com/products/servlet/

Tian, W., Zebedee, J., Zulkernine, F., Powley, W., & Martin, P. (2005, May). Architecture for an autonomic Web services environment. *Proceedings of 7th International Conference on Enterprise Information Systems (ICEIS'05)*, Miami, Florida, (pp. 54-66). Retrieved from http://www.cs.queensu.ca/home/cords/wsmdeis.pdf

Tosic, V., Ma, W., Pagurek, B., & Esfandiari, B. (2004, April). Web services offerings infrastructure (WSOI): A management infrastructure for XML Web services (Tech. Rep.). *Proceedings of IEEE/IFIP Network Operations and Management Symposium (NOMS)* (vol. 1, pp. 817-830), Seoul, South Korea. Retrieved from http://www.sce.carleton.ca/netmanage/papers/TosicEtAlResRepAug2003.pdf

Tosic, V., Pagurek, B., Patel, K., Esfandiari, B., & Ma, W. (in press). Management applications of the Web Service Offerings Language (WSOL). *Information Systems.*

Verheecke, B., Cibrán, M. A., Vanderperren, W., Suvee, D., & Jonckers, V. (2004). AOP for dynamic configuration and management of Web services in client-applications. *International Journal on Web Services Research (JWSR), 1*(3), 25-41.

Wang, H., Huang, J., Qu, Y., & Xie, J. (2004). Web services: Problems and future directions. *Journal of Web Semantics, 1*(3), 309-320.

Web services for management. (2005). Retrieved June 20, 2006, from http://developers.sun.com/techtopics/webservices/management/WS-Management.Feb.2005.pdf

Web service transfer. (2004). Retrieved June 20, 2006, from http://msdn.microsoft.com/library/en-us/dnglobspec/html/ws-transfer.pdf

WS-eventing. (2004). Retrieved June 20, 2006, from http://ftpna2.bea.com/pub/downloads/WS-Eventing.pdf

WE-Trust. (2005, February). *Web Service Trust Language (WS-Trust)*. Retrieved from http://specs.xmlsoap.org/ws/2005/02/trust/WS-Trust.pdf

World Wide Web Consortium (W3C). (2003). *SOAP version 1.2 part 1: Messaging framework*. Retrieved June 20, 2006, from http://www.w3.org/TR/soap12-part1/

World Wide Web Consortium (W3C). (2004a). *Extensible Markup Language (XML)*. Retrieved June 20, 2006, from http://www.w3.org/XML/

World Wide Web Consortium (W3C). (2004b). *The platform for privacy preferences project (P3P)*. Retrieved from http://www.w3.org/P3P/

World Wide Web Consortium (W3C). (2005). *Web Services Description Language (WSDL) version 2.0* (Working draft). Retrieved June 20, 2006, from http://www.w3.org/2002/ws/desc/

About the Authors

José de Aguiar Moraes Filho received his BS degree in computer science from the State University of Ceara (UECe) in 1987 and his master's degree in applied informatics from the University of Fortaleza (UNIFOR) in 2003 (both in Brazil). Since 2003 he has been an assistant professor at UNIFOR. In 2004, he received the Top Ten Master Dissertation Award from the Brazilian Computer Society (SBC). His research interests are information integration, mobile data management, XML (extensible markup language) data management, and query processing. Currently, he is a PhD student at the University of Kaiserslautern, Germany.

Bernd Amann got his engineering degree in computer science from the Technical University of Vienna (Austria) in 1988. He joined the database team (Verso) at INRIA-Rocquencourt (France) in 1989 and obtained his PhD in computer science from the Conservatoire des Arts et Métiers (CNAM), Paris (1994). During the same year, he became an assistant professor at CNAM. He was member of the database team (Vertigo) at the CEDRIC laboratory and a scientific collaborator at INRIA until September 2004, when he obtained a full professorship at the Université de Pierre et Marie Curie (Paris 6) and became a member of the database team at the LIP6 laboratory. His current research activities concern service-oriented data management and integration. In particular, he is interested in database-oriented models and algorithms for service discovery, service composition, and service classification.

Lefteris Angelis received his BSc and PhD degrees in mathematics from Aristotle University of Thessaloniki (AUTh), Greece. He works currently as an assistant professor at the Department of Informatics of AUTh. His research interests involve statistical methods with applications in information systems and software engineering, computational methods in mathematics and statistics, the planning of experiments, and simulation techniques.

Boualem Benatallah is an associate professor at the University of New South Wales, Sydney, Australia. His research interests lie in the areas of service-oriented computing and large-scale and autonomous data sharing. He has been a program committee member of several conferences. He was the program committee chair of several international workshops on Web services. He was the program committee cochair of the Third International Conference on Business Process Management and the Third International Conference on Service Oriented Computing. He was guest editor of several journal special issues on Web services. He has published widely in international journals and conferences including the IEEE TKDE, IEEE TSE, *IEEE Internet Computing*, *IEEE Network*, *IEEE Intelligent Systems*, VLDB, and PADD journals, and IEEE ICDE, IEEE ICDS, WWW, and ER conferences.

Salima Benbernou is an associate professor in the Department of Computer Science at the Université Lyon 1, France. She is a member of the Database and Knowledge Representation and Reasoning (DBKRR) Group. She spent 2 years (1998-2000) in Cap Gemini and the Ernst & Young Corporation. Her research interests include Web services, data modeling, and reasoning. She received her PhD from the Université de Valenciennes, France.

Angelo Brayner received an MS (computer science) from the University of Campinas, Brazil and a PhD (computer science) from the University of Kaiserslautern, Germany (1994 and 1999, respectively). He has been with UNIFOR since 2000 as a full professor and leader of the Advanced Database Research Group (CEARA). His special research interests include mobile databases, advanced transactions models, concurrency control and query processing in multidatabase systems, and query processing in wireless sensor networks.

Panos K. Chrysanthis is a professor of computer science at the University of Pittsburgh, USA, and an adjunct professor at Carnegie Mellon University. His current research focus is on mobile and pervasive data management including Web services and sensor networks. In 1995, he was a recipient of the National Science Foundation CAREER Award for his investigation on the management of data for mobile and wireless computing. His research accomplishments have been published in over 100 papers in journals and peer-reviewed conferences and workshops. In addition, his publication record includes a book and book chapters on transaction processing and data access in distributed, mobile, and Web databases. He is on the editorial board of the VLDB journal, and was general chair and program chair of several workshops and conferences in the field of data management.

Paraskevas Evripidou completed his undergraduate studies in electrical engineering at the Higher Technical Institute of Cyprus, Cyprus (HND, 1981) and the University of Southern California (BSc, 1985). He completed his graduate studies at the University of Southern California (MSc, 1986; PhD, 1990 in computer engineering). He has taught at the University of Southern California (part-time faculty, 1989-1990) and at Southern Methodist University (assistant professor, 1990-1994). His research interests are parallel processing and computer architecture, data-flow systems, and functional programming and parallelizing compilers.

Elena Ferrari is a full professor of computer science at the University of Insubria, Como (Italy). From 1998 until January 2001, she was an assistant professor at the Department of Computer Science of the University of Milano (Italy). She received an MS in computer science from the University of Milano (1992). In 1998, she received a PhD in computer science from the same university. During the summer of 1996, she was a visiting researcher at the Department of Computer Science of George Mason University, Fairfax (Virginia). During the summers of 1997 and 1998, she was a visiting researcher at Rutgers University, Newark (New Jersey). Her research activities are related to various aspects of data-management systems, including Web security, access control and privacy, multimedia databases, and temporal databases. On these topics she has published more than 100 scientific publications in international journals and conference proceedings. She gave several invited lectures and tutorials at Italian and foreign universities as well as at international conferences and workshops. Dr. Ferrari has served as program chair of the Fourth ACM Symposium on Access Control Models and Technologies (SACMAT'04), software-demonstration chair of the Ninth International Conference on Extending Database Technology (EDBT'04), and the cochair of the First COMPSAC'02 Workshop on Web Security and Semantic Web, the first ECOOP Workshop on XML and Object Technology (XOT 2000), and the first ECOOP Workshop on Object-Oriented Databases. She has also served as program committee member of several international conferences and workshops. Professor Ferrari is on the editorial board of the VLDB journal and the *International Journal of Information Technology (IJIT)*. She is a member of the ACM and senior member of IEEE.

Giovanna Guerrini is an associate professor at the Department of Computer and Information Sciences of the University of Genova, Italy. She received the MS and PhD degrees in computer science from the University of Genova (1993 and 1998, respectively). She was an assistant professor at the University of Genova (1996-2001) and an associate professor at the University of Pisa (2001-2005). Her research interests include object-oriented, active, and temporal databases as well as semistructured and XML data handling. She served as program committee member of international conferences like EDBT, ECOOP, ACM OOPSLA, and ACM CIKM.

Dušan Húsek received a PhD in technical cybernetics from the Technical University of Prague, Czechoslovakia (Faculty of Electrical Engineering), in 1983. Currently he is with the Institute of the Computer Science Academy of the Sciences of the Czech Republic where he has headed many international research projects. Dušan Húsek's research interests include neural networks, information retrieval, and the semantic Web. The most recent research result of his and his team is the method of nonlinear Boolean factor analysis based on neural-network attempts. His publication list comprises more than 150 papers in scientific journals and proceedings of renowned conferences. He is a member of IASTED and ISI.

Ioannis Katakis holds a BSc in informatics from the Aristotle University of Thessaloniki, Greece, where he is currently pursuing a PhD in text mining under the supervision of Professor Ioannis Vlahavas. His main research interests include textual data streams, e-mail mining, and Web-page classification. He is a member of the Machine Learning and Knowledge Discovery Group (http://mlkd.csd.auth.gr) at the same university.

Dimitrios Katsaros was born in Thetidio-Farsala, Greece, in 1974. He received a BSc in computer science from the Department of Informatics of the Aristotle University of Thessaloniki, Greece (March 1997), and a PhD from the same department (May 2004). He spent a year (July 1997 to June 1998) as a visiting researcher at the Department of Pure and Applied Mathematics at the University of L'Aquila, Italy. Currently, he is a postdoctoral fellow at the Department of Informatics of the Aristotle University of Thessaloniki conducting research on ad hoc networks. He is also an adjunct lecturer at the Department of Computer and Communication Engineering at the University of Thessaly, Volos, Greece. His research interests span the areas of mobile and pervasive computing, wireless ad hoc networks, wireless sensor networks, and data mining (with an emphasis on structured Web data mining). He is an editor of the book *Wireless Information Highways*, published by IRM Press in 2005.

Mehregan Mahdavi received an MS in computer science and engineering from Amirkabir University of Technology, Tehran. He is currently a PhD candidate at the School of Computer Science and Engineering, University of New South Wales, Sydney, Australia. His research interests are in the Web and databases including Web caching, Web portals, Web services, Web data integration, and versioning. He also does research and development in identity and access management. He is a member of the IEEE.

Pat Martin is a professor and associate director of the School of Computing at Queen's University. He holds a BSc from the University of Toronto, an MSc from Queen's University, and a PhD from the University of Toronto. He is also a faculty fellow with IBM's Centre for Advanced Studies. His research interests include database system performance, Web services, and autonomic computing systems.

Maristella Matera is an assistant professor at Politecnico di Milano, Italy, where she teaches about databases. She has been awarded several fellowships supporting her research work at Italian and foreign institutions; in particular, she has been a visiting researcher at the Graphics, Visualization and Usability Center at the Georgia Institute of Technology, Atlanta, USA. Her current research work focuses on design methods and tools for Web applications design and development. In particular, it concentrates on Web log mining, Web application usability and accessibility, context-aware Web applications, and multimodal Web interfaces. She is the author of about 50 papers on the previous topics and of the book *Designing Data-Intensive Web Applications* (Morgan Kaufmann Publisher, 2002). A more detailed curriculum vitae and the list of publications can be found at http://www.elet.polimi.it/people/matera.

Marcelo Meirelles received a BS degree in systems analysis from the Papal Catholic University of Campinas (PUCCamp) in 1989 and his master's degree in applied informatics from UNIFOR in 2004 (both in Brazil). Since 2005, he was an assistant professor at the Federal University of Ceara (UFC Brazil). His research interests are information integration, XML data management, active XML, query processing, and health-care systems.

Rosa Meo is a professor at the Department of Computer Science at the University of Torino, Italy. She holds a Dr.Ing. degree in electrical engineering and a PhD in computer engineering, both from Politecnico di Torino. Her research interests are in the field of databases, in particular active databases, XML, and data mining. She has been serving as a reviewer for several international conferences and journals such as ACM TODS, IEEE TKDE, TDE, *AI Communications, Computer Journal, Journal of Privacy Technology, Intelligent Data Analysis,* VLDB, ACM KDD, IEEE ICDM, ECAI 2004, ACM SAC, ECML, PKDD, DaWak, AI*IA 2003, XML Database Symposium (Workshop di VLDB 2003), *Database Technologies for Data Mining,* Pattern Representation Management (EDBT Workshops), *Integrating Data Mining, Databases with Information Retrieval,* Logical Aspects and Application of Integrity Constraints (DEXA Workshops), and Knowledge Discovery with Inductive Databases (ECML/PKDD Workshop). She participated in European-funded projects in data mining, such as Mietta (on multilingual information extraction) and cInq (consortium on knowledge discovery by inductive queries).

Marco Mesiti is an assistant professor at the University of Milan, Italy. He received the MS and PhD degrees in computer science from the University of Genova, Italy, in 1998 and 2003, respectively. His main research interests include the management of XML documents, XML schema evolution, and access control mechanisms for XML. He has been a visiting researcher at the applied research center of Telcordia Technologies, Morristown, New Jersey. He co-organized the first and second editions of the EDBT workshop DataX and served as a program committee member of EDBT PhD Workshop 2006, ADBIS Conference 2006, IEEE SAINT 2005, IEEE SAINT 2006, and EDBT Workshop ClustWeb 2004, and as reviewer for international conferences and journals.

Benjamin Nguyen graduated from the Ecole Normale Supérieure de Cachan in 2000. He prepared his PhD at INRIA with the Verso/Gemo groups, and received his PhD in computer science from the University of Paris XI in 2003. Since 2004, he has been an assistant professor at the Université de Versailles et Saint-Quentin-en-Yvelines, France, and is a member of the database group of the PRiSM CNRS Laboratory of the Université de Versailles. He is also an external researcher at INRIA (Gemo Group) and member of the World Wide Web Consortium. His current research activities concern XML data mediation and XML warehousing through the use of service-oriented models.

George Pallis graduated from the Department of Informatics of Aristotle University of Thessaloniki, Greece in 2001. Since November 2001, he has been with the Department of Computer Science of the University of Thessaloniki, Greece, studying toward his PhD. His current research interests include Web data caching, content distribution networks, and data mining and its applications mainly to Web data.

Stavros Papastavrou is a full-time teacher at St. Barnabas School for the Blind in Nicosia and a PhD student at the University of Cyprus, Cyprus. His current research focuses on accelerating dynamic Web content practices, proxy caching, mobile agents, and Java middleware technology. In 1999, his bachelor's thesis received the Best Paper Award at IEEE's International Conference in Data Engineering. He has also published a number of papers in journals and peer-reviewed conferences. He has worked as a senior Web developer for the United States Chamber of Commerce. He is currently developing new techniques for making computer technology and programming interfaces accessible to visually impaired people.

Jaroslav Pokorný received the PhD degree in theoretical cybernetics from Charles University, Prague, Czechoslovakia, in 1984. Currently he is a professor of computer science at the Faculty of Mathematics and Physics at Charles University and the head of its Department of Software Engineering. J. Pokorný has published more than 200 papers and books on data modeling, relational databases, query languages, file organization, and XML. His research interests include also database design, information retrieval, and the semantic Web. He is a member of the ACM and IEEE.

Wenny Rahayu is an associate professor at the Department of Computer Science and Computer Engineering, LaTrobe University, Australia. She has been actively working in the areas of database design and implementation covering object-relational databases, Web and e-commerce databases, semistructured databases and XML, the semantic Web and ontology, data warehousing, and parallel databases. She has worked with industry and gained expertise from other disciplines in a number of projects including bioinformatics databases, parallel data mining, and e-commerce catalogues. She has been invited to give seminars in the area of e-commerce databases at a number of international institutions. She has edited three books that form a series in Web applications, including *Web Databases*, *Web Information Systems*, and *Web Semantics*. She has also published over 70 papers in international journals and conferences.

Hana Řezanková finished her PhD studies at the University of Economics, Prague (VSE), Czech Republic, in 1988. From 1994, she has been an associate professor at the Department of Statistics of the VSE. She was the vice dean in charge of student study programmes at the Faculty of Informatics and Statistics of the VSE from 1998 to 2001. She is a member of the International Association for Statistical Computing. She was a member of the board of directors of the European Regional Section of this association from 2000 to 2004. Her publications focus mainly on categorical data analysis and cluster analysis.

Laura Irina Rusu received her bachelor-of-science degree (computer science, 1996) and a master-of-economics degree (1997), both from the Academy of Economic Studies, Bucharest, Romania. She is currently studying for a PhD degree at La Trobe University, Australia, where her areas of interest are XML data warehousing and mining. During 2004, Mrs. Laura Rusu worked as an associate lecturer at La Trobe University.

George Samaras finished his undergraduate studies at the University of Athens (BSc in mathematics, 1982) and his graduate studies at the Rensselaer Polytechnic Institute, USA (MSc, 1982, and PhD, 1989, in computer science). He has worked in the applied research program of IBM's Communications and Networks Centre at Research Triangle Park, North Carolina (1990-1993), and has taught at the University of North Carolina at Chapel Hill (visiting assistant professor, 1990-1993). He was also a member of IBM's International Standards Committees for issues related to distributed transaction processing (OSI/TP, XOPEN, OMG). His research interests are concerned with relational and object-oriented databases, distributed transaction processing, commit protocols, and mobile computing.

Ismael Sanz has a BSc and an MSc in computer science from Universitat Jaume I, Spain, where he is a lecturer. Previously, he worked for 3 years as a researcher at STARLab, Vrije Universiteit Brussels, Belgium. His research interests include approximate techniques for XML databases, structural clustering of XML, and the integration of information-retrieval techniques in an XML context. Currently, he is completing a PhD thesis on multisimilarity heterogeneous XML systems.

Václav Snášel received the PhD degree in algebra from the Masaryk University Brno in 1991, and was an associate professor in 2001. From 2001 he has been a visiting scientist at the Institute of Computer Science, Academy of Sciences of the Czech Republic. Since 2003 he has been vice dean of research and science at the Faculty of Electrical Engineering and Computer Science. Snášel has published more than 230 papers on ontology, knowledge management, databases, multimedia, information retrieval, neural networks, data compression, and file organization. He is a member of IASTED and AMS.

David Taniar received his bachelor's (honors), master's, and PhD degrees in computer science, with a particular specialty in databases. His research now expands to data mining and mobile databases. He has published research papers in these fields extensively including a recent book *Object-Oriented Oracle*. Dr. Taniar is now a staff member at Monash University, Australia. He is the editor in chief of international journals, including *Data Warehousing and Mining*, *Business Intelligence and Data Mining*, *Web Information Systems*, *Web and Grid Services*, *Mobile Multimedia*, and *Mobile Information Systems*. He is a fellow of the Institute for Management Information Systems (FIMIS).

Grigorios Tsoumakas received a BSc in informatics from the Aristotle University of Thessaloniki, Greece, in 1999, an MSc in artificial intelligence from the University of Edinburgh in 2000, and a PhD in machine learning from the A.U.Th. in 2005. His research interests include classifier ensembles, learning in planning, distributed knowledge discovery and mining text and biological data. He is a member of the Machine Learning and Knowledge Discovery group of A.U.Th. (http://mlkd.csd.auth.gr), the Hellenic Artificial Intelligence

Society, and the Special Interest Group on Knowledge Discovery and Data Mining of the Association for Computing Machinery.

Athena Vakali received a BSc degree in mathematics from the Aristotle University of Thessaloniki, Greece, an MSc degree in computer science from Purdue University, USA (with a Fulbright scholarship), and a PhD degree in computer science from the Department of Informatics at the Aristotle University of Thessaloniki. Since 1997, she has been a faculty member of the Department of Informatics, Aristotle University of Thessaloniki, Greece (currently she is an assistant professor). Her research interests include design, performance, and analysis of storage subsystems; XML and multimedia data; and data placement schemes for multimedia and Web-based information. She is working on Web data management and she has focused on XML data storage issues. She has published several papers in international journals and conferences.

Ioannis Vlahavas is a full professor at the Department of Informatics at the Aristotle University of Thessaloniki, Greece. He received his PhD degree in logic programming systems from the same university in 1988. He specializes in logic programming and knowledge-based and AI (artificial intelligence) systems, and he has published over 100 papers and five book chapters, and has coauthored three books in these areas. He teaches logic programming, AI, expert systems, and DSS. He has been involved in more than 15 research projects, leading most of them. He is currently leading the Logic Programming and Intelligent Systems Group (LPIS Group, http://lpis.csd.auth.gr; more information at http://www.csd.auth.gr/~vlahavas).

Farhana H. Zulkernine is a doctoral student at Queen's University in Kingston. She received her BSc and MSc degrees from Bangladesh University of Engineering and Technology. She has almost 10 years of experience in software development and analysis at different organizations including UNICEF (United Nations Children's Fund), Canada. Her main research interests include Web-services discovery and management.

Index